Churches of Worcestershire

Churches of Worcestershire

by
Tim Bridges

Tim Bridges

Logaston Press

LOGASTON PRESS
Little Logaston, Logaston,
Woonton, Almeley, Herefordshire HR3 6QH

First published by Logaston Press 2000
Copyright © text Tim Bridges 2000
Copyright © photographs (unless otherwise credited) Tim Bridges 2000

ISBN 1 873827 56 3

Set in Times by Logaston Press
and printed in Great Britain by
Hillman Printers (Frome) Ltd

Contents

For my nephews Richard and Matthew

1. Naunton Beauchamp
2. Churchill in Oswaldslow
3. Upton Snodsbury

Upper Arley • Cookley • Churchill • Hagley • Frankley
                              in H'shire
         Wolverley •   • Clent • Romsley
Button Oak •   • Blakedown •   • Rubery
         • Trimpley   • Broome
Far •   • KIDDERMINSTER • Belbroughton
Forest •   Stone   • Lickey • Cofton Hackett
    • BEWDLEY   Fairfield •   Barnt Green • Wythall
         Ribbesford • Wilden Chaddesley • • Catshill
Bayton •   Corbett • Dodford • Blackwell • Alvechurch
Knighton- • Mamble Heightington   Rushock • BROMSGROVE • Finstall
on-Teme •   • Rock • STOURPORT •   Grafton   • Tardebigge • Beoley
Rochford • Eastham Lindridge • Pensax Crossway • Hartlebury Manor   • REDDITCH
            •   • Abberley Green Elmley   • Stoke Prior
TENBURY   Orleton Stockton-   Lovett Elmbridge • Upton Warren
WELLS •   • Hanley William on-Teme • Astley   • Doverdale • Bentley
   • Hanley Child   Stanford- • Shrawley   • Wychbold
Kyre Wyard • Stoke on-Teme • Gt Witley Hampton Lovett • Hanbury
        Bliss Shelsley Shelsley   • Lt Witley DROITWICH • Astwood
Bockleton •   Walsh • Beauchamp • Holt Ombersley   • Hadzor   Bank
         • Harpley • Clifton-   Salwarpe   • Martin Hussingtree • Bradley • Cookhill
    Lower   on-Teme Wichenford • Grimley • Oddingley Himbleton
    Sapey • • Martley   Claines • Hindlip   Dormston
      Doddenham   Broadheath Hallow Tibberton Huddington Kington • Inkberrow
           • Lulsley Broadwas • WORCESTER   Crowle • Grafton Flyford Flavell
      Knightwick • Cotheridge Crown • East   Bredicot • Flyford • Abbots Morton
   Suckley • Alfrick Leigh Whittington Spetchley • Broughton 3 • North • Rous Lench
           Bransford   Norton Hackett • 2 Piddle
                Powick by Kempsey White Ladies Aston 1 Abberton Norton and Lenchwick
         Callow End   Peopleton Bishampton • Church Lench
     Newland   Stoulton • Pinvin Throckmorton   • Harvington Cleeve Prior
   Madresfield Kempsey Drake's Broughton • Wyre Lower Moor Offenham Middle • Pebworth
 West Malvern   Pirton   Piddle Wick • Fladbury   South Littleton Littleton
            • MALVERN   PERSHORE   • Charlton   • Honeybourne
      Guarlford Severn Croome Besford Cropthorne   EVESHAM Bretforton
        Stoke d'Abitot Defford • Birlingham • Bricklehampton Badsey
   Malvern Wells Earls   Gt Comberton • Lt Comberton Netherton Wickhamford
      Hanley Swan Croome   Eckington Elmley Hinton-on-the-Green
Little Malvern Hanley Castle UPTON Hill • Strensham Castle Sedgeberrow Childwickham
   Welland • Hook Croome   Bredon's Norton   • Broadway
         Common   Bredon Overbury Ashton-under Aston
Hollybush Castlemorton Ripple Bredon • -Hill Somerville
      Longdon Queenhill   Kemerton   • Beckford
   Pendock Cross • Birtsmorton
      Berrow Bushley
   Pendock
Eldersfield

0   5   10
miles

Map of Worcestershire showing the location of churches included in this book

Foreword

A lifelong interest in churches has led eventually to the production of this book. It has also come about as a result of lecturing, teaching evening classes and leading guided visits around local churches over the last 12 years.

All the historic Anglican churches of the present county of Worcestershire are included in the text, and several modern churches appear where information has been readily available. A number of late 19th-century mission chapels, together with 20th-century churches which were built also to function as halls, and ecumenical centres are not to be found here, although they play significant roles in their local communities. The book is restricted to Anglican churches, though a growing public interest in the buildings of the Roman Catholics and Nonconformists must be acknowledged. The churches in the book are approached from an architectural and historical viewpoint, reflecting my own interests and knowledge, whilst recognising the hugely significant spiritual and social role of the church in the community, both in the past and at present. Mention is made of key historical figures associated with or commemorated in the churches, but it is of course the thousands of worshippers and visitors over the centuries, about whom little is usually known, who have shaped the churches to their present form and given each its unique atmosphere. It is this atmosphere which can be sensed on approaching a church, and which remains with the visitor long afterwards. The church buildings and their contents, of course, contribute to this atmosphere. Site visits have yielded much information, and its discovery has been influenced by the excellent research of Sir Nikolaus Pevsner in his *Buildings of England* volume on Worcestershire. The *Victoria County History* of Worcestershire provides much invaluable information, supported by numerous local historical books. These are listed in the reference section, which is also intended as a source list for further reading for anyone wishing to examine the churches in more detail than has been possible within the scope of this book. However, the numerous good guidebooks and handsheets to be found in the churches themselves are not included in this list, although their increasing appearance can be seen as a most encouraging response to the growing wish of local people and visitors to know more about these churches. This heightened awareness is also leading to a greater accessibility of churches. The national trend is for improving access and it is hoped that the churches included in this book will, if they are not normally open during the day, be able to make available details of opening times or access arrangements, along with times of services, whilst obviously addressing concerns about security. Every church mentioned here has both features of interest and is a place for prayer and reflection, which is to be treasured both by those who use it regularly and by those who are discovering it for the first time.

Thus, I would like to gratefully acknowledge the work of all those clergy, churchwardens and congregations, in whose care these churches are placed, in all that they do to preserve, maintain and keep them in use. The support, financial and otherwise, of organisations such as English Heritage, grant-making trusts, and local authorities should also be recorded. Some churches are now in the care of other denominations, or are maintained by the Churches Conservation Trust, and their various roles are also significant. However, the maintenance of churches in use is often difficult, and it is the role of the Worcestershire and Dudley Historic Churches Trust to allocate grants and to support churches in the county and diocese of Worcester with their restoration work whenever possible. I have been fortunate to have had the opportunity to serve as a Trustee since 1996, and am aware of many of the problems which are faced by Worcestershire churches in their upkeep. Therefore, I am very pleased that a small part of the proceeds from the sale of this book will contribute towards the work of the Worcestershire and Dudley Historic Churches Trust.

The writing of this book has only been possible with the huge amount of support which I have received from others. I am very grateful to Andy Johnson of Logaston Press for providing the opportunity to write this book and for the great patience and the enormous skill that both he and Ron Shoesmith have shown in editing my work. However, any mistakes or omissions in the text are my own responsibility, and I would be grateful to know of them via Logaston Press. My parents, Harry and Gill Bridges, have always encouraged my interest in churches and have given unfailing support to this project. Several of the photographs are taken from their slides; the remainder are my own, except those on pages 18, 145 and 147 which are reproduced courtesy of Logaston Press.

I am grateful to Worcester City Council for the encouragement I have received to undertake this work outside of my role at Worcester City Museums, and to my colleagues at the Museum for continued support and advice, in particular, Iain Rutherford, Museums, Arts and Heritage Officer. The Trustees of the Worcestershire and Dudley Historic Churches Trust, including the Chairman Michael Shaw and Secretary John Lakeman, have been constantly encouraging, and I am particularly grateful to Michael Wall for his useful suggestions and supply of guidebooks, as well as to John Bailey, who made available his very helpful card index of references to19th- and 20th-century furnishings and glass, from Diocesan Directories and Calendars. Many of these are included in the text. My grateful thanks are also due to Angie Bishop for her expert word-processing of my handwritten drafts, and for resolving many challenging points of legibility and grammar along the way. Michael Tavinor very kindly read the proofs, and I should also like to thank him for making numerous excellent suggestions and improvements. Several friends, colleagues and students have encouraged and advised on my work with churches and this book, but I would like especially to acknowledge the support of Rupert and Julie Bridges, David and Lydia Warner, Mark Renn and Anna Dolecka, Richard Bailey and Gail Simmons, Barbara Ronchetti, Annette Leech and Sandy Marchant. Many people have suggested that this book should be written, and it appears as a response to their enthusiasm and encouragement in the hope that more people will enjoy discovering the often all too little known churches of Worcestershire.

Tim Bridges
March 2000

CHAPTER I

The History of Worcestershire's Churches

The Early Church in Worcestershire to *c*.1066

Worcestershire has many Prehistoric and Roman sites, which have been investigated archaeologically. The Iron Age hillforts of the Malverns and Bredon Hill are conspicuous, whilst the remains of the Roman towns of Droitwich and Worcester are less obvious. With little documentary evidence to assist, it is only possible to gain information about the devotions and beliefs of the people of this area before the 4th century from the results of archaeological work on shrines and burials. Early sacred sites became deep rooted in local traditions, and their subsequent adaptation as Christian with the establishment of churches from the time of the Christianisation of Roman Britain is part of a process of absorption of old beliefs by a new faith. Whilst direct links are nebulous and often dangerous to make, the presence of the church by a spring at Romsley, or within the area of the Iron Age hillfort at Hanbury, would seem to be significant.

A strong Christian presence in late Roman Worcester is also possible. The reported discovery of a bronze Chi-Rho symbol, together with the early origins of the churches of St. Helen, St. Alban and St. Peter the Great, and their locations in relation to the late Roman defences and cemetery, are all evidence, though not entirely conclusive, of an active Christian community at Worcester from the 4th century. However, what happened to such a community during the following centuries is unclear. The advances of pagan Anglo-Saxon culture during the 5th and 6th centuries reached across the river Severn from south-east England, but a lack of pagan Saxon burials to the west of Worcester, and the known strength of the surviving British Christian community in Wales and the west country at this time, points to the possibility that Christianity survived at least in pockets in what is now western Worcestershire. Whilst the river Severn effectively bisects the county, it is unlikely that there was a hard and fast boundary—it was more probably an indistinct border area. Saxon cemetery sites are known in the east, particularly around the Avon Valley, such as at Upton Snodsbury or Beckford. Meanwhile, to the west, the churchyards at Stockton and Knighton in the Teme valley appear circular, and may well have their origins in early British Christian enclosures of which numerous examples can be found in Wales.

The mission to convert the pagan Saxon peoples of England sent by Pope Gregory and led by St. Augustine, arrived in Kent in 597 and its effects gradually spread north and west. The presence of existing Christians to the west of the river Severn is apparent from the meetings of their leaders with Augustine and his missionaries—meetings which are thought to have taken place within the present Worcestershire. Abberley, Rock, Hartlebury and Dodderhill all make claims to be the locations of meeting places. The meetings were to resolve differences which had arisen over the celebration of Easter and the liturgy of baptism, which eventually came to a head at the Synod of Whitby in 664, when the practices of Rome and of Augustine's mission were adopted.

1

The organisation of the church in the later Anglo-Saxon period was built on the work of the mission. Large minster or monastery churches were established in centres of population, whose geographical hinterland then became large parishes from which monks went out to preach and minister the sacraments. At Kidderminster, the presence of a minster has made an obvious contribution to the place name, but there were several others in Worcestershire, including Pershore, Evesham, and St. Helen's church in Worcester with its extensive parish. By 680 the focus of the church in Worcester had reached a point where it

St. Alban's church, Worcester, where the dedication suggests an early Christian foundation

became significant enough for the town to become the centre of a diocese which covered most of the present county, as well as south Warwickshire and most of Gloucestershire. The first bishop, Bosel, was no doubt able to build on a strong sense of Christian tradition which may have extended back as far as the 4th century.

There is little visible evidence today of Worcestershire's Anglo-Saxon minster churches, for they have been rebuilt and replaced in subsequent centuries. However, it is possible to get a sense of the scale of such a church and to see a splendid example of the style of architecture at Deerhurst in Gloucestershire. The large church here, located some three miles from the county boundary near Tewkesbury, still contains much masonry and sculpture from the 8th to 10th centuries. Other local examples of substantial Saxon churches are at Wootton Wawen and Tredington in Warwickshire, Bibury in Gloucestershire and Stanton Lacy in Shropshire. Although foundations have been uncovered in Pershore Abbey, it is also possible that some Anglo-Saxon masonry exists in some larger Worcestershire churches such as Holt, but accurate dating is difficult.

Monks going into the smaller communities of the minster parish would have established a preaching place in a prominent situation, possibly an earlier sacred site. Its location would have been fixed by the erection of a cross. Whilst none of these early preaching crosses have survived, fragments of their successors of 9th and 10th century date are at Frankley, Tenbury Wells and particularly the beautiful cross head at Cropthorne. Throughout the later Anglo-Saxon period church buildings were erected alongside these crosses. Simple stone and wooden structures for worship have disappeared, but an example of the type of building, with its plain nave and chancel, and round-headed doorways and windows, can be seen in Odda's chapel, at Deerhurst, a private foundation of the early 11th century close to the minster church.

The church flourished in late Anglo-Saxon Worcestershire, with large powerful monasteries at Pershore and Evesham, and the diocesan centre at Worcester. The activities of important churchmen such as bishops Oswald and Dunstan at Worcester, and Ecgwin at Evesham, are recorded in documentary sources, as are the development of cults and relics appertaining to these and to Edburga (or Eadburga) at Pershore. The monasteries had great influence over the surrounding lands, and the effects of the politics of the church and the emerging kingdom of England were particularly felt in Worcestershire, with the confiscation of land from Pershore by King Edward the Confessor as an endowment for the foundation of the great abbey at Westminster. Nevertheless, very little physical evidence survived the great rebuildings of the Norman Conquest, although stonework from the earlier cathedral at Worcester may have been

The Anglo-Saxon cross head at Cropthorne

reused in the reconstruction started by Bishop Wulstan, which began with the crypt in 1084.

Numerous other churches were no doubt founded at this time for developing communities. In Worcester itself, the expansion of the defended settlement to the north seems to have led to the establishment of St. Andrew's, St. Swithin's and All Saints' churches. The latter two have been shown to be adjacent to the defences. Today the earliest masonry on these sites is later medieval, but could they have begun as gate chapels in a similar way to St. Michael at the Northgate in Oxford? Out in the county there is little visible defence for later Saxon churches, but fragments of sculpture can be seen at Stoke Prior, Rous Lench and Wyre Piddle, whilst arches at Sedgeberrow and Warndon along with the south wall of St. Alban's church in Worcester are quite possibly related to the pre-Norman churches.

The Norman Conquest in 1066 brought about massive rebuilding, but there are some instances of Anglo-Saxon workmanship and building techniques continuing in use. The crypt of Worcester Cathedral is the most significant example. It was rebuilt by Bishop Wulstan, the only Anglo-Saxon bishop to remain in his see. Several churches show evidence of Saxon type work which may in fact date from after the Conquest, including those churches already mentioned at Warndon, Sedgeberrow and St. Alban Worcester. Indeed very plain round-headed arches as at Hanley William, or over the Gloucestershire border at Great and Little Washbourne, are the product of this transition. Similarly difficult to date exactly in the 11th century is the herringbone masonry of Elmley Castle, which should be compared with Edvin Loach in Herefordshire or Loxley in Warwickshire.

The Norman Period, *c*.1066 - *c*.1200

Almost a hundred—nearly half—of Worcestershire's churches have some Norman stonework. The great contrast in this level of survival to that of Anglo-Saxon churches is in the main due to the zeal with which the conquering Norman lords carried out the wishes of William I in removing existing buildings and culture. Worcestershire, and even more Herefordshire to the west, were very much part of the frontier area bordering Wales, and powerful Norman families such as the Beauchamps and Tosnys were granted land here to help ensure the region's stability. Castles and fortified manors were at the centre of their estates, and alongside them old churches were rebuilt or new ones founded.

The Romanesque style used by Norman builders reflected their power and military strength. The round-headed arches, windows and doorways were set in thick walls which were strengthened by flat buttresses, making their churches simple but solid.

Most Worcestershire villages had a two cell church with nave and chancel, and in remoter parts of the county, like the Teme Valley, churches such as Eastham or Rochford have changed little in plan.

Larger churches existed where there were wealthy and influential patrons or greater centres of population. Some were larger versions of the two cell church such as those at Rock and Holt, whilst others were extended with aisles as at Cropthorne or Overbury. A further group of large churches were those connected to new monasteries, such as Astley, Leigh or Bredon, whilst existing large monastic churches were rebuilt on a grand scale. Wulstan's rebuilding of Worcester Cathedral was no doubt a landmark, but the substantial remains of Pershore Abbey, which can be compared to the better preserved Tewkesbury in Gloucestershire, and the Norman work at Great Malvern must have had an influence on nearby church architecture. Indeed, Kempsey and Powick churches were cruciform with transepts, whilst Beckford and Pirton had central towers. Norman towers at the west end without doorways perhaps reflect a semi-defensive intention, as at Harvington or Fladbury, whereas an apse at the east end was in line with fashion on the continent and monastic churches like Pershore and Worcester. There are no apsidal chancels surviving in Worcestershire, although the foundations of one have been excavated at Kyre Wyard. However, examples of Norman apses can be seen at Moccas and Peterchurch in Herefordshire. Most churches of Norman origin have rather fragmentary remains, such as Huddington or Ashton-under-Hill, which can be best understood by making comparisons with more complete examples. In any case it is the presence of features, such as doorways or windows, that date the masonry to the Norman period. The fragmentary remains of buttresses and a tiny blocked window at Grimley are typical examples, but it is important to be wary of the large number of Norman features, preserved and reset during later work, particularly in the 19th century, when their antiquarian significance was realised. The churches at Badsey and Childswickham have examples of this.

Worcestershire is particularly rich in Norman sculpture from the 12th century. Perhaps the best known is the work of the 'Herefordshire School'. This was a team of sculptors, some of whom had probably worked on Hereford Cathedral, who carried out work for local patrons in the latter part of the century. The origins seem to be with Oliver de Merlimond, Lord of Shobdon in Herefordshire, who founded a priory there at the time that he went on pilgrimage to the shrine of St. James at Santiago de Compostela in Spain. The sculptors who undertook the carvings at Shobdon, of which just the famous arches now survive, were heavily influenced by the sculpture of southern France and northern Spain and worked elements in with more local designs, which are Celtic, Anglo-Saxon and Viking. Shobdon dates from the 1130s, and the work at the well-known church at Kilpeck near Hereford was executed at about the same time. Carving undertaken by these sculptors, or influenced by them, is found across north Worcestershire, and indeed, the easternmost known example is at Billesley near Stratford in Warwickshire. Their Worcestershire work includes doorways at Rochford, Ribbesford and Romsley, a fragment from a doorway and the font at Chaddesley Corbett, the chancel arch at Rock, corbels at Astley and Hagley and carved panels at Eastham and Stockton in the Teme valley.

Other superb sculpture is to be found in the Bredon Hill area, where several churches contain work similar to those on the Cotswolds, and stylistically linked to Gloucester, including doorways at Little Comberton and Netherton, along with doorways and arches at Beckford. These and other elaborate Norman doorways were built as impressive entrances to beautifully decorated churches, with carved zig-zags and rope moulding. Now, the interior paintwork has largely gone, although there is also evidence for the exteriors of churches built from rubble stone being plastered and limewashed, often embellished with red lines to imitiate blocks of ashlar masonry. True ashlar was reserved for the buttresses or the doorways and windows which could then be carved. The carving was probably just part of a more elaborate decorative scheme in paint or with statuary which is now lost. So Norman doorways, such as those which project from the wall at Stoulton, Pirton, Knighton or Bockleton, were probably further embellished. The same is probably true of plain Norman arches as at Astley or Eckington. Indeed fragments of sculpture now reset elsewhere in churches, as at Earls Croome or Elmley Castle, could have formed part of such schemes. The arrangements of red and green sandstone on the nave walls at Martley is indicative of what could be done when funds allowed.

Whilst it is difficult to know much about the interior fittings of Norman churches, there are numerous 12th-century fonts, including those at Holt, Broome, Pinvin and Overbury. Several, such as at Rock and Bayton, have similar forms of decoration. Finally, the exceptional 12th-century stone lecterns at Crowle and Norton provide an indication of the internal beauty of many of these churches.

Medieval Churches, *c*.1200 - *c*.1530

Towards the end of the 12th century, English architecture was transformed by the use of the pointed arch. This had its origins in the architecture of the Middle East, and the Holy Land in particular, and its use became widespread in Western Europe as a result of the Crusades and developing trade links. The pointed arch seems to make its first appearance in Worcestershire with the west end of the nave of Worcester Cathedral, built about 1185. The pointed arches are mixed with round headed ones in the double bays of arcade, triforium and clerestorey. On these and on the arches of this date in Bredon and Cropthorne churches, the decoration is the popular Norman zig-zag, whilst at Leigh the arcade has massive round Norman piers supporting plain pointed arches.

The medieval Gothic styles developed from this, first in a plain but elegant form called Early English. This was the style favoured by the Cistercian monks, whose increasing presence during this period did much to assist its spread, along with an improved understanding of geometrical principles. The main Cistercian monastery in Worcestershire at Bordesley in Redditch survives only in a very fragmentary state, but the remaining parts of Dore Abbey in Herefordshire display characteristic work of high quality. The influence of the Cistercians can be felt in the rebuilt east end of Worcester Cathedral, which was started in 1224. Here, pointed lancet windows appear through arches, with clusters of shafts, many of which are picked out in dark purbeck marble, and have finely carved capitals with increasingly naturalistic foliage. The effect is similar in the east end of Pershore Abbey, whilst some parish churches contain elements of it, such as the south aisle at Bredon. The tower at Stoke Prior was no doubt built by cathedral masons, and has similar detail to the base of the tower at St. Andrew Droitwich. Other Early English work includes the chancel at Kempsey, or the nave and chancel at Ripple, whilst examples of lancet windows in groups and as singles can be seen at Powick, Himbleton and Mamble, or forming simple plate tracery at Beckford.

The vault at the east end of Pershore Abbey, which was erected after 1288 with beautiful naturalistic carved bosses, heralds the coming of the Decorated style. More flamboyant than Early English, the Decorated style derives its chief influence from France, at a time when political and economic links were still very strong. The style is easily discernible through its window tracery, which developed from basic Y-shaped divisions through the use of cusps and ogee curves to make increasingly elaborate designs with trefoil and quatrefoil shapes. Many churches have windows with the simple Y-shaped design, with and without cusps, including Broughton Hackett and Huddington. The chantry chapel added to Broadwas church with a foundation deed of 1344 provides a dateable example of this type of building. More elaborate Decorated windows can be found at Martley and Stoke Prior, but the 14th-century chancel rebuilt for the Corbett family at Chaddesley Corbett contains four windows, each of great individuality. There are some fine 14th-century towers, of which those at Areley Kings and Hampton Lovett include porches, and fine stone spires at Bredon and Castlemorton reflecting patronage.

Much of this work in the parish churches was probably influenced by the rebuilding of the nave of Worcester Cathedral in the Decorated style between about 1320 and 1370. It was a major building project at the heart of the county and diocese. Fine carved capitals and moulded arches are also found in the arcade at Huddington and the nave at Kempsey.

Tomb recesses, complete with cusps, crockets and ogees survive at Mamble and Bredon, and it is interesting to make the link with the same details on the canopies and architectural features depicted in the virtually identical stained glass panels showing the Virgin and Child at Fladbury and Warndon, which date from the early 14th century. There is even some ballflower decoration on a tomb recess in Cropthorne, but apart from prolific quantities on the tower of Pershore Abbey, this distinctive Decorated style motif is less in evidence than in Herefordshire, perhaps as more prestigious Worcestershire churches were built in the 15th century.

The architectural style of the 15th and early 16th centuries was the distinctly English Perpendicular. The economic and political situation at this time served to make England more insular architecturally. The damage to the economy from the Black Death, along with a lessening of ties with France and loss of land held there through the Hundred Years War, all seem to have contributed to an individuality in contemporary architecture. During the second half of the 15th century there was also the civil strife and uncertainty of the Wars of the Roses. The French orientated Decorated style gave way to Perpendicular with its lower and, eventually, flat arches, doorways and octagonal piers. Lower roof pitches were often lined with parapets and battlements, and the style showed a love of pinnacles and large areas of wall space taken up with huge windows containing tracery which included an increasing number of straight lines and right angles, distinct from the curvaceousness of the Decorated style. The clerestoreys at Malvern Priory of about 1420 show the Perpendicular style at its best, but very good quality Perpendicular church buildings were erected in those parts of Worcestershire which were wealthy from the cloth and other industry—in the north at Kidderminster and Bromsgrove, and in the south-east towards the Cotswold Edge. The nave clerestorey at St. Mary, Kidderminster is echoed in miniature at Upper Arley, whilst the Evesham churches have fine Perpendicular features. Claines and Inkberrow churches are almost entirely Perpendicular, and the chancel at Huddington, south aisles at Berrow, Rock, Pebworth and Upton Snodsbury, windows at Alfrick and Cotheridge and the elaborate south chapel with vault at St. Laurence, Evesham are examples of the varying degrees of ornament which the Perpendicular could offer. Additions to churches at this time, often by single or groups of wealthy benefactors include the porch at All Saints, Evesham, the similar porches at Hampton and Honeybourne and the former two storey porch at Cropthorne, as well as chantry chapels at Middle Littleton and Hampton Lovett. These chantries were often separate little structures within the bodies of larger churches, of which that built for Prince Arthur in Worcester Cathedral in 1502 is the only good survival in Worcestershire. Such chantries can be seen on a grand scale at Tewkesbury Abbey in Gloucestershire, and are echoed in the memorial to Joyce Beauchamp at St. Mary, Kidderminster.

Some older churches were modified to become fashionable with lower roof pitches and battlements, particularly on readily visible sides of the building as at Elmley Castle and Broadway, or with heightening of towers like Kemerton and Holt. Others received new towers of which Little Comberton, Overbury, Powick and Leigh are a selection, but the highly ornamental yet diminutive tower at Romsley and the elaborate panelled belltower of Evesham Abbey should not be missed. The Evesham tower, which was begun in 1513, is one of a group of fine Perpendicular towers on large churches in the West Country of which the tower of Worcester Cathedral, which was finished in 1374, is one of the earliest. The mason was John Clyve of Cleeve Prior who had also worked at Windsor. There are great similarities between the tower of Malvern Priory and that of Gloucester Cathedral, both built after 1450, whilst the tower at Little Malvern Priory has some similar panelling. Towers with comparable features such as open-work battlements or panelling are found in Gloucestershire, South Wales, and a well known group in Somerset.

Only a limited amount of structural timberwork has survived as much was replaced in later centuries, but the relative absence of good quality building stone in many parts of Worcestershire together with an abundance of forest, notably Wyre, Feckenham and Malvern Chase, meant that timber could be readily used. There is a timber arch at Oddingley and an arcade at Ribbesford. The timber-framed churches at Bewdley and Whittington have been replaced, that at Newland survives in part, but the 14th-century nave with huge braces at Besford is far too little known, and compares with Melverley in Shropshire or Marton in Cheshire. Timber-framed towers remain at Dormston, Kington, Warndon, Cotheridge and Pirton, whilst the bell frames at Mamble and Knighton-on-Teme are also splendid pieces of medieval timber work. Medieval timber porches include Huddington, Warndon and Crowle, and there are many fine timber roofs of the 14th and 15th centuries, such as those at Stoulton, Rock and Shelsley Walsh.

Most medieval furnishings were of course also of timber, and many have architectural features which can also be found in the structures and in the stonework. There is wooden Decorated style tracery in the west window at Besford church, which is like its stone counterparts, and reflects the carved work on screens, such as those at Leigh or Little Malvern, or the traceried panels on the pews at Cropthorne. However, in order to appreciate the colour of a medieval church interior and the way it was furnished, it is necessary to gather evidence from around the county and piece it together to form an overall picture, for much was swept away during the far-reaching changes of the Reformation years.

The Reformation and after, *c*.1530 - *c*.1800

The arrival of Protestantism brought more than a century of often sweeping reforms to the medieval Catholic church. King Henry VIII's decision to break ties with Rome led to alterations in the form of worship, which, although in their entirety were severe and irrevocable, were spread out over a long period. This period also saw movements to reinstate Catholicism, particularly during the reign of Mary Tudor, and there were interludes when more conservative churchmen, such as Archbishop Laud under King Charles I, reinstated Catholic practice in church worship. This contrasted with periods of more radical Protestant reform, which was perhaps at its most extreme with the government of Oliver Cromwell during the Commonwealth.

These changes had several effects on the churches of Worcestershire. The Dissolution of the Monasteries between 1536 and 1540 saw the disappearance of several major churches in the area—in particular the abbeys at Bordesley and Evesham. Worcester Cathedral lost its priory but remained the seat of the bishop, whilst considerable portions of the monastic churches at Pershore, Malvern and Little Malvern were used as parish churches. The Dissolution of the Chantries in 1547 led to the absorption of chantry chapels into the parish churches, often leaving little trace of their presence except for a piscina in the wall. Worcestershire had a strong tradition of Roman Catholic worship throughout this period, with many wealthy families maintaining a secret Catholic presence often in very difficult and dangerous circumstances. The priest holes and secret chapel at Harvington Hall near Kidderminster survive as a reminder of their determination. If chantries were forbidden, then private chapels for family burial meant that a dominant presence was often kept in the church. The Barneby chapel at Bockleton or the Sheldon chapel at Beoley reflect this. The latter was built in a very late Perpendicular style during the late 16th century and can be compared with the Berkeley chapel at Spetchley, but contrasted with the innovative brick chapel for another branch of the Berkeleys at Cotheridge and the Blount chapel at Mamble.

However, there was little new building during this period of uncertainty. Work was restricted to the adaptation of existing church structures with new fittings and furnishings, of which Wickhamford is a very good example. Images of Christ, the Virgin and saints were removed from walls and windows, and replaced by whitewash and plain glass. The focal point of furnishings became a tall often central pulpit, surrounded by substantial pews, whilst the chancel became more integrated into the body of the church, often with the removal of screens and the installation of communion tables and rails. Aside from the burial chapels, most structural work was necessary repair. A new chancel was built at Ashton-under-Hill in a late Perpendicular style, and damage in the Civil War led to alteration and rebuilding at Castlemorton and Dodderhill, both reusing old material. However, a new east end at Hanley Castle was built in brick in 1674 and, whilst the form of the tower, chancel and chapel is still medieval looking, the surviving sandstone

Little Malvern Priory from the hills, showing the restored medieval fishponds to the right

doorways are square, and the windows have mullions and transoms, which apart from little cusps are like contemporary domestic features. An interesting comparison can be made with the Renaissance style church of similar date at Monnington-on-Wye in Herefordshire.

A growing interest in classical architecture is reflected in many monuments of this period which use motifs copied from Greek and Roman buildings. Pilasters, caryatids, pediments, cartouches and columns can be seen on 17th-century memorials in Rous Lench, Croome d'Abitot and Leigh—pointers towards the extensive number of classical buildings to be erected in Worcestershire in the 18th century, heralded by the tower at Bewdley church built in 1695.

The forms of worship adopted during the later 17th century set a pattern that continued through the 18th, and which is reflected in the church buildings. Medieval churches continued to be altered to update them and traces of their medieval Catholic past further removed. The refitting of the naves at Shrawley and Hanbury with the clearance of tracery from the windows is evidence of this, but elsewhere much has been reinstated or superseded by alterations in the 19th century.

Repairs continued to be made to old fabric as had been done in the 17th century, but there were two major forms of new church building. Urban improvement and change led to much rebuilding, inspired by construction in other towns after serious fires in the late 17th century. The best known example was, of course, London with its elegant streets of fashionable brick houses and classical churches designed mainly by Christopher Wren. The rebuilding of Warwick after the fire of 1694 must also have had great local impact. Certainly Evesham, Pershore, Upton-upon-Severn, Bewdley and Worcester, which were prospering with growth in local agriculture, trade and industry, all saw major refits and rebuilds with Georgian façades and building throughout the towns. This extended to reconstructing the churches at Upton and Bewdley, as well as to four churches in Worcester city. All these buildings have elements of classical architecture, and were beautifully appointed. St. Swithin's church in Worcester by the Woodward brothers remains one of the best examples of a Georgian church, complete with fittings, not just in Worcestershire but in the whole of England.

The second series of major church building projects are found on the country estates of the wealthy land-owning families. Fashions for classical art and architecture in the great houses and their churches derived from visits to the classical ruins of Greece and Rome. Palladian mansions such as Hagley or Croome filled with classical furnishings and pictures were set in landscaped parks which were likewise filled with classical follies and ornaments. Churches which were built as part of these changes were often also classical, with symmetry and proportions which suited the form of worship of the day. Large naves and little or no chancels were usual. Tardebigge church built for the Windsors by Francis Hiorn, and the Foleys' church at Great Witley (see rear cover) are excellent examples of this. However, the baroque flamboyance of the interior at Witley is unlike that of most of its contemporaries, and was designed with a particular project in mind—to house newly acquired treasures of paintings, glass and organ. Other smaller classical churches must have been influenced by these ambitious works, and good examples can be seen at Longdon, Broome and Wolverley, though all were refitted in the 19th century.

Despite the popularity of classical architecture, the Gothic style never disappeared from view during the 18th century. Several churches rebuilt with classical features incorporated existing medieval Gothic work, such as Upton and All Saints Worcester, where parts of towers were retained. These were, of course, expensive to replace, and at St. Swithin Worcester, the medieval tower was recased in a Gothic form but in a matching stone to the rest of the building. At Hanbury a new tower was built in 1793 in a simple Gothic style, to become a prominent feature of the landscape as seen from the Hall, whilst at Stanford-on-Teme and Croome d'Abitot medieval style churches on hilltops brought an element of traditionalism to the parkland.

The Last Two Hundred Years

Increased toleration of other churches and religious groups towards the end of the 18th century, culminating in the emancipation of Roman Catholics in 1829, was matched by a growing religious zeal within the established church. This developed on a background of urban expansion and an absence of churches in some areas, so that in 1818 one million pounds was voted to the Church Commission for building new churches, with further sums following. The early 19th century, therefore, saw a large number of churches being built, often rather cheaply, to house potentially large congregations sometimes in direct rivalry to nonconformist chapels. The name Commissioners Church is generally applied to churches built at this time, and which include spacious naves with numerous pews, often with several galleries, and focused on large pulpits for powerful sermons. These were accompanied by short chancels, and west towers which often had side vestibules giving access to the galleries. The style was no longer classical, but plain Gothic. Long Early English lancets were most often used and can be seen at Catshill, but other styles were experimented with, such as Norman at St. Clement, Worcester or Perpendicular at St. George, Kidderminster.

Whilst the true Commissioners Churches were those built for increasing urban populations, other churches were rebuilt at this time in similar styles, of which St. Michael at Broadway, and the churches in Elmley Lovett and Pensax are all good examples. One architect employed by the Commissioners to build new churches in Birmingham was Thomas Rickman, who devoted much time to studying English Gothic architecture, and indeed first used the terms Early English, Decorated and Perpendicular. Rickman's churches were still essentially Commissioners type buildings, but displayed a greater understanding of the medieval styles used, such as the Decorated style windows in the nave of 1835 at Hartlebury, whilst also being innovative with, for example, cast iron piers at Ombersley and Hartlebury, or unusual flying buttresses of 1825 on the tower at Ombersley. Only Rickman's simple nave of the Catholic church in Redditch is typical Commissioners Early English.

The 1820s and 1830s saw both a Roman Catholic revival in England and a change of direction, encompassing many Catholic ideas, within the established church. The growth of the Oxford Movement and the Cambridge Camden Society were the impetus behind a much greater emphasis on ritual worship. The importance of the altar for a focal point required larger chancels and the pulpit became less dominant.

The classical and plain buildings of the 18th and early 19th centuries were seen as undistinguished, and too similar to most nonconformist churches. Instead there was a preference for churches in the medieval Gothic style. The movement, which became known as the Gothic Revival, was led by the Roman Catholic architect Augustus Welby Northmore Pugin, who produced 14th-century style Catholic churches for wealthy patrons, of which perhaps the best local example is St. Giles' church at Cheadle in Staffordshire. Pugin's work in Worcestershire is restricted to a school at Spetchley for the Berkeleys and the lychgate with some interior fittings at Blackmore Park church, Hanley Swan for the Hornyolds. However, Pugin's son was the architect of the since demolished church at Madresfield. Other architects followed Pugin's ideas, and Gothic Revival churches were designed highlighting the importance of the altar in a separate chancel, that had to be proportionally smaller than the nave and divided from it by an arch, and the whole elaborately ornamented with both carving and painting.

Additional features to these churches included porches, aisles, towers or bellcotes, and a vestry or sacristy. Transepts were encouraged, to make the church cruciform, but these often proved to be useless spaces. Additional symbolism was found in triple lancets or runs of three steps which were considered to represent the Trinity.

All these elements can be seen in Worcestershire churches designed during the third quarter of the 19th century by architects who worked across the country. William Butterfield was closely involved with the Cambridge Camden Society from 1842, and Keble College Oxford begun in 1867 is one of his most famous designs. Butterfield enjoyed experimenting alongside traditionalism, and the polychrome brick-work of the college and his church at All Saints, Margaret Street in London is reflected inside and out at Alvechurch. Butterfield's work at Feckenham and Sedgeberrow shows clearly his fascination for medieval Gothic. Henry Woodyer, who worked with Butterfield in 1844, also produced amazing Decorated style buildings such as St. Michael, Tenbury Wells which, like his church at Highnam in Gloucestershire, show that if the money was available, most things were possible. Other prominent architects designed churches in Worcestershire, notably Richard Cromwell Carpenter at Kemerton, Sir Arthur Blomfield at Upton and Wribbenhall and George Edmund Street at Hagley and St. Peter, Malvern. However, the best known Victorian church architect, Sir George Gilbert Scott, who was deeply involved in restoring and refurbishing Worcester Cathedral between 1864 and 1874, had only one parish church design in the county—that of St. Matthias, Malvern Link, although his family and practice designed the churches at Hanley Swan, Stourport and Churchill in Halfshire. The most elaborate example of a Victorian Gothic Revival church in Worcestershire must be that at Newland designed by Philip Charles Hardwick, who joined his father's London practice in 1843, and whose Great Western Hotel at Paddington Station completed in 1861 set a precedent for imposing station hotels.Hardwick's medieval style at Newland is used with lively 19th-century enhancement both in the Decorated exterior, and in the colourful decoration and fittings of the interior by various artists and craftsmen. The interior at Newland makes the most of the Victorian ability to work iron and fire tiles by improved manufacturing processes as well as to readily import building materials from abroad. However, to keep a medieval authenticity there are Gothic details everywhere and traditional techniques were used in the wall paintings, although these like the glass have a quality distinct from actual medieval work. For all the advances in engineering and technology, Victorian church builders and their patrons chose almost without exception medieval Gothic, and usually the style of about 1300 with its transition from Early English to Decorated.

However, a burgeoning movement of Italianate design, which found popularity in country houses such as Bricklehampton Hall or urban villas and commercial buildings, may have assisted in the sympathetic classical additions of chancels to the Georgian churches at Broome and Tardebigge. These can be compared with the east end of St. Philip's church (now cathedral) in Birmingham. Much Victorian restoration work has been condemned as harsh where older, particularly medieval churches are concerned, and certainly some churches were changed dramatically to conform with the principles of Ecclesiologists. Alterations at Old St. Martin, Worcester, and at Hanley Castle or Naunton Beauchamp were not sympathetic to what was there before, and churches like Bricklehampton or Rous Lench were given features in exaggerated forms of the original styles. However, there was a genuine interest in the buildings and their architecture, which ensured that much detail had a medieval precedent and was archaeologically correct.

This can be seen in additions and rebuildings at churches such as Wick, Belbroughton and Shelsley Beauchamp, and in restorations which only sought to recreate the original, as in the east window at Stoke Prior. By the 19th century many churches had received only minimal and vital structural repairs since the 16th century, yet had often been altered and adapted several times. Similarly towns were still greatly expanding and new churches were built in the growing suburbs of Worcester, particularly in the former parish of Claines, as well as in the fashionable resort town of Malvern.

These various aspects of 19th century churches are also to be seen in the work of local architects. The cathedral architect, Abraham Perkins was employed to construct the church at Doddenham, restore Wichenford and to rebuild Little Witley and Whittington. All four churches are different—Whittington is a Commissioners type church of 1842, whilst Little Witley has exaggerated Early English work of 1867. The diocesan architect, William Jeffrey Hopkins, seems to have worked on most churches in the central eastern section of the county, where his simple Decorated style work at Tibberton or Abberton can be compared with extensive restorations and rebuildings at Upton Snodsbury or Flyford Flavell. Henry Rowe was a noted Worcester architect, though his churches are of a small scale as at North Piddle and Lulsley. Harvey Eginton's Norman style church at Trimpley is also of interest. The most prolific local architect was Frederick Preedy. Born in Worcestershire, Preedy had offices in Foregate Street, Worcester by 1852, and worked on churches all over England, with most commissions in Worcestershire and the adjoining counties. He too favoured the style of about 1300 and good examples of his work can be seen at Hollybush, Madresfield, Crowle and St. Mary Magdalene, Worcester. Like so many other architects of his time, he also designed many pieces of church furnishing and stained glass, as well as undertaking substantial restorations as at Rock and Middle Littleton.

Some rather over zealous restoration, and in particular the scraping of church interiors back to the stonework, brought a reaction towards the end of the 19th century. Whilst scraped stone emphasises hidden features such as blocked doorways or windows, it also involved the destruction of earlier plaster and wall paintings. Thus the Society for the Protection of Ancient Buildings was founded by William Morris in 1877 as a reaction to Scott's restoration and scraping of Tewkesbury Abbey in Gloucestershire. The Arts and Crafts Movement, which flourished towards the end of the century, put a different emphasis on church restoration, with attempts to preserve the historic features found in most old churches. Irregular arches of different stones, floors of varying texture and furnishings from several periods were no longer swept away to be replaced with a uniform style, and churches restored in this more sympathetic manner can be seen at Bransford and Martley. Arts and Crafts architects favoured the light and airiness of Perpendicular churches and the use of well-crafted traditional materials, following the work of George Frederick Bodley whose font can be seen in Worcester Cathedral. The nearest large church by Bodley is Hoar Cross in Staffordshire, but Sir George Aston Webb had several commissions in this area, and his church of St. George in Worcester, with the alterations at Alfrick and Claines reflect the philosophy of the movement. Other architects produced work worth seeing, such as George Fellowes Prynne at St. Martin, Worcester, William Henry Bidlake's tower at Wythall, Walter Tapper at Ascension, Malvern and Temple Moore's chancel at St. Stephen, Redditch. However, the finest Arts and Crafts church in Worcestershire is that by Arthur Bartlett at Dodford. Here both the stateliness and homeliness of the design is enhanced by the often subtle craftsmanship and furnishings by members of the Bromsgrove Guild of Applied Arts.

This unusual group of craftsmen and women was founded by Walter Gilbert, a former art teacher at Bromsgrove School in 1894. Until its demise in 1966, the Guild produced fine works, many of which are in Worcestershire churches, of which Dodford has the finest collection. Furnishings and glass can be seen at Hanbury, St. George Worcester, Tardebigge and Bromsgrove. The Guild's reputation attracted members from overseas, including Louis Weingartner and Celestino Pancheri, and whilst some works were produced individually, many were done anonymously in the name of the Guild. As holders of a Royal Warrant from 1908, the Guild made the gates and railings for Aston Webb's remodelling of Buckingham Palace, the bronze doors of the Bank of England, the lamp standards in Parliament Square all in London, as well as the copper Liver Birds in Liverpool.

The work of the Guild stemmed from an interesting 'fin de siècle' of artistic embellishment in Worcestershire churches, with high quality furnishings and sculpture produced by the Forsyths of Worcester, or the significant amounts of stained glass by Hardman and Co. and Charles Eamer Kempe. The pre-Raphaelite glass at Wilden, designed by Edward Burne-Jones, and work by his successors in this style such as the windows by the Camm family at Hook Common or Strensham are also notable. Throughout the late 19th and early 20th centuries much of the financial backing for restoring, building and enhancing these churches came from local industry, of which Baldwin's ironworks at Wilden and John Corbett's saltworks at Stoke Prior are typical examples.

Restoration of churches in the 20th century has been ongoing, with much necessary structural work being undertaken to the larger churches such as Malvern Priory and Pershore Abbey, as well as to Worcester Cathedral. Churches have been archaeologically recorded to aid future plans, and adapted to keep them useable and up to date. Sometimes this has been done in a very contemporary manner such as with George Pace's chancel fittings of the 1960s at Pershore Abbey. With the huge numbers of churches in existence, maintenance has been a great problem throughout the 20th century, and some churches have been closed to worship. A few, such as St. Peter the Great in Worcester, have been demolished, but many have been converted to another use. St. Andrew, Pershore is now the parish centre, Cow Honeybourne provides housing and St. Helen, Worcester is part of the County Record Office. Other redundant churches are preserved in their entirety by the Churches Conservation Trust, including Pendock Old Church, Croome d'Abitot and Strensham. A near case of closure was at Warndon, but this was avoided by new housing nearby making the church viable, and leading to its extensive restoration. Most churches need huge sums of money to cope with difficult restorations, but many of these have been undertaken after enormous fund-raising efforts—Ripple, Mamble, Cotheridge, Kyre Wyard to name but a few. Financial support is now available from bodies such as English Heritage and the Worcestershire and Dudley Historic Churches Trust, but the care and maintenance along with the use and atmosphere is largely the work of the parishioners. Visitors are generally encouraged and awareness of the history and architecture of these churches has grown throughout the century. It is perhaps a shame that there are not more 20th-century churches to add to those of earlier date, but certainly those at Matchborough in Redditch, Blackwell near Bromsgrove along with Holy Trinity and St. Matthew in Worcester should be seen in the context of their surroundings and communities along with their Norman, Medieval, Georgian and Victorian predecessors.

CHAPTER II

Church Decoration, Fittings and Setting

Furnishings and Fittings

It is difficult today to form an impression of the interior appearance of a medieval Worcestershire church before the Reformation, with extensive stained glass windows and wall paintings all contributing to a dim atmosphere lit by candles; a church in which mass was celebrated, and which formed a focal and very integrated part of the lives of everybody in the community. The fittings and furnishings have changed several times since the end of the Middle Ages, as new movements of thought and changes in the liturgy have been adopted. There are relatively few survivals of medieval church fittings and furnishings in Worcestershire, and to understand them it is perhaps best to explore a typical interior, examining features as they would have been in their medieval context.

The entrance doorway to the nave may contain a medieval door which might be cross battened as at Upton Snodsbury, or medieval ironwork as at Astley. Sometimes there is evidence of greater security than just the lock, with mortices for huge wooden bolts, as at Shelsley Walsh. The holy water stoup at or near the entrance will probably have been broken at the Reformation, but the survival at Shrawley is particularly elaborate.

The font was usually in the nave at the west end of the church, where many still are today. Stone fonts endure the rigours of time more readily than many wooden fittings, and most churches have retained a medieval example. Indeed sometimes they have been preserved in churches which were rebuilt at a much later date, like Broome or Suckley. Round Norman fonts are plentiful, often with elaborate decoration, as at Chaddesley Corbett and Holt, though many are relatively plain like South Littleton and Eastham. Later medieval fonts were often polygonal with decoration, and can be seen at Upton Snodsbury and All Saints, Evesham. The font at Elmley Castle has a fine carved base. Many naves are now filled with pews, though these did not arrive until the later Middle Ages. Early congregations stood or made use of stone seats around the edge of the nave, none of which have survived in Worcestershire. The earliest pews in the county are 15th-century, ranging from plain benches at Warndon to seats with panelled ends and tracery at Cropthorne or the Littletons. There is 16th-century linenfold panelling at Strensham. At the east end of the nave was the pulpit which became popular for preaching with the coming of the friars from the 13th century. Few medieval pulpits survive in and around Worcestershire, but the Perpendicular pulpit at St. Eadburgha, Broadway is a good example.

The nave was divided from the chancel by the rood screen which often supported a loft with the rood or crucifix on a beam, and which was adorned with candles at festivals. Examples of screens are found at Aston Somerville and Little Malvern. A loft survives *in situ* at Besford, whilst that at Strensham is now at the back of the nave (see rear cover). Evidence of access to former rood lofts for singers can be found in the many rood loft stairs, such as Martley or Stoke Prior. At Leigh part of the rood screen survives across

Norman lecterns at Norton (left) and Crowle (right)

the side aisle. The ceiling above was often more elaborate than that of the rest of the nave with carving and painting as a canopy of honour, of which one can be seen at Knighton-on-Teme. Other screens separated chantry chapels, and were known as parclose screens. There is an excellent example at Shelsley Walsh, and the mortice holes which joined many more to the piers of arches can frequently be seen, as at Huddington.

The chancel beyond the screen was the sacred space, divided off to keep it as a sanctuary and apart from secular activities in the nave. Here the priest celebrated mass using a variety of fittings some of which can often still be found. Martley church has part of its stone altar; a medieval reredos can be seen in Pershore Abbey; aumbries or cupboards for sacred items exist at Cropthorne, whilst there is a sedilia at Bredon. Piscinae, where the chalice and paten were washed, can be seen in most churches, with good examples at Salwarpe and Clifton-on-Teme. Huddington has niches for statues, and there are brackets for more statues or candles in many chancels including Sedgeberrow.

Both Bredon and St. Mary, Tenbury Wells have Easter Sepulchres on the north side of the chancel, where the sacrament was kept between Good Friday and Easter Sunday. Churches which were served by a number of clerics had stalls, of which those at Ripple with their carved misericords are an excellent example. These were also used in the monastic communities, and can be seen at Pershore, or Great and Little Malvern, as well as some fine examples dated to 1379 in Worcester Cathedral.

Worcestershire has two fine Norman lecterns now in the naves of Norton and Crowle churches. Wooden and brass lecterns in the form of an eagle, the symbol of St. John the Evangelist, became popular in the later middle ages, but no medieval examples exist in Worcestershire.

The liturgical changes of the Reformation period are inextricably linked to differences in the ways that the buildings were furnished. Little now remains in Worcestershire of extreme Protestant arrangements made during the Commonwealth, whereby the communion table was placed centrally and surrounded by seating and rails in the chancel, though examples can be seen at Hailes and Deerhurst in Gloucestershire, and there are vestiges of the arrangement at Warndon. However, numerous communion tables of this date remain in Worcestershire churches, including Stoke Prior and Spetchley, and there are good 17th-century pulpits at St. Michael Broadway, Ipsley and Naunton Beauchamp, though these have been reduced in size from the large three-decker pulpits which once dominated church interiors. Sermons lasting at least an hour were preached from here and wrought iron stands, to hold the hourglasses to time them, survive at Oddingley and Bishampton. Doors were fitted to the pews making for less draughty box pews, which could be rented, though free seating for those unable to afford this were usually to be found towards the back of the church. Ownership of pews was also frequently attached to property, and changed hands when that property was bought or sold. Some 17th-century box pews survive at Cotheridge, where there is also a fine pulpit, whilst those at Wickhamford, around the surviving three decker pulpit, are in an arrangement laid out during the reign of Charles II. Under Charles II chancels like those at Wickhamford or Huddington were frequently screened off from the naves. Communion tables were returned to the east end and separated by communion rails, often with turned balusters, of which there are many survivals, such as at Castlemorton or Dormston. Medieval furnishings were also often adapted; there is medieval woodwork in the pulpits at Queenhill and Overbury, and the Strensham rood loft was reset at the west end of the nave as a singing gallery. Many medieval fonts received covers which were often quite plain such as at St. Alban, Worcester, but there is a more elaborate example at Shrawley.

Fittings and furnishings continued in a similar fashion through the 18th century, and Worcestershire's new classical churches were equipped with splendid pieces. Much of this disappeared during 19th-century alterations, but there are some good furnishings at the four Georgian Worcester churches, of which St. Swithin has retained its complete interior, including a spectacular three decker pulpit. Elements of the Gothic style were introduced in churches where this was integral to the building design. In particular the remarkable Gothic furnishings at Croome d'Abitot set a precedent for the interiors of the Commissioners Churches of the early 19th century. Box pews, galleries and large pulpits fill the naves of Ombersley and Whittington churches, though the east ends with their prayer and commandment boards have been modified later in the century to emphasise the presence of the altar. A greater use of iron during the 18th and 19th centuries reflects developments in industry in the Severn valley area, with wrought ironwork in the sword rest and communion table at St. Swithin, Worcester, and the cast iron gallery piers at Ombersley and Hartlebury.

These interiors became quite unfashionable with the Gothic Revival and ecclesiological movements of the mid-19th century. Medieval style furnishings preferred by the Victorian patrons, incumbents and architects now fill most Worcestershire churches. The most lavish and colourful extremes of High Church Anglicanism can be experienced at Newland, or a little more plainly at Madresfield and Kemerton.

However, the rows of pitch pine pews, the choir stalls, organs and reredoses which were installed in churches built or restored by architects such as William Jeffery Hopkins at Upton Snodsbury or Flyford Flavell, or Frederick Preedy at Hollybush or St. Stephen, Worcester are typical of the changes in this period. They were following the example of William Butterfield at Sedgeberrow or Henry Woodyer at St. Michael, Tenbury, all of which fit into a distinct national pattern of church interiors. Nevertheless, the story of the furnishings is parallel to that of the fabric of the buildings, and much earlier and particularly pre-Reformation material, such as fonts and pulpits, was retained and adapted to new surroundings.

The close of the century and the growth of the Arts and Crafts movement brought a revival of the use of traditional techniques and materials. Fine quality woodwork and metalwork can be found in the designs of Sir George Aston Webb at All Saints and St. George, Worcester, whilst the screen and altar-piece at Ascension in Malvern complement the architecture of Walter Tapper. Several churches contain furnishings by the Bromsgrove Guild from the first half of the 20th century, particularly Dodford, but fine later metal and woodwork by Guild members including Celestino Pancheri can be found in many churches, such as Tardebigge and Stoke Prior. 20th-century furnishings often with a plain but streamlined finish are present in almost every church, though little is attributed. The chancel furniture in Pershore Abbey, the work of George Pace, is an outstanding example from the 1960s.

Glass, Wall Painting and Tiles

The occurrence of stained glass in Worcestershire churches is similar to that in most other English counties. Medieval glass generally survives in a fragmentary state, with many churches possessing small pieces often collected together in one or two windows. In some cases, at least, a complete panel has been preserved, but apart from one or two instances of exceptional glass, all are overshadowed by the splendid collection of 15th-century windows at Great Malvern Priory. The Reformation years, time and neglect have all taken their toll on Worcestershire's medieval glass, but there are interesting examples of 17th- and 18th-century work, and most churches possess 19th-century windows designed by at least one of the country's leading glass producing firms. Whilst window glass had been used in Britain since Roman times, it was very costly and many windows in early churches were merely shuttered, rebates for which can be seen at Holt and Shrawley.

There are no examples in Worcestershire of early medieval glass except for the poorly preserved figure of St. Mary Magdalene at Himbleton and perhaps some of the saints at Kempsey. Figures of saints and scenes from the Life of Christ were popular by the 14th century, and are shown in distinctive blues, greens, yellows and reds. The increasingly naturalistic details of faces, hands and feet, together with the ornamentation of canopies links the glass closely with the Decorated architectural style. Windows at Kempsey, Bredon, Birtsmorton and Sedgeberrow contain saints, whilst the Virgin and Child at Warndon and Fladbury (see rear cover), seated Christ at All Saints, Evesham and crucifixions at Mamble and St. Peter, Droitwich are all evidence of an increasing desire to illustrate the teachings of the church, which should be seen in context with sculpture, wall painting and manuscript illustration.

Improved glazing techniques allowed greater flexibility in painting and staining glass by the 15th century and apart from the windows at Great Malvern Priory, typical glass with saints figures and biblical scenes from this period can be seen at Holt, Oddingley, Huddington, Inkberrow and Little Malvern. Their delicacy and lightness reflect the large windows of the Perpendicular style. Oddingley has a good collection of donor figures, whilst Queenhill, Dormston, Fladbury and Hampton Lovett have heraldic arms.

No doubt the donor figures and heraldic arms have survived the Reformation because of their secular nature, but many of the other remaining fragments of medieval glass can be found in tracery lights. Glass was expensive, however, and it is known from the surveys of the county by Habington and Nash that much more survived at least into the 18th century. Nevertheless, clear glazing became fashionable, though it was sometimes embellished with heraldic arms as at Eldersfield, and the installation of enamelled glass panels showing saints and religious scenes was allowed during the time of Archbishop Laud and after the Commonwealth, when from 1650 to 1660 stained glass was harshly condemned. 17th-century panels, probably from the Netherlands, can be seen at Abbots Morton and Alfrick.

By the 18th century, whilst clear glass was still the norm, any coloured glass which was commissioned took the form of a painting. One of the most outstanding sets in the country is at Great Witley, where the enamelled painted windows by Joshua Price are to Italian designs. Price came from a family of glass painters in York, a city with a long glazing tradition, and the windows are exceptional in that they were brought by Lord Foley from the Duke of Chandos' fashionable house in Middlesex. Meanwhile much medieval glass was replaced with clear windows for the sake of fashion.

Early 19th-century glass had similar qualities to that of the previous century and is relatively uncommon. The east window of St. Thomas, Dudley in the West Midlands by Joseph Backer showing the Transfiguration is a good local example. However, with the Gothic Revival in the middle of the century, there was a renewed interest in medieval glass and the techniques of its production. Many firms started to produce glass deemed appropriate for medieval settings. Chance of Oldbury was one of the first, producing glass by the early 1860s and examples of their windows, albeit later in date, can be seen at Wichenford and Stoke Prior. James Powell and Sons produced glass in Whitechapel, London for windows at Hagley, and there are windows by Clayton and Bell at Pershore Abbey. Chance's glass was used by John Hardman and Co., and apart from the several windows in Worcester Cathedral, the glass at St. Michael, Tenbury is a considerable display of their work, The style is reflected in the work of many other artists including Michael O'Connor, who produced glass for Pugin, and who was commissioned to design a window in St. Mary, Kidderminster, and William Wailes, also used by Pugin, who designed a window at West Malvern. Glaziers were constantly studying medieval glass and reproducing elements of it. Charles Eamer Kempe produced much that is similar to glass of about 1400 and examples can be seen at Bricklehampton, Bockleton and Wick, as well as at St. Matthias and Holy Trinity churches in Malvern.

However, it was the work of William Morris and Co. which changed the style of glass in the later part of the century with clear, bold designs and areas of colour separated by prominent black leadlines. The firm's glass production is an important part of the pre-Raphaelite movement, and cannot be separated from the production of furnishings, paintings, tiles or tapestries. Many of the designs are by Edward Burne-Jones, whose windows are to be found at Ribbesford and Wilden, partly as a result of family connections, whilst some early Morris glass can be seen at Rochford. The firm's production continued after the deaths of Morris and Burne-Jones, and a later example can be seen at Wolverley.

The influence of the Arts and Crafts movement and Morris and Co. reached into the 20th century. The windows by Christopher Whall, as at Upton-upon-Severn, show this, as does the prolific work of the Bromsgrove Guild, both collectively and by individuals, such as Albert Lemmon's glass at Bengeworth and in the leading of the clear glass at Dodford.

After the First World War, memorial windows were installed in many Worcestershire churches, as at Bradley by Archibald Davies of the Bromsgrove Guild, whilst following the Second World War there were numerous new commissions to replace bombed glass in other parts of the country. However, perhaps the lack of destruction at this time in Worcestershire has contributed to a relative absence of late 20th-century glass in the county, though occasional examples such as the east window at Stoke Bliss are striking and a vital contribution to this continuing heritage.

The decoration of walls should be considered alongside this story of glass. Much medieval wall painting has been lost with the scraping of plaster from the walls of Worcestershire churches during 19th-century restorations. Before then, paintings had frequently been covered with whitewash. The best survivals are at Martley and Pinvin, though clear fragments can also be seen at Kyre Wyard, Belbroughton and Wickhamford. These comprised similar themes to those in the stained glass, but substantial areas were also painted with geometric patterns such as in the chancel at Martley. Painted canopies and drapery help to date them as with glass. Recent restoration work has shown that the chance of survival beneath existing whitewash is likely to be high, and there have been interesting discoveries at Bransford, Strensham and Spetchley.

Following the Reformation, texts and the royal arms were painted on the walls. The royal arms, as at Wickhamford, replaced judgement paintings over the chancel arch and served as a reminder that the monarch was head of the church, but from the 18th century these were mostly carved in wood and incorporated into the furnishings. Fragments of post-Reformation painting have been uncovered at Lower Sapey and Pebworth, which would have been text within a geometric design or associated with painted architectural features. The characteristic 18th-century desire for plainness is quite definitely not reflected in the interior of Great Witley church (see rear cover), where the magnificent paintings by the Italian artist, Antonio Belucci, are set in moulded gilded surrounds, which continue over the walls, giving the church the feeling of a palatial room.

In the quantity of decoration, though not in style, Witley has more in common with the 19th-century interiors of the Gothic revival. In some instances painted text gave way to a recreation of a high level of pictorial wall decoration not seen since the Reformation. The murals by Clayton and Bell at Newland are the most lavish, but their work at Pershore Abbey, the painted arcade at Feckenham (see rear cover) and the surround of the chancel arch at Madresfield are also of this period.

Worcestershire churches are rightly well known for their medieval floor tiles. The production centres at Droitwich, Worcester and most significantly Malvern are the foundation for this reputation. Great Malvern Priory has the county's largest and best collection of both floor and wall tiles, but impressive groups of tiles survive in many churches including Bredon, Cotheridge, Martley, South Littleton, Huddington and Strensham. Designs include heraldic arms, such as those at Middle Littleton, Claines and Warndon, whilst symbols of the church are at Claines and Little Malvern, and inscriptions at Holt, Bredicot and Salwarpe.

There is a fine 17th-century tile floor with a geometric pattern at Bredon, whilst plain quarry tiles of the 18th and early 19th centuries help to give a homely feel to the interiors at Shrawley and Martley. The production of medieval style tiles flourished in the 19th century, not least at Chamberlain's tile works in Worcester—the floor at Worcester Cathedral is a classic example of the reuse of medieval design introducing new colours, often green and blue. Other 19th-century tile pavements are to be found at Newland, Hanbury and All Saints, Evesham, whilst the lower parts of the chancel walls at Sedgeberrow are lined with medieval style tiles of this type.

Memorials

Almost every Worcestershire church contains a collection of memorials to people with whom that church has been associated, and much information about families and individuals can be gleaned from them. Most date from the last 300 years, and many relate to the wealthy, but a look at memorials in the churchyard can reveal gems of information about ordinary local people. Examples of interesting graveyards include Chaddesley Corbett, Leigh and St. Eadburgha, Broadway.

The earliest memorials in churches were carved decorations on stone coffin lids which could be seen on the church floor. A simple relief, often just a cross, was used to commemorate a lord or churchman, and examples have often been reset away from their original location, as at St. Peter, Droitwich. Simple stone sarcophagi were also used—there is a surviving example at Martley.

By the 13th century memorials consisted of life-like effigies in relief, which were set on tomb chests. In Worcestershire, memorials of this type must have been led in style by the effigy of King John in

The 17th-century memorial to Sir Giles Reed in Bredon church

18

The 14th-century chantry chapel at Broadwas

Worcester Cathedral, which dates from about 1230. There are several effigies from this period, particularly of knights, with arms and legs arranged in various ways, as at Martley and Great Malvern, or from later in the century at Mamble and Pershore. However, the 14th-century figures are shown lying rigid with hands together as in prayer.

Later medieval memorials have a wealth of architectural detail of contemporary Decorated and Perpendicular styles in their tomb chests, and in the case of the Beauchamp memorial in St. Mary, Kidderminster, in elaborate canopies. The Perpendicular tomb chest of King John dating from 1529 and the neighbouring chantry to Prince Arthur, begun in 1504, in Worcester Cathedral, again provide useful focal points from which memorials of the local nobility in county churches can be compared. Good examples of late medieval memorials survive at Bredon, Holt, Claines and Stanford-on-Teme. Such memorials might be associated with the foundation of chantry chapels, where prayers could be said for the souls of the deceased, and which became increasingly elaborate up to the 16th century. Interesting traces and examples of chantries can be seen at Broadwas, Martley, Shelsley Walsh and the Evesham churches. Concern about the immediacy of death in the Middle Ages was expressed in representations such as the cadaver at Mamble, whilst the commemoration of a death abroad was often made by returning the heart in a casket for burial in the home parish. Memorials for heart burials can be seen at St. Mary, Tenbury Wells and Bredon. Not everyone could afford lavish stone memorials, and incised slabs as can be seen at Rock, or brasses were very popular. Where they survive, brasses, like effigies, are remarkable references for costume, as at Strensham, Fladbury and St. Mary, Kidderminster. There are often other details such as heraldry or inscriptions. All medieval memorials are now in surroundings which are quite different from what was originally envisaged, and would have been adjacent to wall paintings, stained glass and furnishings, which rarely survive. Meanwhile, most ordinary people were buried simply in the nave of the church or in the surrounding churchyard. Once spaces were filled, bones were collected and placed in charnel pits or ossuaries, of which that at Worcester Cathedral is still preserved.

From the 16th century increasing numbers of merchants and lesser landowners wished to be buried with more elaborate monuments. With the changes of the Reformation there were less opportunities for embellishing parts of the church, and so, particularly amongst recusant Catholic families, highly decorated Renaissance style memorials became popular. Memorials to the Blounts at Astley, Berkeleys at Spetchley, Sheldons at Beoley, Hanfords at Eckington were all in this category, and there are further excellent large 17th-century memorials at Norton, Bredon, Leigh and Cropthorne. There is a wealth of heraldry on these memorials, and the costume of the effigies can be beautifully fashioned as on the Savage memorial at Elmley Castle. An interesting contrast can be made between these and the unusual wooden memorials at Shelsley Walsh and Stockton-on-Teme. There are also several post-Reformation brasses with inscriptions, of which those at Huddington and Eastham are good examples.

By the end of the 17th century, an increasing number of wall mounted monuments and tablets were erected, as at Tardebigge or Leigh, in preference to tomb chests. 18th-century monuments tend to be larger, of black and white marbles, and firmly classical in design. With lengthy epitaphs, striking figures and architectural detail they often dominate the church interiors, as at Croome d'Abitot, Great Witley and Strensham. Marks on the memorials or documentary evidence often record the names of sculptors— Roubiliac and Chantrey at Hanbury, Scheemakers at Powick, or the Bacons at Astley. Many of these fashionable London sculptors were Huguenot French or Dutch in origin, and the standards of craftsmanship are high with a wonderful diversity of ideas from the classical dress at Great Witley to the musical instruments at Powick. Smaller wall tablets were still popular, and many are also beautifully carved with swags of drapery or foliage. Ombersley, Astley and Grimley churches have some good examples.

By the 19th century these tablets became more restrained but also prolific. Groups can be seen at Shrawley, Hartlebury and in most of the Worcester churches, many with interesting inscriptions. However, the Gothic Revival brought a renewed interest in the medieval style chest tombs and the Wolstenholme Prescott tomb at Bockleton is typical. A 19th-century gloss comes in the sentimentality of the imagery, part of the culture of mourning which followed the death of Prince Albert. Medieval style brasses were also popular, with Gothic lettering, such as that to Francis Winnington-Ingram at Ribbesford.

Twentieth-century memorials inside churches tend to be smaller plaques of stone, wood or brass, though, like their medieval predecessors, they are often linked to the donation of a window or piece of furnishing. The bronze Art Nouveau memorial of the early 1900s by Feodora Gleichen at Madresfield is exceptional, but there was often considerable expenditure on memorials to the dead of the First World War. Aside from many attractive and individual interior pieces as at Little Comberton or Stoulton, these often took the form of a community memorial recreating the idea of the medieval churchyard cross, as at St. John, Worcester. Most 20th-century memorials are stones in churchyard and cemetery settings, which along with those of the two previous centuries show a huge variety in materials and architectural detail. An example of a tragic piece of social history can be seen on the slate stones commemorating the deaths on the railway at Bromsgrove. It is interesting to compare the restored 17th-century burial ground of St. Stephen's chapel at Redditch with a complex graveyard such as Feckenham to see changes in fashion and taste for commemorating the dead.

It is unfortunate that so many gravestones have been cleared for ease of maintenance in the second half of the 20th century, especially as several of the stones themselves have been broken up and there is often no record of their original positions. An important postscript to this theme of churchyard protection is the increasing emphasis placed on their roles as conservation areas for wildlife, and not just for the preservation of the stones.

Setting and Context

The structures of communities around the churches have developed along with the roles and settings of the churches within them. Features from different historical periods often remain around the church, in a changing scene which continues to move forward as fresh needs and new interests arise.

Most rural medieval churches were close to the residence of the lord of the manor, who was often also the patron. Earthworks from medieval manor houses, such as Rock and Churchill, or the buildings of their successors such as Huddington and Great Witley, are frequently adjacent to the churches. The village was usually nearby. Sometimes the main settlement has moved or disappeared leaving the church in relative isolation, with further earthworks from the houses in a neighbouring field, as at Pendock, Grafton Flyford or Throckmorton. In both town and country, the church was an important focus of parish life with most public events being held there alongside services. The nave was used for plays and pageants, and would frequently house the church ales which were fund-raising events held by the parish for the main-

The churchyard at Stone showing the cross and timber-framed church house

tenance of the nave, tower, aisles and porch. The chancel was screened off and was the responsibility of the patron, who also appointed the priest. The patron could have been the lord of the manor, or the bishop as at Kempsey, or a monastery like Pershore or Westminster. Chantry chapels were similarly separated by screens and provided for by individual endowments.

Much of the evidence for the life of medieval priests has disappeared since the Reformation. In well endowed parishes they lived in some splendour, and parts of the medieval priests' houses survive in the rectory buildings at Martley and Abberley. Most vestments, books and plate have also vanished, but occasional examples such as the cope at Church Lench or the psalter from St. Helen's Worcester are reminders of the great riches which complemented the architecture, decoration and furnishings in medieval churches. Vestries and sacristies, where these treasures were stored in the Middle Ages grace Stoke Prior and Rock, whilst medieval chests survive at Eckington and Spetchley. A room over the porch, or Parvis, was used as a school or library, and was considered prestigious. An example can be found at Bredon, and they were intended at Severn Stoke, Cropthorne and Fladbury, but never built.

Outside, the churchyard provided a public open space where preaching could be conducted from a cross, of which there are many examples in Worcestershire, now without their heads. However, a carved cross head is preserved inside the church at Dormston. Those at Broadwas, Strensham and Suckley have niches for the pyx to be placed in on Palm Sunday. Here announcements of national events were made, including outbreaks of war and peace, the deaths and accessions of monarchs, and the parish business was conducted. With the increasing popularity of pews in naves by the 15th century, alternative accommodation was constructed near the church for the church ales and other events. Timber-framed church houses can be seen at Areley Kings and Stone.

Following the Reformation, the incumbent's residence frequently came to dominate the environs of the church, depending on the wealth of the 'living' of the parish. Large Georgian rectories were built at Ripple and Hartlebury, and in the 19th century the incumbent's house often formed part of a remodelling of the church's surroundings with a new school, as at Alvechurch. Schools were frequently attached to churchyards, as successors of medieval schools run by priests, which were later endowed through the church, such as St. Mary, Kidderminster or the Chantry School at Martley. During the 19th century, many village schools were built close to the church and continue in use today, as at Longdon, Tardebigge or Upton Snodsbury.

Charitable works by the church, like education, had a physical expression after the Reformation through the provision of boards listing the bequests and trusts which assisted various categories of needy parishioners. Typical boards survive at Warndon and Defford, whilst those from St. Peter the Great in Worcester are now at the Commandery. Such doles and gifts played a significant part in poor relief into the 20th century; doles of bread from Worcester Cathedral are well recorded in Victorian photographs. Generous endowments sometimes led to the foundation of almshouses near churches, which make an attractive and unusual contribution to the surroundings at Hanley Castle, Kyre Wyard and Newland. Church and community have been closely linked over the centuries and this has manifested itself in various ways which can be interpreted when visiting the churches of Worcestershire.

ABBERLEY   ST. MARY

St. Mary is situated to the north of the centre of this pretty village on the Abberley Hills. It replaced the medieval church of St. Michael, part of which still stands in the square. However, it is not the church spire, but the clock tower at Abberley Hall which dominates the skyline when the hills are approached from the valleys of the Severn and the Teme.

The tower and spire are at the south west corner of the church, which has a nave and chancel with side aisles and porch. The church was built by the Moilliet family of Abberley Hall between 1850 and 1852. James Moilliet gave the land and most of the money, and his son John Lewis Moilliet went on to be rector from 1865 to 1904. The architect was J.J. Cole, who also restored the church after a serious fire in 1876.

The doorways, windows and interior features are all in the Early English style of the late 13th century. Inside, the arcades have polished marble columns and stiff leaf capitals, with inset carvings including an ark, a pelican and a dove. There are marble shafts in the chancel, and two light openings into the Moilliet chapel. There are late 19th century furnishings, including the font, pulpit, lectern and miserecords. Amongst the glass and memorials, there is engraved glass in a north window. It commemorates Gilbert Ashton, a cricketer, who died in 1961.

ABBERLEY   ST. MICHAEL

St. Michael, Abberley, showing the ruined nave

The remains of this medieval church stand in a pretty graveyard in the village square at the centre of the village, with the much altered medieval rectory to the east. The tower, nave and aisle are in ruins, but the chancel and south chapel survive intact.

St. Michael is a pre-conquest foundation, and indeed tradition claims that in the 7th century St. Augustine met the British bishops in the parish at Apostle's Oak. The church was one of a group along with Astley and Rock built by the Tosny family, who were powerful Norman lords in this part of Worcestershire. Parts of the remaining sandstone structure are 12th century, including the base of the tower, the north wall and surviving window, the reset south doorway and the former north doorway, which is now at the west end of the chancel. The carving on these doorways is very weathered. In the 13th century the south aisle and chapel were added, and the chancel was lengthened to the east. The Early English east window is of this date. A clerestory was added to the nave in the 15th century, which resulted in severe structural problems. Indeed, the remains of buttressing to the north side is evidence of attempts to rectify the situation. In the end the church was abandoned when St. Mary was built in 1852. The ruins were made good in the 1960s—at this time the early medieval grave slab with carved crosses, and five 14th-century silver spoons, were discovered in the stonework. The spoons are now in the British Museum.

The homely interior of the chancel and the south chapel contains mainly 20th-century furnishings under a 16th-century roof structure. There is a 17th-century wall tablet to the Walsh family, who held the manor after the Reformation.

ABBERTON   ST. EADBURGA

The hilltop church of this small village is a landmark in the east Worcestershire countryside; it was even more conspicuous until the removal of the stone spire from the flightpath of aircraft using Pershore Airfield during the Second World War. The gaunt tower has a parapet and is at the west end of an undivided nave and chancel. There is a south porch and a north vestry. The church was built of lias by William Jeffrey Hopkins in 1881-2 to replace a medieval structure on the same site, the work paid for by William Laslett of Abberton Hall, who was Member of Parliament for Worcester during the late 19th century. The doorways, windows and other external features are in the Decorated style, but the interior comes as a surprise with yellow brick walls and some polychrome work in green and red. The nave is divided from the chancel by a wooden arch. The furnishings are contemporary, though the Norman font is preserved. It is round with bands of carved zig-zag decoration, similar to the font at Wyre Piddle. Some memorial tablets on the walls to the Sheldon family of Abberton Hall date from the 17th and 18th centuries.

The dedication to Eadburga or Edburga is a reminder that Abberton was part of the estates of Pershore Abbey during the Middle Ages—Edburga'a shrine and relics were in the abbey.

ABBOTS MORTON   ST. PETER

Abbots Morton remains quite remote and undeveloped in wooded countryside to the south of Inkberrow, close to the Warwickshire border. St. Peter stands at the west end of the village, which is lined with timber-framed houses and cottages in pretty gardens. In the Middle Ages, Evesham Abbey held the manor, and earthworks from the house and moat remain in the field to the north of the church.

The medieval sandstone church consists of a west tower, nave and chancel with south porch, north transept and 20th-century vestry. Part of the north wall is Norman with a plain blocked doorway, but most of the building is 14th- and 15th-century with a mixture of Decorated and Perpendicular windows. The tower, with a Decorated west window and bell-openings, has battlements and gargoyles around a low saddleback roof. The tracery of the straight-headed Perpendicular side window to the chancel is ornamented with ogees and cusps. The window is next to a plain priest's doorway, and may be the result of a rebuilding of this part of the church in the 17th century; over the east window is a stone dated 1637. The 15th-century porch has medieval seating on either side.

The charming whitewashed interior has been sympathetically restored and has 15th-century timber roof structures. The nave and chancel are divided by a truss which is plastered to form a tympanum. Although the font is Norman and the communion rail is 17th-century, the other furnishings are 19th- and 20th-century, including the screen.

There is a little medieval glass in the north transept window, along with some 18th-century heraldry. The east window contains two medallions of Flemish glass depicting King David, dated 1590.

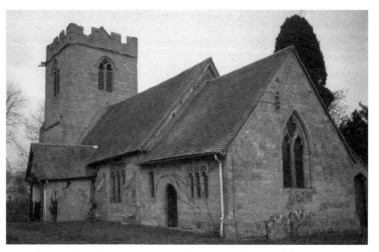

The medieval country church at Abbots Morton

ALFRICK   ST. MARY MAGDALENE

In a large churchyard at the centre of the village stands this attractive red sandstone church, with nave, chancel, north transept, vestry and timber south porch. The timber belfry at the west end has a sundial on the south face and supports a short spire. The nave is Norman with lancet windows surviving in the west, north and south walls. The other windows in the nave and chancel are in a mixture of Decorated and Perpendicular styles. The Decorated east window has reticulated tracery, and a nave south window has a sill used for sharpening scythes. The porch is 15th-century. The north transept and vestry were built in the Arts and Crafts Perpendicular style in 1885 by Sir George Aston Webb, and are similar to his additions to the church at Claines.

The interior is homely and well restored with many features of interest. By the south door are the remains of a holy water stoup. The nave and chancel have no dividing arch, but there is a 19th-century screen containing 15th-century woodwork. The wagon roof to the nave is also medieval, as is the plain piscina in the chancel, but the pulpit is 17th-century. The north transept, now known as the Lulsley Chapel, contains a 17th-century font and a worn 12th-century carving of a man from the redundant church in the neighbouring village of Lulsley. Lulsley and Alfrick were both chapelries in the parish of Suckley until 1912.

Alfrick: the Annunciation and St. Peter with Christ in Dutch glass

The church contains an excellent group of Dutch glass panels dating from the 15th to the 17th centuries, which were given from a private collection in the 1950s. In the nave, the figure of St. Bernard of Clairvaux is 15th-century, whilst those of St. Augustine, St. Ambrose, St. Margaret, and St. Peter with Christ are 17th-century. In the chancel there are 16th-century panels showing the Annunciation, the Adoration of the Shepherds and further Saints. In the north transept the panels which depict Adam and Eve with David and Goliath are 17th-century.

There are several interesting ledger stones and memorial tablets. In the north transept the tablet to William Allies who died in 1818, is by Joseph Stephens of Worcester. The Allies family lived in Lulsley and gave the sundial and weathercock on the tower. Jabez Allies was a noted local historian in the 19th century. The 18th-century memorial to the Estopp family is painted with cherubs. In the chancel a stone plaque commemorates the charity of William Makeam, being a regular gift of bread to the poor. A 19th-century curate at Alfrick Skeffington Dodgson, was the brother of Charles Dodgson, who wrote under the name Lewis Carroll—the author of *Alice in Wonderland*. Carroll visited Alfrick several times. Skeffington Dodgson was later vicar of Vowchurch in Herefordshire.

ALVECHURCH   ST. LAURENCE

This is a large church on top of the hill at the centre of this sprawling suburban village between Redditch and Birmingham. Alvechurch has long been a sizable place. In medieval times it had an annual fair on St.

Laurence's feast day and a weekly market; indeed, today the village centre has the atmosphere of a small town. It was also important in medieval church life; the bishops of Worcester had been granted land in Alvechurch by King Offa of Mercia in 780, and had a residence here until the 16th century.

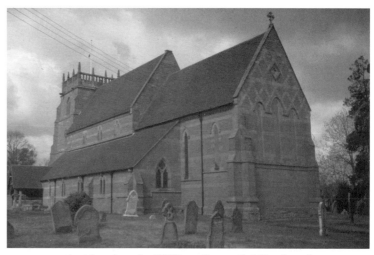

At Alvechurch, William Butterfield's church dominates the earlier tower

The church consists of a nave and chancel with side aisles, porch and vestry, with a west tower. The lofty body of the church was rebuilt by William Butterfield between 1859 and 1861, completely dwarfing the earlier west tower, which was never capped by Butterfield's intended pyramidal roof. The tower itself is mainly 15th-century, but the upper part was rebuilt in 1676 and finished with a balustraded parapet. The sandstone north aisle is mainly 14th- and 15th-centuries, and contains two windows reset from the medieval chancel. The north aisle also has a Decorated east window, and was probably the location of a chantry chapel dedicated to the Virgin Mary. Butterfield used red and buff sandstone to create his favoured polychrome decoration on the exterior of the rebuilt nave and chancel, reminiscent of his famous brickwork at Keble College, Oxford. His work at Alvechurch is a mixture of the Early English and Decorated styles.

The Norman south doorway, with carved saltire crosses on the arch, has been reset to form the main entrance. Its retention is a reminder of Victorian interest in antiquities. The same is true of the reset 13th century priest's door at the entrance to the vestry, and the sedilia of similar date in the chancel. However, the overall impression on entering is of a large Victorian urban church dominated by Butterfield's polychrome brickwork, timber roof and the contemporary fittings. Of these, the font, reredos, and chancel tiles are worth seeking out. The east window glass is of 1873 by Charles Gibbs, and there is other glass of this period by the Worcester designer, Frederick Preedy. The low chancel screen incorporates woodwork from the medieval rood screen.

Amongst the many memorials, the following earlier ones are of interest. In the chancel there is a grave slab carved with a cross and the arms of Bishop Carpenter of Worcester. As Carpenter was buried at Westbury-on-Trym church in Bristol in 1476, whose grave is this? There is also part of a Perpendicular tomb recess. In the north aisle another large late 14th-century recess contains the effigy of a knight, thought to be Sir John Blanchfront. Towards the west end is a brass of 1524 to Philip Chatwin, who was a gentleman usher to King Henry VIII. There are two small 17th-century brasses commemorating Richard and Elizabeth Acton. In the north aisle can be found an elaborate memorial tablet to Edward Moore, who died in 1746.

Outside, the medieval churchyard cross has been resited by the tower. Amongst the headstones is a large cross designed by Butterfield and erected in 1861 in gratitude to the philanthropic Harriet, Lady Windsor of Hewell Grange. It commemorates two of her sons, who had recently died. William, the younger son was killed in a railway accident on the way to his nephew's christening. Butterfield also designed a large polychrome tomb slab for Archdeacon Sandford, the incumbent who had commissioned the rebuilding of the church, and for whom Butterfield had previously designed the nearby school and former rectory. Alvechurch is a classic example of church and associated buildings, designed by one architect for the Victorian parish priest.

ASHTON-UNDER-HILL   ST. BARBARA

*Ashton-under-Hill showing the chancel
which was rebuilt in the 17th century*

The limestone church stands at the foot of the eastern slopes of Bredon Hill. It can only be approached by footpath from the medieval village cross in the long and attractive street. The unusual dedication to St. Barbara was first mentioned in the 18th century, but appears to be derived from the medieval priory at neighbouring Beckford, which once held the manor of Ashton. Beckford Priory was under the control of the monastery of St. Barbe-en-Auge in Normandy, which may have endowed an altar to St. Barbara in the church. Earlier sources refer to the church as dedicated to St. Andrew.

The west tower, porch, north aisle and chancel are attached to a Norman nave of which the south wall survives with the simple doorway. This wall now contains a mixture of windows, including a large Perpendicular one. The plain base of the tower is 13th-century, though the upper stage, with its Perpendicular bell-openings, gargoyles, battlements and pinnacles, is 15th-century. The 14th-century porch has Decorated windows, seats and the remains of a stoup. The north aisle was rebuilt in the 19th century, but the chancel was reconstructed in 1624. The style is 17th-century Gothic, and the unusual design of the east window incorporates a pair of carved dolphins, which formed part of the arms of the patron, Sir John Franklin.

A particular feature of the interior is the lower east end, on account of the sloping site. The north arcade is Perpendicular with characteristic octagonal piers. The font is of similar date and is elaborately carved with flowers in quatrefoil panels and pendants of foliage. Pieces of 12th-century carved stones are set in the chancel wall, and there are memorial tablets to the Baldwyn family, who are understood to have named Paris, the hamlet on their nearby lands, in recognition of their Norman origins. Aside from a panel of medieval glass in a south window, and the 17th-century communion table, the remainder of the fittings and glass are 19th- and 20th-century. These include a copy of Holman Hunt's *Light of the World*, and a Madonna designed by the Arts and Crafts artist Florence Camm.

ASTLEY   ST. PETER

St. Peter is an attractive red sandstone church situated on the crown of a hill next to the former Georgian rectory along narrow lanes. It is located about one mile west of the present village centre and Astley Hall, the former home of Prime Minister Stanley Baldwin.

The Norman nave and chancel still form the principal part of the church. At different dates a west tower, porch, north aisle and chapel have been added. The south wall of the nave shows that the Norman church was a prestigious building. Between the lancet windows, there are buttresses comprising two semi-circular shafts up to the level of the string course, which then rise as single shafts to the corbel table. The corbels are carved heads of the Herefordshire School type. Why was this church so heavily ornamented? The reason appears to lie in the foundation of a priory here by Ralph Tosny, who was granted the land of this parish along with Abberley and Rock at the Norman Conquest. The priory was directly linked to the Abbey of St. Taurin, near Rouen in France, and was suppressed with other 'alien' monasteries in 1414. Apart from the church there are now no other remains of the priory above ground, though the nearby well is probably associated with the religious foundation.

Other Norman features to be seen outside include the lancet windows on the south side of the nave and chancel, though these were much restored in the 19th century. The south doorway is partly hidden by the 20th-century timber porch. It is fine Norman work with much carved zig-zag decoration to the arch, with a plain tympanum, which was probably originally painted. The doorway stands in a projecting section of wall like several others in Worcestershire churches, such as at Martley and Stoulton. Remains of medieval mass dials can also be traced on this wall.

The Perpendicular north chantry chapel and tower, which has battlements and pinnacles, were probably added after the manor passed to the Beauchamps in 1385. At about this time the chancel was extended to the east, and the windows here as well as in the tower and north chapel are Perpendicular, though the east wall of the chancel had to be replaced in the 20th century. The north aisle was also rebuilt in the Perpendicular style, but the present larger structure dates from about 1838. Indeed the church underwent much restoration in the 19th century; the chancel and north chapel received new roofs in about 1840 after a fire, and the nave roof has been lowered, leaving a conspicuous roof line on the east wall of the tower.

The interior is made rather dark by the combined effect of the scraped sandstone walls and the richly coloured glass. The chancel arch is Norman, but rebuilt in the 19th century. It has a plain arch resting on trumpet scallop capitals. The Norman north arcade is a little later with lovely round piers and abaci also with scallop capitals. There is a reset carved Norman face on one of the piers. On the north wall of the chancel a Norman window, which was covered over by the building of the north chapel, is only visible from the inside. The arches to the tower and the north chapel are Perpendicular, though the latter could be a rebuilding of the previous Norman opening. The blocked medieval stair to the former rood loft is also entered from this chapel.

The date of the font is debatable, but would seem to be of Norman origin, though reworked in the later Middle Ages. The iron south door furniture is also medieval, and there is a 17th-century pulpit, the surviving part of a three decker.

The remainder of the fittings and glass are Victorian and later, but the interesting collection of monuments, mainly to owners of the manor, span several centuries. Most colourful are the recently restored Blount tombs in the north chapel, of which the earliest was the work of Robert Guildo in 1577. Guildo was a Hereford mason of Dutch origin, who designed several monuments for the local gentry, and his work at Astley can be compared to memorials in the churches at Bosbury and Madley in Herefordshire and Abergavenny in Monmouthshire. This chest tomb commemorates Walter and Isabel Blount who died in 1561 and 1562. They are shown wearing contemporary costume, as are their children, who are depicted in mourning below. Heraldry on the tomb includes the Blount family crest, the sun and slipper.

A second chest tomb is to Robert and Anne Blount. It has balusters and wreaths with roses on the sides. Robert died in 1573 and the tomb is in typical late Tudor style. There are wall memorials to Samuel and Anne Bowater of 1696 and 1686, which look earlier in style. The north chapel is dominated by the white marble monument, with an urn and obelisks, to Sir Thomas Winford, who died in 1702. The beautiful memorial to Sarah Winford, who died in 1793, was the work of John Bacon, the chief designer at the Coade stone factory in Lambeth; the figures of Benevolence with a pelican and Sensibility with flowers are shown by an urn. The memorial to Sarah Freeman, who died in 1806, and to Harriet Winford, who died in 1801, are similar, with figures seated by urns, and were designed by John Bacon junior. The adder which killed Harriet is shown around her arm.

A simple ledger stone in the floor of the nave commemorates John Watson, the architect of Glasshampton House in the parish. The house has gone but the early 19th-century stables are now used by the Society of St. Francis. The incumbents of Astley included Martin Buckle from 1894 to 1914, who was the architect of the restoration of Castle Frome church in Herefordshire, and William Havergal from 1816 to 1841, who was also rector of St. Nicholas church in Worcester. He was the father of Frances Ridley Havergal, singer, author and hymn writer, who is buried in Astley churchyard.

ASTON SOMERVILLE   ST. MARY

At the end of a long lane in this small Vale of Evesham village, St. Mary is almost hidden from view from the road. The village was associated with the Norman family of Somerville until the 19th century. The parish is in the diocese of Gloucester, and was in Gloucestershire until the boundary was redrawn in the mid-20th century.

The limestone church has a nave, which may have Norman masonry, to which the tower and chancel were added in the 13th century. The priest's doorway and some chancel windows are Early English, but the other windows are Decorated, apart from the Perpendicular east window. There was a late medieval south chapel, which was demolished around the 17th century, leaving a blocked arch. The top of the tower has 15th-century pinnacles and battlements with gargoyles.

The church is entered through the medieval north doorway inside the porch, which dates from the restoration of 1908. The interior has bare stone walls, scraped at the same time. The arch to the tower is of about 1200 with round piers, whereas the chancel arch is Perpendicular. It is fitted with a contemporary wooden screen with pretty Perpendicular tracery. This is a lovely survival, above which can be seen the mortice holes in the arch which once held the rood beam. There was also a loft, to which the stairs can still be seen in the south wall. The font has a 12th-century base, but the top appears to have been retooled at a later date, perhaps after the Reformation. There are also some fragments of medieval glass in a nave north window. The pulpit incorporates 17th-century woodwork, and the chancel panelling of the same date is from the former box pews.

The tall effigy of a knight wearing chain mail is probably Sir John Somerville, dating from the 13th century. A local story tells that it was recovered from a field. It is certainly damaged and has been used for sharpening blades, but it is more probable that it was once in the demolished south chapel. A wall memorial commemorates John Parry, who died in 1714 after being rector here for 54 years, and his wife, Rebecca, who died in 1709. They endowed the church with communion plate.

ASTWOOD BANK   ST. MATTHIAS AND ST. GEORGE

This large village developed in the 19th century with the growth of the needlemaking industry in neighbouring Redditch. Today cottages and factories are mixed with suburban development on the ridge with the church at the northern end. The village was once in the parish of Feckenham.

The chancel and base of the south tower were built in the Decorated style to designs of William Jeffrey Hopkins in 1884. The tower was never completed, and so the church does not dominate views of Astwood Bank as it should. Today the base is covered by a sweeping roof, and a small bellcote rests on the roof between chancel and nave. The rendered nave and aisles have long lancet windows, arranged in pairs to the sides and west end. They were added in 1911 by W. Cogswell.

The interior is large and barn-like. The west end reflects the Arts and Crafts movement with attractive arcades of the Perpendicular style, and octagonal piers without capitals. There are many 20th-century fittings.

BADSEY   ST. JAMES

*The restored medieval church at Badsey
has a Perpendicular tower*

Badsey is a large Vale of Evesham village, with red brick villas and terraced houses built in the late 19th century for agricultural workers. However, evidence of Roman settlement has been found, and the church is probably of Saxon foundation. There were strong links to Evesham Abbey in the Middle Ages, when the Manor House was used by the monks for convalescence. This pretty stone and timber building stands close to the church in the centre of Badsey.

St. James is mainly medieval and built of limestone, though it was much restored in 1885. The nave and chancel have a south aisle with porch, and a north transept with vestry. The tower is at the west end. There is much Norman masonry in the nave, especially the north wall and doorway, which has carved cable moulding on the lintel and zig-zag on the arch. The Norman lancet window was moved here from the south wall in 1885, but nearby is the surviving jamb of another lancet, now lost. The chancel and north transept, which is otherwise known as the Aldington Chapel after the neighbouring village of Aldington, are both 14th-century with Decorated windows, though the rounded head to the east window is a 17th-century alteration. The fine 15th-century tower is built of ashlar and is crowned with gargoyles, battlements and eight pinnacles. The bell-openings and west window are Perpendicular, and there is an 18th-century clock face.

Entering through the reset medieval south doorway, past the broken remains of the stoup, several medieval features can be found amongst the Victorian restoration. The Perpendicular tower arch is very elegant, and the west window contains fragments of medieval glass, including a quarry showing a chalice which has been placed upside down. The font has a 14th-century stem with carved foliage, and the pulpit contains linenfold wooden panels, which were purchased in 1529. The 18th-century communion rails were the gift of William Seward of Seward House. The nave arcade and chancel arch date from 1885, and at this date the box pews of 1730 were made into panelling for the walls. The east window contains some 19th-century glass of the pre-Raphaelite type.

On the north side of the chancel is the fine but worn monument to Margaret and Richard Hoby, who died in 1617. The Hoby family acquired the manor at the Dissolution of Evesham Abbey. The couple kneel at a desk, with a skull and hour glass to remind onlookers of death and the passage of time. The arms above include an ascending hawk or hobby—a pun on the family name. The children face west, being two sons, Richard and Gerard, and a daughter, Margaret, from Margaret Hoby's first marriage to John Newman of Chaddesley Corbett. It is thought that the monument became worn when the east gable collapsed in 1654 and left it exposed. There is a tablet with a carved surround of 1685 to William Jarrett in the nave. Memorials to the two World Wars are prominent, and the tower screen also commemorates those who served.

Outside, two 12th-century carved stones can be seen in a pier of the churchyard wall. These were probably from the Norman nave and were placed here during the 1885 restoration.

BARNT GREEN   ST. ANDREW

The church stands on a slope amongst suburban housing at the centre of this large village, which grew up towards the end of the 19th century around the railway station on the estate of the Windsors of Hewell. The parish was formed out of Alvechurch. St. Andrew is a red brick structure with a chancel, nave with aisles and clerestorey and louvered bellcote at the east end. The church is styled after an Italian basilica, and was constructed between 1909 and 1914 to the designs of A.S. Dixon. It is similar to his church of St. Basil at Deritend in Birmingham. Inside the light falls through coloured glass in the clerestorey windows, whilst the war memorial outside at the west end shows Christ crucified, with a soldier and sailor to either side. This unusual piece is the work of the Bromsgrove Guild.

BAYTON   ST. BARTHOLOMEW

Bayton is on the north-western edge of Worcestershire, and there are dramatic views from the village towards the Clee Hills in Shropshire. Around the church, the groups of timber-framed and brick cottages give little indication of the extent of open cast coal working here in the 19th century, though Clows Top to the south-east does have a more industrialised feel.

St. Bartholomew consists of a sandstone nave with porch, chancel with organ chamber and a west tower. The nave is Norman, and the round-headed arch of the south doorway is ornamented with zig-zag and lozenges. The antiquarian John Noake records the existence of a tympanum in the 19th century and this may have had Herefordshire School type carving, given the proximity of the work at Rock.

In 1817 the wide nave was lengthened to the west, and the tower rebuilt with simple Y-shaped tracery to the bell openings, replacing a timber belfry similar to that at Knighton-on-Teme. The chancel and east window were much rebuilt in the Perpendicular style in 1905.

The attractive interior gives a taste of the Arts and Crafts movement from the 1905 restoration. The great timber roof is medieval, though the wooden arch and framing at the division between nave and chancel is of 1905. The Norman font is drum-shaped, carved on the bowl with scrolls and beads above a rope moulding, and on the stem with leaves, in a similar style to the font at neighbouring Rock church. In the chancel there is a grave slab with a Latin inscription dated 1654, whilst the pulpit and stalls contain 17th-century panels. The early 20th-century glass in the east window shows shafts of light from the risen Christ descending onto the church, and was presented by the Meysey family of nearby Shakenhurst Hall, whose hatchment from the 19th century hangs in the nave. The tower contains a 15th-century bell dedicated to St. Nicholas.

BECKFORD   ST. JOHN THE BAPTIST

Between the A46 and the lower eastern slopes of Bredon Hill, this large village spreads out from a wide central street, although the village is not as picturesque as nearby Ashton or Overbury. The place has much of archaeological and historical interest, with Iron Age and Saxon sites, and the fascinating Hall on the site of an alien priory held by the monastery of St. Barbe-en-Auge in Normandy. At Grafton in the northern part of Beckford parish is a cottage containing several Norman features including an arch; it was once a chapel of Beckford Priory.

St. John is a most attractive church, which stands between the Hall and the street. It is built of limestone and consists of a nave and porch with a central tower, chancel and vestry. The nave is Norman, with two extremely beautiful doorways, and probably dates from between 1160 and 1175. The south doorway is inside the 15th-century porch. The jambs with shafts are accompanied by bands of carved projecting zig-zag. This has been built into the porch wall on the eastern side, where there are also the remains of a stoup. The capitals are carved with beautiful scallop trumpets, and the tympanum is supported by two corbels each carved with a pair of heads, of which two face outwards and the other two face each other across the top of the entrance. This a most unusual feature in this area, but is similar to the Prior's Door at Ely Cathedral. The tympanum

Beckford: the interior looking towards the chancel

above has simple carvings of a cross, above which are a circle and a bird, and two beasts to the sides. It would have been most dramatic in its original painted state, and could show horselike beasts in adoration of the Trinity, if the circle represents the eye of God and the bird is the dove of the Holy Spirit. However, it has also been interpreted as showing the triumph of the Church, with the cross rising above evil beasts which have large ears or horns. The north doorway is exposed and worn by comparison. This tympanum shows the Harrowing of Hell, with Christ forcing his cross into Hell's mouth. His other hand holds a leash to a man, possibly Adam. Similar designs can be seen on the much eroded carvings at Shobdon Arches in Herefordshire. The lintel has a frieze of carved foliage, and includes two carved heads, which have been compared to heads surviving at Malmesbury Abbey in Wiltshire.

One small Norman window remains in the south wall of the nave, and parts of two further Norman windows can also be found in the west wall, where there is also a Perpendicular window. The other nave windows are Early English and Decorated. The base of the tower is also Norman, and has the blocked arch to the destroyed south transept. The middle section of the tower is Early English and the top with battlements and pinnacles is 18th century, replacing a spire removed in 1622. The 13th-century chancel has pairs of Early English lancets on the side, and the three eastern lancets have small roundels above, making an excellent example of Early English plate tracery. The 15th-century north chantry chapel now houses the vestry and has a 17th-century east window.

The interior was scraped in 1911, but remains very atmospheric. The eye is immediately drawn to the Norman tower arch, with its carved zig-zag decoration, scallop capitals, and frieze to each side. On the left are set a carved centaur and two human heads. This seems to be another Italian style feature and is again reminiscent of Herefordshire carving. The spur at the base of the shaft has a further head. One

Beckford: the tympanum and arch above the south doorway

of the shafts has been removed, probably in the 17th century to make way for the former three decker pulpit. The other arches are Early English, along with the springers for the vault. The chancel roof contains medieval timbers, whilst the nave has a wagon roof. The 12th-century shaft with capital in the nave would appear to be the jamb to one of the Norman windows. The Perpendicular font is octagonal with carved four-leafed flowers, and there are some 15th-century bench ends with Perpendicular tracery, like those at Cropthorne. Apart from some 17th-century woodwork in the chancel screen, the remainder of the fittings are 19th- and 20th-century. There is also a panel of 17th-century Flemish glass in the Norman window showing Christ carrying the cross.

BELBROUGHTON   HOLY TRINITY

The church stands on a bank close to the centre of this attractive village in the prosperous countryside between Bromsgrove and Stourbridge. Belbroughton was a centre of scythe making, but it is now mainly home to commuters from the Black Country towns. To the east of the village, in the grounds of Bell Hall, is a simple Norman chapel, which has long been used as a barn. It retains its Norman doorways and windows on the north and south sides, but the east and west ends were renewed in the 17th century.

When approached from the south, Holy Trinity appears deceptively compact. It is built of sandstone, and the west tower with spire, nave and south aisle with chancel, conceal a very large north aisle. The church's Norman origins are reflected in the reset window in the south aisle, some stonework in the south door, and roll moulding of the priest's door, which was rebuilt in the 16th century. The spire is octagonal with Decorated lucarnes, and rests on the tower, which has been restored several times between the 17th and 20th centuries. There are battlements and gargoyles at the top but the Perpendicular style tracery to the west window dates from the great restoration of this church in 1894-5. Indeed the porch, vestry and substantial north aisle were added at that time, when the Decorated ogee-headed doorway and one window were reset from the former medieval north wall. Most other external features are either medieval or Victorian Decorated in style, but the south aisle east window is Perpendicular.

The interior is scraped and rather dark, but the large number of arches is very noticeable. The Perpendicular north arcade has continuous chamfers and no capitals to the octagonal piers, and is probably a little earlier than the south arcade, which has concave sides to the piers, similar to those at St. Mary's church, Kidderminster. These arcades were much restored in 1894, when the north arcade was discovered in the former north wall. The Victorian arcade, which was to be positioned there, now forms a curious series of blind arches in the present north wall.

The chancel arch and sedilia are also Perpendicular, though restored between 1847 and 1852. In the south aisle a 13th-century piscina is close to the Perpendicular font, which is octagonal with flowers in quatrefoils. At the east end of the aisle are three reset medieval consecration crosses. On the north side of the chancel is a 14th-century recess with a carved ogee head, which was probably the tomb of the patron, and would have served as an Easter sepulchre. On the south side is an aumbry or blocked low side window. Some reset medieval stonework makes up the sedilia in the north aisle. The nave roof is 14th-century, though the dates 1654 and 1677 carved on the tie beams show when these were replaced. Indeed, the chancel roof was entirely renewed in the 17th century.

The chancel has undergone many changes. No medieval woodwork survives but the rood loft stairs can be found to the south of the chancel arch. After the 1894 alterations, the medieval chancel housed the organ. The pulpit and lectern contain 17th-century woodwork, including parts of a dragon frieze. The 17th- and 18th-century panelling in the reredos is inscribed HP 1721, a reference to the local landowner, Humphrey Perrott, of Bell Hall. The vestry screen was made in 1977 by Robert Pancheri of Bromsgrove, and indeed all the other furnishings are 19th- or 20th-century.

A delightful medieval survival can be found in the remains of a painting of the Virgin and Child at the east end of the south aisle on the north wall, which may indicate that this was the Lady Chapel. There are further faint traces of painting in the nave. Fragments of medieval glass are reset in a window in the north aisle, including part of a scene showing a man tending his pigs, an image which was used in medieval art to represent September or October in the Labours of the Months.

The other glass is 19th- and 20th-century, including the late Victorian south aisle east window and a south window of 1905 by Charles Eamer Kempe. The south chancel windows were also installed by Kempe after 1874 as a memorial to the W.B. Woodgate, rector from 1837.

There are many memorial tablets, including one of the 17th century to the Tristram family in the south aisle. Outside, the medieval churchyard cross base was given a new shaft and head in 1900 as a memorial to Rector Woodgate's son, Edward, who was killed at Spion Kop in the Boer War.

There is a mass dial on the south-east corner of the church. The Lychgate is of 1912, by the Bromsgrove Guild and commemorates a missionary, Henry Charles Goodyear, who died in Africa in 1889. Across the road to the east the late medieval timber-framed tithe barn now serves as a village hall.

BENTLEY   ST. MARY

Bentley is a scattered settlement of houses and farms in the lanes to the east of Stoke Prior. It was once a chapelry in the parish of Tardebigge, and the present church built in 1874-5 replaces a lost medieval chapel. The church is of brick and was paid for by Lord Windsor of Hewell.

BEOLEY   ST. LEONARD

St. Leonard stands close to the line of Roman Icknield Street, in a striking setting on the side of a hill near to the Vicarage, Beoley Hall and the site of the castle. This has long been an important site. The castle was held by the powerful Beauchamp family, though it passed to the Sheldons during the reign of Richard II. The Sheldons were important in the later history of Beoley, and their memorials are to be found in the chapel which they added to the church in the late 16th century. The sandstone church has a west tower, nave with aisles and porch, a chancel and large north chapel. To the north is a large parish room, the Tapestry Room,

Beoley church showing the Sheldon Chapel to the right

built in 1975, reflecting an expanding population with the encroaching housing estates of Redditch.

The church was founded in about 1140 by Hawise de Limsey and her son Geoffrey, and although there are Norman remains in the nave and chancel, nothing is visible externally. The masonry at the east end of the 13th-century chancel indicates that it was lengthened between 1230 and 1250. At this time the eastern section of the present north aisle and the narrow south aisle were also built.

In the early 15th century the tower was added, with the west doorway, west window, stair windows, bell openings and an image niche all heavily ornamented with crockets. It is very similar to the towers at Clent and Cleeve Prior, as well as those at Beaudesert in Warwickshire and Yardley in Birmingham, and thought to be the work of the medieval mason, William Dowland. At about this time the north aisle was extended, the south aisle partly rebuilt, new windows installed in the chancel, and the north door rebuilt with an image niche. This would have been the principal entrance from Beoley Castle and Hall in medieval times, and around the doorway can be seen remains of some carved figures and animals.

The chancel east window is Perpendicular, and in about 1580 the Sheldons built the north chapel with its large east window in a late Perpendicular style. The tracery is very straight and square. In 1686 a dormer window was put into the south aisle to give extra light to the pulpit. 19th-century restoration included the rebuilding of the nave east gable and the south porch replaced a timber structure in 1885.

The interior is full of interesting features. The plain Norman chancel arch survives over five steps leading from the nave, a result of the hillside site. The south arcade is early 13th-century, and one round pier has two shafts. The north arcade dates from later that century with quatrefoil piers and nailhead decoration to the arches.

The round font is late Norman, and has four large carved female heads under the bowl, linked by tresses of their hair. In the south aisle a Norman carving shows an abbot wearing mass vestments, with his arm raised. He is possibly a representation of St. Leonard and was formerly outside. The communion table is 17th-century, but apart from the medieval lectern base, most other furnishings are 19th-century. The box pews were fitted in 1845, and have holes in the poppy heads for candleholders. The 19th-century tower screen was brought from Tanworth-in-Arden church in Warwickshire, and the ringing chamber was installed in 1970. Robert Pancheri of Bromsgrove made the font cover in 1947, and the frontals chest and cupboard are also his work from 1977.

Fragments of medieval glass can be found in a north aisle window, including part of a canopy with the White Rose of York and the Sun in Splendour, dating it to the 15th-century. In the south aisle further fragments of the same date show a head of St. James and the Christ child. There is also a copy of a 13th-century Italian painting of the Crucifixion; the original was brought to the church by a vicar in the 1920s and proceeds from its sale in 1973 helped to finance the Tapestry Room.

It was William Sheldon of Beoley Hall who brought tapestry weaving to Beoley. The Sheldons became wealthy from weaving cloth and had continued the work of the monks, who had been weaving at nearby Bordesley Abbey before the Dissolution. William is buried with his wife, Mary Willington, with a memorial of 1570 in the Sheldon chapel to the north of the chancel. The Willington family had estates at Barcheston in South Warwickshire, and William Sheldon also established tapestry weaving there after sending his son, Ralph, to Arras in the Netherlands. He was accompanied by Richard Hickes, who learnt the art and on his return was placed by William in charge of weaving at Barcheston with some Flemish weavers. As well as ordinary tapestry hangings, William Sheldon produced a series of large tapestry county maps, known today as the Sheldon Tapestries. William's monument is next to that of his son, Ralph, and his wife Anne Throckmorton. Ralph died in 1613 having built the Sheldon Chapel.

The interior of the Sheldon Chapel

The Sheldon family were recusant Roman Catholics, and Ralph Sheldon's chaplain probably celebrated Mass at the portable altar now incorporated into the 16th-century stone altar at the east end. The monuments to William and Ralph Sheldon are similar in style with large arched canopies above the effigies, all of which are beautifully carved. Other memorials worth seeking out are those to Edward Sheldon, who died in 1643, in the chancel, William Sheldon, who died in 1659, in the nave, and above the entrance to the Sheldon Chapel, the tablet to another Ralph Sheldon, who died in 1684 and whose Latin inscription translates 'Once Ralph Sheldon, now ashes, dust, nothing'. The Sheldon family are buried in a vault beneath the chapel, which also contained a skull long thought to be that of William Shakespeare. Also in the chapel is a 13th-century coffin lid with a foliated cross which was once over the grave of a priest. The catholic faith of the Sheldon family also ensured the survival of medieval vestments from Bordesley now at Downside Abbey, and the medieval processional cross from Beoley now at Mount Carmel Roman Catholic Church in Redditch. In the nave are hatchments of the Holmes Hunter family who acquired the manor from the Sheldons in the 18th century.

In the churchyard, the 14th-century cross base is decorated with quatrefoils, and on the steps is a 17th-century shaft for a sundial. The Vicarage incorporates 16th-century work. Nearby is the grave of Police Constable James Davies who was murdered by a poacher, Moses Shrimpton, in 1885. Shrimpton was executed at the last public hanging in Worcester. Davies' death is also commemorated by a plaque near the tower arch.

BERROW   ST. FAITH

The rugged tower and Perpendicular south aisle at Berrow

Berrow is a scattered community, and St. Faith is placed picturesquely below the eastern slopes of the south end of the Malvern Hills in a large churchyard. The dedication is the same as St. Faith's church, Overbury, under whose patronage Berrow existed from the 12th century until the Reformation.

The church is built of lias and has a west tower, nave with south aisle, porch and chancel. The Norman north wall to the nave and chancel survives, and the plain north doorway has a shaft each side and an uncarved tympanum. There is an Early English lancet, and the chancel was lengthened and given Decorated windows in the 14th century. There is also an altered low side window. The south aisle is Perpendicular, as is the tower, which appears quite rugged, has a higher square stair turret and battlements, and looks like many Welsh church towers. The timber north porch is probably 15th-century, and the Norman doorway contains a medieval door which opens into the church.

The interior is similar to other county churches. It has been scraped, and was much restored in 1858. The arcade is Perpendicular but has been altered at the west end. The tower arch is similar to the north arcade at Belbroughton, with continuous chamfers and without capitals. There is no chancel arch; the Norman arch was probably removed when the chancel was lengthened and replaced by a screen, which does not survive.

Although most of the fittings date from 1858, there is a Norman font, shaped like a cauldron and ornamented with beaded cable patterns. The pulpit is 17th-century on a later base. The glass is an assortment of 19th- and 20th-century work. Outside are the remains of the medieval churchyard cross.

BESFORD   ST. PETER

Hidden away in the narrow lanes north of Defford, this remarkable church is far too little known. The village is scattered and the church stands amongst farm buildings next to a Georgian farmhouse with its serpentine garden wall. It has a nave and chancel, with porch and vestry and a bell turret at the west end.

The 14th-century timber-framed nave at Besford

When viewed from the east, the lias Decorated style chancel and vestry of 1880-81 by William Jeffrey Hopkins conceal the 14th-century timber-framed nave. This is now unique in Worcestershire. The nave framing is of large square panels, some of which are strengthened by diagonal braces. Original features include the blocked north doorway, with its ogee head, and the tracery of the west window, which is similar to the tracery on medieval wooden furnishings. The timber porch is 15th-century, whilst the bell turret and other windows were restored by Hopkins in 1880.

The interior is dimly lit and full of atmosphere, with much exposed timber-framing and the medieval nave roof structure. The chancel is divided from the nave by the medieval rood loft, a rare survival in this county. The open screen below dates from 1919, but much of the carved panelling on the loft, with quatrefoils, rosettes, and vines is 14th-century.

The font, south door hinges, and the glass quarries in the west window are other medieval survivals.

The interior of Besford showing the rood loft

However, most of the other furnishings date from 1881, when the 17th-century pews were adapted as panelling for the nave walls. The 17th-century communion rail runs in front of the altar from the tomb chest of Richard Harwell of Besford Court, who died aged 15 in 1576. The memorial has an alabaster effigy, surrounded by a much damaged, but most unusual wooden lattice. The panelling above the tomb has traces of painting, and there are carvings of a child and coats of arms, which include the family's distinctive rebus of a hare, on the chest below. Before the construction of the vestry, a painted wooden triptych hung on the wall to the west of the monument. This is now in the nave, and probably commemorates Richard and the other children of Edmund Harwell, who died in their infancy at the end of the 16th century. The painted panels are much damaged, but traces remain of images of death and the passage of time, which were so much favoured on memorials in this period; it is a remarkable survival of vernacular painting. The monument on the south side of the chancel is a tablet to Sir Edmund Sebright, who died in 1679. The helmet hanging opposite, along with the other arms, banners, and hatchment, are all relics of the Sebright family, who occupied Besford Court until 1885.

BEWDLEY   ST. ANNE

*The view up Bewdley's Load Street
is closed by St. Anne's church*

The name Bewdley means beautiful place, and this pretty town has grown up in a narrow wooded part of the Severn Valley. It has long been a place of strategic importance and indeed Tickenhill House above the town incorporates part of a medieval royal palace associated with the Council in the Marches which had its apogee in the last half of the 16th and early 17th centuries. Today, the view west along Load Street from Bewdley Bridge is one of the most attractive pieces of Georgian townscape in Worcestershire. St. Anne's is the focal point at the west end, standing in the centre of the street. The 18th century saw the town's period of greatest prosperity, gained from the river trade before the construction of the canal at Stourport. The re-building of the nave and chancel of the church between 1745 and 1748 reflects this wealth.

The architect of the sandstone church was Thomas Woodward of Chipping Campden, who also rebuilt St. Swithin's church in Worcester and St. John's church in Gloucester in a similar plain classical design. The main façade is at the east end, with a Venetian window and a short balustrade below the hipped roof. There are five round-arched windows to each side.

The nave was attached to the tower, which had been built in 1695 of a rougher stone. It too has round-arched windows with surrounds typical of the late 17th century. The balustrade at the top, surmounted by urns on the corners, completes the overall classical appearance of the church. The building of the tower was financed by the local Member of Parliament, Salwey Winnington.

The interior is white, light and very spacious, a sense heightened during recent restoration. There is an absence of memorials; a reminder that the church was a chapelry of Ribbesford and that Bewdley did not become a separate parish until 1853. The plaster vault in the nave is carried by large Tuscan columns with a cornice, whilst the short chancel has a lower ceiling, and is entered through the segmental chancel arch.

18th-century furnishings include the inlaid pulpit, the west gallery, and the pews which have been adapted from the box pews. Later furnishings include some from the demolished church of St. Andrew at Dowles. Outside, in the east window of the tower, hangs the sanctus bell, thought to have come from the previous medieval chapel.

Bewdley chapel was served by Ribbesford church from the 15th-century, but before that the town was an extra-parochial sanctuary. The chapel must have been a fascinating building, being timber-framed and integral with other buildings. It was on first floor level, with businesses on the street below, and was approached from the street by a stairway which divided the chancel from the north chapel. At the end of the 16th century, the historian Thomas Habington records it as having aisles to the chancel and nave, with the two bay north chapel housing a chantry of St. Anne to the east and the chapel of the Guild of the Holy Trinity to the west. The south aisle had the cordwainers chapel dedicated to Our Lady. The church of Holy Trinity in the Market Place at Richmond in Yorkshire would seem to be the closest surviving comparison to this curious chapel. Dedications to St. Anne were often associated with wells and springs, such as St. Anne's Well in Malvern, and this connection with water extended to river crossings, where chapels were often dedicated to her for prayer for a safe passage, as seems to be the case here at Bewdley.

BEWDLEY   ALL SAINTS, WRIBBENHALL

Wribbenhall is Bewdley on the east bank of the River Severn, and has timber-framed cottages and houses mixed with early 19th-century warehouses between the embankment of the Severn Valley Railway and the river. It had a thriving pewter and brass industry in the 19th century. A burial ground with a lychgate off Westbourne Street marks the site of Christchurch built in 1701 as a chapel of St. Mary, Kidderminster. It was demolished in 1879 when the present church, All Saints, was built on Kidderminster Road. The land was given by Walter Hemming of Spring Grove, now the West Midlands Safari Park.

The church was designed by Sir Arthur Blomfield, and is in a similar early Decorated style to his church at Upton-upon-Severn. It is rock-faced in red sandstone, and has a nave with a south aisle and sweeping roof, a chancel with an octagonal bell turret and short spire on the north side above the vestry, and a porch.

The interior is spacious and has many 19th-century fittings. The chancel screen and reredos of iron and gilded mahogany were designed in 1899 by Robert Alexander Briggs, and can be compared with his reredos in the Jesus Chapel of Worcester Cathedral. The Lea memorial window has glass of 1884 by Burlison and Grylls, and another window by them of 1886 is a memorial to the family of Walter Hemming, donor of the site. The west window, in memory of Slade Baker, of 1886 and the Ritchie memorial window of 1893 are by Heaton, Butler and Bayne, whilst the Baugh memorial window has glass by Hardman & Co.

BIRLINGHAM   ST. JAMES THE GREAT

During the Middle Ages, Birlingham was a chapelry of Pershore Abbey in the charge of the rector of St. James church at nearby Nafford—whose church had disappeared by the 16th century after that village was abandoned.

Today, the churchyard of St. James at Birlingham is renowned for its show of snowdrops and crocuses. It lies at the centre of the quiet village by the River Avon to the south of Pershore. The sandstone church has a west tower, with an aisled nave, chancel, organ loft, porch and vestry. It is approached from the south through a gateway, which is the former Norman chancel arch. This is the earliest survival on the site. It is decorated with shafts to each side, scalloped capitals and projecting zig-zag.

The 15th-century Perpendicular tower is positioned at the west end of the present large south aisle. The middle stage was adapted as a dovecote, with flight ledges on the north and south windows and nesting

Birlingham's medieval tower contains a dovecote

holes inside. Doves were an important source of food in the Middle Ages, and similar dovecotes can be found in the county in the church towers at Overbury and South Littleton, as well as at Collingbourne Ducis in Wiltshire. The higher stair turret and pinnacle were added during the re-building of 1871-2 by Benjamin Ferrey, who was also the architect of Fairfield Church near Bromsgrove. This 14th-century style structure replaced previous re-buildings of 1784 and 1833.

Inside, the Perpendicular tower arch contrasts with Ferrey's polychrome work of red sandstone and grey limestone in the Decorated style arcades and chancel arch. There are 14th-century style timber roofs.

Two medieval corbel heads are preserved in the church, and a brass plate survives commemorating Thomas Harwell, who died in 1603, with several members of his family. The kneeling figures are shown in contemporary costume with coats of arms. A brass plate in the chancel showing an old man holding a chalice commemorates a rector, Robert Rashleigh Duke, who was responsible for the 1870s rebuilding of the church. The extraordinary lectern, now at the back of the church, is a life-sized angel with the bible open at the beginning of Acts by Theodore Pfyffers, and most of the remaining fittings are of the period of re-building. A window in memory of Henry Bernard, who was killed in 1942, shows St. George and the dragon and is by Archibald Davies of the Bromsgrove Guild.

At the west end of the church are preserved the village stocks.

BIRTSMORTON   ST. PETER, ST. PAUL AND ST. THOMAS

Few churches can claim such a tranquil setting as Birtsmorton; in a churchyard with plentiful trees, and next to the picturesque moated timber-framed Court, which was home to the Nanfan family from the 15th to the 18th centuries.

The lias church has a west tower, nave and chancel with transepts, and a porch. It is unusual in being almost entirely Decorated in style, with original 14th-century windows in the nave, and replacements of 1877 in the chancel and transepts. The porch also dates from 1877, and the plain 15th-century tower was restored in 1895. While the exterior is attractive, it is inside that there are particular features of interest.

The entrance is through a doorway of 1877, but the door retains some medieval ironwork and a sanctuary ring. The whitewashed interior is generally quite plain, with arches to the chancel and transepts dating from the 1877 restorations, when a medieval piscina was also discovered and renovated. The furnishings include a 12th-century tub font, and whilst they mainly date from 1877, the pews, almsbox and pulpit all contain much 15th- and 16th-century woodwork. The former communion table by the south door was given by the third Earl of Bellemonte. It is 18th-century with a marble top on wrought iron supports, and is very similar to the communion table in St. Swithin's church, Worcester. The stained glass includes many medieval fragments, some of which have been moved from the Court.

There are the arms of the Ruyhall family in the nave windows, whilst the east window contains an unusual medieval panel showing the baptism of St. Christopher, which was installed in about 1970 for the Dawes family of the Court. The royal arms of King George IV hang in the church, along with a hatchment to Lord Coloony, the unmarried son of the third Earl of Bellemonte, who died in 1740.

The Earls of Bellemonte were associated with Birtsmorton through the marriage of Richard Coote, who became Earl of Bellemonte, to Catherine Nanfan, the last of a line of Nanfans at the Court. Catherine was

The restored 14th-century cruciform church at Birtsmorton

married four times before her death in 1737, and her second husband's memorial is in the chancel. He was Admiral William Caldwell, who died in 1718, and his effigy is on a tomb chest, with his flagship carved on the front. Above there is a rococo cartouche with carved navigational instruments and military trophies. The most intriguing memorial is a large early 16th-century tomb chest, with the indent of a lost brass on top, and carved kneeling figures to the sides under crocketed arches. It is most probably the memorial erected by Jane Nanfan to her three husbands. Born Jane Coleshill, she married Sir John Nanfan, who acquired Birtsmorton Court in 1425, and was Sheriff of Cornwall and Worcester. She was also married in turn to Sir Renfrey Arundell and Sir William Houghton. The kneeling bishop on the side seems to be her son, John Arundell, who was Bishop of Lichfield from 1496 to 1502. Other figures shown are members of the Nanfan, Arundell, Houghton and Lygon families. The inscriptions have disappeared, but St. Mary Magdalene and St. Mary of Egypt can be identified amongst the figures. Above the tomb is a tablet dated 1572 with the Nanfan coat of arms, and the initials W.N. and G.N. for William and Giles Nanfan. Other tablets include that to Bridges Nanfan, who died in 1704, carved by Thomas White, and one to a rector, R. Pilson who undertook the two restorations of the church in the 19th century.

Of the four bells in the tower one is medieval and dated to 1450. On its side are the initials RC next to the inscription, and it may have been made by Robert Crowch of London.

BISHAMPTON   ST. JAMES

St. James stands at the very north end of the mile long village street, which has a mixture of timber-framed cottages and 20th-century houses. There are most attractive glimpses of the church tower across the field from the road to the north east. The church was once a chapelry of Fladbury and was formerly dedicated to St. Peter.

The sandstone and lias building has a nave and chancel with porch, vestry and west tower. The medieval style church was rebuilt by Frederick Preedy in 1870-71, except for the commanding 15th-century Perpendicular tower with its battlements and tall pinnacles. Much medieval masonry was reused by Preedy. Both 12th-century doorways were preserved. The south doorway has carved trumpet scallop capitals, and keeled roll moulding to the arch, with an animal head at the top. The north doorway is similar but much more plain. A Norman window has been reset on the south side. In a bell opening there hangs a small bell, perhaps a sanctus (similar to one at Fladbury), which was given by William Kite in 1620.

The inside is white and feels similar to the other churches designed by Preedy, with most fittings and glass dating from around the time of the rebuilding. The font, however, is 12th-century, shaped like a cauldron, and ornamented with crosses, rosettes and cable similar to the fonts in South

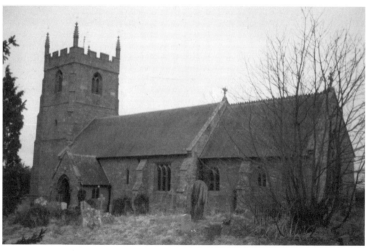

Bishampton was rebuilt by Frederick Preedy in 1870-71

Littleton and Bricklehampton churches. A medieval architectural fragment now in the church is part of the reticulated tracery from the former stone screen in Worcester Cathedral. There is also a 17th-century iron hourglass stand, like that in Oddingley church, and amongst the memorial tablets, one to John Callow, who died in 1810, and was formerly a Governor of Quebec.

BLACKWELL   ST. CATHERINE

At the centre of this village of commuter homes close to the Lickey Hills, St. Catherine comes as something of a surprise in leafy surroundings opposite the Gothic Methodist church, which is itself of interest for it contains a remarkable set of wall paintings. The church was built to replace a mission church of 1882 on a site given by Lord Windsor of Hewell, and was designed by H.L. North to look like a Scandinavian church with white rendered walls to a nave, aisles and chancel with steep pitched tiled roofs, and a central tower with a steep saddleback roof. The windows are pointed, though the west window is circular to represent the wheel of St. Catherine. It is a 1930s design and was built by Braziers of Bromsgrove between 1939 and 1940, indeed special dispensation was required to finish the building after the outbreak of the Second World War. The light interior has painted beams, and benefits from the open effect of the central lantern tower.

BLAKEDOWN   ST. JAMES

Blakedown is a prosperous commuter village situated in a hollow on the main Kidderminster to Hagley road. It developed during the latter part of the 19th century after the coming of the railway, and Victorian brick cottages and villas are clustered around the church, with larger 20th-century houses beyond. Indeed Blakedown was part of the parish of Hagley before St. James was opened.

The church is of sandstone with a nave, aisle and porch with vestry, organ loft and chancel. The timber west bell turret supports a short spire. The church was originally designed in 1866 by George Street, the architect of St. John's church, Hagley. Much of Street's walling remains, but the church was remodelled in 1905 when the aisle, vestry and organ loft were built.

This remote sandstone church is hidden away in the countryside and lanes south of Tenbury Wells, in a small arm of the county which projects into Herefordshire. Surrounded by a large churchyard, St. Michael consists of a nave with west tower and a chancel with north chapel.

Whilst the church is of Saxon foundation—footings thought to be from an early building have been found in the churchyard—the present church has some easily recognisable Norman features. Typical flat buttresses and round-headed lancet windows can be seen on both sides of the nave with two beautiful doorways, which stand proud of the walls with blind arcading above, making splendid entrances. The doorways are decorated with shafts and scallop capitals, with rolls to the arches, surrounded by crenellation and lozenges. The blind arcading has intersecting arches decorated with billets. There are five intersecting arches above the north doorway, but only four over the south. They are very similar to those over the south doorway at Eastham church and probably date from between 1160 and 1170.

The chancel was rebuilt in the 13th century, and retains its two-light Early English windows with pointed trefoil heads on the south side. The east window was rebuilt in the Decorated style by Henry Woodyer in 1862. The plain north chapel was built by the recusant Roman Catholic Barneby family in about 1560 in a simple late Perpendicular style. It was a private chapel which remained in the ownership of the lords of the manor until it was restored and handed over to the church by the Prescott family in 1959.

The fine Norman north doorway at Bockleton

The 19th-century Prescott tomb

Inside, the main impression is of a Victorian Gothic Revival church, and indeed most of the furnishings, including the piscina, sedilia, screen, pulpit, pews and font date from the restoration of 1867. The arcade leading from the chancel to the north chapel was also built at this time. However, the nave north-east window contains pieces of medieval glass, showing the Virgin and Child. The striking east window glass was designed by Charles Eamer Kempe in 1905, as a memorial to the vicar, Richard Mence, who died in the previous year. The dark colouring of the

Bockleton: the 17th-century Barneby tomb

window is typical of Kempe's work, and shows scenes from Christ's early life and St. Michael killing the Devil.

Two monuments in the north chapel are very interesting. In 1594, Richard Barneby erected a fine classical memorial, three years before his death. He has a fine effigy, next to that of his wife, Mary Habington, cousin of the historian of Hindlip. They are both in contemporary costume with a helmet between their heads and lie on a rolled mat above the tomb chest, which is faced with heraldry between supporting caryatids. Above the tomb, a large panel supports obelisks, and a pediment with carved *memento mori*—Father Time is shown with his scythe on the right, whilst on the left a boy is blowing bubbles to mark the passage of time. The keystone has a carved skull with a winged hourglass and scales. The inscription is on the panel with their children on each side—five sons and four daughters, the smaller effigies representing the children who predeceased their parents.

Close by, the monument to Thomas Wolstenholme Prescott was carved in white marble in 1867 by Thomas Woolner. It is a moving piece of Victoriana, with Prescott's effigy lying on the tomb chest, which is carved with a relief showing the young Prescott holding the hand of an older man on his deathbed; he caught a fatal fever, whilst nursing his dying gamekeeper. There is also a plain monument to Charles Baldwyn who died in 1706, and on the north side of the nave is a medieval recess which once contained a memorial.

There are two lychgates on the paths leading into the churchyard from the lane. The eastern gate is the reconstructed 15th-century timber-framed porch of the church.

BRADLEY   ST. JOHN THE BAPTIST

At the southern end of this straggling village between Hanbury and Feckenham can be found this isolated church. It stands in a pretty field setting approached only by footpath, close to Shell Brook and the former Victorian school. It is a green sandstone building with a nave and north porch, attached to a chancel with a north-east tower and broach spire, which was built in the early Decorated style by William Jeffrey Hopkins in 1864-65. The east window has tracery typical of Victorian architects working in this style, whilst at the west end is a rose window. Bradley was a chapelry to Fladbury church until 1866, and the present structure succeeded an 18th-century brick church, which in turn replaced a medieval timber-framed chapel.

Inside is fitted in a manner typical of the 1860s. There is a round stone pulpit and the bare walls are patterned using contrasting red stone. The glass in the west rose window is a memorial to men of the parish killed in the First World War, and shows their regimental badges with the Agnus Dei above. It was designed by Archibald Davies of the Bromsgrove Guild. In the porch are preserved two 14th-century grave memorial slabs with carved crosses.

BRANSFORD

ST. JOHN THE BAPTIST

Many people are unaware that Bransford has a church, as it stands alone on a hillside, down a lane almost a mile south of the village which lies on the busy Worcester to Hereford road. St. John the Baptist is a chapelry to Leigh, and the building is small and simple with a nave and chancel under one roof, and a porch. The timber bell turret rises above the gable to the west wall, which abuts on to the lane. On the other sides the church is surrounded by a small meadow. This is a country church of great charm.

Bransford's plain east window and timber bell turret

The earliest part of the building would seem to be a sandstone western part of the south wall of the nave which has an Early English lancet of the 13th century. The Decorated south and blocked north doorways, along with the north and west windows, are 14th-century. The chancel and rest of the nave south wall are 15th-century, though the other nave window is a 19th-century replacement. The east end of the church was patched with brick in 1812 when the three light east window was removed, and the chancel now has curious, but very attractive, domestic style east and south windows, similar to those on many local farmhouses. A dormer window, which was removed in 1957, was probably installed at this time to throw more light onto a gallery. The timber porch is probably 16th-century, and the weatherboarded bell turret a century later, although it contains a 14th-century bell. Traces of a medieval mass dial can be seen on the south wall.

Inside, the massive timber supports to the turret are hidden from view by a fine timber-framed partition, which separates the west end of the nave from the body of the church, similar to those at Mamble and Knighton-on-Teme churches. The lovely plain and peaceful interior is the result of a restoration in 1957 by Robert Potter. Many of the furnishings are 19th- and 20th-century, but the 17th-century communion rail and table are retained. A medieval piscina, which has been cut away, was positioned on the south side of the nave for a secondary altar. The wagon roof timbers are also medieval, and exposed traces of medieval wall paintings on the north wall of the church suggest extensive survivals beneath the whitewash. There is a 14th-century Decorated canopy in the glass of the north window of the nave.

BREDICOT

ST. JAMES THE LESS

Although it is only three miles east of the centre of Worcester, the hamlet of Bredicot is still surprisingly remote, despite having been bisected by the railway in the 19th century. St. James stands to the west of the line in the grounds of the Old Rectory. It is a very small field church, with a 13th-century sandstone nave and chancel under one roof. The timber porch is probably 16th-century, and the bellcote was added in the 19th century to replace a timber turret. The church was restored in 1843, but the late Early English window tracery survives, Y-shaped in the side windows and intersecting in the east window. The plain south doorway is probably also 13th-century.

The interior is simple with mainly 19th- and 20th-century fittings. However, the font has a 14th-century bowl, the piscina has a 13th-century trefoil head and there are some 14th-century tiles in the porch, some of which formed part of a pattern with an inscription which would have read as a prayer.

BREDON   ST. GILES

The spire of St. Giles is a conspicuous landmark for miles around. Motorists on the M5 approaching Worcestershire from the south enter the county from Gloucestershire to a view of the spire, close to the medieval tithe barn of the monks of Worcester by the River Avon, with the slopes of Bredon Hill as a backdrop. In the village, the church stands at the west end of the street, across the churchyard from the rambling Tudor former rectory.

Bredon has long been an important ecclesiastical centre. A monastery was founded here, probably on the site of the church, in about 716 by Eanulph of the Mercian royal house. It was endowed by his grandson King Offa, but had become a possession of Worcester Monastery by the 10th century.

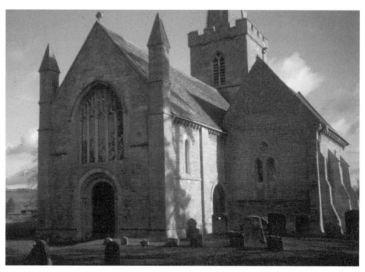

The exterior Norman features to the nave and the Early English south chapel at Bredon

The medieval church is large and constructed of limestone. It consists of a nave with side chapels and a north porch, central tower and chancel with vestry. The nave and porch are fine late Norman work, with echoes of nearby Tewkesbury Abbey in Gloucestershire. The entrance arch and string course above are ornamented with zig-zag, and the grand porch interior has a vault supported by shafts with trumpet scallop capitals. The parvis chamber above is later medieval. The Norman arch to the north doorway is decorated with projecting zig-zag, whereas that of the south doorway has linked lozenges. The west end of the nave has Norman buttresses, string course, corbel table and lancet windows on each side. The west front is impressive with two square pinnacles on the corners, as at Ledbury church in Herefordshire. The west doorway is of similar type to the others, but the front was altered by the insertion of a large Perpendicular window.

The eastern part of the Norman nave is hidden from view by the side chapels. The south chapel has pointed lancet windows, which along with the tiny quatrefoil window on the west wall are Early English. Heavy buttressing has been necessary here because of subsidence. The tower and chancel were rebuilt about 1300, and the north chapel added a little later with Decorated windows. During the 14th century the spire was added to the tower, rising to a height of 161 feet. Scratch dials can be traced on the nave walls, and there is a Decorated image niche on a chancel buttress.

The interior is attractive, spacious and light. In the Norman nave, the inner arches to the three doorways have unusual roll moulding. The arch to the tower from the nave is contemporary, and is the key to the late 12th-century date, being pointed, yet having zig-zag decoration and trumpet scallop capitals. This is very similar to the two west bays of Worcester Cathedral nave which date from about 1185. They may, of course, be the work of the same mason, as Bredon was a possession of Worcester.

The south arcade is typical Early English work with quatrefoil piers, and the south chapel windows are enhanced inside with detached marble shafts, as can also be found in the eastern part of Worcester Cathedral. This was the Mitton Chapel, built for the Lords of the Manor of Mitton, now in Tewkesbury. The north arcade, however, is Perpendicular, and later than the Decorated windows of the north chapel. The chancel arch, aumbry, sedilia and piscina are all Decorated, whilst the Easter Sepulchre on the north side with crockets and ballflowers was restored in the 1960s.

The fittings and monuments are of great interest with many medieval survivals. The font is Perpendicular with a 17th-century cover. The pulpit is 20th-century but is a copy of the medieval pulpit at Southwold Church in Suffolk. Sadly, the painted medieval rood loft, which stood across the tower arch, was removed in 1840, though the stairs can still be seen. There is some 13th-century wall painting with a red masonry pattern in the chancel, and on the altar steps is a group of over 80 fine medieval floor tiles. Most are heraldic, showing the arms of England, Castille, Léon and France, together with those of families including Beauchamp, Fitzalan, Warenne, Bohun, Mortimer, de Vere, Cantelow, Newburgh, Clare, Hastings, Berkeley, Graunson and Stapleton. Others show birds, animals and foliage. The remainder of the church floor is a chequer of hexagonal tiles which create a delightful optical illusion. The communion rail is 17th-century with long pendants between the balusters. The 20th-century altar is by Sir Ninian Comper.

The glass in several of the chancel windows is 14th-century. There are figures of St. Mary Magdalene and St. Mary of Egypt, as well as quarries with foliage designs of ivy, maple and oak with acorns. The heraldic glass, including some from Hadzor Church, shows arms of the Beauchamp, Bellingham and Tattershall families. The 19th-century glass includes the east window, which depicts the Epiphany and the arms of Bishop Prideaux, who is buried here. Of similar date are the arms of the Dukes of Portland, former patrons of the church. Sir Ninian Comper designed the 20th-century glass for the tower windows.

The memorials in this church are fascinating. In the Easter Sepulchre there is a reset medieval stone grave slab with a cross and traces of ballflower decoration. On the south chancel wall is a beautiful early 14th-century coffin lid. It shows a Crucifixion with a rugged cross, above the arms of which are unidentified male and female busts separated by two doves. The fine canopies at the top are carved with cusps and crockets. The adjacent 14th-century tomb with effigies of a man, woman and child, could be to William and Katherine Reed of Mitton. Notice the indented slab in front of the altar which once contained a brass, and to the right the brass of Bishop John Prideaux of Worcester and his wife. Prideaux died in poverty at Bredon rectory, the house of his son-in-law, having been removed from office by Oliver Cromwell, as he had been chaplain to King Charles I.

In the south chapel, there are three arched tomb recesses. The smaller eastern one contains a slab carved with a shield and two arms clasping a heart. It is likely that this commemorates the burial of the heart in a casket of a member of the Mitton family who died abroad, possibly on crusade. A second recess now contains a medieval stone cross from the lost chapel of the Holy Cross at Mitton. The south chapel is dominated at the west end by the huge memorial to Sir Giles Reed of Mitton, who died in 1611, and his wife

The interior showing the 12th- and 13th-century arches

47

Catherine Greville, the daughter of the great Warwickshire landowner, Sir Fulke Greville. The monument is of alabaster with the effigies on a chest between black columns. The arch above is beautifully decorated, as is the rear wall, on which there is an inscription. The children are shown on either side. The upper part of the monument is crowned with cherubs, obelisks and a black eagle.

BREDON'S NORTON   ST. GILES

St. Giles is accessible by footpaths from the surrounding block of lanes, which are bounded by limestone walls and cottages in this pretty village on the western slopes of Bredon Hill. That this church has the same dedication as neighbouring Bredon is more than a coincidence, as Bredon's Norton was originally a chapelry to its neighbour's larger church.

The limestone church is long and comprises a nave and chancel with porch and west tower, which is capped by battlements and a pyramid roof. The earliest parts are Norman, with some surviving masonry reset as the south porch entrance and the south doorway. The carvings are late 12th century and include trumpet scallop and zig-zag. The present nave and chancel were originally built in the 13th century, and inside can be seen the chancel arch of that date with carved, stiff leaf capitals. At the west end of the nave is a lancet window, which must be earlier than the 13th-century tower by which it is now obscured from external view. Part of the east window and a lancet in the nave are also reset 13th-century work.

The interior, with its mainly 19th-century fittings, is very much the result of the extensive rebuilding work by Worcester architect Frederick Preedy in 1883. Amongst the memorials, a large tablet typical of the late 17th century, with two columns and a pediment, was probably erected just after the death in 1685 of the wife of William Hancock. He was the founder of the Bluecoat School in Bredon and died in 1719.

BRETFORTON   ST. LEONARD

The church is at the centre of this straggling Vale of Evesham village. The situation is pleasant, being at the opposite end of the square from the famous Fleece Inn, which is in the care of the National Trust.

The archaeological interpretation of St. Leonard is more complex than it first appears. There is a tower at the west end of a nave and chancel which are surrounded by aisles, transepts and a porch, all built of limestone. The Norman nave was probably first given aisles during the late 12th century. At the east end, the chancel was rebuilt and consecrated in 1295. The lancet windows, the east window—which despite restoration in 1855 still has three lancets under one arch—and a south window, with cusped Y-shaped tracery, are all typical of the transition from the Early English to the Decorated style. Architecture from this transition can also be seen at nearby Honeybourne church. The Decorated north transept is, however, 14th-century, whilst the nave and north aisle wall were rebuilt in the Perpendicular style of the 15th century. At this time the ashlar west tower was added, topped with pinnacles, battlements and gargoyles of demons and a lion. The north and south doorways and transept east windows were all also replaced in the 15th century. Medieval mass dials can be found on the exterior of the chancel, and there is early graffiti on the tower walls. In the porches of 1847, both north and south doors are 15th-century, with several original iron fittings.

The interior is scraped to the stonework, which makes the church dark, but it has assisted in the understanding of the archaeological development. The nave arcades are basically late 12th-century and have round piers. The south arcade is a little earlier, with large trumpet scallop capitals and simple arches. The arches of the north arcade are chamfered, and the nailhead decoration and carvings of the capitals suggest a 13th-century date. At the west end, there are a bishop and three knights, probably representing the murder of Archbishop Thomas Becket, by the knights of King Henry II, whilst in the middle, the dragon with St. Margaret has leaves sprouting from its tail, and is very similar to the dragon on the font at Elmley Castle church. A contemporary stone with nailhead decoration can also be found reset in the south window of the south transept.

The west end was altered in the 15th century and again during the restoration of 1847. On the south side a Perpendicular arch and a half arch were built at the west end, suggesting that a short south aisle was extended westwards when the tower was built. The north arcade, however, runs the full length of the north wall.

At the east end of the nave, the rood loft stair survives beside the chancel arch, marking the position of the rood screen, which was removed in the 19th century. It is possible that the tie beam on the roof truss above supported a plastered tympanum, which may have been painted with a Last Judgement scene in the Middle Ages. The font is Norman, though the cover dates from 1721.

There is an unusual medieval piscina in the south transept close to some 17th-century woodwork reused in the squire's pew. The panel by the pew door is dated 1615, and the carved blank arches and almost classical figures are typical of this period. The other pews and furnishings are late 19th-century, including the choir stalls which came from a church at Stratford-upon-Avon in Warwickshire. The stained glass includes some medieval fragments in the north aisle and transept windows, amongst which can be found a head of Christ. However, most of the other glass is Victorian, including that in the east window of 1855.

BRICKLEHAMPTON   ST. MICHAEL

This tiny community beneath the north side of Bredon Hill boasts the longest English place name without any letters repeated. The village is of Saxon origin, and archaeological finds of that date were made here in the 19th century. Bricklehampton was among the estates taken from Pershore Abbey to endow Edward the Confessor's abbey at Westminster in the early 11th century, and the church remained a chapel of St. Andrews at Pershore during the Middle Ages. The church is reached by a path from the lane through the village, and has a nave, tower, chancel, vestry and porch. The tower is built into the west end of the nave, and has a saddleback roof, giving it a French appearance. It dates from 1876, when the east wall was also rebuilt and the timber porch added.

However, the masonry of the nave is Norman and the south doorway is ornamented with shafts and projecting zig-zag. The trumpet scallop capitals have floral decoration like those on the entrance arch at Bredon church. The nave also has a blocked Norman lancet window, and two further lancets with trefoil heads of about 1300.

The interior very much reflects the 1876 restoration, but the nave wagon roof is medieval, as are the stoup and image bracket. The round font is Norman and has tapering sides decorated with two crosses and two rosettes. It is very similar to the fonts in Bishampton and South Littleton churches. In the chancel, the piscina is medieval, and the 19th-century sedilia incorporates medieval stone arm rests. The glass in the west window, and the four chancel side windows of 1888, is by Charles Eamer Kempe. There is a tablet in the nave to Francis Palmer who died in 1715.

BROADHEATH   CHRISTCHURCH

Broadheath is famous as the birthplace of the composer Sir Edward Elgar, and the house can be seen about a mile from the church, which stands at the west end of the sprawling village of Lower Broadheath. It is of dark red sandstone and is surrounded by trees. The tower stands at the west end of the nave, with aisles, porch and chancel and vestry. The present church was built in 1903-04 and the architect was Charles Ford Whitcombe, who used the Perpendicular style favoured by the Arts and Crafts movement at that time. The church replaced an earlier building of 1837, which was a chapel of ease to Hallow, and this in turn is now part of the school to the south-west of the church.

Inside there is much contemporary early 20th-century woodwork, including the reredos and the communion rails, which have carved vine decoration. Ford Whitcombe designed the glass of the east window in 1904, which shows St. John and the Women at the Holy Sepulchre. Other chancel windows show Ruth and Naomi, and a nave window showing Christ by the sea is a memorial to Admiral Richard Britten. The tower is surmounted by a gilded weathervane of a galleon, and houses a 15th-century bell brought from the old church at Hallow.

BROADWAS   ST. MARY MAGDALENE

At the end of a quiet lane, off the busy main road through the village near the River Teme, this red sandstone church can be found standing in a graveyard, surrounded by trees. The lengthy nave and chancel are under one roof, with a chapel and porch on the south side and a timber bell turret at the west end carries a short spire.

The nave and chancel were probably rebuilt in the early 13th century. There are several lancet windows of this date and the south doorway has a pointed arch supported by carved waterleaf capitals. The north doorway is earlier, from the late 12th century and has a round arch. The nave was extended westwards later in the 13th century to enclose the belfry. The Decorated style east window is 19th century, but there is a restored 15th-century window on the south side of the chancel.

The most beautiful part of Broadwas church is the south chapel (see illustration p.19), a chantry dedicated to the Blessed Virgin Mary in 1340. It was endowed with 120 acres of land in Cotheridge, which paid for the maintenance of a chaplain, who was to say mass regularly for the souls of six local benefactors—William de Kydesby, Peter de Grete, Margery Drew, John and William de Howselle and John de Broadwas. The chapel was open by 1344 and is a fine piece of Decorated architecture, and although restored it is an important piece of work which can be dated from documentary evidence. Between the steep end gables the chapel has its own pitched roof, below which the buttresses are capped by gables with cusped ornament. The two-light windows on the south side have ornate cusped Decorated tracery, and the east windows comprise a pair of lancets with cusped heads beneath a round window filled with ogee tracery. Originally the chapel would have had a stone altar at the east end, and been screened off from the nave. It was probably decorated with elaborate wall-paintings and stained glass. The fireplace at the west end of the chapel is later, probably 19th-century.

The interior has been scraped to the stone and is rather dark, but the lovely arcade to the south chapel is noteworthy. It has two arches with quatrefoil piers and typical Decorated mouldings. The nave and chancel are themselves no longer divided by an arch, which seems to have been removed during the 15th century, when the eastern part of the nave north wall was rebuilt. Perhaps the addition of the chapel had weakened the structure. At the west end of the nave, the timber work of the belfry was entirely replaced in the 20th century, and is divided from the body of the church by openwork timbering.

Among the mainly 19th- and 20th-century fittings, some earlier pieces can be identified. There are medieval piscinae in the chancel and south chapel, and on the chancel floor can be seen some late medieval tiles. Some once formed the border to a pattern, whilst some of the remainder show the arms of the Berkeley family and Abbots Elyot and Nailhart of Gloucester, arms which can also be found in neighbouring Cotheridge church. The medieval font has a plain octagonal bowl on a stem which is decorated with scallops. Woodwork from the 17th century includes some plain benches at the west end by the balcony railing of similar date.

At the east end, the chancel has 17th-century panelling, close to the pulpit of 1632, which has carved scrollwork and the names of the churchwardens, William Noxon and Roger Price. The tester above is inscribed 'Blessed are they that hear the word of God and keep it'. The east window glass was produced in 1899 by Burlison and Grylls. There are some 17th-century ledger stones at the west end, and a monument by William Stephens of Worcester to Henry Roberts who died in 1761 has classical ornament surrounding a draped urn.

The belfry contains a 14th-century bell, and outside the churchyard cross has a medieval base with a niche for the pyx, though the upper parts are 20th century.

BROADWAY

ST. EADBURGHA

St. Eadburgha, Broadway: the Norman church was much extended in the 15th century

From the 10th century until the Dissolution of the Monasteries in 1539, Broadway was held by Pershore Abbey. The relics of St. Eadburgha or Edburga were held in a shrine at Pershore, and Broadway church was dedicated to her, along with the churches at Abberton and Leigh. St. Eadburgha is the old parish church at Broadway, and stands about one mile south of the present village centre and present parish church of St. Michael, on what was the medieval route over the Cotswold edge from Worcester to London. The church is very attractive, built from local limestone, in a pretty churchyard with many large trees.

The church has a nave with aisles, central tower with transepts, and chancel. The earliest parts of the building are the Norman nave and chancel, of which the flat buttresses on the east and west walls can be seen outside. The tower was built into the nave in the 14th century, with the north transept added at the same time. The south transept had been built a century before. The upper parts of the tower are 15th-century Perpendicular with battlements and pinnacles above typical square headed bell openings. These are similar to several chancel windows, and of the same date as the rebuilt aisles, with their windows and battlements. The Norman chancel had been given new lancet windows in the 13th century—these have been blocked up on the south side, and replaced by an 18th-century Gothic window. There is a blocked late Norman doorway on the north side of the chancel, and other blocked entrances around the church gave access to family pews and staircases to galleries in the 17th century.

The construction of St. Michael's church in the early 19th century meant that St. Eadburgha has remained almost unaltered since that date, with two sympathetic restorations in 1866 and 1916. The interior has a very special atmosphere with some lime-washed walls and a jumble of stone arches beneath medieval wagon roofs. The floors are made up of uneven stones and quarry tiles. The late Norman church was aisled, and the arcades date from about 1200. The round piers support capitals with scallop trumpets,

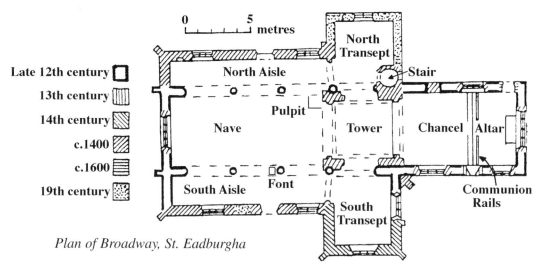

Plan of Broadway, St. Eadburgha

Late 12th century

13th century

14th century

c.1400

c.1600

19th century

from which rise the plain pointed arches. The 14th-century crossing under the tower incorporates parts of the eastern arches of the arcades, and the capitals given battlements to form brackets, possibly for statues. The tower and chancel arches are 14th-century, though the latter includes Norman imposts. The interior of the tower is lit by small Perpendicular lancets above roof level, and has a stone vault with eight ribs, in the same style as Hampton church. This was opened up in 1916 with the removal of the post-Reformation ringing chamber.

The font is a plain Norman tub with tapering sides, and there is an Early English trefoiled piscina in the chancel. The pulpit is Perpendicular with traceried panels which have been stripped of paint. The blocked entrance to the rood loft is in the north east corner of the tower, and parts of the medieval screen have been reused to form the screen in the north transept. There are some 14th-century benches in the chancel, but most of the pews are 19th-century and come from St. Michael. The wooden pillar almsbox by the pulpit is also medieval. The tiles on the steps by the font are 15th-century, and there are some fragments of medieval glass. Part of a panel with the arms of the Sambach family survives in the east window, and there is a face, possibly of Christ, in the west with pieces of borders with crowns in several others. The communion rail and chandelier in the chancel are 17th-century and there are royal arms of Charles I dated 1641, over the tower arch. In the chancel a photograph shows a carved oak panel with images of saints, which may be a medieval Flemish chest front, and is no longer preserved in the church.

There are several memorials in the church. Two parts of a 13th-century effigy of a priest are in the south transept. On a panel north of the altar is a modern copy of a stolen brass to Anthony Daston of Broadway Court who died in 1572. This is a palimpsest brass with part of a Flemish brass on the back, the rest of which is at Westerham church in Kent. Daston had married Ann Sheldon, who had two sons by her previous marriage to Francis Savage of Elmley Castle, and the Broadway estates remained in the Savage family until 1795. The memorial tablet to Walter Savage, who died in 1641, is typical of the period. Most other tablets are to the Phillips family who subsequently acquired the estate. The tablet in the south transept to William Taylor, who died in 1741, has columns, pediment, and cherubs with a skull below. There is also a brass plate in the chancel to John Treavis, who died in 1641. He probably added the gabled front to the Lygon Arms in the village in 1626. Many other memorials to the Sheldon family, who were Lords of the Manor before the 17th century were destroyed in 1866.

Part of a memorial with a *memento mori* inscription is reset in the south transept, and there are several fine headstones of limestone outside, as in so many Cotswold churchyards over the border in Gloucestershire. At the entrance to the churchyard can be found a 17th-century mounting block.

BROADWAY   ST. MICHAEL AND ALL ANGELS

St. Michael, Broadway—the church of 1840 in the Early English style

This is the church which is immediately visible to visitors to Broadway. It stands just south of the Green in this popular tourist village. The centre of Broadway shifted northwards from the end of the Middle Ages to its present setting along the main route from Worcester to London, and by 1608 a chapel of ease to St. Eadburgha had been built and dedicated to St. Michael. This building was replaced in 1840 by the present church, which was constructed in the fashionable bold Early English style by the local architect, Harvey Eginton, who had designed the similar church at Catshill in 1838. It was proposed to demolish St. Eadburgha at this point, but this was fortunately never undertaken.

St. Michael has a west tower, aisled nave and a short chancel which was extended to its present size in 1890. It is built of local limestone and blends well with the surroundings, although the long lancets which dominate the exterior and are paired for the substantial bell openings give the exterior a severe appearance. The top of the tower has a solid parapet and four heavy pinnacles. The chancel windows of 1890 have tracery in contrast with the lancets.

Inside, the church has many 19th- and 20th-century fittings, but the fine pulpit with its carved 17th-century woodwork comes from St. Eadburgha. There is some interesting 20th-century glass reflecting Broadway's development as an arts and crafts centre. The east window is a memorial to the Boer War, produced in 1901 by Clayton and Bell, and shows the risen Christ, with St. Michael and Joshua dressed as soldiers. The Payton memorial windows date from 1959, and show St. Michael and St. Eadburgha, designed by Joseph Nuttgens, who also produced the baptistry windows in 1965. The Brown and Patrick memorial windows are also good examples of 1960s glass.

In the churchyard lies the grave to the architect Sir Arthur Blomfield who designed the Worcestershire churches at Upton-upon-Severn and at Wribbenhall in Bewdley, and who is well known as the architect of Selwyn College, Cambridge and the Royal College of Music in London.

BROMSGROVE   ALL SAINTS

All Saints was built on the Birmingham Road at the north end of the centre of Bromsgrove, to serve a town which was expanding rapidly in the late 19th century. It is a large sandstone church with aisled nave, transepts, chancel with polygonal apse, and a north-west tower. The body of the church was built between 1872 and 1874 to the designs of John Cotton, the architect of Finstall church and the hall at Bromsgrove School. It is built in the late 13th century Early English style, but Cotton took the unusual step of making the end windows of the transepts look sufficiently later to give an impression of chronological development which might be found in a genuine medieval church. The tower with parapet and pinnacles was added in 1888 in the 14th-century style to Cotton's design, although this had to be revised from his original plan for a spire because of the poor quality of the ground below. The builder was Jonathan Brazier of Bromsgrove.

The interior is faced with yellow brick with some polychrome detail, especially to indicate the position of the transepts at the east end of the nave arcades, as the church does not have a true crossing. The fittings are mostly contemporary, but the rood beam, sedilia, panelling, credence table and wrought iron gates and screen are early 20th-century work by the Bromsgrove Guild. The glass includes a window which was installed to commemorate Queen Victoria's Diamond Jubilee of 1897 by Hardman & Co., and the Amphlett memorial windows of 1901 and 1902 by Jones and Willis. The memorial window to the architect Henry Yate is by Arthur Clarke and Archibald Davies of the Guild, while the Brighton memorial window was designed by Albert Lemmon of the Guild in 1927.

BROMSGROVE   ST. JOHN THE BAPTIST

The spire of the parish church dominates views of the town of Bromsgrove. St. John is a large church, and stands on a hilltop away to the west of the High Street and the town centre where the famous public school is located. Bromsgrove was an important medieval market town, which developed as a manufacturing centre chiefly for nails into the 19th century. Today it is one of several affluent towns in the north-east of Worcestershire, close to the West Midlands conurbation.

The most attractive approach to the church is by a flight of steps from St. John Street, which lead into the spacious churchyard through a 17th-century timber lychgate. The red sandstone church has a west tower and spire, aisled nave with porch and chancel with vestry, and is similar to

The Perpendicular nave and aisles of St. John the Baptist

the medieval churches of other prosperous West Midlands towns. The exterior architecture is mainly Early English and Perpendicular, but the south doorway has some reused Norman stonework. The chancel is a fine late 13th-century structure. The priest's doorway, side windows of two lancets, and east window of five stepped lancets are good examples of the Early English style. The aisles were added to the nave at this time and embrace the west end of the chancel. The south aisle has an Early English east window, whilst on the north side there are a doorway and stepped lancet windows of the same date.

The lower part of the tower is Decorated, but the belfry and spire are 15th-century Perpendicular. At this time a new west window and three niches, now with statues of St. Peter, St. Paul and St. John the Baptist, were placed lower down to bring a sense of unity. The bell openings are joined by continuous blind arcading around the belfry, with much carved decoration, similar to the towers at St. Mary, Kidderminster and King's Norton church in Birmingham. Panelled battlements and pinnacles surround

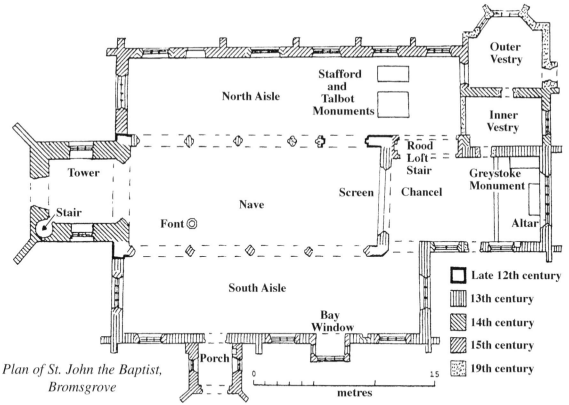

Plan of St. John the Baptist, Bromsgrove

Late 12th century
13th century
14th century
15th century
19th century

the base of the soaring octagonal spire. The aisles were remodelled at this time and the clerestorey was added to the nave, all of which have battlements and pinnacles, and there are many characteristic square-headed windows. The south aisle windows also include two with pointed arches at the east end, one of which is blocked, either side of the unusual Perpendicular square bay window, which was intended to take a burial, like the later example at Spetchley church. The inner vestry on the north side of the chancel is 14th-century, while the outer part was added in the 19th century. The church was restored in 1858 by Sir George Gilbert Scott, and like many sandstone Midland churches has much Victorian stonework on the exterior.

The church is entered through the 15th-century porch, which has a Perpendicular roof, niches and a stoup. Inside, the general appearance is largely the result of the Victorian restoration, but parts of 12th century piers at the east end of the north arcade, perhaps from an arch to a lost transept, show the large nave at the core of the church to be Norman work, which has since been continuously altered. The chancel arch is Early English, with carved nailhead decoration, and contemporary with the rest of the chancel. The piscina at the east end of the south aisle and the main part of the north arcade, which has quatrefoil pillars, are also Early English, though the small arch, second from the east end, was inserted in 1858. The south arcade, tower arch, and the panelled arch between the chancel and north aisle, are Perpendicular.

The fittings are almost entirely late 19th- and early 20th-century, but the stair to the former rood loft, and the stonework quatrefoil panels to the sedilia, which probably come from the Stafford memorial, are medieval. The lectern is 17th-century, and the Arts and Crafts pulpit was designed in 1903 by Charles Ford Whitcombe, architect of Broadheath church. An altar and other fittings were made at this time by Bromsgrove Guild craftsmen. Several windows contain Victorian glass made by firms of note. The east window of 1861 and the south aisle east window of 1867 are by Lavers and Barraud. The west window has glass of 1870 by the Belgian, Jean-Baptiste Capronnier and the windows of the bay in the south aisle were glazed by Ward and Hughes in 1883. An early 20th-century window in the north aisle showing Dorcas, Anna and the education of Timothy is by Amy Walford of the Bromsgrove Guild.

The collection of monuments is very impressive. In the south aisle bay window there is a coffin lid carved with a foliated cross. At the east end of the north aisle are the alabaster effigies, with fine costume, of Sir Humphrey Stafford and his wife, Eleanor Alesbury. The Staffords lived at Grafton Manor, south of the town, and Sir Humphrey's death at Blackheath near London during the Jack Cade Rebellion in 1450 is mentioned in Shakespeare's *Henry VI*. The priests of the Stafford Chantry were required to keep a school, which forms the basis of the present Bromsgrove School. Close by are the effigies of Sir John Talbot and his two wives, Margaret Troutbeck and Elizabeth Wrottesley. Sir John died in 1550, having inherited Grafton Manor from his father, Sir Gilbert Talbot, who had taken the Manor over from the Stafford family in 1486, after Sir Humphrey's son, also Sir Humphrey, was executed for treason for supporting Richard III at the Battle of Bosworth in 1485. The Talbot inscription has disappeared from the monument, but enough remained in 1856 to help Lord Talbot establish a claim to the Earldom of Shrewsbury. There are also the defaced effigies of a woman and a man in prayer.

In the chancel, next to the altar is the memorial to Elizabeth Greystoke, who until her death in 1490 was the first wife of Sir Gilbert Talbot, to whom Grafton was granted in 1486. The effigy has contemporary costume and the tomb chest is decorated with Gothic panels and deacons holding shields, very much in the fashion of the late 15th century. The tablet to Bishop John Hall of Bristol, who died in 1710, has an inscription which refers to him having been Master of Pembroke College, Oxford, and there are two 17th-century brass memorial inscriptions, one to Bridget Talbot who died in 1612, and one to her sister, Margaret Lygon, who died in 1632.

In the south aisle stands the large monument to George Lyttleton who died in 1600, who is shown reclining and wearing his robes as sergeant-at-law. Under the arch to the back of the memorial, the decoration of fruit and flowers is very similar to that on the Wylde monument in St. Peter, Droitwich. The Boer War memorial tablet in the south aisle is by Amy Walford of the Bromsgrove Guild.

Outside in the churchyard there is a defaced 17th-century effigy, and two restored slate headstones to Thomas Scaife and Joseph Rutherford, railway engine drivers who were killed in an accident in 1840, when a boiler exploded. On the stones are illustrations of early steam engines and unusual epitaphs. The stones serve as a reminder of Bromsgrove's position close to Lickey Incline, which trains could at one time only climb with the assistance of a second engine.

BROOME   ST. PETER

Close to the Clent Hills and south of Hagley, Broome is a pleasant but little known scattered village. The church too deserves wider acclaim. The site is medieval and the former 13th-century church was a chapelry to Clent. However, it was rebuilt in the late 18th century, and is a most attractive brick building with a west tower, nave and chancel, in a churchyard with yew trees.

The small nave has two round-headed windows on each side with clear glazing, typical of the 18th century. The low west tower has similar

The small brick Georgian church at Broome

round-headed bell openings and a pyramid roof. The short chancel was extended eastwards to double its length in 1861, but using similar brick and keeping the 18th-century style, which was most unusual in the age of the Gothic Revival.

The Georgian interior is quite plain, though the furnishings are the product of the 19th-century refurbishment. However, the small round Norman font has survived. It is carved with 15 arches, with beaded decoration, and six grotesque heads with large eyes. The monument to Anne Hill, who died in 1804, is by John Flaxman. He was well known for his memorials in Georgian times, and also produced the Knight memorial in Wolverley church. Anne Hill is shown in profile seated on the ground, reading a book.

BROUGHTON HACKETT   ST. LEONARD

Passing through the village on the road from Worcester to Alcester, it is the converted hopkilns which attract attention. The church is tucked away from the main road on the lane towards Crowle, in an extensive churchyard.

St. Leonard is a small, simple east Worcestershire field church with a nave and chancel built of lias under one roof, which carries a pretty weatherboarded bell turret at the west end. There is a timber south porch. Although the 14th- and 15th-century church walls were much rebuilt in the 19th century, the west wall is medieval with a text book example of a 14th-century Decorated style window, with Y-shaped tracery ornamented with cusps and a quatrefoil. The very plain whitewashed interior has 19th-century fittings, but there is a 17th-century communion table, an 18th-century chantry board and some ledger stones to the floor. In the bell turret, there are two 14th-century bells, which may have been made by a foundry in Warwick, and are similar to contemporary bells at Beaudesert and Whitchurch in Warwickshire.

The classic Decorated style west window at Broughton Hackett

BUSHLEY   ST. PETER

Bushley is on the southern edge of Worcestershire with views south east across the meadows towards the River Severn and Tewkesbury. The church is beside the lane in the centre of the village surrounded by timber framed and brick cottages and houses. It is built of lias and has a west tower and short spire, nave with chancel, transepts and vestry.

There was a medieval church on the site which was replaced by Edward Blore in 1843 for the Dowdeswell family, who lived in the large house to the north of the village, formerly Pull Court, but now known as Bredon School. The house was also rebuilt by Blore between 1836 and 1846. Indeed, two 14th-century windows from the previous church were incorporated into a folly on the estate. The nave and tower of the present church are Blore's work, and are of the Commissioners type in the Early English and

19th-century Bushley church with Edward Blore's nave and Sir George Gilbert Scott's chancel

Perpendicular styles, which were favoured in the 1840s. The short apsidal chancel was replaced with the present chancel and transepts in 1856-57 by Sir George Gilbert Scott in an early Decorated style with large windows below pierced quatrefoil parapets and pinnacles.

The interior contains many mid- to late 19th-century fittings, although the font may be late 12h century. Glass in several of the windows was installed for the Dowdeswell family. The south transept window of 1888 is by Hardman & Co. of Birmingham, as is the window on the south side of the chancel of 1877, which shows the Resurrection. However, it is the numerous Dowdeswell memorials which are the dominant feature of the interior. Among them, the tablet to Roger Dowdeswell, who acquired Pull Court in 1628 and who died in 1633, is an early example of the classical style with a pediment. The memorials to Judith Dowdeswell, who died in 1666, and William Dowdeswell, who died in 1683, have urns on columns, whereas the tablet to Richard Dowdeswell, who died in 1673, and his wife, Ann Pleydell, is surrounded by twisted columns. To the side, the memorial to another William Dowdeswell, who died in 1775, is by John Hickey, and shows a woman leaning against the base of an urn with wreaths. He was Chancellor of the Exchequer, and was anxious to prevent a war of independence in America, which in fact, began in the year of his death. The long inscription was written by Edmund Burke. There is also a tablet to one of William's sons, a further William, who was Governor of the Bahamas and Commander-in-Chief of the forces in India.

In the nave is the earliest memorial, a brass to Thomas Payne and his wife Ursula. He died in 1500 and they are shown in contemporary costume; she has Latin inscriptions on her head-dress and girdle. They lived at Paynes Place, a fine late 15th-century timber-framed building which still stands to the south of the village. It is a local tradition that Queen Margaret of Anjou found refuge in this house with the Paynes after her defeat at the Battle of Tewkesbury in 1471.

BUTTON OAK   ST. ANDREW

This small corrugated iron and timber mission church on the Shropshire border serves part of the parish of Dowles in Wyre Forest. It contains some items from the Georgian church of St. Andrew, which stood near the River Severn at Dowles near Bewdley, until it was demolished in the mid-20th century.

CALLOW END   ST. JAMES

This sprawling village between Powick and the Old Hills is overshadowed by the large brick church and buildings of Stanbrook Abbey. It is easy to miss the west gable of St. James on the side of the main road, close to the village hall and school. The church was built as a chapel of ease to Powick church by the sixth

Earl Beauchamp of Madresfield in 1888. It has a brick nave and chancel with a small louvered bell turret on the roof. The two windows at the west end are of an unusual Perpendicular type, but the side windows are more domestic in style.

CASTLEMORTON   ST. GREGORY

The church spire can be clearly seen on views across Castlemorton Common from the Malvern Hills. St. Gregory is at a road junction in the centre of this scattered village, and across the field to the south of the church can be seen the earthworks of the Norman castle of the Foliot family, from which the village takes its name.

The tower and spire stand at the west end of the nave and south aisle, east of which there is a chancel and south transept. The Perpendicular north porch is of timber but the rest of the church including the spire is built of grey sandstone. The red tile roofs give the building a homely appearance, especially with the hipped roof to the transept. The Norman origins of the church are evident outside. There are two windows in the chancel north wall, some reset pieces of a string course with cable moulding on the east wall, and the north and south doorways. Both have scalloped capitals and zig-zag protruding from the wall, similar to many other doorways as at Bricklehampton or Earls Croome. The tympanum to the north doorway has a carved Agnus Dei, and may be the work of masons from Dymock—identified as the Dymock School of Sculpture. The south doorway has been reset in the 13th century south aisle and has a plain tympanum. The south transept was added later in the 13th century and has a large south window with lovely intersecting tracery. The east wall of the transept has two lancets with trefoil heads, beneath a hood mould which links them above and is finished by a carved head at each end. Such a nicely ornamented transept must have been added as a chantry chapel.

The Norman doorway and Decorated window on the south side of Castlemorton church

In the north wall of the nave are a Decorated and a large Perpendicular window. The tower is also in the Perpendicular style with niches for statues in the angle buttresses, and topped by battlements with gargoyles, around the base of the octagonal spire. The tower is recorded as being built in 1387 whilst the spire is a 17th-century replacement.

The rather dark scraped interior reveals many features of interest. Above the arcade on the south side of the nave are further Norman windows. The arcade itself, like the spire, was rebuilt in the 17th century when the church was repaired after Civil War damage. Some of the funds for these repairs were raised from the sale of materials from the demolished bell tower at Worcester Cathedral. There is mixed Norman and Decorated masonry in the pillars and arches. The three light Perpendicular north window has a fine canopied niche on either side, and seems also to have been introduced during the 17th-century alterations. It is thought to have come from Little Malvern Priory. Although the chancel arch was rebuilt in 1879, the doorway to the medieval rood loft stair can still be seen. In the transept the 13th-century piscina would have been used in the chantry chapel. Close by is a broken font which dates from the early 17th century, and came from Deerhurst church in Gloucestershire. The present font, which presumably replaced it, is a baluster type with acanthus leaves on the bowl, which dates from around 1700, along with the cover. The communion rail is dated 1683 and 1684 and has flat open-work balusters.

The other furnishings are 19th- and 20th-centuries. The pulpit was designed by William Butterfield in 1858 for a church in Smethwick, but brought here in 1873. The reredos and lectern were made in 1900 by Richard Houghton of Worcester. The east window has glass also of 1900 by Hardman & Co., and there is a window in the transept of 1927 showing the Annunciation, St. Cecilia and St. George. The south window of the chancel has some 15th-century quarries. Amongst the memorials is a tablet to Richard Cocks who died in 1821, by Sydney Gregg of Ledbury, which shows a woman in mourning, holding a torch by an urn. Outside in the churchyard, the medieval cross base now supports a 20th-century wooden war memorial.

CATSHILL   CHRISTCHURCH

Catshill—a Commisioners church

Christchurch stands in the centre of the large suburban village of Catshill, which grew up in the 19th century to the north of Bromsgrove. The building is of local red sandstone and has suffered badly from the effects of weathering.

The west tower and nave were built in 1838 by Harvey Eginton. This was a Commissioners church, and the heavy Early English style of the lancets in the wide nave and tower is typical. The tower with its plain parapet and pinnacles is very similar to Eginton's tower at St. Michael, Broadway. The chancel was rebuilt in 1887 with side chapels. The windows have plate tracery of a later Early English type favoured at the time.

The contrast between the eastern and western sections can be seen inside, where amongst the many 19th-century fittings, the small white earthenware font with Perpendicular detail is unusual. At the east end two windows showing St. Luke and St. John were designed as memorials by Hardman & Co. in 1887. The north chancel window which shows the Christ and Virgin was installed by Burlison and Grylls in 1889.

Interest in this church is aroused through its associations with the poet and classical scholar Alfred Edward Housman, who was born nearby at Fockbury in 1859. He was baptised at Christchurch, where his grandfather had been the first vicar.

CHADDESLEY CORBETT   ST. CASSIAN

Chaddesley Corbett has a most attractive village street of brick and timber framed houses dating from the 17th and 18th centuries. At the south end is the large and interesting church of St. Cassian, built and enlarged in the Middle Ages to serve an extensive forest parish between Kidderminster and Bromsgrove.

The dedication to Cassian, a 4th-century bishop, is highly unusual. Constructed in red sandstone, the church consists of an aisled nave, chancel with north chapel and vestry, and a west tower with spire.

Outside, the only evidence of the building's substantial Norman origins is the blocked north doorway. This was in fact reset from the south side in 1826, and has scallop capitals to the shafts and rich zig-zag ornamentation. Part of the former tympanum is now inside the tower. The north chapel of about 1280 is the next part of the exterior to be seen in date order. The Y-shaped tracery of the north windows, and three stepped lancets under one arch at the east end are typical Early English work. It is probable that the roof level of the chapel was lowered and the parapet added when the vestry was built on the east side in the 16th century. South of this chapel, the chancel was rebuilt in the 14th century, probably by William Corbett, the last member of this family to hold the manor of Chaddesley. Pevsner describes the chancel as 'the most spectacular piece of the Decorated style in any Worcestershire parish church'. The large east window and three south windows have a superb range of exotic Decorated tracery with flamboyant cusps and ogees making up a range of trefoil and quatrefoil designs. In one south window there is a wheel of mouchettes, echoing a French rose window, near to the fine priest's doorway. The south aisle has a Decorated west window, but the other windows and battlements are Perpendicular, dating from the heightening of the aisle in the early 16th century. In the heavily buttressed south wall, there is a Perpendicular tomb recess, with a very fine but weathered ogee canopy.

The tower and spire date from 1777. They are Gothic in style and were designed by James Rose, who also rebuilt Stanford-on-Teme church in similar Georgian Gothic. The tower at Stanford retains its west entrance, which was blocked in favour of a south doorway at St. Cassian by William Butterfield in his restoration of 1863-64. Butterfield rebuilt the north aisle in the Decorated style and restored the east end of the south aisle.

The tall Norman nave arcades are the most striking feature of the church interior, and appear to have

The Norman font at Chaddesley Corbett

been built in phases. The three eastern bays of the north arcade with their round arches, date from about 1150, and the rather wider south arcade with pointed arches a little later. The west bay of the north arcade is a puzzle. It has a pointed arch, and seems to relate to the extension of the nave to the west, sometime after 1150. The exact reasons and sequence for building work on these extraordinary arcades are debatable.

The medieval tower arch dates from around 1400 and surrounds the 18th-century one, whilst the chancel arch has been much altered during 19th-century restorations, when the doom painting, rood screen, loft and stairs were removed from it. The arches leading into the north chapel have been restored but essentially date from the building of the chapel in about 1280. The chancel retains several Decorated features. There is an image niche on either side of the east window, and sedilia, piscina and aumbry, all with elaborately carved crocketed ogee canopies. The supporting brackets of the sedilia are carved with heads of a king, a queen, a bishop and a lady. The foliage at the base of the niches includes a figure, probably a Green Man.

The imposing font dates from between 1160 and 1170. It was carved by Herefordshire School masons, and the bowl has four dragons surrounded by bands of plaiting and intersecting tendrils. The dragons may represent evil, to be overcome by the power of the church symbolised by baptism. The carving is very similar in style to that on the great Herefordshire fonts in Castle Frome and Eardisley churches. The same type of carving can be seen on the fragment of the tympanum of the former south doorway, which is now preserved by the west window of the tower. Part of Christ in Majesty holding a book can be seen, with drapery much like those on the surviving complete tympana at Rowlestone church in Herefordshire, and at Pedmore church in Stourbridge. Almost all the other fittings are the result of Butterfield's restoration of 1863-64, though the organ which dates mainly from 1817, was resited on a new west gallery in the 1960s, when the north chapel was refurbished. Medieval fragments of glass can be found in the east and west windows of the south aisle. The chancel east window was given in 1864 by William Perrins, who with his partner John Wheeley Lea had set up the chemists shop in Worcester in 1823, that later grew into Lea and Perrins. The middle window of the north aisle showing children gathering flowers at the feet of Mary, was installed by the Bromsgrove Guild glazier, Archibald Davis, in 1926 in memory of Doris Faller.

The monuments include an effigy of a knight dating from the end of the 13th century. He is shown cross-legged, wearing a chainmail hood, with a later border of flowers. The effigy is very similar to one in Pershore Abbey, and another at Draycott-le-Moors church, Staffordshire. He may be Roger Corbett, Lord of the Manor, who died in 1290. Another Roger Corbett, who became rector in 1306, may be represented in the damaged effigy of a priest in vestments. Better known is the brass to Thomas Forest, his wife Margaret, with their five sons and six daughters. Forest died in 1511 and was Keeper of Dunclent Park at Stone, part of the Royal Forest of Feckenham. The shields above the heads of the couple show a hunting horn and a pack of arrows. The words of the inscription are separated by arrows, horns, roses, acorns and leaves, and in the corners are the symbols of the four Evangelists.

The classical tablet to Humphrey Pakington, of nearby Harvington Hall who died in 1631, is of fashionable black and white marble with columns and a pediment. It is placed above a tablet to his wife Abigail Sacheverell, who lived on until 1657. There are also simpler tablets to their daughters Dame Anne Audley and Lady Mary Yate, who died in 1692 and 1696. They both lived at Harvington Hall and so were probably responsible for the construction of the many hiding places in that house for Roman Catholic priests. A further tablet, with interesting heraldry, of 1647 is to Elizabeth Holt of Aston Hall in Birmingham who probably died at Harvington whilst visiting the Pakingtons.

Outside in the graveyard is a collection of beautiful Georgian table tombs near the restored medieval churchyard cross. There are the remains of a mass dial on the south wall of the church, whilst the low brick building with Gothic windows on the north side of the graveyard is the former schoolroom of 1809.

CHARLTON   ST. JOHN THE EVANGELIST

Charlton is a popular residential village near the River Avon between Cropthorne and Evesham. St. John is a small church in the village centre, constructed in the local lias, with just a nave and chancel under one roof with a bellcote at the west end. Its position by the roadside is explained by the fact that the church was a conversion from the medieval tithe barn of 1872, which was consecrated in 1883. It was paid for by Henry Workman of Evesham and was undertaken by the Forsyths of Worcester. The interior is plain and whitewashed, with several contemporary fittings.

CHILDSWICKHAM   ST. MARY

St. Mary stands at the end of a lane on the edge of this Vale of Evesham village, in a churchyard surrounded by fields. The honey-coloured limestone reflects the closeness of the Cotswold edge, and the parish is in the diocese of Gloucester. The attractive view of the church spire behind the medieval village cross on the green is deservedly well-known and much photographed.

The church has a nave, chancel, north transept and west tower with spire. A reset window in the transept is the only external evidence to the Norman parts of the building, and most of the transept and chancel masonry is 13th-century. There is also an Early English window of two lights with plate tracery in the transept. The ashlar west tower is 14th-century, with a Decorated doorway and south window, but the octagonal spire with lucarnes behind a battlemented parapet is Perpendicular. The north and south walls of the nave are 19th-century, and there is a sanctus bellcote at the east end.

The entrance through the tower leads to an interior which appears to be much the product of the Victorian restoration, but the west wall of the nave is Norman and has a plain doorway with shafts and scalloped capitals. The Early English chancel has groups of triple shafts on the walls, of which those in the middle shafts are keeled like similar shafts in Pershore Abbey. These carry trumpet scallop capitals, of which the easternmost pair have small leaves, like the capitals at Dore Abbey in Herefordshire. It was thus intended that the chancel should have been vaulted, which would have made it a grand structure. On the north side a blocked Perpendicular arch led to a former north chapel. There are also Perpendicular image niches in the nave with canopies of carved foliage. Apart from the 19th-century fittings, the font probably dates from the 1660s and there are some fragments of medieval glass in a south window of the chancel. Outside are the remains of four mass dials, and in the churchyard is a headstone to Mary Lane, who is said to have died at the age of 133 in 1741.

CHURCHILL (IN HALFSHIRE)   ST. JAMES

Churchill, in the medieval hundred of Halfshire, is a quiet village in attractive arable farming country, north of Blakedown. The commuter housing and restored cottages give little hint of an industrial past based on ironworking.

The red sandstone church, at the centre, has a nave, porch, chancel and north tower in a secluded churchyard surrounded by trees and hedges. The building was erected in 1868 by William Jeffrey Hopkins to replace a dilapidated medieval church, with a timber bell turret. It is a typical church of the period with early Decorated style windows. The rather plain tower is surmounted by a parapet.

Inside there is a characteristic interior of the 1860s with Decorated style features, including a recessed seat with canopy to the east of the chancel arch. The screen of 1930 was made by Bromsgrove Guild craftsmen in memory of Hakewill Tresyllian Williams. The east window has glass of 1877 installed by Clayton and Bell as a memorial to Lord Lyttleton of Hagley, while a window showing St. George is in memory of soldiers killed in the First World War is by Archibald Davies of the Bromsgrove Guild.

CHURCHILL (IN OSWALDSLOW)   ST. MICHAEL

Once this was part of the large Anglo-Saxon parish of St. Helen, Worcester. Today, St. Michael is an isolated church on top of a hill in this scattered hamlet south of the Worcester to Stratford road. It stands next to the remains of the moat to the former manor house, and has just a nave and chancel built of lias, with a timber porch and small bell turret. The exterior is simple, and most of the features, including the windows, date from the restorations of 1863 and 1910. It is now in the care of the Churches Conservation Trust.

The church has plain south and north doorways of about 1300, and the atmospheric interior with its scraped nave and whitewashed chancel has been little altered this century. The Decorated chancel arch and piscina are 14th-century, and the nave wagon roof is medieval. The octagonal font is 15th-century. The chancel is entered by a low screen, and has 17th-century panelling and communion rails. The pulpit is also 17th-century, but the octagonal font is Perpendicular. The remaining medieval glass in the east window is the Wysham family arms. In the nave there is a carved stone lion in two parts, which may once have been a gable ornament. The memorial tablets include one to Thomas Barker, who died in 1688, which has a skull with bat wings at the base as a *memento mori*. A further memorial in the graveyard commemorates the burial of English nuns of the Order of Poor Clares, who were banished from France at the Revolution in 1789, and who were given a home at Churchill Wood Farm by the Roman Catholic Robert Berkeley of Spetchley.

CHURCH LENCH   ALL SAINTS

Church Lench is the largest of the Lenches group of villages and stands on a prominent ridge to the north of Evesham. All Saints stands at the west end of the village in a commanding position, and the tower is visible for miles around. The church is grey, of the local sandstone, and has a chancel with vestry and nave with south aisle and a porch, with the tower at the west end.

Evidence of the Norman nave can be found in the reset south doorway, with its shafts and moulded round arch, and the

The restored medieval church of Church Lench

plain north doorway. In the 14th century the chancel was built and the eastern part of the south aisle added as a chantry. This was extended westwards a century later when the south doorway was repositioned. The Perpendicular nave clerestory was also added and a large window inserted in the north wall. The tower with its battlements and large pinnacles was added around 1500. The church was extensively restored by Frederick Preedy between 1854 and 1858, when the porch was constructed and the chancel was rebuilt. The vestry and organ chamber were added in 1888.

The interior is a good example of a Victorian High Church refurbishment of a medieval church. The arcade has a 14th-century arch at the east end, with two smaller 15th-century arches to the west. The earlier arch gave access to the chapel and a Decorated niche for a saint's statue survives at the east end of the aisle. The chancel arch is Perpendicular and has the rood loft stair nearby. The collection of 19th-century furnishings include several designed by Preedy such as the font and cover with pulley installed in 1858 and the stone pulpit of 1888. The oak reredos, carved in 1888 depicting the Feeding of the Five Thousand is by J. Bridgeman. The lectern, to Preedy's design, was produced by Rattee and Kett of

Cambridge in 1852. Over the chancel arch the large wall painting of Christ in Glory surrounded by angels is of about 1888, possibly by Hardman & Co.

In a glass case is displayed an early 16th-century blue velvet cope, which was later reworked into an altar frontal. Nearby, the tympanum of the blocked north doorway contains a small window where fragments of medieval glass have been reset, including the heads of Christ and the Devil. The 13 windows glazed by Preedy include five in the chancel and three in the nave of between 1854 and 1858 mainly in a simple 13th-century style. The earliest was Preedy's first window. In 1867 the Reverend William Chafy of Rous Lench Court gave five further Preedy windows in the nave showing the Annunciation, Nativity, Adoration of the Magi, Baptism, the Good Shepherd and St. Martin of Tours.

Preedy restored the medieval churchyard cross in 1864, which is close to the medieval font now serving as a sundial.

CLAINES   ST. JOHN THE BAPTIST

The setting of Claines church retains a remarkably rural feeling, despite being very close to the A449, and its recent inclusion within the boundary of the City of Worcester. The church stands on a low hill of clay, from which the name Claines is derived. It was at the centre of a very large parish, which included much of what is now northern Worcester, and the present rural area sandwiched between the River Severn, Ombersley and Fernhill Heath.

The Perpendicular church of Claines on the edge of Worcester

The medieval sandstone church has a nave, with aisles, porches and a second north aisle, a chancel with chapels and vestry, and a west tower. The outside appearance is remarkably uniform with Perpendicular windows, many of which are straight-headed, but with ogee curves to the tracery. The steep pitch to the roofs of the nave, side aisles and chancel is less usual for the period than the parapet to the low pitched roof of the south chapel, which has pinnacles and carved quatrefoils. The tower is also crowned with battlements and pinnacles. The dormer window which throws more light into the south aisle was restored in 1840, and the outer north aisle, porch and vestry were added by Sir George Aston Webb in 1886-87. The sympathetic Perpendicular style work closely resembles his additions to Alfrick church of the previous year. Webb reused the medieval Perpendicular windows from the north aisle and preserved the unity of the exterior.

Cupboards in which bread was placed for distribution to the poor are preserved in the entrance porch which leads to the scraped stone interior. There are tall octagonal piers to the Perpendicular arcades with plain arches, similar to those leading to the tower and the chancel. The arcade leading from the chancel to the north chapel is a little more elaborate, with squints to the piers. The rood loft entrance is close to the chancel arch and the main timbers of the nave roof are medieval. Almost all the fittings and decoration are 19th-century. Much of the window glass shows scenes from the life of Christ, and both the east and west windows of 1899 are by Burlison and Grylls. The unusual 19th-century tile pavement in the chancel shows a Tree of Jesse, but several 15th-century tiles are reset on the wall by the north entrance, and include several designs, particularly inscriptions of animals and fleurs de lys.

The memorials include an early medieval coffin lid now placed by the font. The elaborate effigy of John Porter of Portersmill who died in 1577, is shown with contemporary civilian costume lying on a tomb chest with carved Gothic panels and shell arches. A classical tablet commemorates Mary Porter who died in 1668, and has a pediment above with an angel's head below. There are several tablets from the later 17th and 18th centuries, some of which are of wood with classical surrounds typical of the period. Many 19th-century memorials are to wealthy families from the developing north end of Worcester. Amongst them, Sir Harry Wakeman of Perdiswell Hall gave the organ to the church. He died in 1831 and his memorial has a bust on a draped sarcophagus carved by Peter Hollins of Birmingham. The lectern is a memorial to the brother of the author Dame Barbara Cartland, Ronald Cartland, who lived in the parish, and was killed in the First World War.

Outside, the extensive churchyard is bisected by a short track leading to the Mug House, a timber-framed inn to the south of the church, which is the successor of the medieval church ale house.

CLEEVE PRIOR   ST. ANDREW

Cleeve Prior is a village with many brick and lias stone houses with several attractive corners and greens and lies on a prominent ridge to the south of the River Avon, close to the Warwickshire border. There is archaeological evidence for settlement in the parish since prehistoric times. The name Cleeve is derived from the Anglo-Saxon word for cliff, to which Prior was added to show that this was the property of Worcester Priory, as opposed to Bishop's Cleeve, now in Gloucestershire and once held by the bishop. The church is near to the imposing stone Tudor Manor House, which has an attractive round dovecote.

The tall tower at the west end makes the body of the church appear low. The medieval lias nave and chancel were flanked by north and south transepts, but that to the north has long disappeared. The nave is essentially Norman, with a simple north doorway, and a buttress to the north-east corner. In the 13th century the south wall was given a new doorway and windows in the Early English style. The south transept was rebuilt in brick in the 18th century. It was given Gothic windows in 1863, whilst the chancel was extensively rebuilt in 1908, when the 14th-century windows were reset. The tower is the most interesting exterior feature, with late 14th-century bell openings which reflect the transition from Decorated to Perpendicular, with both flamboyant tracery and transom bars. There are many crockets on the openings, as well as on the stairway lights, image niches, and the west window, though the window tracery has been replaced. The tower is topped by battlements with eight pinnacles, and grotesque gargoyles.

The interior contains several medieval survivals. The nave has a simple Early English arch to the south transept, and another has been closed off on the north side. The chancel arch is 14th-century, as is the piscina at the east end. The nave roof timbers are medieval, over a 14th-century octagonal font, and some 15th-century traceried bench ends. The remarkable large dugout chest is also medieval.

In 1886 the reredos was installed in the chancel with Minton tiles, and the chancel windows contain some good glass by Frederick Preedy. The north lancet windows of about 1863 show Christ's charge to Peter, whilst the east window of about 1870 depicts the Corporal Acts of Mercy, and the south window is a fine representation of the Supper at Emmaus. Other Victorian windows show Simeon and Dorcas.

Outside in the churchyard are some fine 18th century headstones and there is a medieval scratch dial on one of the buttresses.

CLENT   ST. LEONARD

The Clent Hills form a barrier of high ground between north-east Worcestershire and the Black Country, and form good walking country with superb views in every direction. To the south-west lies the scattered village of Clent now inhabited mainly by commuters. The church is near the dual carriageway from Hagley to Bromsgrove at Church Town, a little way from the main centres of population at Holy Cross and Lower Clent. From Norman times Clent was a royal manor in the care of the sheriff of Staffordshire, and was only transferred to Worcestershire in 1844.

The church is built on a considerable slope which causes quite a dramatic rise between the west tower and the chancel at the east end. In between is an aisled nave, whilst there is a chapel to the north of the chancel. The church is built of dark red sandstone. Its origins are Norman, but now the nave aisles and porch are as rebuilt by Kirk and Parry in 1864-5 in the Decorated style, whilst the east end and tower are Perpendicular survivals. Indeed, the chancel is very late Perpendicular, probably 16th-century, with a transom bar across the east window at the level of the springing of the arch. The south priest's doorway has a Latin inscription commemorating the burial of John Cleye, who is otherwise unknown.

The interior of the nave has a late Norman south arcade of three bays, with round piers and trumpet scallop capitals. Though there are medieval roofs in the nave and chancel, Perpendicular tower and chancel arches, and 15th-century piscinae in the chancel and the south aisle, the overall feel of the interior is Victorian. The north arcade is typical of this period, and was constructed during the Kirk and Parry restoration to replace arches on cast iron columns from the former north aisle of 1837. The furnishings are mainly 19th- and 20th-century, with those in the chancel dating from 1956. The chancel also contains several memorial tablets to the Amphlett family, lords of the manor, including one to John Amphlett who died in 1656 which has twisted columns and a pediment. The Victorian glass includes one window of 1885 by Heaton, Butler and Bayne, and one of 1897 showing Mary of Bethany by Lavers and Westlake. There is also a window of 1920 by Archibald Davies of the Bromsgrove Guild showing a grape harvest and commemorating the Treaty of Versailles.

CLIFTON-ON-TEME   ST. KENELM

The River Teme flows through the valley to the east of the village, which stands on a hilltop at 600 feet. There are many fine timber-framed and brick houses and cottages along the main street, the layout of which reflects unsuccessful attempts to develop a borough and market here in the Middle Ages. The church spire is a conspicuous landmark and rests on a massive tower. Together with the nave, chancel, aisle, porch and vestry, it is constructed of rubble sandstone with some tufa dressings.

The lower parts of the tower with an Early English lancet window, the nave with a blocked north doorway and the chancel are 13th-century. The south aisle was built in the 14th century, though most of the windows, the porch and vestry were added by James Cranston between 1847 and 1853. The shingled broach spire dates from the 17th century, and replaced a medieval one which was blown down. The belfry at the top of the tower also had to be repaired and given new windows at that time.

The interior is whitewashed and was much restored in the 19th century, though the 14th-century south doorway contains a medieval door. The south arcade has Decorated octagonal piers and typical arches. The 14th-century piscina bowl from the south aisle chantry chapel is now in the chancel in a 19th-century recess. The hexagonal font is 13th-century and has the remains of a 17th-century lock. The Victorian organ arch marks the site of the destroyed founder's tomb and Easter Sepulchre, an example of which can be seen in St. Mary's church, Tenbury Wells. The east window of the south aisle contains the arms of the Poynings, Wysham and Warren families set in 15th-century Grisaille in the tracery. Below is Frederick Preedy's Coucher memorial glass of 1862 showing scenes from the life of Christ. The Moncrieff memorial window at the east end of the chancel was given in 1882.

There is an interesting collection of memorials. The earliest is a 14th-century effigy of a knight to be found in the south aisle, the east end of which was formerly the chantry chapel of the Wysham family of Woodmanton, where parts of the medieval manor house still survive at Woodmanton Farm. It probably commemorates Sir Ralph Wysham who died in 1332, and had been Steward of the King's Household and Justice of North Wales. The cross-legged effigy, which was once painted, is similar to those at Pershore Abbey and Chaddesley Corbett church. On the north wall of the nave, the tablet to Henry and Elizabeth Jeffreyes of Ham Castle by the Teme, is from the workshop of the famous sculptor Grinling Gibbons in 1689, and for which the contract still survives. The neighbouring tablet of 1718 to Elizabeth Jeffreyes who became Lady Winnington is by Thomas White, who carved much of the sculpture on Worcester Guildhall. Both tablets have drapes to the sides and a cherub's head at the top. The tablet on the south wall of the chancel to John, Francis and Edward Ingram is by Richard Westmacott. There are several ledger stones, including one by the chancel steps to Sir William Jeffreyes who died in 1658.

The churchyard cross has a medieval base with a niche on the west side to house the pyx during processions, but the top is modern. The lychgate dates from about 1860.

COFTON HACKETT   ST. MICHAEL

The parish lies on the east side of the Lickey Hills, near the source of the River Arrow, and close to the county's border with the West Midlands. Indeed, much of the housing is for Birmingham commuters, and the church is only a stone's throw from the southern end of the Longbridge car works, itself alongside the Worcester to Birmingham railway. Nevertheless, this is an ancient place mentioned in Anglo-Saxon charters, and the setting of the church and nearby hall along a narrow lane remain remarkably secluded. The white painted part-Georgian Cofton Hall was held by the Leycester family until 1525, and incorporates a late medieval timber-framed great hall.

The red sandstone church is of late Norman origin, but the earliest surviving masonry is late medieval. The nave and chancel are mostly 14th- and 15th-century, with a Decorated east window, and several Perpendicular side windows. The unusual bellcote with three pinnacles is 16th-century, and the timber porch has late medieval upright posts. The church was restored in 1861 by Henry Day, who also restored Feckenham church and designed the nearby church at Lickey. He rebuilt the west end and renewed many of the windows.

Inside, amongst the Victorian restoration and fittings, there is a Decorated piscina with an ogee arch, and the pulpit contains some medieval woodwork, possibly from the former screen. The wooden reredos, a memorial to Henry Sadler, an organist, is the work of Bromsgrove Guild craftsmen. There is one window in the chancel of 1881 by Charles Eamer Kempe. The monument to William Leycester who died in 1508 is impressive. He is commemorated with his wives, Eleanor Wyrley who died in 1514, and Anne Hoord, on an incised slab, showing the figures in contemporary costume, with a younger man and woman below, and the family arms above. The memorial tablets include four to successive members of the Joliffe family, who lived at Cofton Hall in the 17th and early 18th centuries. Another tablet commemorates William Babington, who died in 1625, and his wife Eleanor Littleton, who lived for a further 43 years. The Biddulph family were the last to hold Cofton Hackett before it was sold to the earls of Plymouth in 1813, and there is a tablet to Thomas Biddulph who died in 1795.

Outside, the large churchyard is surrounded by trees and contains a medieval cross base, decorated with large quatrefoils.

COOKHILL   ST. PAUL

Along the ridgeway which forms the border with Warwickshire, New End and Cookhill form a continuation of the line of settlement from Astwood Bank into the parish of Inkberrow. The village has a mixture of timber-framed and brick cottages, with the remains of the chancel of a Cistercian nunnery now incorporated into an 18th-century house, appropriately called Cookhill Priory, at the southern end.

The large, urban looking church is in the village centre on land given by the Marquess of Hertford of Ragley Hall in Warwickshire and was built as a chapelry of Inkberrow in 1876. The architect was Frederick Preedy, who designed a nave and chancel, with vestry and porch. There is a bellcote at the west end. The single and double lancet windows are Early English style. Inside there are typical contemporary furnishings, as well as some early 20th-century stained glass.

COOKLEY   ST. PETER

North of Kidderminster, Cookley grew up by the Stourport to Birmingham Canal as an iron working centre in the early 19th century. The village is a mixture of Victorian brick terraces and more modern housing with the church at its centre. The parish was part of Wolverley until 1845.

The red and blue brick church consists of a nave and chancel with aisles, organ chamber and a porch. There is a tower at the west end with battlements. It was designed in 1849 by E. Smith, and then enlarged in 1872 by J. Meredith, the architect of Kidderminster Town Hall. Smith's work is similar to his contemporary, Thomas Rickman, architect of Ombersley and Hartlebury churches, in that it shows a more correct interpretation of Gothic architecture than in the Commissioners churches in the area, though the brick tower with its Early English style lancets is very much of the Commissioners type.

Inside, the box pews with their poppy heads are part of this same movement towards closer interpretation of medieval gothic. There are other contemporary and more recent fittings, and the stained glass in the east window dates from 1850.

COTHERIDGE   ST. LEONARD

Set in meadows close to the River Teme, Cotheridge church stands beside a lane just south of the Worcester to Bromyard road. Cotheridge Court stands a little to the west and is an attractive brick and timber-framed house which was once home to a branch of the Berkeley family. The village is small, consisting largely of a scattering of houses and farms.

St. Leonard's church is most unusual and picturesque. The exterior of the nave, chancel and part of the north chapel are whitewashed, but the church is dominated by the large

Cotheridge church

weatherboarded timber south tower, which is capped by a pyramid roof. There has been much debate over the date of the walling of the lower part, which is made up of vertical timber planks, held together by tongued and grooved joints. It is probably early 14th-century. The nave and chancel are basically Norman, and parts of the flat buttresses survive. The existing Norman windows appear to have been slightly refashioned in the 18th century. The large Perpendicular south window with fine tracery was inserted in the 15th century, and would have thrown more light onto the screen and pulpit. The chancel east window is Decorated, next to the straight-headed mullion window with round arches of the north chapel which was added to the chancel in 1620 by the Berkeley family. Like the Blount chapel at Mamble church this is an early example of the use of brick in Worcestershire. In 1947 the nave roof collapsed, and the surviving furnishings were crammed into the chancel.

The present entrance into the north chapel leads through what is today a spacious vestry, down steps into the chancel and one of Worcestershire's most extraordinary church interiors. It is a cosy composition with whitewashed walls, 17th-century box pews and communion rail. On the floor are a collection of medieval tiles, some of which have arms of Berkeley, Elyot and Throckmorton. During the restorations of 1947-61 and 1979-87 the chancel arch was fitted with wooden doors, and the openings to either side were glazed. These give access to the bare white nave with its Georgian style plaster ceiling. The nave houses the greater part of the three decker 17th-century pulpit with its attractive carved decoration, of which the tester is also preserved. The small Norman chancel arch has a shaft to each side with a scallop capital, and is decorated with a beaded spiral band. It is an unusual survival, but the openings to either side would have improved visibility of the chancel from the nave in the 18th century. A similar example is at Wyre Piddle church, but most such arches and openings were removed in the 19th century. A pretty Georgian door opens to the base of the tower, where the lower parts of the timber-framing can be seen.

The only pre-Victorian glass is the 17th-century arms of the Berkeleys in the north chapel window. The east window glass was installed in 1872 by Frederick Preedy, and shows scenes from the life of Christ. The chancel contains several memorial tablets and some fine ledgers in the floor. On the south wall, the memorial to Thomas Berkeley carries an inscription recording his sickness and death in 1669, whilst he was travelling near Constantinople with the English ambassador to Turkey.

CROOME D'ABITOT   ST. MARY MAGDALENE

Croome church is a Georgian Gothic gem in the grounds of Croome Court. It stands in a prominent site on a ridge to the north-east of the house, though it can be approached by a footpath across a field from the lane by the Pershore Lodge. This walk does not prepare the visitor for the view to the west on reaching the church of the north front of the Court and across the grounds to the Malvern Hills. The estate was owned by the Coventry family from 1570 to 1949, and in 1763 the sixth Earl replaced the medieval church which had stood to the west of the Court, with this church—its site and design chosen to form part of the landscape of the park as viewed from the house. This landscape was laid out by Lancelot 'Capability' Brown and includes numerous features and follies, which are being restored by the National Trust. The vesting of the church in the Churches Conservation Trust in 1975 and its subsequent restoration has ensured its survival as part of the park, after many years of neglect.

Capability Brown designed the limestone exterior in the Gothic, rather than the Classical style that was more usual in the 18th century. He had previously used Gothic on the stables at Burghley House near Stamford in Lincolnshire. The church would thus appear in views across the park as a typical medieval parish church. The west tower is the most visible feature, and the most elaborate. It is Perpendicular in style with pinnacles and traceried battlements above large bell-openings. Below the belfry there are small quatrefoil windows, and at the west end a large arch opens into the lower part which forms an entrance porch with fine wrought iron gates. The porch interior has niches and a Gothic vault, and the west door is decorated with Gothic motifs. There are blank image niches either side of the tower on the west end of the nave with projecting ogee canopies. The nave has Decorated style windows, but is on a Georgian Classical plan with three bays. The low pitch roof with battlements and pinnacles are Perpendicular in style. The chancel is larger than on other churches of this type, as it was built to contain the family memorials from the previous church. The east window has simple Decorated style intersecting tracery.

The interior was designed and planned for the sixth Earl by Robert Adam, though not all of his ideas were carried out. The result is a plainer version of the Georgian Strawberry Hill Gothic interior at Shobdon church in Herefordshire. The wide spacious nave is in fact a hall church, with slender piers and a cornice dividing a central nave with a coved ceiling from side aisles with flat ceilings. The chancel arch with crocketed plasterwork has an ogee headed recess on either side, containing Commandment and Creed boards, and leads into the chancel which is filled with four large monuments. The walls are cream

The tower at Croome d'Abitot

washed, the window plain glazed, and there is a black and white marble floor. Gothic details appear on most of the 18th-century stained furnishings, including the pews and communion rails. The pulpit has a Georgian Gothic presence, with a splendid gabled and pinnacled tester surmounted by a huge central

crocket. The wooden pedestal font is more classical in design and probably early 19th-century.

The monuments reflect the wealth and power of the Coventry family from the 17th century. On the south side, Thomas, the first Lord Coventry, who died in 1639, is shown semi-reclined in his robes on a large free-standing black and white marble memorial. In front of the effigy is a mace on a cushion, and beside him are figures of Virtue and Justice—he was Lord Keeper of the Great Seal of England, which is shown being held by Justice. Above is a large arch with

The Georgian Gothic interior at Croome d'Abitot

two more allegorical figures, shown reclining. It is possible that this memorial was made by the sculptor, Nicholas Stone. Two of the other large memorials show Thomas, the second Lord Coventry, with robes and coronet, who died in 1661, and his wife, Margaret, Lady Coventry, who died in childbirth, and is shown holding a baby, with two children by her feet. John, the fourth Lord Coventry, who died in 1687 has a remarkable memorial for which there is a contract signed in 1690 with the sculptor, Grinling Gibbons. His work is evident in the beautiful garlands at the top, and there are fine Corinthian pilasters behind the semi-reclined effigy with figures of Hope and Mercy to either side. A similar monument to the first Earl of Coventry was intended for Croome church in 1700, but was placed at Elmley Castle church instead.

The numerous memorial tablets in the nave include a large piece with a pediment and caryatids to Sir Henry Coventry, who died in 1686, by William Kidwell. The memorial to the sixth Earl, who built the church, and who died in 1809, is by John Bacon Junior, and shows a kneeling woman bent over the pedestal of an urn, similar to a memorial by him in Astley church. The tablet to the ninth Earl records him holding the title for almost 87 years until his death in 1930.

Although the fortunes of the Coventry family may have declined, a visit to this church and the surrounding park give a strong impression of life on a great country estate in the 18th century.

CROPTHORNE   ST. MICHAEL

The village street at Cropthorne runs over a hill parallel to the River Avon between Pershore and Evesham. St. Michael's church is at the top of the hill in a well-kept churchyard, surrounded by timber-framed and brick cottages and houses. The church, too, is attractive and built of limestone with a west tower and an aisled nave with porch and chancel.

The tower is late Norman, and has lancet windows set in central buttresses on the walls of the exposed sides. The belfry is Perpendicular with elaborate bell openings, battlements, pinnacles, gargoyles and a pyramid roof. Much of the nave masonry is Norman, but this is concealed from the outside by aisles of the 13th century and later, replacing the original Norman ones, and the 16th-century Perpendicular clerestorey. This was much replaced on the north side in the 18th century, and the chancel was rebuilt in 1894, though an Early English north lancet, north doorway and blocked south priest's door were reused.

Cropthorne church

The east window has 19th-century tracery in a 14th-century frame. The main south doorway is also Early English, and is entered through a 15th-century porch which once had two storeys.

The attractive whitewashed interior is dominated by the beautiful Norman arcades. They are four bays long, with round piers and plain round arches. The north arcade dates from about 1120, and the southern one from 30 years later. The Norman chancel arch piers with scallop capitals survive, but the pointed arch was added in about 1300. The tower arch shows the transition from Norman to

Gothic at the end of the 12th century, with nailhead decoration and chamfering on a solid pointed arch, which is not unlike the tower arch in Bredon church. In the south aisle is a blocked doorway high on the south wall, which once gave access to a chamber over the porch.

The interior contains many interesting fittings. In the chancel, there are medieval image brackets, an aumbry and a 13th-century piscina. A further piscina denotes the site of a chantry in the south aisle. The benches have many fine panelled ends with tracery of about 1500 and there are traces of figures in a medieval wall painting on the north wall of the nave. The font dates from about 1850, and the stone chancel reredos with a carved scene of Christ in Gethsemane was given in memory of Francis Holland who restored the chancel in 1894. In the 1930s the same family gave another reredos in the south aisle with an Annunciation and Nativity scene.

In the north aisle is preserved an Anglo-Saxon cross head which was discovered during the 19th-century reconstruction of the chancel (see illustration on p.3). Was this once the top of the preaching cross outside an Anglo-Saxon church on this site? It dates from the early 9th century, is of limestone, and is beautifully carved. The arms and top have cusps similar to the Northumbrian crosses, but the decoration has links to other carving in this region; fantastical birds and animals are shown on foliage, in a similar manner to the decoration of contemporary manuscripts and metalwork from northern Europe, demonstrating England's strong links with society on the other side of the channel by the 9th century. The design may represent the triumph of the Church shown in the cross and the foliage—the vine possibly representing Christ—over evil in the form of unknown beasts. It bears great similarities to the remains of a cross at Acton Beauchamp church in Herefordshire.

Close to the cross in the north aisle is a 14th-century recess with an ogee head, decorated with ball-flower ornamentation, and containing a coffin lid with a cross, which once covered the grave of a priest. At the east end of the aisle is the large painted chest monument to Francis Dingley of Charlton, who died in 1624, his wife Elizabeth Bigg, and their 19 children. The effigies lie side by side with an inscription on the back wall. The children are shown kneeling on the side of the chest. Five sons and one in a cradle are followed by seven daughters, including twins, and a further cradle, four more sons and a third cradle beyond. The second coloured monument is placed awkwardly at an angle by the chancel arch, having been removed from the chancel during the rebuilding. Edward Dingley died in 1646, and is shown kneeling at a prayer desk opposite his wife, Joyce Sandys. Behind is an inscription, and above a canopy supported by black columns. Below are kneeling their four sons and three daughters. The Dingley family held Charlton until the 18th century, when family quarrels led to a murder, after which the eccentric last descendant in the direct line died without children.

Outside the base and shaft of the medieval cross survive in the graveyard. This may be the successor to the Saxon cross, which itself makes Cropthorne church so important to the history of Worcestershire.

CROSSWAY GREEN   ST. MARY

Correctly known as St. Mary, Bishop's Wood, this small church stands beside the busy A449 dual carriageway a little to the north of the Mitre Oak Inn. This is an ancient Christian association, and the Mitre Oak was reputed to be one of the sites where St. Augustine met the British bishops in the 7th century. It is more probable that it marks a boundary of the medieval bishop's manor of Hartlebury on the route to Worcester.

The church has a chancel and nave with a porch and bell turret at the west end. It is rendered and decorated with beams to give a mock Tudor appearance, for the church was built as a mission by Bishop Henry Philpott in 1882 for the southern part of Hartlebury parish. For many years the churchyard was used as the parish burial ground and the church became the cemetery chapel. However, it was restored in

1987 and rededicated for use by Bishop Philip Goodrich. The lychgate is a memorial erected to Bishop Philpott in 1892. It was designed by Vale of Wolverhampton and has a commemorative inscription in mosaic by the workshop of Antonio Salviati of Venice over the entrance.

CROWLE   ST. JOHN THE BAPTIST

Today Crowle is a sprawling village set in undulating countryside east of Worcester. St. John's church lies back from the main street at the southern end of the village. The proximity to Worcester was reflected in medieval times when this was a manor held by the priors of Worcester. Today Crowle Court is a farm with a twentieth century house, but the moated medieval site to the west of the church contains the ruins of a sandstone building, and the nearby substantial remains of the lias tithe barn is an important reminder of the visits of priors, like William More, whose accounts and journals record many details of life at Crowle in the early 16th century.

The sandstone church has a west tower with nave, transepts, chancel, vestry and a north porch. Externally, only the porch is medieval. It is a fine 14th-century timber construction, with a carved boss to the interior roof timbers, and a carving of the Annunciation over the entrance. The tower was rebuilt in two phases, along with the rest of the church, in the Decorated style between 1881 and 1885 by Frederick Preedy and has a reset image niche on the east face.

Inside, the Victorian interior incorporates some interesting medieval features. The tower arch is late Perpendicular with typical hollow mouldings and capitals. The octagonal font is also Perpendicular, ornamented with cusped panels on the sides of the bowl, foliage on the underside, and traceried panels on the stem. Most interesting is the limestone lectern which dates from about 1200 (see illustration on p.14), and was discovered in 1845 in the churchyard. It is thought to have come from the chapel of the priors in the Court, and may have been deliberately buried at the Reformation. It is one of the two oldest to survive in the country; the other is also in Worcestershire in Norton church. The stem is 19th-century, and some of the foliage carving has been reworked, but the projecting figure of a man holding vine stems, kneeling and looking at the congregation, is impressive. The 19th-century fittings include a medieval style rood screen, a mosaic reredos depicting the Holy Sepulchre, and the Victorian east window glass shows the Crucifixion. The 19th- and 20th-century memorial tablets include one to a Colonel Davison with contemporary lettering and colour.

Outside, a medieval stone coffin in the graveyard was placed here during the rebuilding of the church.

CROWN EAST   ST. THOMAS

This small church stands by the side of the Worcester to Bromyard road, a short distance from the end of Worcester's western bypass. It is easily missed, but is in fact the church serving the parish of Rushwick. The name Crown East seems to be derived from 'crow's nest', referring to its position on a hill.

A chapel is recorded here during the 13th century, but no trace remains. The present church, which opened in 1876, succeeds an earlier 19th-century building, which stood in the grounds of Crown East Court (now Aymestrey Court), and was the chapel of the Bramwell family. It is built of brick with windows and doorways in the Decorated and Perpendicular style. The south tower porch has an open timber belfry and a short spire.

The interior has many contemporary fittings, but the font is Norman. It was discovered in the 19th century, buried in the yard of Manor Farm at Lower Wick in Worcester, and probably came from the church of St. Cuthbert, itself now incorporated in a barn.

DEFFORD   ST. JAMES

The black and white church tower stands on top of the hill surrounded by the substantial village and looks towards Bredon Hill across the River Avon. The Worcester to Cheltenham railway passes close to the church.

The church was once a chapelry to Pershore and consists of a west tower with short spire, nave and porch with a chancel. The church's Norman origins are evident through the south doorway which has Norman jambs and a keystone carved with a small but unusual crowned female head, which has been compared in style with carving on the Portail Royal at Chartres Cathedral in France, and the west doorway to Rochester Cathedral in Kent. The tower has a 14th-century stone base, but the timber belfry and short spire date from the early 20th century. The chancel was rebuilt in the 19th century, though the lias nave walls appear to be medieval, but with two 17th-century windows, and a dormer above which lights the gallery. The blocked north doorway contains a 19th-century window.

The interior is whitewashed and contains mainly 19th- and 20th-century fittings, though a tie beam from the medieval roof is still visible, and there is an 18th-century west gallery. There is a large Decorated style chancel arch from the 19th-century restoration, and a heavily moulded octagonal font. 19th-century benefaction boards survive under the tower, and the striking east window glass of 1898 shows Christ with St. James and St. Peter. Two impressive 18th-century ledger stones are now mounted on the nave walls. In the tower, there is a mid-15th-century bell.

DODDENHAM (and KNIGHTWICK)   ST. MARY

The setting of this little church close to Knightsford Bridge over the River Teme at the foot of Ankerdine Hill is extremely attractive. By the entrance is a floodmark showing the level of the Teme in the floods of 1886. The church was built in 1856 to replace the chapel at nearby Knightwick, where there is now a cemetery chapel (see separate entry), and a medieval church of St. Andrew at Doddenham about one mile to the east, of which nothing now remains.

Abraham Perkins, architect of much of the restoration of Worcester Cathedral, as well as of Little Witley and Wichenford churches, designed this building. It has a nave with chancel, a north porch and vestry, and a pretty polygonal bell turret and spire to the west gable. The style is early Decorated and typical of this architect.

The interior has many contemporary fittings, including the lectern of 1882 carved by William Forsyth. The glass in a window showing St. George and St. Michael is by Christopher Whall who continued to work to the principles of William Morris in the early 20th century. The church contains a plain Norman font.

DODFORD   HOLY TRINITY AND ST. MARY

Dodford is a heavily wooded parish between Bromsgrove and Chaddesley Corbett. A priory of Augustinian Canons was founded here by Henry II at the end of the 12th century, and the remains are incorporated into a farmhouse near the church. The church is, however, a product of 19th-century Dodford. Feargus O'Connor, leader of the Chartist movement, acquired the Dodford estate in 1848 to establish a settlement offering people an affordable opportunity to purchase smallholdings, become self sufficient and, as property holders, to be able to vote. Dodford is one of four villages in the region laid out by the Chartists, and many of the distinctive single-storey cottages remain. Though O'Connor's original scheme was economically unsuccessful, landowners in Dodford found that the heavy clay soil was suitable for growing strawberries, which were produced here in great numbers into the 20th century.

The present church in Priory Road was built between 1907 and 1908, to replace a wooden building in Church Road dating from 1863 which was served by a curate from Bromsgrove. It was endowed by the first vicar, Walter Grenville Whinfield, and was built in the Arts and Crafts Perpendicular style by little known architect Arthur Bartlett, whose other works include a vicarage and school buildings in Bromsgrove and the chapter house at Southwark Cathedral in London. It was constructed by Brazier of Bromsgrove.

The church has a long nave and chancel, with a tower on a south transept and the exterior is mainly rendered. The tower has a round window with a Greek cross design to the tracery at the end of the transept. There is a Celtic cross feature worked into the bell openings, and a saddleback roof. The space to the south of the nave by the tower is filled with an unusual courtyard with an open air pulpit surrounded by a wooden cloister. This was a memorial to the vicar's elder brother, and was much used during Whinfield's time. There is a north transept to accommodate the organ, whilst the baptistry at the west end protrudes from the nave gable, and where there is a statue of the Good Shepherd by Louis Weingartner of the Bromsgrove Guild.

Indeed, the beautiful, light and spacious interior houses a remarkable collection of Arts and Crafts fittings created mainly by members of the

Dodford church exterior (top), interior looking east (centre) and window detail (below)

Dodford church.
Details of Art and Crafts work:
plaster panel from the nave vault (top
left), carved detail from the organ loft
(top right) and from the rood beam
(lower left)

Bromsgrove Guild of Craftsmen. The whitewashed nave is spanned by great arches of concrete faced with stone, and decorated with plaster panels showing animals, fruits and produce from Dodford. These were designed by Leopold Weisz of the Guild, who was killed on the Titanic, and modelled by Charles Bonnet. Fruit is also carved on the wall plate. At the front of the nave, six carved bench ends represent the words of the Benedicite, a canticle of praise, and were probably made by Richard Haughton of Worcester. Two of these are a memorial to John Bungay, thought to have been the first child born in the Chartist village in 1849. The lectern is also Houghton's work, but the remaining pews were made by Celestino Pancheri of the Guild during the 1930s. The pulpit with carved panels depicting a fisherman, a shepherd, a sower and a hunter, along with the organ loft, where the panels have a musical theme, showing David with his harp and St. Cecilia at the organ, are also Pancheri's work. The organ itself was made by Nicholson of Worcester, a firm owned by the vicar's brother.

The rood beam, which divides the nave from the chancel was carved with Christian symbols by Herbert Henry Martyn of Cheltenham, and is surmounted by a cross of hammered copper showing the tree of life by Amy Walford of the Guild. Another Guild member, Richard Tapp, designed the altar, while the communion rails and reredos were made by Celestino and Robert Pancheri in 1972. The choir stalls were designed by Arthur Bartlett, whilst at the west end, the font is 18th-century and was brought here from the previous church, though it probably came originally from St. John's church in Bromsgrove.

One of the most striking features of the interior is the lack of stained glass. Although some windows have mosaics of coloured glass, the lead lines are the main feature of the windows, which include emblems of the Church such as a dove and a crown of thorns. These windows were produced to designs by Joseph Sanders in the studio of Archibald Davies, a prominent member of the Bromsgrove Guild.

DORMSTON   ST. NICHOLAS

Dormston church, showing the timber-framed tower and porch

On the southern side of the Forest of Feckenham, Dormston is a small scattered settlement spread along narrow lanes close to the Worcester to Inkberrow road. The former forested nature of the parish is reflected in the number of timber-framed buildings, of which the 17th-century Moat Farm with its dovecote is particularly well known.

Timber is also dominant in the church. The short west tower has close-studded timber-framing similar to the tower at Warndon church, and a saddleback roof like the neighbouring church at Kington. The timberwork is set on a stone base and dates from around 1450. The timber-framed porch is of about the same date, and was glazed in 1899. The small grey sandstone nave is Decorated, and may incorporate older masonry, but the north window and blocked north doorway are 14th-century. The chancel was rebuilt in 1837 using medieval material.

Near to the exterior of the south doorway is a medieval holy water stoup. The interior is pretty, despite having been scraped back to the stone in the 19th century. At the west end a 14th-century lancet window and the former west door, which now opens into the tower, show that the tower post-dates the body of the church. The tower interior contains massive timber braces, some of which are very crudely worked. The nave retains its medieval roof timbers, but all traces of wall paintings referred to in previous guide books have gone. The octagonal font is 14th-century, and both the south nave windows contain fragments of medieval glass including the arms of the Lovell family. There are some 16th-century pews with open backs in the nave, and the communion rail is 17th-century. Reset in the chancel wall next to the altar is the finely carved head of the medieval churchyard cross, with figures of Christ and the Virgin. This is a rare survival; so often there is little evidence for what was on the many existing cross bases. The tower contains two bells of the 17th century and one of the late 15th century.

DOVERDALE   ST. MARY THE VIRGIN

Along a lane to the east of Dunhampton on the A449, lies the small village of Doverdale. By the side of the church a moated site is all that is left of the manor house of the Doverdale family who held the estate from the 11th to the 15th centuries. The small red sandstone church now stands alone but near farms, almost a mile from the Georgian Doverdale Manor.

The Norman origins of the church are evident in the blocked north doorway of the nave, which still has some Norman masonry. Whilst the nave windows contain some stonework which could be 15th-century, but more probably 17th-century. The church was almost entirely rebuilt by Frederick Preedy in 1860, his work including the Decorated style east window of the chancel, the conversion of the south porch to a vestry, the construction of the timber bell turret with small lead spire at the west end over a short porch and the circular west window.

The interior is stone-faced and divided by the chancel arch—a typical interpretation by Preedy of the 14th-century style. The fittings are almost all of the time of rebuilding, though the panelling on the nave walls incorporates 17th-century woodwork. In the north window, there is restored 15th-century glass showing the Virgin, surrounded by quarries with scrolls inscribed 'Emmanual' on top of flowers, of a similar pattern to the glass in the window of the Great Hall at The Commandery in Worcester. The east window contains glass by Hardman & Co. of 1860. The bell turret contains a 15th-century bell dedicated to St. Thomas.

DRAKES BROUGHTON   ST. BARNABAS

This suburban village between Pershore and Worcester is largely a creation of the 1970s. Amongst this recent development are a few older houses and cottages near the church, which was built to serve this expanding community and the adjacent village of Wadborough as a chapel of ease to Pershore Abbey.

The church was constructed in lias by William Jeffrey Hopkins in 1857 and has a nave and chancel with porch and vestry. In the south-west corner a narrow, short stone tower is surmounted by a timber belfry and spire, which was rebuilt after collapsing spectacularly during a gale in 1977. There are Decorated style windows alongside some Early English style lancets. The interior is faced with brick, and the chancel is given prominence with carved capitals to the trusses. It is divided from the nave by a timber arch structure.

DROITWICH   ST. ANDREW

St. Andrew's church stands at the heart of Droitwich. By the River Salwarpe to the north are the sites of the brine pits from which salt was extracted from prehistoric times until the 19th century, and which made Droitwich a significant Roman settlement. This importance continued through the Anglo-Saxon period and into the Middle Ages. The church may stand on the site of a Saxon minster church, though it is possible that the minster became the church of St. Mary, Witton, which stood on the hill to the south of the town. This church has long disappeared, but the site is marked by a graveyard off Lyttleton Road. St. Andrew stands at the corner of High Street and St. Andrew's Street adjoining several historic buildings, in a part of the town which still retains much of its pre-19th-century character. The church contains 13th-century work which survived the town fire of 1293.

The church does not dominate the town centre as well as it did before 1911, for it was then that the tower had to be reduced in height for safety, as a result of structural problems related to the extraction of

The truncated tower of St. Andrew, Droitwich

brine. The 13th-century base of the tower is on the north side and has two fine lancet windows with shafts which, like those on the tower at Stoke Prior church, are very similar to work at the east end of Worcester Cathedral. The north and south aisles have separate roofs to the nave resulting in an attractive west front of three gables. The aisles were built in the 14th century after the fire, although the north wall was rebuilt in about 1910, and the nave west window dates from 1800. The chancel was shortened in the 18th century and the east wall rebuilt in 1928. To the east of the tower is a Perpendicular north chapel, which was a chantry chapel dedicated in 1491 to St. Richard de Wych, also known as St. Richard of Chichester. St. Richard was born at the manor house on the site of the present Raven Hotel about 1197. He went on to become Bishop of Chichester, but according to legend returned to Droitwich to bless the main brine pit at Upwich when it dried up, and the brine flowed once more.

The interior is attractively divided by the arcades and arches into several irregular spaces, giving the whole a rather jumbled feeling. The three tower arches and the chancel arch are all 13th-century with keel mouldings, and have beautiful crocketed capitals with foliage and heads. The south capital to the chancel arch has trumpet scallops like the arches at St. Augustine's church (see next entry). The nave and south chapel arcades are all early 14th-century with octagonal piers and chamfered arches. There are carved heads thought to be of the mason and King Henry III on the arch leading from the south aisle into the south chapel. The chancel has blocked medieval windows and a priest's doorway and a small arch on the north side gives access to the former chantry of St. Richard. Here there are 15th-century brackets on the east wall for images and an aumbry under the tower. The chancel roof has Perpendicular timbers, and there is a 14th-century piscina in the south chapel. At the west end the font is 17th-century, and shaped like a goblet with geometric designs on a square stem. It is very similar to the font in St. Peter's church. The wooden cover has turned balusters. A gallery at the west end was removed in 1880, which had been used by the inhabitants of the Coventry Hospital, almshouses in the Holloway to the east of the town centre.

There is little pre-19th-century glass, but one window in the south chapel contains some 17th-century arms. The interior walls carry many memorial tablets. One of 1680 commemorates Mary Clifford, and there is a tablet to John Browne, collector of salt duties during the 18th century. A large memorial by the chancel arch commemorates Coningesby Norbury who died in 1734. He fought in the West Indies with Admiral Benbow, and negotiated for the release of slaves in Morocco on behalf of the Government.

DROITWICH ST. AUGUSTINE, DODDERHILL

Dodderhill is today the northern suburb of Droitwich, but in medieval times the parish was large and included Elmbridge and Wychbold. The church is at the very southern end of the parish and dominates the centre of Droitwich, standing on a steep outcrop high above the River Salwarpe, canal and railway. The site is ancient, and in Roman times a fort guarded the northern side of this important centre of salt production; remains of Roman occupation have been found around the church. The church site is amongst the claimants for the meeting place of St. Augustine and the British bishops. The later Saxon church was part of an important holding of Earl Godwin of Wessex.

The church now consists of a chancel, crossing, north transept, massive south tower and vestry. Much of the exterior is of blackened red sandstone, but the transept and chancel north wall were faced in brick in about 1840. The present structure incorporates the remains of the church consecrated in 1220, which had an aisled nave and central tower at the crossing and was described by Thomas Habington in the early 17th century. But in 1646, during the Civil War, whilst royalist troops attempted to remove roundhead soldiers occupying the church, the nave and south transept were destroyed by fire. The west wall of the nave remained standing into the 18th century and appears on an engraving of the church. The south transept was rebuilt as a tower to replace the central one in 1708, but reusing 13th- and 14th-century materials from the nave, including windows which are now the bell openings. The chancel east and side windows are early 14th century, and date from the rebuilding of the east end prior to the dedication of new altars in 1332. On the south side of the chancel, by the priest's door, a vestry was added in 1845 on the site of the 18th-century porch.

Inside, the church is confusing because of its truncated shape, but has a uniform appearance in contrast to the exterior, as the walls were scraped back to the sandstone in the 19th century. The heart of the church is still the crossing, which has trumpet scallop capitals and keeled shafts supporting pointed arches from the 1220 church. Only the north west pier has stiff leaf carving, and nearby a blocked doorway once gave access to the stairs of the central tower. The beautiful early 14th-century chancel windows have stone shafts, and there are the remains of a blocked low side window, also with shafts. The piscina and sedilia are of similar date, but have ogee arches, and have a curious appearance as the west part of the sedilia is blocked and now contains masonry from the destroyed parts of the church.

Many of the fittings were presented by the Droitwich 'Salt King' John Corbett during the 19th century. The tile floor, pews and organ are all of this time. The font dates from 1854 and the pulpit with its wrought iron openwork was installed by 1890. The reredos of 1905 shows the two St. Augustines. The earliest window glass is in the north transept east window, where fragments of medieval glass were assembled in the 18th century.

Corbett presented the south window of the tower showing the Good Samaritan and the Baptism of Christ, the west window showing St. Augustine's mission, the north window in the transept showing the Ascension, as well as the south and east windows of the chancel showing the Crucifixion, and King Solomon with the Queen of Sheba by Samuel Evans of Smethwick. The south east window dates from 1904 and shows the Resurrection.

There are many memorial tablets including a group from the 1600s. One is to the children of both Edward Phillips and Arthur Phillips who died respectively in 1656 and 1664. A brass plate under the tower of 1630 commemorates John and William Brace. The remains of the monument on the north side of the chancel to Gerald Dannet of Elmbridge, who died in 1615, and his family has the figures of his four children with their initials under the family arms.

DROITWICH   ST. NICHOLAS

The present sandstone Victorian church on Ombersley Road gives little indication that it is the successor to a medieval church which stood at the corner of Friar Street and Winnetts Lane. The first church was built in the mid-12th century but was destroyed in the town fire of 1293. A second church was built in the early 14th century by the Nunnery at Westwood, who held the parish until the Dissolution of the Monasteries. During the Civil War the church was used to billet soldiers and was ruinous by 1651. The tower and some walling survived until the site was finally cleared in 1828. A Decorated window and other masonry including carved heads were incorporated into the façade of the Old Cock Inn in Friar Street. An incised slab was excavated near the site in the 1970s and is preserved in the Heritage Centre. It shows parts of the figures of a man in armour with a woman, thought to be members of the Rudying family, who held considerable rights to extract salt in Droitwich during the Middle Ages.

With the expansion of the town to the west after the arrival of the railway in 1852, a third church dedicated to St. Nicholas was proposed in 1864 for a site in the new suburb. In 1867 the foundation stone was laid and the church was built to the design of a local architect, John Smith, and opened in 1869. It was never completely finished—the spire was not built on the south west porch tower, which instead has a pyramid cap. There is a nave, south aisle and chancel, to which a north aisle and vestry were added in 1872-3. The vestry is the work of Lewis Sheppard, the architect of Wychbold church. The style is Early Decorated with both plate and bar tracery to the windows.

The inside is lightly painted with many 19th- and 20th-century fittings, including a font and pulpit by William Forsyth and the stalls and communion rail of 1923 by Sprague and Evans of Worcester. There is a Nicholson organ of 1891. The Decorated style arches have several capitals which have never been carved. The glass in the east window shows the Ascension, and four others with the Nativity, Crucifixion, Resurrection and Pentecost were all installed by Frederick Preedy in 1869, though the Crucifixion has since been removed. There are several memorial tablets, but one larger work by Francis Williamson from Esher, Surrey, with a white angel and a white rock commemorates George Edward Penrice McConnel who drowned, aged 14, in 1886 in the lake in Westwood Park. The tower contains a set of tubular bells installed by Harrington, Latham and Co. of Coventry in 1903.

DROITWICH   ST. PETER

The unusual rooflines of St. Peter, Droitwich

The best approach to St. Peter's church is on foot from the lido and across the park. The path crosses St. Peter's Fields to the church which stands almost one mile south-east of the town centre. More correctly known as St. Peter-de-Witton, this church served a second manor in Witton, the other being St. Mary which was absorbed into St. Andrew's parish. St. Peter's was a largely rural parish until the housing developments of the 20th century, although the church served the central areas of Queen Street and Hanbury Street. Next to the church is St. Peter's Manor House, a fine 17th-century timber-framed building, which was home to Treadway Nash, the Worcestershire historian, who was also vicar of this church.

The various rooflines to the nave, chancel and transepts of the church indicate a building of great interest. The chancel contains much Norman work, and three Norman lancet windows can be seen on the north wall. Below them is a 14th-century doorway. The blocked arches on the south side of the nave reflect a reduction of the church during the 16th century with the removal of the 13th-century aisle. The former east window to this aisle can be seen on the east side of the Decorated south transept—it stands out as an Early English window of three stepped lancets. The two blocked arches on the west wall of this transept perhaps indicates that there was a south chapel beyond the south aisle. The north transept is decorated, with a fine north window containing reticulated tracery. The Perpendicular west tower, with good examples of bell openings and a west window, has a rather blunted appearance due to the solid parapet. The nave was heightened in the 16th century by the addition of an unusual close-studded timber-framed clerestorey. In the 19th-century the porch and vestry were added on the south side, and in 1972 a large room known as the Winslow Vestry was built to the north of the nave.

The interior is equally intriguing. The Norman chancel arch survives with coupled columns and scallop capitals. Above it the triple arch is a 19th-century addition. The blocked arches to the aisle have 13th-century capitals carved with heads and stiff leafs. The Perpendicular timber nave roof has moulded beams and floral bosses, and at the west end the line of the previous roof can be seen on the tower wall. A medieval roof boss carved with the head of Christ survives in the south transept. There is a 14th-century piscina and the former Perpendicular priest's door now leads to the vestry. The font is a 17th-century goblet, similar to that at St. Andrew's, and around it are medieval floor tiles. There is another group of tiles in the Vestry, all of which have the remains of inscriptions and the arms of the Beauchamp, Hungerford and Throckmorton families. Part of the medieval altar stone was used to make a credence table in the chancel in 1853.

The east window of the south transept contains yellow and dark green glass of the early 14th century, which includes a Crucifixion and parts of canopies. The chancel east window glass was installed in 1853 by Frederick Preedy and also shows a Crucifixion scene. The west window glass is by Michael O'Connor of 1868, and the memorial window to Mrs Lea is of 1884 by Burlison and Grylls.

The families who lived at St. Peter's Manor between the 16th and 18th centuries are represented in the many memorials. Under the tower is a 16th-century stone to John and Isabel Wythe. Blocking a 14th-century window of the north transept is the large memorial to George Wylde, who was Sergeant-at-Law and died in 1616. He is shown robed and lying on one side. Above is a flat arch supported by two columns, and the back face is decorated with fruit and flowers. A boy blowing bubbles is also shown as a reminder of passing years, along with Father Time with his scythe. A naïve tablet with allegorical females and another boy blowing bubbles commemorates Richard Nash who died in 1690. In the nave, a 20th-century plaque made by the Bromsgrove Guild is a memorial to Edward Winslow, who was baptised here in 1595. He was one of the Pilgrim Fathers who sailed in 1620 to New England on the *Mayflower*.

The tower contains a 15th-century bell, and in the south transept is a medieval coffin lid with a carved cross. This may have come from the grave of one of the priors of Studley in Warwickshire, who were patrons of this church. A headstone in the churchyard commemorates John Courtney Lord, who died in 1921 having campaigned to establish separate law courts for children. As a result of his work, the first juvenile court met in Birmingham in 1905. An inscription in the porch makes a poignant connection to salt, the source of Droitwich's wealth: 'Remember Lot's Wife'.

EARL'S CROOME   ST. NICHOLAS

The leafy approach to the village and church from the road between Upton and Pershore is heralded by the crucifix-shaped war memorial, standing on the corner like a continental wayside shrine. The church is across the lane from Earl's Croome Court, the gabled timber-framed house of the Jeffrey family, now occupied by the Earl of Coventry.

The lias Norman church has a compact nave and chancel, with a north vestry. The present squat west tower was built in the Norman style into the west end in 1832, and has a contemporary Norman style west door. The north and south doorways are both of the 12th century. The north doorway is well preserved and has the remains of a frieze in the surround, similar to carving at Leigh church. It was formerly sheltered by a porch. Both doorways have columns with incised zig-zag decoration and scallop capitals. The arches have both roll moulding and carved protruding zig-zag. There is a Norman north window to the chancel, and on the east gable a tiny Norman window above a string course. The main east window is a 13th-century lancet representing an enlargement of the 12th century opening, and on the south side of the chancel is a further Early English lancet. The nave has an unusual 15th-century window on the south side, with a wooden frame with carved trefoil heads.

The present entrance is through the tower, but the south doorway retains its medieval door. Inside, the church is whitewashed and was much altered in the 19th-century restoration, when a vestry was added and the gallery installed. However, the Norman chancel arch is very fine. The columns are similar to those on the doorways, and there is a similar carved interlace to that in Beckford church. The northern capital is carved with a leaf, whilst that to the south has a lion entwined in trails of foliage. A trinqueta and more entwined foliage are carved on panels to the side, similar to the chancel arch at Rock. The pulpit and prayer desk contain 16th-century linenfold panelling, and the font bowl was brought from Ripple church when the medieval font was reinstated there. A large painting of the Holy Family hangs in the nave. A north window contains some 14th-century glass in the tracery lights, and the glass below was installed as a monument to Rector Philpott in 1874 by Lavers, Barraud and Westlake. The oak-framed window contains some medieval glass, especially around the border.

There are several memorial tablets and ledgers, especially in the chancel. Many of them commemorate the Jeffrey family, including Thomas Jeffrey who died in 1650. His secretary, Samuel Butler from Strensham, was the author of *Hudibras*, a famous 17th-century satire.

EASTHAM   ST. PETER AND ST. PAUL

Eastham church stands in the farmyard of Eastham Court in the Teme Valley. This isolated settlement is approached across the river from the Worcester to Tenbury road by an 18th-century brick bridge. There are few houses and the place has a timeless atmosphere.

The west tower of the church is eye-catching because it is of red brick. It is short with large lancet bell openings and pinnacles, and dates from 1825 when it was built in the contemporary Commissioners style to replace a timber framed structure. By contrast, the nave and chancel with vestry are grey and built of tufa from near Shelsley Walsh. The nave is 12th century Norman, and has a spectacular south doorway with blank arches intersecting above on a projection, similar to the doorways at Bockleton church. The doorway has a column to each side with block capitals, and the arch is decorated with a roll moulding and a line of Saltire crosses, like the doorways at nearby Martley, Knighton and

The Norman church at Eastham is built mainly of tufa

Stockton-on-Teme churches. The adjacent reset panels of sculpture of the Herefordshire School type show Sagittarius and Leo. The simple north doorway with a keeled roll moulding probably dates from about 1200. There is a Norman window in the north wall of the nave, but the other windows are 13th and 14th century. The present east wall is now blank, except for a small round window in the gable. It is in a similar position to a Norman window at Earl's Croome church, and so may be the successor of an earlier opening.

The blank east wall was formerly painted behind the altar, but today the entire interior is scraped back to the tufa. The view east is dominated by the 19th-century Norman style chancel arch, which replaced an original Norman arch, the bases to the pillars of which can be seen near the lectern and pulpit. The former rood loft stair is to the side and there are also Norman panels showing an Agnus Dei in a roundel, and a monster formed from two beasts, but with a single head. The chancel contains a sedilia and piscina, and has a low side window of uncertain but medieval date. The font is a large Norman cauldron with rope moulding below the bowl set on a 19th-century base. Much of the woodwork is 17th-century including the lectern, pulpit and choir stalls, whilst the chancel panelling appears to be reused from furnishings such as a bedhead. This must have been common practice, and other similar examples are at Kinnersley in Herefordshire. One carved wooden roundel is early 16th-century. The naïve painting of the Crucifixion over the south door dates from about 1700, and there are royal arms to George I and II. There is much 19th-century glass.

The memorial tablets include one of 1690 to Edward Soley of Orleton which is painted with his arms. Nearby in the chancel are two small 18th-century brass plaques with sad inscriptions that commemorate infant burials.

The churchyard has many trees and attractive views along the valley. By the path are the overgrown remains of a preaching cross base.

ECKINGTON   HOLY TRINITY

Eckington is a large village below the north-western side of Bredon Hill. It was an Anglo-Saxon settlement, with lands held by Pershore Abbey until they were passed to Edward the Confessor's abbey at Westminster. There is a fine medieval bridge across the River Avon, and numerous timber-framed cottages amongst more modern dwellings around a compact network of lanes. In 1840 the railway bisected the village and market gardening thrived as a result. The limestone church stands on the main street, a short distance from the restored medieval village cross.

The substantial tower is a local landmark, standing at the west end of the south aisle, and with the gables of the nave and north aisle comprises an imposing west front. At the east end there is a large chancel. The nave is Norman, and has a beautiful west doorway which was moved from the north side in 1831, when, unfortunately, some stones were lost. The late 12th century date is confirmed by the stiff leaf capitals on the shafts to either side. The arch above is carved with a form of interlocked triangular crenellation, with lozenges across the angles and bears similarities to carvings on the doorways at nearby Bredon church and Netherton chapel. The original west doorway would have helped create an interesting west front in early medieval times as the remains of an arrangement of adjacent lancet windows show, though these have been partly obscured by the large Perpendicular west window and the staircase buttress to the tower. The Perpendicular tower is crowned with battlements and eight gargoyles, and when it was built the south aisle was also widened. The position of the late 13th-century aisle east window gives an indication of its previous width. The chancel is 14th-century and has a Decorated lancet with carved ballflower, whilst the east window lights have trefoil heads. Two 14th-century windows were reset in the organ chamber in 1887. The north aisle was built of brick in 1831 to accommodate a growing population, but perhaps as a result of some local opposition remains unconsecrated. Buildings belonging to the work-house to the north of the church were demolished in 1836, and the aisle extended to make a vestry, with a stone west gable.

Inside, arches divide spaces of different character reflecting the architectural changes in the building. The south arcade with round pillars and arches has trumpet scallop capitals typical of the late Norman period. The western part of the nave north wall is Norman, though the north arcade and chancel arch date from 1887 in the Norman style. The tower has Perpendicular arches to the nave and south aisle, with a niche at the corner that has a vaulted canopy below a carved leopard's head, and nearby is a corbel showing an angel clasping a heart. The Perpendicular nave roof has beams carved with foliage and dragons, and in one scene a monster is shown swallowing a man.

Sadly, the medieval rood loft, which was still in the church in 1848, was removed soon afterwards and destroyed, but there is a font possibly of 13th-century date. Apart from a medieval dugout chest of elm, there are a communion table dated 1663, a royal arms, and an 18th-century clock mechanism under the tower. The remainder of the furnishings are 19th- and 20th-century, and include misericords showing the Prodigal Son and the Good Samaritan carved by Florence Camm, as well as a prayer desk of the 1920s by craftsmen from the Bromsgrove Guild. One chancel lancet window has 14th-century glass showing a kneeling woman and St. Elizabeth, and there are further fragments in another lancet. The Adoration by the Shepherds and the Kings in the east window of 1925, and an Annunciation in the south aisle, are by Walter Camm. The Holy Trinity window in the north aisle was installed in 1969 by Joseph Nuttgens.

The most imposing memorial is that to John Hanford of Woollas Hall, the manor house on the slopes of Bredon Hill. The Hanfords were a Catholic family and had a chapel in the house. John died in 1616 and is shown with his wife Anne Rake kneeling opposite each other across a prayer desk. Their ten children and three step-children are shown kneeling on the base. The costume is remarkably detailed; one unusual touch is the wrinkled stockings of Sir John and the elder sons. The memorial is thought to have been carved by Epiphanius Evesham, and certainly bears resemblance to his work on the Bigg tomb in Norton church. The tablet to Thomas Thornbery of 1771 shows his coat of arms. In the south aisle is a small Italian Della Robia porcelain plaque of the 16th century, which was installed in the church in memory of the Reverend Edwin David Annand, who was vicar here between the First and Second World Wars.

Outside, on the south wall of the chancel, the remains of a mass dial can be traced near the priest's door.

ELDERSFIELD   ST. JOHN THE BAPTIST

In the south-western-most part of the county, the grey spire of Eldersfield church is a feature of the land-scape in the views from the Upton to Gloucester road towards Malvern. The village is a scattered commu-nity with a centre of population at Corse Lawn; all on the east side of the wooded Gadbury Hill. The church stands near the Court and Pigeon House Farm, both of which have fine dovecotes. In medieval times land in the parish was thought to have been held by the Whittington family from nearby Pauntley in Gloucestershire. The family included Richard or Dick Whittington, the near legendary Lord Mayor of London. The Whittington arms appear on the font, but the only confirmed association is through the marriage of Dick's mother, Joan, to Thomas Berkeley of Eldersfield.

The lias stone church has a west tower, nave and chancel with a north aisle, south chapel and porch. The 13th-century tower is massive and supports the tall Perpendicular octagonal spire. It is a somewhat primitive structure with corner buttresses, simple pinnacles, as well as empty image niches on the north and south faces, with carved quatrefoils to their sides. A niche on the south-west buttress contains the figure of a knight with shield and sword. The south chapel is also Perpendicular and has a low pitched roof, and was built as a chantry chapel dedicated to the Virgin Mary by Thomas Holford. These represent

15th-century additions to the church, which are rather more modest than other local examples of that period. The nave is mainly Norman, and in the porch is part of a doorway with one shaft and part of a zig-zag arch, with a 15th-century doorway set into it. The chancel has 13th- and 14th-century windows.

The interior is whitewashed and light. Further evidence of the Norman church is apparent in the chancel arch which, although greatly restored, retains the shafts to the sides and large plain abaci carved with simple zig-zag decoration. Similar examples can be seen on arches at Great Malvern Priory. Also restored is the 14th-century north arcade with its Decorated quatrefoil piers and pointed arches. In the south chapel are medieval image brackets carved with grotesque faces with their tongues out.

The font is carved with arms of local landholding families, including Bridges, Beauchamp, Berkeley, Despencer and Whittington. It is Perpendicular, though much reworked, and some 16th-century pews also survive with linenfold panelling. Parts of the medieval screen are incorporated into the 17th-century pulpit and lectern, whilst fragments of a medieval stone altar have been reused in the south wall, and are visible in the porch. The commandment boards are placed over the chancel arch.

There are six panels of 17th-century armorial glass. A memorial to Henry Savage, who died in 1672, records that he was Master of Balliol College, Oxford and Chaplain to King Charles II. The epitaph to his mother, Winifred Savage, who died in 1615, likens her qualities to various women in the Bible. Near the tall tower arch is the memorial stone to William Underhill who died in 1647, from where money from his charity was distributed twice yearly to the poor until the 20th century when it ceased to be viable.

The churchyard contains several 18th-century monuments, as well as a medieval stone coffin which was once inside the church.

ELMBRIDGE   ST. MARY

*Elmbridge church was rebuilt in 1873
but retains its 12th-century doorway*

On a low hilltop north of Droitwich, Elmbridge is a group of houses and cottages set amongst farms. The parish was formed in 1877 out of part of Dodderhill, and for most of its history Elmbridge was a chapelry to St. Augustine's church, now in Droitwich. Indeed, the Dannett family whose memorial is in that church held much land at Elmbridge during the 16th century. Purshull Hall, a large brick and timber-framed house in the parish, was associated with the planning of the Gunpowder Plot, and indeed was bought by a recusant Catholic priest in 1750.

The church is a small red sandstone building with a nave, chancel and north aisle. There is a rather oversized bellcote on the west gable which gives the first impression that the church is 19th-century, as is the case with many north Worcestershire sandstone churches. It was indeed much rebuilt in 1873, but the south doorway is late 12th century. It has two shafts on either side with simple capitals. The arch has carved projecting zig-zag with lozenges, and an unusual trapeze ornament. Above is a small 19th-century gable.

The small and whitewashed interior also gives the impression of a Victorian church. Although the arches of the north arcade are 19th-century, the round piers and plain capitals are late Norman. There is a 17th-century communion rail and table brought from the Catholic chapel at Purshull Hall, but the remainder of the fittings are mostly 19th- and 20th-century. There is glass in the east window by William Forsyth of Worcester and another window with glass by Ward and Hughes. There are several memorial tablets, including one to Edmund Purshull, who died in 1650, with garlands and a skull at the top, and batwings underneath.

ELMLEY CASTLE   ST. MARY

Elmley Castle is one of the prettiest and best known villages in Worcestershire. It lies under the steep north slope of Bredon Hill, and has a main street with timber-framed, stone and brick cottages running from a medieval cross at the north end to the church at the south. The village takes its name from a castle belonging to the Despencer and Beauchamp families which stood on the lower slopes of the hill a little to the south-east. It was ruinous by the 14th century, and today the site is marked by earthworks and a few

Elmley Castle church from the north

masonry fragments. The subsequent 17th-century manor house of the Savage and Davies families has also been demolished. This stood to the south of the church, which is hidden by trees from the street.

The limestone tower has battlements, as do the north aisle, porch and north transept, which have low pitched roofs. Beyond this, the nave and chancel have steep roofs, and on the south side there is another aisle. The low pitch roofs and battlements represent improvements to the medieval church between the 15th and 17th centuries, and so it has a Perpendicular appearance on the north side. Indeed, the 14th-century north aisle was refurbished in the 15th century when the north transept was added. It was given large square-headed windows, some with attractive tracery. The porch was rebuilt in a similar Perpendicular style in 1636 and has an image niche over the doorway. However, inside the porch is a 13th-century Early English doorway, and the substantial tower base with lancet windows is of about the same date. The Perpendicular upper part of the tower has typical bell openings. The chancel is possibly the earliest part of the present structure, having herringbone masonry in the north and south walls that dates from before 1100. The south aisle was rebuilt in the 16th century and is much plainer than the north. Facing away from the village and street it would have been hardly seen. In 1863 the chancel was renovated by Ewan Christian and given Decorated style windows, and in 1878 the church was restored by Frederick Preedy, who repaired the walls and much of the window tracery.

The scraping of the interior back to the stone was also undertaken in 1878, giving it a rather harsh and dark appearance. Much of the stonework is nonetheless medieval. The Perpendicular arcade has octagonal piers and chamfered arches, though the eastern arch is plainer and could have led to an earlier north transept. The curious south arcade has two bays at the east end divided by an octagonal Decorated pier, and then two individual western arches cut through the earlier wall. It has been suggested that this is

The reset carved stone in the porch depicting a rabbit

Anglo-Saxon masonry, and could be part of a long narrow church with typical proportions of that period, to which the chancel with the herringbone masonry was added at about the time of the Norman Conquest. However, it is also possible that the condition of the south wall and arches is linked to the 16th-century reconstruction of the

The font with dragons carved on the base

south aisle. By contrast the Gothic chancel arch is 19th-century, probably by Christian.

The porch contains reset carved stones showing a rabbit and a pig, and other Norman worked stones can be seen in the masonry of the church. The font is a 15th-century octagonal bowl carved with arms of the Savage and Beauchamp families and the Prince of Wales. It is set on a 13th-century base with menacing dragons entwined in their twisted tails, which bears great similarity to a carved capital in Bretforton church. The entrance to the rood loft stair is by the north transept arch. Some plain medieval bench ends were restored by Preedy when he refitted the pews and installed the pulpit in 1878. The north window of the north transept contains some red and white fragments of medieval glass, and there is a pre-1603 royal arms in a south aisle window. The east window was installed by Powell & Co. in 1878, who also made the Rhoades memorial window in the south aisle in 1897. The painting of the pregnant Madonna by Donald Pass dates from the late 1960s.

There are several 17th- and 18th-century memorial plaques and ledgers around the church, but the north transept is filled by the great monuments. William Savage died in 1616 and is shown with his son Giles, who died in 1631, on a delicate alabaster monument against the west wall. Giles' wife Catherine, is also

The Coventry memorial

shown, though when she died in 1674, she was buried in Great Malvern Priory. The effigies are beautifully carved, and Catherine nurses a baby holding a ball. Their four sons are shown kneeling at their feet by a stag's head. Above are plaques and hanging armour, but there is no superstructure, unlike the memorial on the east wall which blocks the former east window. This is to the first Earl of Coventry, who died in 1699, and should have been placed with the rest of his family memorials in the church at Croome d'Abitot, but his widow had married Thomas Savage and came to live at Elmley. The second Earl, her stepson, refused to have the memorial at Croome because the inscription made false claims about the pedigree of her family. The monument is the work of William Stanton and dates from the very early 18th century. It is of black and white marble, and shows the first Earl semi-reclining and wearing a wig. His coronet is next to him. Above are two columns and a large curved pediment, with allegorical figures above and beside him.

The tower contains a medieval bell, and outside in the churchyard are two elaborate limestone sundials from Elmley Castle House. They are 16th-century, and the one by the path has the Savage arms carved on the side. The rest of the carving is chequer work. They were restored in the 1970s and stand amongst a fine group of 17th- and 18th-century headstones and two table tombs made from limestone.

ELMLEY LOVETT   ST. MICHAEL

In the lanes to the east of Hartlebury, Elmley Lovett remains an isolated hamlet despite the encroaching development on the site of Air Ministry camps and sheds from the Second World War. Like nearby Hampton it takes its name from the Lovett family who held land here after the Norman Conquest. The church stands on a low hill and the spire can be seen from some distance across the fields.

The tower and spire are of sandstone and stand at the west end of the nave and chancel. The spire has roll mouldings on the angles and along with the tower dates from the 14th century. Much of the stonework in the church is medieval but it was largely rebuilt in the Commissioners style in 1839 to 1840 by John Mills. There are long lancet windows to the sides and three large stepped lancets at the east end in the favoured Early English style. The walls have battlements and the roof is low pitched. Since the demolition of St. Peter the Great church in Worcester, this is the only example of work in the county by this architect.

The interior is plain with mainly 19th-century fittings, but the base of the medieval cross survives in the churchyard.

EVESHAM   ABBEY PRECINCT AND BELLTOWER

Evesham Abbey was an Anglo-Saxon foundation, but little remains of it today. It was at the heart of this busy market and waterside town, which lies on the River Avon at the centre of the Vale of Evesham, renowned for its fruit and vegetable cultivation. The foundation of the Abbey by St. Ecgwin or Egwin, then Bishop of Worcester, in 701 followed a vision of the Virgin on the site reputedly by Eoves the Swineherd. During the Middle Ages the abbey became a great centre of pilgrimage to the shrine of Ecgwin, but after the Dissolution in 1539 the abbey buildings were mostly demolished leaving just fragments of the church, the gateways, some precinct wall, the almonry and the great abbey belltower for which Evesham is justly famous. Evesham's two medieval parish churches, All Saints and St. Lawrence, stand within the precinct, to the north of the site of the abbey church. The east end of the abbey church has now been marked out on the ground, and gives a sense of scale to the adjacent belltower. Despite the

huge losses and changes, there is still the sense of a close here, to which the limestone belltower must have been the final addition before the Dissolution, forming a gateway which connected the parish graveyard to the eastern part of the abbey precinct. Indeed the vaulting in the gateway at the base of the tower was never completed. The tower was built between 1524 and 1532 by Clement Lichfield who had become abbot in 1513. It is in the finest Perpendicular style with panelling on the east and west faces. The bell openings are also typical Perpendicular work, and are below a crown of openwork battlements with pinnacles in the style of Gloucester Cathedral. The original clock given by Lichfield had wooden quarterboys to strike the chime. They are now preserved in the Almonry Museum. The tower was restored by Frederick Preedy in 1876.

Abbot Lichfield left his mark on the architecture of the two churches as well, particularly with the foundation of chantry chapels, and had also endowed the Grammar School, parts of which survive in nearby Merstow Green. He fought to save the abbey from dissolution but was unable to prevent closure or the immediate destruction of the church and buildings. He retired to a former manor at nearby Offenham, and was buried in All Saints church. The belltower was purchased by the townspeople and so survived.

The Perpendicular abbey belltower

EVESHAM   ALL SAINTS

All Saints is the northern of the two churches in the abbey precinct, and was initially the parish church for the eastern part of the town. Today it is Evesham's parish church, and has an aisled nave and chancel with transepts, with a large porch at the west end adjoining the tower and spire. The church is built of limestone and most of the exterior features are Perpendicular.

The porch has entrances on the north and south sides, with openwork battlements and pinnacles. The west wall of the porch has a five light Perpendicular window and the stonework is panelled and

All Saints, Evesham, showing Abbot Lichfield's chantry chapel

ornamented with carved quatrefoils and emblems of Prince Arthur, the eldest son of Henry VII who died in 1509, and Katherine of Aragon, his wife—three feathers of the Prince of Wales, a pomegranate and a rose. This early 16th-century date points to the work of Abbot Lichfield, and indeed the most conspicuous feature on the south side is Lichfield's projecting chantry chapel. It is higher and more ornate than the surrounding aisle with large transomed windows and openwork battlements. The remainder of the nave and transepts have Perpendicular windows of both three and five lights. There is no clerestorey to the nave, but at the east end are two small windows over the chancel, which were inserted by Frederick Preedy during the restoration of 1872-76. At this time the chancel was much rebuilt and given a Decorated style east window, and the north aisle and transept were extensively restored. The slender tower has an octagonal spire recessed behind battlements and pinnacles. The piecemeal nature of the exterior results from sporadic additions culminating in the work of Abbot Lichfield and contrasts to the uniformity of St. Lawrence.

Entrance is through the porch, and under a Perpendicular vault with an oak pendant carved with the symbols of the Passion. There is a stoup on the tower door jamb with a niche above, and a 1946 sculpture of the Virgin and Child. The west doorway from the tower into the nave survives from the Norman church. The arches to the chancel and the north transept are Decorated, though the chancel arch was rebuilt and heightened by Preedy. The arcades are Perpendicular, with projections to the piers separated by hollows. The south arcade is a little higher than that on the north. The most lavish medieval feature of the interior is Lichfield's chantry. It is entered by a panelled arch, and below the windows are carved quatrefoils and large flowers. The vault has a pendant hanging below the arch, carved with the initials CLP for Clement Lichfield Prior (similar to the pendant with rebus in the Morton Chapel at Bosbury church in Herefordshire). This indicates that the chapel was built between 1510 and 1513 whilst Lichfield was still prior, and before he became abbot. Evidence for the slightly earlier building date of the south transept comes with the former west window of the transept which now opens into the chapel.

The Perpendicular font is octagonal and carved with quatrefoils and flowers, and there are several pieces of sculpture from the abbey, including roof bosses and an early 14th-century seated figure of Moses. The north transept roof with its carved bosses dates from about 1500. No other medieval fittings survive, and all the 17th-century fittings were removed when Preedy restored the interior in 1872. This is unfortunate in that the church was noted in the 17th century for the preaching of its puritan incumbents. However, the woodwork of the chancel screen was carved locally by C. and H. Salmon, and the iron and copper gates were worked in the Arts and Crafts style in 1910 by Blunt and Wray of Holborn, London. The figure of Christ was carved in Oberammergau, Germany, to designs by Charles Ford Whitcombe, architect of Broadheath church, and the statues of the Virgin and St. John are by Richard Houghton of Worcester. The wooden reredos in the Lichfield chapel is by Bligh Bond, and that in the chancel is by Richard Boulton and Son of 1875. Of the same date are the tiles by Godwins of Lugwardine in Herefordshire in the chancel.

In a north window is a 14th-century glass panel showing a seated Christ, but the remaining glass is mostly Victorian. Between 1872 and 1876, Preedy designed the east window showing the Life of Christ, a north chancel window showing Cain murdering Abel, and the Martyrdom of St. Stephen, and the east window of the north transept with the Corporal Acts of Mercy. The transept north window is of 1882 by the Belgian Jean-Baptiste Capronnier. A history of Evesham Abbey is shown in the 1883 windows of the south transept and Lichfield chapel by Powell & Co. of London, who also produced glass in 1900 for the south-east window showing Saints Ambrose, Lawrence and Stephen. Also in 1900, Shrigley and Hunt produced the west window with the four Evangelists and the glass for the small windows over the chancel arch. A further window contains glass by Percy Bacon of similar date.

The numerous memorial tablets include a stone to Adam Cave, who died in 1698, carved by Thomas White of Worcester, and another to Elizabeth Cave, who died in 1728, by Richard Squire, architect of All Saints church, Worcester. A wreathed urn with an obelisk commemorates Elizabeth Baylies who died in 1754, and whose husband went on to become a physician at the court of Emperor Frederick the Great. A simple slab marks the site of the grave of Abbot Clement Lichfield on the floor of the chapel built as his chantry.

EVESHAM   ST. LAWRENCE

The Perpendicular church of St. Lawrence from the east

St. Lawrence stands a few yards south of All Saints, very close to the site of the nave of Evesham Abbey. Historically this was the parish church of the west side of the town, and was much used up to 1540 as it housed several chantries endowed by wealthy merchants. However, it lost its endowments with the Dissolution of the Chantries in 1548, and fell into a poor state of repair. Despite attempts to renovate it in the 18th century, much of the nave had collapsed before it was restored in 1836 to 1837 by Harvey Eginton for the Rudge family of Abbey Manor. The church is today vested in the Churches Conservation Trust. The limestone building appears mostly Perpendicular, with an aisled nave, a chancel, a south chapel, and a west tower with a short octagonal spire.

The tower with its stair turret, battlements and pinnacles was built as a piece in the early 15th century, but the spire is by Eginton. There is a defaced crucifixion carved on the north side. The Perpendicular nave and chancel have a large east window, which has elaborate ornamented panelling to the sides and on the buttresses, and has transom level tracery. The sanctuary windows to either side are similar. When Eginton rebuilt the north aisle he removed the higher walls and longer windows installed in about 1737, when a north chapel had also been demolished. The south aisle is all 15th-century, except for Eginton's windows in the east and south walls which mark the location of a former charnel house under the east end. The south chapel was added before 1509 and dedicated to St. Clement like the porch to All Saints, almost certainly by the future Abbot Clement Lichfield. The chapel has fine Perpendicular windows and openwork battlements. The chapel west wall was left blank as it adjoined a walkway linking the church to the abbey and the south aisle wall was altered when this walkway was removed after the Dissolution.

The entrance under the tower, beneath a 15th-century tierceron vault, leads to the well-proportioned Perpendicular interior through a panelled arch. The south arcade is 15th-century, whilst the north is Eginton's copy. Above is the Perpendicular clerestorey, which is not visible behind the aisle roofs on the exterior. Flat piers three bays from the east end mark the site of the former rood screen which divided the nave from the chancel, and there is also panelling below the clerestorey. The beautiful interior of the south chapel also has a panelled arch, niches by the windows, whilst the site of the reredos is marked by the higher sill to the east window. The fan-vaulted roof has a large central pendant. The font in the chapel is a copy of a Perpendicular one.

In general, the interior is a plain contrast to that of All Saints. Eginton refitted the church for the Rudge family in 1836 according to the principles of Protestant fashion, and the pulpit had a reading desk. However, the church was reordered in 1892, but still in a low church way, without the numerous endowments of furniture to be found at All Saints. However the pulpit of 1906 and parclose screens of 1910 are the work of Charles Ford Whitcombe. There is a much altered 17th-century communion table. In the south wall is a piece of sculpture found in 1931 containing the arms of the abbey. The organ of 1840 is by Nicholson and is housed in Eginton's case.

The fan vault in the south chapel at St. Lawrence, Evesham

No medieval glass survives but there is evidence that between 1461 and 1483 the east window was filled with armorial glass. The present glass is of 1862 by Thomas Willement. The side windows of the chancel contain glass of 1864 by Alexander Gibbs. The south window of the south chapel is of 1863 by Hardman & Co., whilst the east is of 1931 by Evans of Smethwick. The east window of the south aisle was glazed by Michael O'Connor in 1847, and there is a Frederick Preedy window of 1866, the others being from between 1930 and 1960 by A.L. Wilkinson, P. Woodroffe, and F.W. Skeat. The Pentecost east window of the north aisle is of 1862 by Preedy, and the other five windows on this side are by G. Webb and F.W. Skeat from between 1930 and 1960.

There are many memorial tablets, and the floor at the east end of the south aisle was lowered to make a vault for the Rudge family in the 1830s.

EVESHAM   ST. PETER, BENGEWORTH

Bengeworth developed in medieval times as the suburb across the River Avon from Evesham. Indeed the main thoroughfare, Port Street, is a direct continuation over the bridge from Evesham's Bridge Street. At the top of Port Street stands St. Peter, a large 19th-century urban church, which replaced a medieval structure which stood to the south of Port Street, lower down the hill. The graveyard of the old church still exists as an attractive green space with trees and memorials, and contains the only surviving part of the church, the base of the west tower porch. This is late 14th century, and has a west doorway, arch and springers for a vault in the Decorated style. The demolished upper parts once supported a spire. The church itself was a sprawling building with a nave, and an aisled chancel with a north transept.

During the 19th century the church fell into a poor state of repair and despite much local opposition was demolished in 1870. The new church was built between 1870 and 1872 on land given by Lord Northwick. It has a nave with aisles, and chancel with transepts, and a large south-west tower porch with a commanding spire. The architect was T.D. Barry, who used the fashionable Decorated style, as can be seen in the elaborate tracery of the east and west windows. There are similarities to Barry's other Worcestershire church at Christ Church, Malvern.

The interior has many contemporary features, such as the arcades with columns of Westmorland granite, and the pulpit of Caen stone with carved heads of Christ, St. Peter and St. John. From the fittings of the old church, the font, 17th-century communion table and a little glass survive, along with some interesting memorial tablets. The small early classical memorial to the charitable benefactor, Thomas Watson who died in 1561, has columns, a foliage frieze, strapwork and skull on a pediment. The larger marble memorial to Alderman John Deacle, woollen merchant of the City of London, who died in 1709, shows the figure in contemporary costume with wig, reclining on a sarcophagus. The back wall is ornamented with pilasters and a pediment, and the inscription is surrounded by carved drapery. Deacle is recorded as establishing a charity school in his native Evesham.

Other fittings in the church are Victorian and later, and the windows are filled with late 19th- and early 20th-century glass. Much of this shows scenes from the New Testament including the large west window with the Corporal Acts of Mercy. Three windows are by Albert Lemmon of the Bromsgrove Guild. One shows a carpenter at work with Mary and Joseph, a second the Good Shepherd with the Good Samaritan, whilst the third shows the Virgin appearing to Eoves the Swinesherd, being the story of the foundation of Evesham Abbey. Although so much was destroyed when the old church was pulled down, a window and other masonry were reused in the church at Norton, and aside from much woodwork which was incorporated into local inns and houses, the communion rails were incorporated in furniture at Hampton (see entry below).

EVESHAM   ST. ANDREW, HAMPTON

On the south side of the River Avon, and now a suburb of Evesham, Hampton is a settlement of Saxon origins. Land in the vicinity was held by Evesham Abbey from the 8th century, and Hampton Ferry was an important crossing point to those lands from the town. The present bridge to the east of the village was not opened until the 20th century.

The church was in the patronage of the abbey, and the present structure is probably to the plan of the 12th century church. The nave and porch, central tower and chancel of lias and limestone, are medieval, whilst the north transept and vestry were added in 1904. The chancel was rebuilt by Abbot John de Brockhampton in 1282, but all the features of the church are Perpendicular, and there was much restoration, particularly of the east window, in the 19th century. The Perpendicular tower has square bell openings with battlements and pinnacles. The south porch is a fine Perpendicular work with a large stone slab roof. It is very similar to the porch at Honeybourne church. The doorway has a square hood mould stopped by large grotesque heads, which are possibly earlier and reused. There is carved foliage to the spandrels of the arch.

The doorway inside the porch also has leaf spandrels, similar to the doorway at Upton Snodsbury church. Three chamfered arches support the porch roof, again like the Honeybourne porch. In 1981 a new stoup was installed by Robert Pancheri of Bromsgrove. The interior is whitewashed and dominated by the massive Perpendicular arches which support the tower. The arches are chamfered and without capitals, whilst the tower vault has eight radiating ribs from a central circle through which pass the bellropes.

The eastern arch has brackets for the vanished rood loft which was once accessed from the tower stairs. The font is plain and could be twelfth century and there are some medieval tiles which were discovered during the alterations of 1904. The communion table is made up from the 17th-century altar rails from the old church in Bengeworth. The other fittings are mainly Victorian and include an early 19th-century pulpit, which was repaired by Clarkson of Worcester in 1893. The west window glass of 1890 is by Burlison and Grylls, and in 1902 the south-east window of the chancel was installed by John Hardman to designs of William Lunn. The east window was the gift of Henry Workman, Mayor of Evesham and shows the bridge across the Avon to Bengeworth which he sought for many years to have built. A charity board records the gifts of John Martin, a local landowner, who, when he died in 1713, endowed a school which stood on the west side of the churchyard until the early 20th century.

Outside in the churchyard the 19th-century cross shaft stands on a medieval base. There are two steps with an octagonal level decorated on each side with a quatrefoil design, but having the remains of a carved seated figure on one face. Nearby is the carved table tomb commemorating the burial of the benefactor John Martin in 1713.

FAIRFIELD   ST. MARY

An expansive village to the north of Bromsgrove, Fairfield was once in the parish of Belbroughton. The sandstone church was built in 1854 by Benjamin Ferrey, who also designed Birlingham church. The nave and chancel have a bellcote at the west end. The style is late 13th-century Early English, with plate tracery to the windows, which are more elaborate in the chancel.

FAR FOREST   HOLY TRINITY

This scattered village lies to the west of Wyre Forest on the Shropshire border. The parish is more correctly Bewdley Far Forest, and was formed in 1845 from parts of Rock and Ribbesford, along with part of Stottesdon in Shropshire. The small church was built in 1844 by Abraham Perkins, architect for Worcester Cathedral. It is in the favoured Early English style, and has a nave and chancel with transepts, porch and west bellcote. The windows are typical lancets.

FECKENHAM   ST. JOHN THE BAPTIST

The former royal Forest of Feckenham extended from Droitwich through to Warwickshire, and a medieval royal hunting lodge and forest prison stood to the west of the present Green in the village. Up to the early 19th century, Feckenham was an important needle-making centre, which was eclipsed by the growth of Redditch, and the parish now forms the rural part of Redditch District Council. Today there is a fine collection of timber-framed and brick houses and cottages which line the Green and two main streets, amongst which are the remains of workshops and needle mills from the village's industrial past.

The church lies in a large churchyard behind the houses on the north side of the Green. It is of dark grey sandstone, and has a squat square west tower, nave with north aisle, porch, and chancel. The lower part of the tower is 14th-century with a 15th-century belfry below panelled Perpendicular battlements and short crocketed pinnacles. The west window is also Perpendicular. The porch and nave south wall were rebuilt by Henry Day in 1866 to 1867. On the south-eastern corner of the nave is a staircase turret which gave access to the former organ loft. The chancel was rebuilt by William Butterfield in 1853, but incorporates two Norman windows at the west end of the north wall, and has two 13th-century south windows. The north aisle is Perpendicular with a typical east window, but it too was much restored in the 19th century.

The spacious interior has a fine north nave arcade dating from about 1250, with round piers carrying octagonal abaci and chamfered pointed arches. One capital has stiff leaf decoration and a carved head.

The arches are decorated with a painted geometrical pattern in red and black—a 19th-century recreation of a medieval design, traces of which were discovered on the easternmost arch (see illustration on rear cover). The arches to the chancel and the tower are 14th-century.

Most of the fittings are 19th-century, including the font cover. However, in the east end, the panelling is 18th-century woodwork, and the benches are reworked from box pews. The glass in the east window was designed by Frederick Preedy in 1867 and shows scenes from the Life of Christ.

The church also possesses some late medieval communion wafer tongs which were discovered on the site of John of Feckenham's family house. In the glass of the aisle east window of 1905 by Charles Ford Whitcombe, John is shown holding a representation of Evesham Abbey. He was a monk of Evesham until the Dissolution, after which he remained a Roman Catholic. John was also present at the execution of Lady Jane Grey, became chaplain to Mary Tudor, and was made Abbot of Westminster when the monastery there was briefly re-established during her reign.

Aside from several 18th- and 19th-century memorial tablets, there is a large monument to Robert Boulton Walden, a local benefactor, who died in 1823, showing a young woman with a child in her arms standing by a pedestal. On the north wall of the chancel is an inscription to Sir Martin Culpeper, (ancestor of Thomas Culpeper who assisted the exiled Charles II), his wife Joyce and their family, which was on a table tomb standing on the south side of the chancel until 1853. Their effigies are thought to have been buried beneath the chancel floor. Sir Martin died in 1604, and had lived in Astwood Court, in the eastern part of the parish. Part of the house is incorporated into a moated farmhouse.

Outside, in the churchyard, the base of the medieval cross survives, though now with a 20th-century shaft and head. The war memorial is by craftsmen of the Bromsgrove Guild.

FINSTALL   ST. GODWALD

Although Finstall has medieval origins, today it is largely the result of industrial expansion around Bromsgrove since the Victorian period, and includes much 19th- and 20th-century suburban housing to the east of Bromsgrove station. The origins of the 19th-century church are interesting. In 1884 it replaced a sandstone building of 1773 constructed by the Brettell family of Finstall Park, which stood close to the railway, but which was only finally demolished in 1971. This was the site of a medieval church also dedicated to St. Godwald. Godwald, who is often known as Gudwal, was an obscure Celtic abbot who is said to have inhabited a monastery on an island off the coast of Brittany in the 6th century. His cult grew up in Worcester in the early medieval period, and a chapel at the Commandery was dedicated to him. Land at Finstall and Stoke Prior was held by Worcester Cathedral, and so St. Godwald came to be venerated here.

The present church consists of a nave and chancel with a south transept. The proposed north transept was never built. The vestry was added in 1924. The church was designed in the early Decorated style by John Cotton, the architect of nearby All Saints church in Bromsgrove, and was built by Brazier of Bromsgrove.

The interior is faced with yellow brick, in a similar manner to Abberton church. The mainly 19th-century furnishings include a reredos of 1897 in Caen stone by Jones and Willis in memory of the rector, J. Bainbrigge, who caused the present church to be built. A carving by Celestino Pancheri of the Bromsgrove Guild commemorates the D-Day landings of 1944, which took place on 6th June, St. Godwald's feast day; Pancheri had previously reworked the reredos. The lady chapel window showing the Annunciation of 1937 is by Albert Lemmon, also of the Guild.

FLADBURY   ST. JOHN THE BAPTIST

Fladbury church

Fladbury is a large sprawling village beside the River Avon between Pershore and Evesham. There is much 20th-century housing but many brick and timber-framed houses survive along the street and towards the mill on the River. The church is by the Green, next to a housing development on the site of the Georgian vicarage. The village was the site of a 7th-century monastic foundation which passed to Worcester Cathedral in the 9th century. The resulting large medieval parish included Throckmorton and Wyre Piddle, as well as Bradley near Feckenham.

The limestone church stands in a pretty churchyard surrounded by yew trees. The tower is at the west end of the aisled nave to which is attached the porch and chancel. The base of the tower is Norman with flat buttresses to the corners and centre. Those in the centre contain lancet windows. It was heightened in the 14th century and an extra stone wall was built internally to reinforce the structure. The belfry openings are Decorated, but the panelled battlements and pinnacles are thought to have been added in the 18th century when the wooden spire was removed. The nave and aisles are mostly Perpendicular, but much rebuilt in the 18th century. The chancel and vestry were designed by Frederick Preedy in 1865, but incorporate medieval material, including a piscina on the wall outside the vestry, which may once have been in a sacristy, to which entry was gained through the north door of the chancel.

The 14th-century porch has a Decorated arch and a rib vaulted ceiling. There was once an upper floor which was entered by a doorway in the south aisle. The interior is spacious, and the whitewashed chancel contrasts with the scraped stonework in the nave and western parts. The tower interior has pointed arches to the Norman windows in the reinforcing wall, and a chamfered Early English arch opening into the nave. The nave arcades are Decorated with octagonal piers and chamfered arches. At the east end of the south aisle a piscina and aumbry mark the site of the chantry chapel founded by Eleanor Throckmorton in memory of her husband John whose brasses are in the base of the tower. The coved nave ceiling is Georgian and painted white, and the chancel arch dates from the alterations of 1865 by Preedy.

For much of his young adult life in the 1840s, Frederick Preedy lived with his family in Fladbury, and so it is not surprising that apart from his work on the chancel, many of the fittings were designed by him. The pews, pulpit and reredos are his work of between 1864 and 1871. The font is also 19th-century, and the tower screen was made up in 1953 from panels from the former west gallery. There are several medieval tiles with coats of arms reset in the chancel and south aisle. The 14th-century heraldic glass in a north chancel window probably came from Evesham Abbey, and shows the arms of the Boteler, Montfort and Despencer families. Reset in a cross on the south aisle altar is a fine panel of 14th-century green and gold glass showing the Virgin and Child beneath a canopy with decorated cusps and crockets (see illustration on rear cover). This was made from the same pattern as the virtually identical panel in the east window of Warndon church. Preedy designed windows in the north aisle and chancel as family memorials showing saints and scenes from the Life of Christ between 1850 and 1882, and installed the east window in 1869 which shows the Feast at Cana, the Miracle of the Draught of Fishes and the Resurrection.

There is a large collection of monuments. Most striking is the tomb chest under the tower with brasses set in a Purbeck marble slab. This commemorates John Throckmorton, who died in 1445, and his wife Eleanor de Spiney of Coughton in Warwickshire, still the home of the Throckmorton family. He was Under Treasurer of England and is shown in armour next to Eleanor dressed as a widow. The tomb chest is carved with quatrefoils in panels. There are three further brasses. A half figure of a priest in vestments is Thomas Morden who was Treasurer at St. Paul's Cathedral, London, and who died in 1458. The brass of Sir Edward Peyto, who died in 1488 survives close to the matrices for the brasses of his family. Another brass with a priest in vestments commemorates William Plowne, rector, who died in 1504. A medieval memorial stone records Godith Bosom whose daughter married the son of John and Eleanor Throckmorton.

In the chancel is a large memorial to Bishop William Lloyd with flowers, foliage and a figure at the top, by James Withenbury. Bishop Lloyd died aged 90 in 1717 having been Bishop of St. Asaph, Lichfield and then Worcester. He was one of the Protestant bishops who confronted the Roman Catholic King James II over the second Declaration of Indulgence in 1688, believing it not to demonstrate tolerance of non-conformists but the reintroduction of Catholicism. Bishop Lloyd was buried at Fladbury, as his son was rector here. Other tablets to note include one with a bust on top to Elizabeth Charlett, who died in 1746, by John Ricketts junior. A tablet with a sarcophagus is in memory of George Perrott of Craycombe House who died in 1806, and whose family hatchments are in the north aisle. A further tablet of 1834 commemorates the rector, Martin Stafford Smith, whose curate William Pruen has a memorial by the side door. Pruen was a preacher who used to entertain John Keble, one of the 19th-century founders of the Oxford High Church movement. Pruen died of a stroke in the pulpit whilst preaching in Stratford-upon-Avon. Many of Frederick Preedy's family are also commemorated on tablets in the church.

In the south belfry opening of the tower hangs a sanctus bell of about 1555, similar to that at Bishampton church. It is inscribed with a dedication to St. Catherine in prayers for the rector, Edward Gregson, who died in 1557.

FLYFORD FLAVELL   ST. PETER

The alliterative place name is curious, and is indeed two versions of the same words, the former Saxon the latter of Norman origin. It refers to Flaed's woodland, and is a reminder of the southern extent of the wooded area which formed the Forest of Feckenham. The village centre is on the top of a hill south of the Worcester to Stratford road, and has a mixture of older houses and cottages amongst twentieth century properties. The church stands along a side lane in a pretty churchyard.

The west tower is attached to a nave with timber porch and north transept, and chancel to the east, and all are built of a mixture of grey and red sandstone. But the Perpendicular tower with battlements and pyramid roof, and square headed bell openings, is the only part of the medieval church to remain intact. The rest was rebuilt by William Jeffrey Hopkins in 1883 using Early English and Decorated styles in an ecclesiologically correct fashion, of which the three lancets in the east wall are typical. Hopkins reused some medieval masonry, particularly the Norman doorway which was blocked and reset in the north wall.

The interior is typically Victorian Gothic Revival with many medieval style fittings, such as the piscina in the chancel. There are some earlier features, such as the Perpendicular octagonal font, two 17th-century benches and some fragments of medieval glass in a south window. Some medieval heraldic tiles including one with the arms of the Heryn family now in the base of the tower.

The tower contains a 15th-century bell, and the base of the medieval cross lies in the churchyard.

FRANKLEY

ST. LEONARD

In the north-east of Worcestershire, Frankley is the last enclave of rural landscape before the edge of Birmingham. The green fields and hilltop clump of trees known as Frankley Beeches provide a great contrast to the estates and tower blocks on the eastern side of the parish. Frankley Service Station to the west is a well known landmark on the M5. The church is in a hollow, close to the reservoir which forms a key link in Birmingham's supply of water from Wales.

The nave, chancel and tower are of dark red sandstone, with a timber porch attached. The sandstone masonry of the walls is mainly medieval, and the east window is 15th-century, though most of the remaining windows are 18th- and 19th-century. The small tower was built into the nave in 1751, using stone from the adjacent manor house of the Lyttleton family which was burnt down during the Civil War. The church was restored in 1873 and again after a fire in 1931.

The compact interior has a Perpendicular wagon roof, and the west end is dominated by the three arches which support the tower. The 20th-century font has a large cover.

The cross in the churchyard has part of a very worn but remarkable Anglo-Saxon shaft with traces of a carved design of scrolls and interlace.

GRAFTON FLYFORD

ST. JOHN THE BAPTIST

The church stands on a hilltop to the north of the Worcester to Stratford road, next to a farmhouse, the former school and the former vicarage. The present village centre is about a mile to the north, and the parish contains some interesting timber-framed houses, of which Rectory Farm is medieval. The field immediately north of the church is a well recorded deserted medieval village site.

The red sandstone tower with its battlements and gargoyles to the corners carries a most unusual short octagonal spire. The tower is Decorated but much of the church was rebuilt by William Jeffrey Hopkins in 1875. There is a nave and chancel with north chapel and a porch. Much medieval material was reused, particularly two Early English lancet windows in the north chapel.

The interior is plain and whitewashed, and contains mainly 19th-century fittings. However, in the chancel there are a plain medieval sedilia and a piscina. The simple 15th-century pulpit has carved arched panels. Two paintings on square boards are 16th-century showing the symbols of St. Mark and St. John. There are fragments of medieval glass in the east and west windows. Several memorial tablets include one dated 1645 with an inscription to Roger Stonehall, a former rector.

GRAFTON MANOR

CHAPEL

Whilst always a private chapel, this interesting building is included as an example of medieval non-parochial church building. This was the chapel of the Stafford and then Talbot families and is attached to their manor house which is now an hotel. It stands at the end of a short lane west of Worcester Road at the south end of Bromsgrove, where it can be seen from the outside.

The brick manor house was mainly rebuilt after a fire in 1710, but it retains its 16th-century front, with a frieze and inscription, and a projecting porch built in 1567. The sandstone chapel has a nave and chancel with a bellcote, and is a 15th-century Perpendicular building. It is linked to the house by rooms which were once the sacristy with a priest's accommodation above.

The chapel windows contain some 16th-century glass, showing the arms of England and Worcester, and panels of Flemish glass with biblical scenes. The chapel was reroofed following the fire, and has a west gallery of about 1800 supported by three ogee arches. There are monuments to key members of the Stafford and Talbot families in St. John's church, Bromsgrove. The house and chapel were used as a Roman Catholic mission during the 19th century under the auspices of the Earl of Shrewsbury, a member of the Talbot family who inherited the property.

GREAT COMBERTON   ST. MICHAEL

The Combertons lie at the foot of the northern slopes of Bredon Hill. Land in Great Comberton was held by Westminster Abbey from the 11th century and passed to the Beauchamp family, who held Elmley Castle in the later Middle Ages. The village is arranged around a group of lanes and has many thatched timber-framed cottages clustering around the church.

The tower of the limestone church forms an attractive feature in the view from the lane across the field to the west. It is Perpendicular, and was set into the nave in the 15th century, with square headed bell openings, gargoyles, battlements and pinnacles. To the east lie the nave, chancel and vestry. The nave walls are Norman, but the windows date from the 14th and 15th centuries. It has been suggested that the nave was originally the chancel, and that the tower replaced a crossing tower, but it could equally have replaced an earlier timber belfry. The chancel has a priest's doorway of about 1400, with crowned heads forming stops to the hood mould. The chancel with the east window and vestry were rebuilt in 1862 by Sir George Gilbert Scott.

Entry is through the west doorway which, with its hood mould and stops carved with a man and a woman, together with the window above, is 15th century. Inside, the west end is complex. A small lobby has a doorway with a pointed arch leading into the base of the tower. Arches to the sides under the tower, which are rounded in the Norman style, support the idea of a crossing, and a very crude arch to the nave appears unfinished. The whitewashed interior contains a 19th-century chancel arch, whilst the nave roof is 14th-century.

The octagonal font is Perpendicular with quatrefoils and blank shields, and there is a 14th-century piscina. The 16th-century benches are plain and massive, and there is panelling to the stalls and a Communion table from the 17th century. The brass lectern was made in 1841 by John Hardman, and three windows contain glass by Clayton and Bell—the east window of 1895, a chancel window showing St. Francis and St. George of 1897, as well as the Good Samaritan window of 1900.

Outside, in the churchyard, a marble pillar commemorates the family of Edmund Smith who were killed in the shipwreck of the *Royal Charter* on the coast of Anglesey in 1859.

GREAT WITLEY   ST. MICHAEL

Witley Court and church form a magnificent group. The Court, in ruins since the fire of 1937, is now in the care of English Heritage and much work is being done to preserve the standing remains and to recreate the landscape setting of this remarkable country house. A medieval manor house on the site was held by the Cokesey and Russell families until it was sold to Thomas Foley, ironmaster of Stourbridge in 1655. The Foleys developed the estate during the 18th century, before it was sold in 1837 to Lord William Ward, owner of much of the Black Country who became Earl of Dudley in 1860. The property was sold in 1920 to Sir Herbert Smith, a Kidderminster carpet tycoon, but after the fire the court was stripped down and left to decay. Restoration began in 1972.

St. Michael's church (see illustration on rear cover) is often mistaken as a private chapel for the house. It has an unusual, opulent baroque interior which is not suggested by the plain exterior. A medieval church stood a little to the west, of which nothing remains above ground, except for part of a pillar incorporated into a churchyard gate. The third Thomas Foley to inherit the estate was created Lord Foley in 1711. He planned the rebuilding of the medieval church, but died in 1732 before work had begun, and the building was paid for by his widow. It was completed in 1735 when Lady Foley herself died.

The church is a brick building, but like the Court it was faced with limestone by the Gloucester architect, Samuel Daukes in the 1850s. It is thought that the architect of the church might have been James Gibbs, a famous London architect who designed St. Martins-in-the-Fields church in Trafalgar Square. It consists of a nave with a short chancel between transepts. The tower is set into the west end of the nave, between lobbies and gallery space and is crowned with a cupola, and beyond which is a porch consisting of a small portico with columns and a pediment. The whole is built to classical proportions with round-headed windows beneath blank round arches. The east window is Venetian in type, and the low pitched roof is surrounded by urns and a balustrade.

The interior is unforgettable. From a lobby under the tower, the entrance reveals the complementary white and gilded walls and ceilings, with their magnificent paintings, and the brightly coloured glass to the windows. The second Lord Foley bought the paintings, glass and organ from the Duke of Chandos' house, Cannons at Edgware in Middlesex, recreating their setting using papier maché stucco with gilt. The ceiling paintings are by Antonio Bellucci, an Italian artist who worked in England between 1716 and 1722, with the Nativity to the west and the Descent from the Cross to the east. There are also ten oval medallions with angels holding the Instruments of the Passion, and ten further medallions with cherubs.

The organ from Cannons has a fine baroque case which forms an integral part of the west wall. It was built by Abraham Jordan and is said to have been played by Handel. The organ was refitted between 1858 and 1860 by Nicholsons of Worcester. The font is by James Forsyth of Worcester, who also worked on the Perseus Fountain in the grounds in about 1860. It has a bowl supported by three angels and a wooden cover with a figure of St. John the Baptist. The box pews were replaced in the 1850s by pews and woodwork by Daukes, in a style which curiously mixes gothic and baroque. The pews have medieval style poppy heads, but with acanthus leaves, whilst there is a baroque pulpit with panels by James Forsyth with an 18th-century wrought iron stair rail. The reredos is a mosaic by the workshop of Antonio Salviati of Venice, brought back by Countess Dudley in 1913.

The glass from Cannons fills every window. It was painted in 1719, except for one in 1721, by Joshua Price, to the designs of Sebastian Ricci, a Venetian painter. The pictorial windows are extremely colourful and show the Annunciation, the Visitation, the Adoration of the Shepherds and of the Magi, the Baptism of Christ, the Miraculous Draught of Fishes, the Resurrection, Healing the Lame and the Supper at Emmaus. The only Old Testament illustration is of the Worship of the Golden Calf.

The most striking memorial is to the south of the altar. It commemorates the first Lord Foley and his family, and is the work of the Dutch sculptor Michael Rysbrack, who also undertook work at Badminton House in Gloucestershire and Blenheim Palace in Oxfordshire. The memorial is one of the largest in England and was completed in 1743 over ten tears after Foley's death. It has a huge grey marble sarcophagus on a plinth, above which rises a large pedestal against the background of an enormous grey marble obelisk. Lord Foley is shown semi-reclining with his widow seated beside him. Five of their children who predeceased them are also shown as statues; the surviving children are not shown. Everyone is in classical costume. There are three tablets from the previous church, commemorating the first Lord Foley who died in 1677, Thomas Wright, rector, who died in 1701, and William Cliffe who died in 1695. Beneath the church is the Foley family vault, where the first Earl of Dudley is also buried.

GREAT WITLEY   ST. MICHAEL'S CHAPEL

This brick chapel stands at the centre of Great Witley village and about one mile north-west of Witley Court. It was originally constructed in 1882 to the designs of Abraham Perkins, the cathedral architect, but was much enlarged in 1895, and a vestry added to the south side in 1897. The chapel has a nave and chancel under a single roof with a bellcote at the west end. From the 1940s to the 1960s the chapel was used as the main place of worship, as the parish church was in a poor state of repair following the fire at the Court. However, following the restoration of the parish church, the chapel was closed in 1977 and stripped of its furnishings, and has since served as a meeting place for Scouts and Guides. The adjacent burial ground contains a Garden of Remembrance established by the Dudley family from the Court.

GRIMLEY   ST. BARTHOLOMEW

Close to the River Severn north of Worcester, Grimley was an important medieval manor held by the priors of Worcester until the Reformation. Little now remains, but the village is a cluster of houses and farms by the church along a cul-de-sac east of the Worcester to Tenbury road.

The red sandstone church has a west tower, nave with north aisle and south porch, and a chancel. The south porch is the most striking feature on the approach to the church. It is in a Norman style, but of 19th-century date with a sloping arcade of short columns to the west supporting the roof for a staircase to the west gallery. The porch shelters a restored but genuine Norman doorway which has scalloped capitals and is set in a projecting section of wall, like the doorways at Stoulton. The south nave wall contains much rough Norman masonry including remains of flat buttresses and a blocked tiny lancet window towards the east end, close to a larger early 14th-century window. The chancel dates from about 1200 and has lancet windows to the sides and flat buttresses at the east end; the east window is Perpendicular. The Decorated style tower with large bell openings and battlements was built in 1845 to replace a timber-framed structure. The north aisle and vestry were added in 1886.

The interior is whitewashed and feels 19th-century. It is dominated by the arcade of 1886 and the predominantly Victorian fittings. However, the octagonal font is 15th-century, and the north aisle windows contain 15th-century glass showing St. John the Evangelist with God the Father, and a window in the nave contains a 15th-century Annunciation. The east window has glass of 1865 by Clayton and Bell.

Amongst the memorial tablets, one by Stephens and Bott of Worcester commemorates Martha Farmer, who died in 1781, in a typical late 18th-century style. The tower contains one 15th-century bell, and the base of the medieval cross survives in the churchyard. The ashes of Samuel Baker were interned in the churchyard. He was a 19th-century traveller who explored the interior of Sri Lanka and several tributaries of the River Nile, including an inland sea which Baker reached in 1864 and named Albert Nyanza. He subsequently served the Khedive of Egypt for many years, leading an expedition to suppress slavery and annexing the Upper Nile area to Egypt.

GUARLFORD   ST. MARY

Guarlford is a small village on a bend in the Malvern to Upton road with several 19th- and 20th-century houses and farms grouped around the church. The wide grassy verges are a vestige of common land in Malvern Chase. Farmland was held by Great Malvern Priory in the Middle Ages, but then passed into the hands of the Foley family.

In 1843 Lady Emily Foley laid the foundation stone of St. Mary's church, as a chapel of ease to Malvern; there was no church here before that date. The architect was Thomas Bellamy of London who used the Early English style in the nave and chancel with pointed lancet windows, as seen in so many contemporary Commissioners churches. The walls are of Malvern granite, cut to give the appearance of crazy paving. In 1877 Earl Beauchamp of Madresfield paid for the addition of the vestry and organ chamber, and in 1906 the west wall and present west window was rebuilt. At this time, the bell turret was removed and the bell hung in a tree as a temporary measure—though it is still there!

The interior is brighter than the gaunt exterior would suggest. The walls are whitewashed and there are many 19th- and 20th-century fittings. The windows are filled with colourful, largely 19th-century glass, most of which are memorials to local people, including Earl Beauchamp. One window of 1868, a memorial to the Wathen family, is by Lavers and Barraud, and the windows in memory of Thomas Need and Elizabeth Bullock date from 1884 and are by Charles Gibbs of London.

HADZOR   ST. JOHN THE BAPTIST

Mention of Hadzor church today usually refers to the Roman Catholic church on the lane to the village from Droitwich. However, the small former parish church stands next to Hadzor House. It is no longer accessible to the public for it is privately owned and has been used as a store since it was closed in 1970. It is a curious building which is just visible next to the house across the park from the Droitwich to Hanbury Road. The small bellcote tower is at the west end of the nave and chancel, all built from green sandstone. Hadzor was the seat of the Amphlett and then from the early 19th century the Galton family, but the House has been much altered and is now a company headquarters.

Much of the masonry of the church is 14th-century and in the Decorated style, but the Galtons more or less rebuilt it in 1835 and again in 1866. The architect of the later phase was probably George Street. The bare interior still contains the large Gothic revival monument to John Howard Galton, who died in 1862. The three north windows of the chancel contain glass by Hardman & Co. of 1868. When the church was closed, the parish was united with Oddingley, and several fittings were moved to the latter church, notably the organ and a brass to Richard Cameron Galton. A panel of 14th-century glass showing the Virgin is now in the Stained Glass Museum at Ely Cathedral in Cambridgeshire.

HAGLEY   ST. JOHN THE BAPTIST

The manor of Hagley came into the hands of the Lyttleton family in 1564. During the 18th century the first Lord Lyttleton rebuilt the Hall and laid out the park, and it is this park, which stretches up to the obelisk on the western slopes of the Clent Hills, that gives the older part of Hagley its character. The village expanded westwards during the 19th century, but St. John's church and the Hall still stand in an idyllic parkland setting, approached from the busy Birmingham to Kidderminster road through the core of the old village.

The Palladian Hall contrasts in style with the striking Gothic church, though both are built of the same red sandstone. The medieval church was expanded and altered by George Street between 1858 and 1865 to form a model Decorated style church for the estate, so fashionable during the Gothic Revival. The cost was covered by a gift to Lord Lyttleton by the county in recognition of his services as Lord Lieutenant of Worcestershire. The outside appearance echoes Henry Woodyer's large estate church at Highnam in Gloucestershire, and has a west tower with a broach spire attached to an aisled nave with porch, and a

St. John the Baptist, Hagley, with Hagley Hall on the left

chancel to the east, all with separate roofs. The vestry is on the north side. All the details are in the style of the end of the 13th century, but the masonry of the south aisle is actually medieval, with Decorated work at the east end. The medieval chancel had already been rebuilt in 1754, and the north aisle was added in 1826 by Thomas Rickman, who also designed the estate church at Ombersley. During his rebuilding Street lengthened the nave westwards by one bay and built the tower.

The corbels on the east side of the south porch are reset voussoirs from a Norman arch. Carved beakheads and chevrons possibly come from a late 12th century doorway, similar to the south doorway at nearby Romsley church. Along with a carved lion inside, these form the only visible evidence for a Norman church on the site. The carved Decorated heads of angels also on the porch, and on the south aisle east window suggest that in the 14th century the church was elaborately ornamented under the patronage of the de Hagley family.

The interior has a typical Victorian feeling, but the octagonal piers with carved foliage decoration on the steps to the south arcade are Decorated. Reset in the south aisle east window is a Norman stone panel carved with a lion, which has a foliated tail. It appears to be very similar to the Herefordshire School sculpted panels at Stockton and Eastham churches. Nearby is a medieval piscina, and a carved head possibly of a priest. The north arcade dates from the time of Rickman's aisle of 1826. Victorian fittings include a round stone pulpit by Street, an ironwork screen, and glass of 1876 in the south aisle designed by Henry Holliday and made by Powell & Co. The south aisle east window was completed by Powell in 1908, whilst the main east window glass by William Wailes of 1857 was replaced by Charles Eamer Kempe's glass in 1901 and shows scenes from the Life of Christ.

The earliest monument is a 13th-century coffin lid from the nave reset into the north aisle in a recess which also contains some medieval work. The lid is carved with a foliated cross which is piercing the head of a dragon. The Lyttleton monuments were moved from the chancel to the base of the tower during the rebuilding. Lucy Fortescue, wife of Sir George, subsequently first Lord Lyttleton, died in 1747 aged 29 and a monument, inscribed 'Luciae', with an urn and a seated cherub was designed by Sir Charles Frederick and carved by Louis Francis Roubiliac. Her husband was Lord of the Treasury between 1744 and 1754, and served briefly as Chancellor of the Exchequer in 1755 under William Pitt. He had the Hall built between 1754 and 1760, and laid out the park, extensively using the services of Sanderson Miller who had recently produced the similar fashionable house and park at Croome. The memorial was erected by his son, the second Lord Lyttleton, in 1808, to a design by Sir John Soane who also designed the British Museum.

HAGLEY   ST. SAVIOUR

The large village of Hagley developed with the arrival of the railway in the 19th century, and consists mostly of Victorian, Edwardian and later 20th-century housing. The area known as West Hagley was provided in 1882 with a mission church that was replaced by a large Perpendicular style church with a high aisled nave and chancel in 1908. The grey stone building is built very much in the tradition of the Arts and Crafts movement. A proposed north aisle was never built, but today there is a large church room on the north side. Inside, the wide interior has many 20th-century fittings, including a reredos decorated by Elsie Matley Moore of the Greyfriars in Worcester. The heavy square capitals of the unused and blocked north arcade remain uncarved.

HALLOW   ST. PHILIP AND ST. JAMES

Hallow is a large village north of Worcester and on the west bank of the River Severn. The settlement developed around the site of the medieval church, the deserted graveyard of which is to the east of the Green. There is an attractive mixture of houses and cottages around the Green, though the large amount of 19th- and 20th-century building is due to proximity to Worcester.

South of the village centre is Hallow Park. The present Edwardian house is on the site of the manor house held by the Habington family during the 16th century, made famous when Queen Elizabeth I hunted in the park whilst visiting Worcester in 1575.

The medieval church was rebuilt in the 1830s, but this church was also demolished after the construction of the present church in 1867, which stands by the Worcester to Tenbury road in a corner of the park. It is a sandstone building with a commanding west tower rebuilt in 1879 and spire added in 1900, which can be seen from some distance. There is an aisled nave with a porch, and a chancel and vestry to the east. The church was built by William Jeffrey Hopkins in the early Decorated style, and the aisles have flying buttresses built in the roofs beneath the unusual rounded nave clerestorey windows with tracery, which is reminiscent of his tracery in the east window of Old St. Martin's church in Worcester. All the other windows and doorways are in the style of about 1300.

The sandstone interior soars into the interesting roof structure. The arches carrying the weight of the roof are carved with Decorated style corbels. The tall chancel arch rises to tracery features with cusps, which is then copied into the adjacent roof trusses. The arcades of four bays with pointed arches have simple carved capitals.

There is a wealth of Victorian fittings. The unusual font was carved by William Forsyth in about 1870, and is decorated with two small figure reliefs and strips of tiles. The reredos is particularly striking, and is by Richard Boulton of Cheltenham. With the loss of the reredos in Holy Trinity church, Worcester, this is an important local example of his work. Beneath a vaulted canopy, which is decorated with coloured stones, is a carved crucifixion scene, whilst seven angels support tall candlesticks above. There is glass of 1935 designed by Archibald Davies of the Bromsgrove Guild, showing Christ with his disciples.

Memorials transferred from the old church include that of Edward Hall, of Eastbury Manor in the parish, who died in 1616 and is shown kneeling in contemporary costume. A tablet to John Pardoe, who died in 1680, has carved fruit, flowers and a cherub's head. A plain tablet with an urn and coat of arms by William Stephens of Worcester commemorates Richard Harrison who died in 1795. In the north aisle is a memorial to the Scottish surgeon, Sir Charles Bell, who died of a heart attack whilst visiting Hallow in 1842, and is buried in the old churchyard. Bell made pioneering studies of the brain and nervous system and gave his name to the type of facial paralysis known as Bell's Palsy.

The clock and bells in the tower along with the spire were the gift in 1900 of the Wheeley Lea family of Parkside in the parish, who were great local benefactors, using their great wealth and fame from Lea and Perrins Worcestershire Sauce.

HAMPTON LOVETT   ST. MARY

The Droitwich to Kidderminster railway line passes by the east side of the churchyard, but the church is concealed from the main road that runs through the parish, and is at the end of a narrow lane. The setting is remarkably rural considering the church is so close to the industrial estates on the north side of Droitwich. The medieval manor house held by the Lovetts and the Blounts lay east of the church; it passed to the Pakington family who then built a hunting lodge some two miles to the south-west at Westwood Park, on the site of a nunnery which they had acquired at the Dissolution. When Hampton Lovett Manor was destroyed during the Civil War, the Pakingtons rebuilt Westwood on a grand scale. Westwood was divided into flats in 1949, but the Pakington association with Hampton Lovett has continued through the monuments in the church.

The red sandstone church has an unusual plan. The nave and chancel have a large chapel on the north side with a vestry, and to the south of the nave is a tower porch, similar to that at Areley Kings church. The nave is basically Norman. The west wall includes the remains of a flat buttress and the north wall has two further buttresses. The north doorway is also Norman with a round arch of roll moulding and a plain shaft to each jamb. The windows in the nave are all Decorated and there is a sanctus bellcote on the east gable. The tower is also Decorated and has a typical doorway and bell openings. On the top are battlements surrounding a small saddleback roof, which was once open at the gables and contained a bell. The chancel also includes a Norman buttress on the south wall, but the windows are Perpendicular. The fine Perpendicular north chapel was originally added for Lady Alice Stury of the Blount family in 1414, but was rebuilt for the recusant Roman Catholic Pakington family in about 1560. The chapel east window is large and square. To the north is a 19th-century vestry.

The interior has been scraped back to the sandstone and contains mainly 19th-century fittings. There are some medieval traceried panels reused on some of the benches, which are from previous benches or a screen. 19th-century screens divide the chapel from the body of the church, and there is a 19th-century carved white Italian Pièta. A north window contains some heraldic glass of 1561 showing the arms of the Pakingtons and associated families. The chancel east window has glass by John Hardman of 1859, and the north chapel east window is of 1882. Other north chapel windows have glass by the Camm family of the Bromsgrove Guild, showing Courage and Diligence with Saints' figures and sporting motifs, which were installed as memorials to Sir Edward and Sir Oswald Partington, the first and second Lords Doverdale.

The monuments are mainly in the north chapel. A much altered Perpendicular tomb chest commemorates Sir John Pakington, who died in 1551, and his wife Anne Dacres. Much restored in 1858 to 1859, the monument is in a recess with carved panelling to the wall and a depressed arch with cresting above. Another Sir John Pakington who died in 1727, is shown as a semi-reclining effigy, in period costume, and wearing a wig. The memorial has a reredos behind, is by Joseph Rose senior, and was originally built on top of the 1551 tomb.

A brass by Hardman showing a woman kneeling by a cross commemorates Lady Diana Pakington who died in 1878. In the nave there is a tablet with an inscription in both Latin and Greek to Dean Henry Hammond, and signed by Joshua Marshall. Hammond was chaplain to King Charles I and found refuge at Westwood after the king's execution. He died in 1660 after writing several Biblical tracts.

It is interesting that William Thomas, rector in the mid-17th century, became Dean and then Bishop of Worcester, and entertained the Roman Catholic King James II at his palace. However, Thomas refused to distribute the Declaration of Indulgence which was issued by James II to all clergy. Thomas subsequently refused to be bound by the Oath of Allegiance to King William III and Queen Mary, but died in 1689 before he could be deprived of his see. Outside the church, traces of a mass dial are apparent on the nave wall, and the cross in the churchyard is a memorial of 1841 to Lady Pakington.

HANBURY   ST. MARY

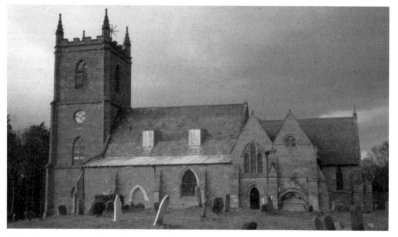

Hanbury—medieval nave, Georgian tower and Victorian east end

The isolated hilltop setting of this church allows fine panoramic views over south Worcestershire to be enjoyed from the churchyard. Indeed, the site was originally an Iron Age hillfort, and in the Saxon period Hanbury's importance as a local centre is reflected in the Minster status of its church. During the Middle Ages lands in Hanbury were held by the bishops of Worcester, but in the 16th century the manor passed to the Leighton family, who sold it to the rector's son, Edward Vernon in 1631. His grandson Thomas, a London barrister, completed the present Hall in 1701. This beautiful red brick William and Mary house stands in parkland about one mile to the south-west, and the Vernon family, who lived here until 1962, contributed much to the present appearance of the church.

The red sandstone church comprises a west tower, aisled nave, and chancel with a south chapel and north vestry. The nave and aisles are medieval, but the tracery was removed from the windows and the south doorway blocked during the 18th century. The roofline of the medieval south porch can be seen above the doorway. The west tower was added in the Gothic style in 1793. Many of the details are reminiscent of Croome D'Abitot church; the west doorway has an ogee arch, whilst the west windows and bell openings have Y-shaped tracery and the top is crowned with battlements and pinnacles. By contrast, the circular side windows are typical classical features of the 18th century. The chancel, chapel and vestry were designed by George Street in 1860-61, and have lancet windows and other features of Early English style.

Entry to the church is via the base of the tower, where there is a dole cupboard built to take loaves for the poor supplied by the Sir John Hanbury charity. The interior of the nave and aisles is an excellent example of the adaptation of a medieval church for 18th-century prayer book worship, and box pews engulf the arcades. The south arcade is 13th-century, with round piers and pointed arches, and even one scalloped trumpet capital. The north arcade is Perpendicular. With the exception of the pews for the Vernons' servants and the Bearcroft family pew, the box pews of 1795 were reduced in height during the 19th century. Of similar date are the west gallery and baroque chandelier. The panelling in the north aisle includes some 17th-century woodwork. The Georgian style Royal Arms of Elizabeth II were added to the Gallery in 1953 by Celestino Pancheri of the Bromsgrove Guild.

The chancel and south chapel are a contrast to the nave in Victorian High Church Gothic. The ceiling decoration is Street's and there is a large ornamental case to the Nicholson organ. The 19th-century reredos of the Last Supper is alabaster. Other furnishings include a 17th-century communion table from St. Helen's church, Worcester, and a 16th-century German relief showing the Adoration of the Magi, which was formerly in Hanbury Hall. In the north aisle hang the artist's models for the Nativity and Resurrection panels on the reredos of Liverpool Cathedral by Walter Gilbert and Louis Weingartner also of the Bromsgrove Guild. The font is of 1860 by Street.

The nave windows are filled with leaded panes of clear glass, but there is a variety of 19th- and 20th-century stained glass in the chancel and chapel, including windows showing St. George, St. Hubert and St. Martin, as well as a Crucifixion scene of 1920 showing Sir Harry Foley Vernon as a soldier, and his wife, Lady Georgina, as a nurse.

The monuments to the Vernon family are in the chancel and south chapel. The earliest is to Richard Vernon, the rector, who died in 1627, and his wife Frances Wylde. They are shown kneeling to face east in a memorial on the wall with pilasters and a straight top. Thomas Vernon, the builder of the Hall, who died in 1722, is shown as a semi-reclining figure in Georgian costume on a large standing monument of white and grey marble. To the sides are seated the figures of Justice and Learning, and at the back are two Corinthian columns either side of an inscription embellished with carved drapes. His cousin, Bowater Vernon, who inherited Hanbury but squandered much of his wealth, died in 1735, and is commemorated by his statue, shown leaning on a pedestal holding a book. He wears Georgian costume below the waist, but is Classical above. A medallion portrait of his wife, Jane Cornwallis, is held by a cherub in front. The monument is often attributed to Louis Roubilliac, but was probably designed by Henry Cheere. Bowater Vernon's son, Thomas, died in 1771 and has a memorial with a female figure and an urn. The memorial to Thomas Taylor Vernon, who died in 1837, is by Francis Chantrey, and shows the profile of a kneeling woman with two weeping children. There are many other tablets to members of the Vernon family, as well as some to the Bearcroft family of Mere Hall. On the south arcade at odd angles are two beautiful 18th-century tablets to John Watkins and Thomas Chetle.

Outside, on the south wall of the chapel is a medieval style recess and memorial to Thomas Bowater Vernon who died in 1859 aged 27, just before the chancel and chapel were built. There is also a mass dial scratched on to the south-west buttress of the nave. The Gothic style railings and gates at the entrance to the churchyard are 18th-century.

HANLEY CASTLE   ST. MARY

Hanley Castle church showing the brick east end of 1674

Hanley Castle lies one mile to the north-west of Upton. The pleasant frontages to the main road give little indication that this was a medieval place of some importance in Malvern Chase. The castle, from which the village takes its name and now just earthworks to the south of the church, was built in the 13th century and held by the powerful Despencer and Beauchamp families during the Middle Ages. Hanley was also the centre of a thriving medieval pottery industry and had a flourishing quay on the River Severn. Indeed, the large medieval parish included Hanley Swan and Malvern Wells.

The village centre at Church End is dominated by the buildings of the school, which is the successor of the grammar school that can trace its origins to the late 15th century. The mixture of 17th-century timber-framing and later brick in the group of buildings next to the church gives the village centre an unusual atmosphere. The main entrance to the churchyard is from the Green with its cottages and inn, and the substantial church is otherwise surrounded by trees which make it less visible from the surrounding roads.

The church has a large north chapel and aisle with porch, behind which are the nave, central tower and chancel. The western part of the building is of sandstone and lias, but the tower, chancel and north chapel are built of brick with sandstone dressings. The earliest surviving part of the church is the twelfth century nave masonry, of which the only obvious Norman feature is the south doorway. The north aisle and most of the nave windows are 14th-century. The brick tower is massive with battlements, stair turret and a low pyramid roof and dates from the rebuilding of the east end of the church in 1674, as a result of the fall of the previous tower and damage during the Civil War. The date is recorded on a plaque above the north chapel doorway. The windows on the south side of the tower and chancel, along with the east window are Decorated style replacements installed during the restoration of 1858 by George Street. Original windows survive in the north chapel and as bell openings on the tower. These windows are rectangular with mullions and transoms, which look like the windows on contemporary domestic buildings. Only the cusps below the transom bars, and the tracery lights of the north chapel east window give the windows an ecclesiastical feeling. The north chapel doorway and entrance to the tower stair turret are square headed. The timber porches were added to the church in the 19th century.

The first impression of the interior is one of darkness, as a result of many of the windows containing deep coloured 19th-century glass. An impression of the light plain interior of the 17th century remains in the north chapel, where there are white painted walls and clear leaded glass panes in the windows. The north nave arcade is Decorated with chamfered arches on round and octagonal piers, and the tower arches appear also to be of this period and retained from the previous structure. The main timbers of the nave and aisle roofs are medieval. The furnishings date mainly from the 1858 restoration, but the octagonal font is 15th-century, and the Communion rail in the north chapel is 18th-century, with alternating twisted and plain round balusters. The glass in the west window showing the Last Judgement is by Clayton and Bell of 1860, and the east window was replaced in 1878.

The Lechmere family of Severn End undertook the restoration in 1858, at which time Anthony Berwick Lechmere was vicar. His alabaster tablet in the nave is rendered in sgraffito to show him kneeling before Christ. In the north or Lechmere chapel there are several other monuments to the family, including an undated but 17th-century kneeling figure of Winifred Lechmere, the memorial to Nicholas Lechmere, lawyer and MP, who died in 1727, and a tablet to his brother, Edmund, killed in the War of the Spanish Succession. The Lechmeres were a recusant Roman Catholic family into the 17th century, and became patrons of the church in 1674 when the east end was rebuilt. They succeeded another recusant family, the Hornyolds of Hanley Swan.

Outside in the churchyard is the grave of Thomas Attwood, a supporter of the Reform Act of 1832, who later went on to become a member of the Chartist movement. The war memorial incorporates the shaft of a medieval cross from the north end of the village. On the south-west corner of the church is scratched a medieval Mass dial. The almshouses at the entrance to the churchyard are recorded on the 18th-century charities board in the church. An interesting footnote is the existence of part of a Saxon tombstone, probably from Hanley Castle, and now incorporated into the house called Severn End. It shows a semi-circular head and is carved with a cross on one side and a figure of Christ on the other. Debate continues over the date, put at between the 9th and the 11th centuries, but it may well be the earliest evidence for a church here.

HANLEY CHILD   ST. MICHAEL

The village consists of a scattering of houses around a group of lanes forming a cul-de-sac high above the Teme Valley. The approach to the church is by way of a grass track with views west into Herefordshire and Shropshire.

The church is on a medieval site. It was rebuilt in red sandstone in 1807 in the Commissioners style with a nave and chancel with a west porch and bellcote. This porch is the base of the former slender tower which collapsed in 1864. The church is very plain and simple with Early English style lancet windows. The east window is a little more grand with Y-shaped tracery.

The interior is a primitive version of the large Commissioners churches—light with clear glass and walls painted white and blue. Most of the early 19th-century fittings survive including the communion rail.

HANLEY SWAN   ST. GABRIEL

Hanley Swan lies towards the western end of the parish of Hanley Castle. By the mid-19th century a considerable community had grown up around the Swan Inn and Swan Green. It is close to Blackmore Park, the seat of the Hornyold family who remained Catholic after the Reformation, and who built themselves a Roman Catholic church at the edge of the village. Today the village is a mixture of timber-framed cottages, early 19th-century villas and 20th-century housing around the attractive green and pond.

St. Gabriel's church was built on a site given by the Lechmere family to the west of the green, and was paid for by Samuel Martin, a retired merchant from Liverpool. It opened in 1873, though for the previous 12 years services had been held in the school. It is a large building of Malvern stone, with an aisled nave and porch, chancel and north-east tower with a commanding broach spire. The architect was Sir George Gilbert Scott, who used the later Early English style in the windows, doorways and arches. The nave has circular clerestorey windows, whilst other windows have plate tracery and the east window consists of five stepped lancets.

The interior is spacious but plain, and has many fittings of the late 19th-century. The reredos was given by Sir Edmund Lechmere, and made by Powell & Co. to designs by Clayton and Bell. There is attractive tilework to either side.

HANLEY WILLIAM   ALL SAINTS

To the north-east of Hanley Child, and the larger settlement of Hanley Broadheath, lies Hanley William. The name William refers to a William de la Mare who held Hanley around 1200. The church, together with a few farms and cottages, lies along a narrow lane near to the 18th-century Hanley Court.

All Saints church is one of a group of small, but largely unaltered Norman churches to survive in the Teme Valley. It consists of a sandstone nave and chancel with a timber porch. On the west gable is a small timber bell turret with a short shingled spire. The Norman nave was lengthened to the west in the 13th century, when the original south doorway was blocked up and replaced by the present more westerly entrance. One Norman single light window remains in the north wall of the chancel, and there are some Early English lancets, but some of the windows were replaced in the 19th century. Over the south door is a carved Norman stone panel showing the Agnus Dei of the Herefordshire School type, similar to examples at Eastham and Stockton-on-Teme.

Despite the addition at the west end, the interior gives a good sense of the scale and simplicity of many small Worcestershire churches in Norman times. This feeling is enhanced by the survival of the plain, small round-headed chancel arch with uncarved capitals, which is very similar in style to many 10th- and 11th-century arches. There are plain whitewashed walls and many 19th- and 20th century fittings. The plain font is 12th century. The lectern contains some 17th-century woodwork possibly reused from a pulpit, and the present pulpit is an unusual three-sided screen with imitation Elizabethan ornament. The glass in the east window is possibly by John Hardman. A small collection of memorial tablets includes one by Joseph Stephens of Worcester, showing a sarcophagus, to James Charlett who died in 1838. In the bell turret hangs a medieval bell, inscribed with a dedication to St. Catherine.

HARPLEY   ST. BARTHOLOMEW

Over one mile west from the old church at Lower Sapey, Harpley church stands in a churchyard with a group of large conifers on a hill. The site was given by the Bickerton Evans family as more convenent than the old church. It was designed by a Herefordshire architect, Frederick Kempson, in 1877 and has a nave and chancel, with south porch and a twin bellcote on a flat projection at the west end. The lancet windows of the nave and chancel are Early English in style. To give a sense of age through irregularity, they are differently spaced on the north and south walls. The chancel windows are grouped under hood moulds to make the east end more elaborate.

The interior is typical of the period, with mainly 19th-century fittings. The font from the old church is plain, but probably Norman. There is an 18th-century communion table.

HARTLEBURY   ST. JAMES

This straggling village to the south of Kidderminster grew up in the centre of a large parish, which formerly included parts of Stourport and Wilden. The approach to the village from the west is across the sandy expanse of Hartlebury Common and past Hartlebury Castle, a residence of the bishop of Worcester. The bishops held land in Hartlebury from the 9th century, but Bishop Giffard fortified a house here in the 13th. Their other main residences were at Alvechurch, which was demolished in the 17th century, and the Palace in Worcester which remained the principal residence until Bishop Hough remodelled Hartlebury between 1717 and 1743. Subsequent bishops in the late 18th century made further improvements to make the Castle the impressive house it is today. The centre of the village clusters around the church on the eastern side of the Castle grounds, and to the east on the hill is the substantial mainly 20th-century development around Waresley Hall and Hartlebury station.

The church stands on a rise in a large graveyard and is of deep red sandstone. The west front is dominated by the west tower and porch, to the side of which are doorways into the aisles, which are under a single roof with the nave. At the east end is the lower chancel with north and south chapels. The main feature of the church is the large aisled nave designed by Thomas Rickman in 1836-7, which replaced the medieval structure. On the north and south sides are huge three light windows with Decorated style tracery. Battlements above conceal a low pitched roof, and there were pinnacles on the corners until the end of the 19th century. At the west end the doorways are in pairs with rose windows above in the style of the entrances to Early English chapter houses in several cathedrals. Rickman favoured this design which he also used at the west end of the nave at Hampton Lucy church in Warwickshire. Above the doorways are further circular windows with elaborate Decorated style tracery. At the east end three rose windows are in the wall above the earlier chancel and chapels. The south chapel and chancel have been much altered by Rickman, this time in 1825, but the walls of the north chapel are medieval. This was built as a chantry for John de Rodborough, rector, in 1325, and has a Perpendicular east window. The tower was rebuilt in 1587 by Bishop Edwin Sandys in the Perpendicular style, to which Rickman added the west

porch with a long Perpendicular style window, making this the main entrance and replacing the former north doorway to the nave. The arms on the west side of the porch are those of Dean John Peel from Waresley, who gave the money for it. Further pinnacles on the tower and porch have been subsequently removed.

The large impressive interior is whitewashed, though there was once 19th-century stencilling in the chancel. The medieval work in the chancel and north chapel contrasts with Rickman's adventurous structure of the nave and aisles. These are of the same height, forming a hall church with vaulted plaster ceilings, divided by a thin Perpendicular style arcade with iron piers. The height is accentuated by the galleries behind the piers in the aisles with their Gothic details and supported by their own iron piers. A further gallery at the west end was removed in 1908. The medieval north wall of the chancel contains an early Decorated two bay arcade with a quatrefoil pier, which is echoed by Rickman's arcade into the south chapel.

There are numerous 19th- and 20th-century fittings. Many of those in the chancel and the nave pews were installed by Bishop Henry Philpott between 1877 and 1880. The bench ends have the names and arms of the Bishop of Worcester added by Bromsgrove Guild craftsmen, and the small bishop's throne in the chancel of

Rickman's huge three light windows in the nave of Hartlebury church

113

1925, also by the Guild, replaced a much larger one formerly in the nave, parts of which are now in the vestry. There is some 17th-century panelling in the south chapel, and the lower part of the font is 12th-century with carved lozenges, although the upper part is a copy of a Norman bowl. The glass in the east window was installed by Burlison and Grylls in 1882 and depicts scenes from the Life of Christ. The south chapel east window has glass by Clayton and Bell showing the Resurrection.

There are numerous memorial tablets in the church, including several in the chancel that commemorate bishops of Worcester. Four bishops—Richard Hurd, Robert Carr, Henry Pepys and John Perowne—are buried in the churchyard. A further memorial commemorates William Robert Skinner, the son of Bishop Skinner, who died in 1695.

The base of the churchyard cross is medieval and has carved quatrefoils on the sides and single spurs to the corners, very similar to the base of the cross at Ombersley church. To the north of the church is the large Georgian former rectory, built for James Stillingfleet, an 18th-century rector, son of Bishop Stillingfeet. The parish church has had close links with the bishops throughout its history.

HARVINGTON   ST. JAMES

Harvington is a Vale of Evesham village close to the Warwickshire border. The main street has many timber-framed cottages, and benefits from being bypassed by the A46. The church is at the centre, on a low hill.

The green copper spire is very conspicuous and was added to the west tower by Frederick Preedy when he restored the church in 1854-55. The church is of lias with limestone dressings, and otherwise consists of a nave with porch and chancel. A vestry was added in 1853 by Preedy and a second one built in 1961 on to the nave. The tower is Norman with lancet windows and double splays of round-headed lancets for bell openings. The gargoyles on the corners are 15th-century. The nave was rebuilt in the late 13th century and has windows with cusped Y-shaped tracery of about 1300. The chancel has unusual 14th-century lancets with straight tops above ogee curves, but the east window was replaced by Preedy, and the former window erected as a feature in the garden of the rectory.

The interior has scraped stone walls with 19th-century roofs. The arch to the tower looks 13th-century and is pointed with chamfering to the arch. It is perhaps a remodelling of the Norman arch undertaken when the nave was rebuilt. A medieval piscina in the nave south wall marks the site of a chantry chapel, and the wide chancel arch leads to the east end where there is a 14th-century piscina with a shelf, decorated with ballflower under the projecting drain. There is also a plain circular Norman font. The glass in the east window showing the Resurrection was installed in 1855 by Preedy. Other glass, and indeed fittings, are of 19th- and 20th-century date.

The memorial tablets include a pair to a father and son, both called Thomas Feriman. Both were rectors, the father from 1569-1618 and the son from 1618-22, and Thomas the elder was also an historian. The tablets are ornamented with strapwork.

HEIGHTINGTON   ST. GILES

High above the road from Stourport to Great Witley, Heightington is a collection of houses and farms on the edge of Wyre Forest. It is in the parish of Rock, and the first record of a chapel seems to occur in 1325. However, the structure of St. Giles' chapel indicates earlier origins, and consists of a nave and chancel built of local stone and under one roof, with a bell turret at the west end. There is one Norman lancet window, but the other windows date from the 14th to 16th centuries, with an occasional later domestic style window as well.

The simple interior is mainly whitewashed, though traces of medieval wallpainting have been uncovered, including part of a figure and a foliage border at the east end. The medieval roof is low and supported by heavy tie beams. The mainly 20th-century furnishings incorporate the medieval stone altar which was rediscovered and placed under the present altar in 1933. At the west end is a singing gallery installed in the 18th century. In 1890 Italian glass showing the Assumption was inserted in the east window. It was covered up by a rector with Protestant leanings, but was reopened in the 1960s by Bishop Charles-Edwards.

HILL CROOME   ST. MARY

Although less than a mile from the M5 and the M50, Hill Croome remains remarkably tucked away. Baughton, one mile to the north, is the parish's centre of population. The church stands on a west-facing hillside, and at the bottom of the churchyard stands a timber-framed farmhouse, Glebe Farm, which originated as the parsonage. Adjacent to the house is a 14th-century timber-framed dovecote, of cruck construction, a reminder that doves and pigeons were an important food

Hill Croome church

source in medieval England. The church is very much the English country church, and was depicted as such in an oil painting by the Victorian artist Benjamin Williams Leader.

The medieval lias stone exterior has been much restored during the 20th century, whilst the hillside setting has led to heavy buttressing. At the west end is a short narrow west tower with a saddleback roof. The nave and chancel are under one roof, and there is a 20th-century timber south porch. The tower lancet and the east window are Early English, and there are mullioned 17th-century style windows in the nave.

The interior has an atmosphere of rural simplicity, which has been maintained by sympathetic restoration. Many of the roof timbers are medieval, and the floor is made up of quarry tiles. The east end is dominated by the massive 14th-century piscina, set at an oblique angle with a crocketed limestone canopy. It appears to be reset, perhaps from a monastery, like the window and canopies in Castlemorton Church, but its position has given rise to discussion as to whether the east end was once apsidal, or whether the chancel has been widened at some stage. There are some 16th-century benches, a 17th-century communion rail, pulpit with tester, and a 17th-century font cover now under the tower. The plain font is Norman, but with a 20th-century cover. In the tower is a 14th-century bell, inscribed 'Ave Maria'.

HIMBLETON   ST. MARY MAGDALENE

Estates at Himbleton were held by Worcester Cathedral Priory throughout the Middle Ages, and a church has existed here since at least the Norman period. It stands at the end of a long lane of timber-framed cottages and farms on the north end of the village, though the most attractive approach is by footpath from the lane to Bradley, across a meadow and Bow Brook. The lias and sandstone church is an unusual shape with a nave, north aisle, south transept, chancel and a large north vestry connected to the aisle by a short passage. The south porch is of timber and at the west end of the nave there is a large timber bell turret with a hipped roof.

The nave is partly Norman, and the small round arched south doorway has one waterleaf capital indicating a late 12th century date. The chancel is 13th-century with an Early English triple lancet east window. The south transept is 14th-century with a typical Decorated south window, but the transept east window is 16th-century. This transept is the Shell Chapel, probably founded as a chantry chapel in the 14th century, but then used by the inhabitants of the hamlet of Shell in the north of the parish, after the separate chapel there passed out of use in the mid-15th century. Many of the remaining windows appear to be late Perpendicular with mullions and rounded arches, though the square windows at the west end of the nave and one on the north side of the chancel are probably of about 1600. The south porch is 14th-century, and has bargeboards decorated with quatrefoils. The 15th-century bell turret was part faced with shingles and part with half-timbering when the western part of the nave was extensively rebuilt in 1893. This was part of a restoration by Ewan Christian, who also restored the church at Norton-by-Kempsey. The building work was done by Thomas Collins of Tewkesbury, whose work in Worcestershire includes additions to St. Matthias church, Malvern. Christian's work was generally sensitive and several internal features were conserved. In 1903 the vestry was added by Charles Ford Whitcombe in an Arts and Crafts style, reflected also in his construction of Broadheath church and the restoration at nearby Huddington church.

The Norman doorway has a 14th-century door with panelled quatrefoils, which gives access to the interior with its medieval roofs and plain plastered walls. The north arcade is late Perpendicular with octagonal piers. There is no chancel arch, and the 13th-century chancel is a straightforward extension of the Norman nave. It was formerly divided by a rood screen and loft, and the blocked rood loft stair doorway can be seen in the north wall of the chancel. The nave and chancel have Perpendicular wagon roofs, with wallplates, which, in the chancel, are carved with battlements, in the nave with foliage and heads. The main font is 12th-century and square, with a carved medallion showing a lamb and cross, not unlike the panels on the churches at Eastham and Stockton-on-Teme. A second 18th-century font is in the Shell Chapel, where there is also the remains of a medieval piscina. Most of the fittings date from the 1893 restoration, though the organ of 1910 is by Nicholson, and the communion rail of 1967 by Robert Pancheri of Bromsgrove.

There are traces of wall painting in the Shell Chapel, but most significant are the substantial remains of the royal arms on the east wall of the chancel, possibly those of Elizabeth I. There is a remarkable survival of medieval glass. The top right corner of the east window contains a 13th-century figure of a female saint, thought to be St. Mary Magdalene, and some quarries painted with leaves. These corroded fragments are possibly the earliest glass in the county, and are now set in a beautiful window, glazed in the late 13th-century style by George Ostrehan in 1904. In the previous year Ostrehan had also restored the glass in the east window of the Shell Chapel, which has 15th-century fragments showing the Crucifixion,

*The glass in the east window
at Himbleton*

116

the Virgin and St. John, with donor figures below, who are named in an inscription as Henry and Agnes Goddi. They are otherwise unknown. In a north chancel window are more 15th-century fragments, which include parts of figures of St. Anne and possibly St. Christopher. The initials TH probably refer to the benefactor, Thomas Hartlebury. One of the north aisle windows also contains glass of this date. A figure of St. John, now without a head, holds a chalice, and there are parts of St. George and the dragon, St. Catherine, and the arms of the Cokesey and Wintour families. At the east of the north aisle the window contains glass by Charles Eamer Kempe of about 1900 showing the Nativity, and the figures of the two St. Johns on the south side of the chancel are of about 1910 by Christopher Webb.

There are several memorial tablets, particularly those in the Shell Chapel to the Fincher family of Shell. The memorial to Philip Fincher, who died in 1755 is by John Laughton of Cleeve Prior. There is an unusual cast iron memorial on the floor to another Philip Fincher, who died in 1660, and his wife Joan.

Outside in the churchyard, a large cross marks the grave of Sir Douglas Galton who died in 1899. He was an engineer and keen promoter of public health, who worked towards the establishment of the Red Cross after visiting casualties of the Franco-Prussian War. There is a large sundial on the south wall of the nave, whilst the Lychgate was built in 1931 as a copy of the timber south porch.

HINDLIP   ST. JAMES

This sandstone church now stands amongst the building complex of the headquarters of the West Mercia Constabulary, who took over Hindlip Hall in 1946. The Hall was rebuilt in the 19th century by the Allsop family, who were brewery magnates, to replace the great 17th-century home of the Habingtons. This family were recusant Roman Catholics, and numerous priests' hiding places were intricately worked into the structure. Most famous was Thomas Habington who, after being presumed guilty of conspiracy in the Gunpowder Plot in 1606, was banished to Worcestershire for the rest of his life. Over the following 40 years he wrote the first detailed history and description of the county. The Habingtons had succeeded the Solley family, whose 15th-century manor house now forms the timber-framed cottages to the west of the church.

Hindlip, which includes part of Fernhill Heath, is very much an estate parish, but without a village centre.

Saxon and Norman churches on this site were chapels to St. Helen's church in Worcester. Of the medieval church only some masonry in the north wall of the nave and the Perpendicular west tower survive. The tower is simple with a Perpendicular west window restored in 1864, and 17th-century bell openings below battlements. In 1864 the new nave and chancel with a south transept were built to designs by William Jeffrey Hopkins for Henry Allsop, the first Lord Hindlip. The transept was replaced in 1888 by the second Lord Hindlip, who added the Lady Chapel and south aisle, enlarged the chancel, and built a vestry. The church was reroofed and pinnacles, now lost, were added to the tower. The second Lord Hindlip refitted the interior in a lavish High Church style, reflected also in his work on the chapel at his Worcester home, Mount Battenhall, and his benefactions to the Jesus Chapel in Worcester Cathedral. There is a marble mosaic floor, and much heavily carved woodwork designed by Lewis Sheppard, including the sedilia, organ case, Lady Chapel screen with saints, and stalls with Old Testament figures. The reredos with the Last Supper and pulpit with saints were carved in Caen stone by Roddis of Birmingham in 1877. The 19th-century metalwork is also of note, especially the chancel screen. Medieval tiles survive and are preserved under the tower, showing arms of the abbeys at Westminster, Gloucester and Bristol. The tower also contains a 16th-century bell.

A wooden memorial to the Habingtons has also been retained and is painted with the arms of the Habington family and successive owners of Hindlip Hall. Several members of the Allsop family are buried in the churchyard, but are commemorated in the window glass which is mainly by Hardman & Co.

The east window of 1877 has scenes from the Life of Christ, with the emblems of the Passion in the tracery. The windows to either side of the altar depict the first and last verses of the hymn 'Lead Kindly Light'. The nave windows of 1878 show Christ as Lord of the Sea, whilst the west window of 1887 shows the Life of St. James the Great, with Christ's transfiguration in the tracery. The south aisle windows of 1888 show Naaman with Elisha, the healing of Hezekiah along with Christ and the centurion, female figures from the New Testament, including the appearance of Christ to Mary Magdalene, and a window of 1878 showing Christ as Lord of the Earth. The west window of the aisle depicts the first council at Jerusalem, the founding of a new school of the prophets and St. Paul's departure from Tyre to found a mission, and commemorates the fourth Lord Lyttleton.

HINTON-ON-THE-GREEN   ST. PETER

Hinton is a small village on a loop road in the Vale of Evesham to the east of Bredon Hill. In the 19th century the village expanded around the railway station as a centre of asparagus growing. The church is situated next to the remains of the manor house on a hill at the east end of the village. The lias manor house was damaged in the Civil War and is now a farm, but is approached through an unusual 17th-century stone gatehouse, consisting of two dovecotes linked by a pair of round arches.

St. Peter's church is approached from the village street along an avenue lined with lime trees. It has a nave and chancel with a west tower and porch, and is built of lias and limestone. The nave is basically Norman, with the north and south doorways having single shafts and capitals decorated with scallops, similar to the south doorway at Beckford church. The arches have roll moulds, and the north doorway has a tympanum with a carved trellis design. The nave has Perpendicular style windows, inserted by Frederick Preedy in 1863, but the battlements and gargoyles are 15th-century. The tower, also with battlements and pinnacles, is Perpendicular. Preedy had adapted the east end of the nave as a chancel, but in 1895 a new chancel was built in the Arts and Crafts Perpendicular style by John Dando Sedding, the only work by this architect in Worcestershire. The south porch is also 19th-century.

The interior is very much the product of these 19th-century alterations, although, the tower arch is clearly Perpendicular. The nave roof and many of the fittings are Preedy's work, but the octagonal font is 15th-century and the medieval rood loft stair and a trefoil piscina also survive. The glass of the east window depicts Christ enthroned and surrounded by saints. There is an incised alabaster slab to William Holford, Abbot of Bordesley Abbey in Redditch from 1452. His tonsured head lies on a cushion below an elaborate canopy and is surrounded by the symbols of the evangelists. He is shown in a monk's habit with a cowl behind. Holford died whilst visiting Hinton in 1490 and was buried there. The stone is well preserved as it was used as an altar before the present chancel was built.

HOLLYBUSH   ALL SAINTS

Hollybush has grown up where the road from Tewkesbury to Ledbury cuts through the Malverns by Midsummer Hill. The church is situated on the common to the east of the steep slope, and was consecrated as a chapel of ease to Castlemorton in 1869. Many of the funds were raised by a local benefactor, Mary Selwyn, who built the church for workers at nearby Hollybush Quarry. By 1911, when the church gained parish status, it had acquired a squatters title to the site on the common.

The church is built from local Malvern stone with limestone dressings. It has a nave and chancel under one roof with a bellcote at the west end. A vestry and south porch are attached. The architect was

Frederick Preedy, who used the late Early English style. The windows are a mixture of lancets and plate tracery, particularly in the east window whilst there is a rose window at the west end. The church was extended a little at the east end in 1929.

The whitewashed interior is a good example of Preedy's interpretation of the early 14th century, with Decorated style roof trusses. The fittings are mainly his work, of which the font, pulpit and communion rail are typical Gothic revival. The reredos and credence table are carved alabaster, with three panels containing angels and a cross. The east window glass designed by Preedy showing the Resurrection and Ascension was given by Mary Selwyn, and her aunt, Countess Beauchamp, in 1869, in memory of her parents.

HOLT   ST. MARTIN OF TOURS

The Norman north nave wall at Holt church (above)
and arch to the south doorway (below)

The parish of Holt to the west of the River Severn consists mainly of farmland. There are three main centres of population—by the bridge at Holt Fleet, on the crossroads at Holt Heath, and, isolated amongst the gravel workings, by Holt Castle and church. The castle is a mainly Georgian house which incorporates a 15th-century hall and a 14th-century tower with battlements. It was held by the Beauchamp family from the 12th to the 15th centuries, before becoming the property of the Bournes and the Bromleys until the 18th century, after which it passed to the Foleys and Wards of Witley Court.

The red sandstone church has a nave and chancel with a south chapel and north vestry, and a tower at the west end. Most of the masonry of the nave and chancel is Norman work, but the carvings are easily confused with copies and imitation work which were installed in the 19th century. A foretaste of this confusion comes with the Norman style lychgate, on the approach to the church. The church was much restored and embellished between 1847 and 1897 by the rector Charles Sale who, with his wife Mary, was a great patron of the arts. Their bequest of water-colours to Worcester City Art Gallery

The interior at Holt showing the Norman chancel arch above which is a copy of a 4th-century Italian mosaic

forms a significant part of the permanent collection. At Holt, the Sales acquired pieces for the church, and Mrs. Sale did much stone carving herself, both for this church and for Little Witley.

The genuine late 12th-century carving can be seen on the south doorway, although it was slightly truncated when the south chapel was built, and there is evidence of reworking in the zig-zag decoration of the arch, where a weathered voussoir has been inserted off-centre. The capitals show the Devil laughing at and assaulting those who enter the church. The style is similar to the Herefordshire School of Sculpture. The north doorway is simpler and less restored. The arch has projecting zig-zag decoration, and the capitals show a fox with a stork drinking out of a barrel from *Aesop's Fables*. There are two plain Norman lancets, which are rebated to take shutters, but the larger elaborately carved lancets on the north and south sides of the nave date from the restoration of 1859. There are Norman flat buttresses and a string course. The chancel is mainly late 12th-century, with long round-headed lancet windows on the north side. It was extended eastwards in the 14th century, and given an east window of two lights with Decorated tracery. The south chapel also has Decorated windows and dates from about 1360. The Norman tower was refaced in the 15th century, when the Perpendicular west window was installed. The belfry projects slightly and has Perpendicular bell openings, battlements and short pinnacles. It is possible that the east wall of the tower contains late Anglo-Saxon masonry—there is a small tapered opening into the nave roof-space, which is only normally visible from inside the upper parts of the roof tower. This could be similar in date to the blocked openings on the south wall at St. Alban's church, Worcester.

The interior is lofty and has walls scraped back to the sandstone, making it quite dark. The Norman nave and chancel are divided by an arch of about 1160, carved with zig-zag and battlement designs, including triangular merlons. There is a hood mould with carved chain links and dots, and a beast's head at the top of the arch. The jambs are asymmetrical and the capitals carved with grotesque heads. The arches to the south chapel from the nave and chancel are also round headed, and would seem to be an unusual survival into the 14th century of a style of about 1200. On the north side of the chancel leading to the vestry is a Norman style doorway, which is the work of Mrs. Sale. There is a tall Perpendicular arch to the tower, whilst the nave roof is 15th-century.

There are several medieval fittings. The font is a splendid piece of Norman sculpture. It is drum shaped with a round stem, carved with a spiral design, not unlike the decoration to the nave piers in Durham Cathedral. On the bowl are monster heads linked by their tongues. The staring eyes contain sockets for coloured glass decoration, and the paintwork has been scraped off giving the font a rather newer appearance than it should have. There are a medieval piscina and an aumbry in the chancel, whilst those in the south chapel have been reconstructed during 20th-century restoration. On the chancel floor is a collection of medieval tiles, with the arms of the Beauchamp and Talbot families, and a group from the former tomb of Walter Scull who died in 1456. These are decorated with the names of the Evangelists and a prayer, and were reset in the floor when the monument was removed from the chancel in the 18th century. In the glass of the south-east window in the south chapel are the remains of a 15th-century Annunciation with an inscription. The jewelled cloak of the Virgin is particularly beautiful. The presence of the Talbot arms in glass indicate that this was a chantry chapel of the Beauchamps at the time that they were connected by marriage to the Talbot family.

The fittings and furnishings which can be linked to Rector and Mrs. Sale begin with the mosaic over the chancel arch. This is a copy of a 4th-century mosaic of the Good Shepherd in the Mausoleum of Galla Placidia at Ravenna in Italy. The Sales purchased it in 1859 along with the mosaic angels in the chancel and installed them at Holt in the face of considerable opposition, both then and since. The pulpit, and the lectern which has been removed, were carved in Norman style by Mrs. Sale. The *Building News* of 1858 reads 'We refuse to criticise, as they are the work of a lady and it is pleasing to find them taking an interest in these matters'. The east window glass was designed by Charles Eamer Kempe and made by Bryans of London as a memorial to Rector Sale in 1896, and

The Norman font with monster heads linked by their tongues

the Flemish glass pieces in the north chancel window, which show the Transfiguration, were bought by Mrs. Sale at Nuremberg in Germany, and installed in 1906. The communion rails were given in 1877 to mark the 30th year of Rector Sale's ministry in Holt.

The medieval effigy with restored paintwork in the south chapel, is thought, because of the coat of arms, to be of Margaret Beauchamp and came from a memorial in the chancel. Above is a helmet and tabard of the Bromley family who held the Manor from 1575 to 1750. The tablet to Henry Bromley, who died in 1683, and his wife Mercy Pytts from Kyre, who died in 1704, has twisted columns and cherub heads typical of about 1700. An earlier tablet commemorates Sir Henry Bromley, who died in 1615. There are also several ledger stones on the floor of the chancel and south chapel.

On the outside walls of the chapel are the remains of a Mass dial, and two blocked medieval squints, one on the south wall, and one to the west, both of which would have given a view of Mass being celebrated at the altar within.

HONEYBOURNE   ST. ECGWIN

There are two churches in this sprawling village which lies to the south of the Cotswold railway line and station. St. Ecgwin's church in Church Honeybourne is now the parish church, and has long been in Worcestershire, although it is in the diocese of Gloucester. In medieval times it was in the patronage of Evesham Abbey, and after its foundation in 1295 was dedicated along with Bretforton church, by the Bishop of St. Asaph. St. Ecgwin was the founder of Evesham Abbey and several churches on the former abbey estates bear his dedication.

The church adjoins fields at the end of a short lane, with views towards the Cotswolds. It is built of limestone, and has a nave, with porch, chancel, and west tower with spire. Most of the church appears to be 13th-century and probably dates from the foundation. The chancel windows are lancets with cusps, the east window is made up of three grouped together under one arch, and there is a priest's doorway. The nave windows have simple Y-shaped tracery, and the two windows from the short south aisle seem to have been reset in the blocked arches when the aisle was demolished. The south doorway and blocked north doorway are both Early English. The Decorated belfry with pinnacles and octagonal spire were added to the earlier tower in about 1365. The spire has three sets of

The porch at Honeybourne church

lucarnes with Decorated tracery. The weight of the belfry and spire have caused the tower to lean dramatically, and a large north-west buttress was added in the 19th century. The Perpendicular south porch has a stone roof with four arches, very similar to the porch at Hampton church. The entrance has a hood mould and pierced tracery either side of the doorway, with an image niche above. A clerestorey was added to the nave in the 15th century, with flat topped windows on the south side, and a new window was inserted in the nave by the porch. The hood mould is similar to that of the entrance.

The interior is high, and whitewashed, with much clear glass in the windows. The 15th-century low pitched nave roof is contemporary with the clerestorey and rests on corbels carved with angels. The Early English chancel is well proportioned, and has a trefoil piscina. The fittings are 19th- and 20th-century, but there are fragments of medieval glass in a window at the west end of the nave.

HONEYBOURNE   COW HONEYBOURNE CHURCH

At the west end of the village of Honeybourne is a second church. This was, until the 1970s, the church of Cow Honeybourne. The bucolic name can be interpreted as the brook by which honey was gathered, to which Cow was perhaps added to describe the agricultural nature of the land here. Cow Honeybourne, west of the Roman Icknield Street, was in Gloucestershire until 1931, and in medieval times was part of the estate of Winchcombe Abbey. From the later Middle Ages the church was served by the vicar of St. Ecgwin's church in the other part of Honeybourne, but had become almshouses by the 17th century. It was rebuilt, apart from the tower, between 1861 and 1863 by William Jeffrey Hopkins, but ceased to be used by the 1970s when it was converted into three houses.

The west tower is Perpendicular with square headed bell openings, gargoyles battlements and a single pinnacle. The body of the church with a nave, chancel, north porch and vestry has Decorated style windows. One larger north window has Perpendicular style tracery, unusual for Hopkins' work. The roof now has several wooden dormer windows.

There was a late 16th-century pulpit in the church, which was brought here at the time of Hopkins' rebuilding work. This is now preserved at St. Ecgwin's church.

HOOK COMMON   GOOD SHEPHERD

This small church stands on a ridge about one mile north-east of Welland and in the rural western part of the parish of Upton-upon-Severn. It is a chapel of ease to Upton church and is built of lias with a nave and chancel. A bellcote stands between them, and there is also a porch and vestry. The church is in the early Decorated style with plate tracery windows, and was consecrated in 1870. The architect was the local George Clarke, who also designed the neighbouring former school and the cemetery chapel in Upton. The work was paid for by the Lord of the Manor, George Martin, of Ham Court near Upton, and was much embellished by the Grice-Hutchinson family of the Boynes at Hook Common.

     The interior is cream washed and has a scissor braced roof. Most of the fittings are late 19th-century, and included a reredos of 1871 to a Preedy design made by Richard Boulton of Cheltenham, with tiles by Godwin & Sons of Hereford, which has since been removed. However, there is a good collection of Arts and Crafts stained glass. The east and south chancel windows are by Heaton, Butler and Bayne, and the west window of 1906 depicting the Good Shepherd (see illustration on rear cover), is by Robert Payne, a pupil of Christopher Whall, one of the best known glaziers of the early 20th century. The glass showing the Old Testament figure of Ruth in the north nave window is by Robert Payne and Son, whilst Payne's pupils, Walter, Florence and Robert Camm produced the memorial window to Charles Grice-Hutchinson, who died from war wounds in 1949.

HUDDINGTON   ST. JAMES

The chancel at Huddington, showing a medieval niche between the two windows

St. James' church has a picture book setting across the lawn from the moated and timber-framed Huddington Court. Once a chapelry to St. Helen's church in Worcester, Huddington was held by the Commandery, Worcester, until it passed to the Wintour family. The Wintours came to Huddington when Roger Wintour married the wealthy Joan Hodington in the 15th century, and it belonged to the Wintours until 1658. The Wintour family were prominent recusant Catholics at the Reformation, and two brothers Thomas and Robert were executed for their role in the Gunpowder Plot.

    The nave and south aisle are of lias, whilst the chancel is of sandstone. There is a timber porch and small bell turret. By the late 19th century the church was on the verge of collapse, and in 1900 it was restored in an Arts and Crafts manner by Charles Ford Whitcombe, the architect of Broadheath church and the vestry at Himbleton church, . The nave is Norman and has one lancet at the west end of the north wall. The small plain Norman south doorway has been reset in the rebuilt wall, and the 15th-century north doorway seems to incorporate a former Norman inner arch. One north window has simple cusped tracery of about 1300, whilst the second window is a later replacement. The south aisle was probably built as a chantry for the Hodington family, but by 1900 only the eastern part survived and was treated as a transept. Ford Whitcombe rebuilt the west end. The windows reflect this story, with a Decorated east window and simple windows to the south and west. The Perpendicular chancel dates from the rebuilding of 1535 by Roger and Elizabeth Wintour. There are square-headed side windows, whilst the east window has stepped lights with tracery above. To the south is a blocked priest's door. The north porch is a beautiful Perpendicular timber structure, very similar to the porches at nearby Crowle and Himbleton.

The interior was scraped to the stone at the restoration of 1900, but maintains a powerful atmosphere. The aisle is divided from the nave by a two bay Decorated arcade, with rich mouldings to the piers, capitals and arches. The chancel arch dates from the 1535 rebuilding, and there are 16th-century wagon roofs in the nave and chancel. In the chancel, there are canopied image niches to each side of the east window, with blank stone shields above, which perhaps once carried the arms of Wintour and Cokesey—the Wintours had inherited great wealth from the Cokesey family, and their emblems appear elsewhere in the church. In the south wall there are a damaged piscina and an aumbry. It is possible that parts of the medieval screen were reused in the chancel panelling, as it contains 14th-century style trefoil openings, which seem once to have served as squints. The panelling formed part of box pews in the 17th century— perhaps the woodwork was reused in a manner similar to the Lulham pew at Madley church in Herefordshire? There are mortice holes marking the position of the medieval parclose screen in the arcade, but the chancel screen is 17th-century with balusters, and along with the communion rail probably dates from the time of Archbishop Laud. Some of the chancel stalls have linenfold panelling of about 1520, whilst others are 20th-century. In the aisle are a 17th-century communion table, and the Royal Arms of George III. The carved Last Supper is from a former 19th-century reredos. Set in the west wall are 15th-century tiles, including some with the arms of the Wintour family, and others with parts of a design which may have made up a large cross, similar to that at Shelsley Walsh. The plain octagonal font is 14th-century. Nearby are commandment and benefaction boards.

The south aisle windows contain many medieval fragments of glass, including arms of the Wintour and Cokesey families. The tracery of the chancel side windows has 16th-century glass with the initials of the founders, R and E, and the rebus of the Cokesey family, a cook's table on a boat. The east window contains several pieces of 16th-century glass which make up figures of the Virgin and St. John with a Crucifixion. These appear to be either Cornish or European glass and were installed in 1933.

In the chancel is a brass with a Latin inscription to Adrian Fortescue, who died in 1653. Plain rectangular brass plates commemorate Frances Wintour, formerly Talbot, who died in 1641, Mary Wintour, formerly Carrington, who died in 1642, successively wives of George Wintour who died in 1658. George Wintour is also commemorated with his third wife, Mary Kemp, by a black and white marble tablet in the aisle. As his only daughter predeceased him, George was the last of the Wintours at Huddington, and the estate passed to the family of his first wife, Frances Talbot—the Earls of Shrewsbury.

Outside a Mass dial is scratched on the east wall, and the former south door has medieval metalwork. By the lychgate a crucifix in wood and bronze marks the site of a grave discovered in the early 20th century. It contained a man's body together with coins of Charles I. He is thought to have been a Royalist soldier who fled from the defeat at the Battle of Worcester in 1651.

INKBERROW   ST. PETER

This large village has much 20th-century suburban housing around a central core of older buildings, many of which face the village green. Behind the timber-framed Old Bull Inn, St. Peter's church is on the edge of the village with views to the east across a small valley. The parish is large and rural, extending eastwards to the Warwickshire border at Cookhill. To the north of the church are the brick Old Vicarage and converted tithe barn. In the keeping of the incumbent is a book of maps, which was left at the Vicarage in 1644 by King Charles I as he travelled with his army through Worcestershire before the Battle of Naseby.

The church is built of the local grey sandstone, and consists of a west tower, nave, north aisle with porch, south transept and chancel with north chapel. The first impression of the church from the north is that it is a Perpendicular building. The tower and north side of the church have typical windows, low pitch roofs, gargoyles, battlements and pinnacles. The tower was funded by the Dyson family of Nobury. It is probable that the north chapel is a little later than the rest and built on the site of the former vestry—there are no cusps to the window tracery which suggest a 16th-century date. The porch was rebuilt in 1887 but incorporates large late 15th-century gargoyles, and the doorway is surmounted by a prominent hood mould. The nave is mainly 15th-century, but contains a reset Early English doorway on the south side. The south transept was added in the 14th century, but the present structure dates mainly from 1784. The chancel was rebuilt in 1887, when the church was restored by Ewan Christian; his work can also be seen at Kempsey church. However, there is a 13th-century priest's door surviving in the medieval lower courses of masonry.

The interior is light and spacious with an elegant late Perpendicular arcade. The tower arch is of the same date. The arch to the south transept is Decorated, and there is a very restored 13th-century piscina and sedilia. The 19th- and 20th-century fittings include riddle posts and a vestry screen by Celestino Pancheri of the Bromsgrove Guild, and his son Robert, carved with Charles I in armour before the Battle of Edgehill, with his head shown severed from his body. The pulpit of about 1800 has Georgian Gothic panels. The square font, which dates from the end of the 12th century, is carved underneath with a dogtooth design, and has panels to the sides with rosettes and the lamb and cross. In the tracery of the west window of the north aisle are fragments of 15th-century glass including figures of St. Catherine, St. Helen with a cross, and an angel. Further fragments are in the east window of the north chapel and in a south window of the nave. There is much 20th-century glass, including figures of St. Anne and St. Francis.

There are numerous memorial tablets including one to Frances Sheldon of Nobury, who died in 1690, and another to George, son of Sir Francis Edgioke of Shurnock Court, who died in 1638. Sir Francis's servant, William Willis, is also buried nearby. The most imposing memorial is the Savage tomb in the south transept. The Savage family lived in the 17th century at neighbouring Dormston, and the south transept, which was probably built as a chantry by Thomas Colman in the 14th century, seems to have become known as the Dormston chapel. Sir John Savage of Edgioke died in 1631. In his alabaster effigy he is shown wearing a ruff, with his head resting on a tasselled cushion and with beautifully decorated armour. The family are shown kneeling around the tomb chest. Above are columns supporting a canopy with early Gothic style panels, which have quatrefoils and cusps. The monument has been damaged, probably during the Civil War period, or when it was moved here from the chancel at the rebuilding of 1784. There are many similarities to the Savage memorial at Elmley Castle church, and to other monuments of this date as in Leigh and Wickhamford churches.

Outside, there is a 15th-century mason's mark at the east end of the north aisle, and a reset Mass dial on the south side of the transept. To the west of the porch is a memorial to Thomas Dyson, who died in 1651.

KEMERTON   ST. NICHOLAS

Kemerton is one of a group of attractive villages on the southern slopes of Bredon Hill. Until 1933 the parish was in Gloucestershire and the church remains in the diocese of Gloucester. The parish includes the Iron Age fort on the summit of the hill, which can be reached by a footpath leading from Bell's Castle at the top of the village. Bell's Castle was built in the early 19th century with battlements and observation posts as home for Edmund Bell, a sailor, who was locally reputed to have made his money from smuggling.

At the lower end of the village stands the limestone church in a large graveyard. The tower is at the west end of the nave, which has aisles under separate gabled roofs, beyond which lies the chancel. There is a north vestry and south porch, whilst a north porch appears to have been proposed but never built. The entire church, except the tower, was built to designs by Richard Carpenter between 1847 and 1849 using the Decorated style; Carpenter's most famous work includes Lancing College in Sussex. The lower stages of the tower date from around 1200 and have lancet windows. They were unbuttressed until the addition of the belfry in about 1500. The square Perpendicular bell openings have hood moulds, above which are battlements and pinnacles.

The interior is Victorian 'High Church', and still very much as it was intended to look by the benefactor Thomas Thorp, Archdeacon of Bristol. From 1839 Thorp was president of the Cambridge Camden Society, which spearheaded the 19th-century Catholic revival in England. Thorp became Rector of Kemerton in 1844, and began to make plans for rebuilding the church according to the 'Tractarian' principles of the society. After a difficult local legal dispute over the plans, the church was consecrated in 1847, but the north aisle was not completed until 1849.

The medieval Early English tower arch survives, but the remainder of the arches and features are in the Decorated style. The fittings are typical of the Tractarian movement, and include a piscina, sedilia, screen and stalls in the chancel. At the crossing is a corona by Hardman & Co., whilst the font is decorated with arcading, flowers, foliage and lions' heads.

The glass in the large east window shows the Crucifixion, with the Virgin, St. John, St. Stephen and St. Alban. It is by Thomas Willement, a pioneering early 19th-century glazier, who treated glass like mosaic. Other good local examples of his work can be seen at Hampton Lucy church in Warwickshire. The side windows by Hardman include figures of St. Augustine, St. Wulstan, St. Nicholas and St. Etheldreda, the latter reflecting Thorp's Cambridge connection. Other windows show the Doctors of the Church—St. Augustine of Hippo, St. Ambrose, St. Gregory, to which St. Jerome was added under the tower in 1903 in memory of Thorp's successor, the Reverend Jerome Mercier. On the east wall is a copy of a medieval Italian painting showing angels, whilst the north aisle fittings were altered in the 1960s with the installation of a stone altar.

Thomas Thorp was buried in 1877 outside the south wall of the chancel, but an effigy was placed in a recess inside in the medieval style, though it is inlaid with Italian marble.

KEMPSEY   ST. MARY

Today Kempsey is a sprawling suburban village to the south of Worcester. However, the area around the church was settled in Roman times, and by the Middle Ages Kempsey was an important manor of the bishops of Worcester. The manor house stood to the north of the church, but had entirely disappeared by the 17th century. Around the church are several timber-framed cottages, and the lane leading south from the church has a ford across Hatfield Brook, which formed the route from Worcester to Tewkesbury until the present main road was cut through the village in the 19th century. To the west lies the large Ham Meadow and the River Severn.

The Early English chancel at Kempsey

St. Mary's church is large and built of red and grey sandstone. It has a west tower, nave and aisles under one roof with a north porch, north and south transepts, chancel and vestry. The earliest parts of the building are late Norman; indeed the western lancet and flat buttress on the south aisle, along with another flat buttress on the east wall of the north transept, survive from what was a large cruciform church of about 1200. There is similar evidence for a church of this type at Powick across the river. The chancel was rebuilt very elegantly in the Early English style between about 1250 and 1260. The east window is made up of five lancets under a single arch, and on the north wall are three pairs of smaller lancets under arches. It is likely to be the work of masons from Worcester Cathedral and bears great resemblance to the architecture of the east end of the cathedral, which was begun in 1224. The north and south transepts have large Perpendicular windows on the ends, and there are further Perpendicular windows in the south aisle. The Perpendicular tower has a recessed west window, and battlements with pinnacles above the typical bell openings. The church was restored in 1865 by Ewan Christian, when the vestry was added south of the chancel, the east wall of the south transept rebuilt, the north aisle window renovated, and the porch added.

The polychrome banding of alternate red and white sandstone in the Decorated nave arcades gives an initial impression of a Victorian interior, but the arcades are medieval, and the piers on the north side are slightly differently shaped to those on the south. The arcades also give access to the transepts; there is no separate crossing. The chancel arch is 19th-century, but the chancel has several Early English features—the east window has shafts to the interior, the piscina has a trefoil arch, whilst the sedilia arches are cusped and carry the insignia of William Cantelupe, Bishop of Worcester from 1237 to 1266. It is believed that Simon de Montfort heard Mass in the chancel just before his defeat and death at the Battle of Evesham in August 1265. The south transept contains another trefoil piscina, whilst that in the north transept is Decorated with an ogee arch. The Perpendicular tower arch is panelled.

Most of the fittings date from soon after 1865, including a Nicholson organ of 1872, although there have been some 20th-century additions and changes. Kempsey church should however, be much better known for its medieval glass. The chancel side windows include eight panels with figures. They are arranged on two levels with the 14th-century ones above the 13th. On the upper level to the north are St. Margaret with a dragon and St. Thomas Becket, shown as an archbishop with a crozier. On the upper level to the south are St. Catherine and St. Cuthbert with St. Oswald's head. One the lower level to the north are a bishop with a crozier and another St. Catherine, and on the lower level to the south are another bishop and a king, probably St. Edward the Confessor. The east window contains glass in three lights by Edward Frampton of 1890, but the panels depicting the Last Supper were installed in 1958.

The largest monument is to Sir Edmund Wylde who died in 1620. He is shown wearing armour, lying in front of a shallow arch above which is an unusual balustrade and his arms with a helm. His two sons are shown below in contemporary costume. Sir Edmund was the nephew of George Wylde, whose monument in St. Peter's church, Droitwich, is quite similar. In the 19th century a chestnut tree sprouted from the top of the monument, and is thought to have grown from a conker confiscated from a boy during a service; the tree died in 1895. Other monuments include a standing memorial to Mrs. Eaton who died in 1790, with a sarcophagus and urn shown in front of an obelisk designed by William Stephens of Worcester. A bust of Thomas Foley who died in 1821 is by Joseph Stephens, and another bust in bronze, with a modelled beard and moustache, commemorates Sir Richard Temple, Governor of Bombay, who died in 1902.

Outside in the northern part of the churchyard is a cross discovered during the restoration of 1865, part of which is medieval.

KIDDERMINSTER   ST. MARY AND ALL SAINTS

The large Perpendicular church of St. Mary and All Saints

Renowned internationally over the last two centuries for the production of carpets, the centre of Kidderminster still has numerous Victorian factory buildings which serve as a reminder of the extent of the industry at its peak, and of its decline in the late 20th century. This church, the parish church, stands to the north of the centre, beside the ring road and now separated from historic Church Street. It has several factory buildings around it, but the ground slopes steeply away to the west to the canal and River Stour. The fast flowing river was one of the reasons for Kidderminster's development as a cloth producing centre in the Middle Ages, and wealth from the cloth trade certainly accounts for the scale and appearance of this great church.

The name of this town is a reminder of the presence of an Anglo-Saxon minster church, and emphasises that this was then a place of some influence locally. The exact site of the minster is uncertain, but there was certainly a church on this site by the 12th century. The present building of dark red sandstone is mainly 15th- and 16th-century in the late Perpendicular style, but it was heavily restored in the 19th century. The tower is in an unusual position at the south-west corner of the aisled nave and there is a chancel, north transept and chapels. At the east end is the vestry and a chantry chapel, making this a church of great length at 215 feet.

Today, the tower acts as a porch, though the medieval porch stood on the tower's east side and had a first floor chamber. It makes an impressive entrance, and would have been more so, had the intended spire been added as at Bromsgrove. The tower was refaced in 1893, and has a large south doorway with traceried spandrels, and large Perpendicular windows to the south and west. On the south side, around the window are three image niches which now contain statues of the Virgin, St. Peter and St. Paul. The belfry has openings in the centre of each side of two lights with transom bars, either side of which are similar blind openings. On the top are pinnacles and elaborate panelled battlements. The nave clerestorey was also refaced in 1893, and comprises a row of fine Perpendicular square-headed windows, with a low pitch roof, and panelled battlements to each side. A plain clerestorey was also added to the nave of nearby Upper Arley church at this time, which must have been influenced by this beautiful structure. In the south-

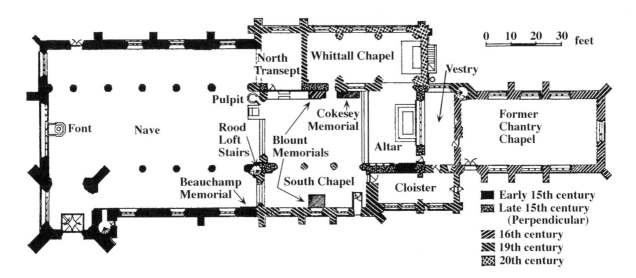

Plan of St. Mary and All Saints, Kidderminster

east corner of the nave is the battlemented turret for the rood loft stairs. The west window is 19th-century Perpendicular. The chancel south chapel was rebuilt in the Decorated style in 1847, when the chancel was restored. The north transept was built as an organ chamber in 1874. The north chapel was added in the Perpendicular style in 1922 by Sir Giles Gilbert Scott, as a memorial chapel for the Whittal family, Matthew Whittal from Kidderminster founded Whittal Carpets in Worcester, Massachusetts, USA.

The eastern part of the chancel is enclosed on the south side by a short cloister built in 1887 as a memorial to the first Lord Dudley to lead to the vestry, which was added in about 1790 between the church and the chantry chapel. The chapel was built by a London merchant, Simon Rice, in the early 16th century. The concept is very similar to the contemporary Lady Chapel placed beyond the east end of Long Melford church in Suffolk. The chapel became a school endowed by Thomas Blount following the Dissolution of the Chantries, and was refounded by King Charles I in 1636. In 1847 a new school building, now the Registry Office, was built in Bewdley Road, and eventually the chapel was renovated as a church room in 1967.

The church is entered through the tower which was given a lierne vault in 1895. The interior walls are of dark sandstone, but reorderings during the late 20th century have given a sense of space. The arcades of about 1500 in the nave have typical concave sided octagonal piers, again similar to those in Upper Arley church. Most of the features of the chancel are 19th-century, but the entrance to the rood loft stairs, on the south side of the chancel arch, is a faint reminder of what once must have been spectacular medieval fittings. The second pillar from the east on the north side has marks which show where a new pulpit was installed in 1621, the gift of Alice Dawkes. This fine pulpit with tester is now in the Victorian Unitarian chapel, known as the New Meeting, in Church Street, but is notable as the pulpit from which Richard Baxter, who was appointed curate here in 1641, preached his sermons. Baxter was a puritan who found himself to be a dissenter at the Act of Uniformity in 1660, and unable to preach in the Church of England. He died in Middlesex in 1691, but is commemorated in Kidderminster, where he was a popular preacher, through the Baxter Memorial Church (now United Reformed) in the Bull Ring, which contains the 17th-century communion table from this church. The 19th-century fittings include the reredos in the chancel designed by William Jeffrey Hopkins in 1880 and made by Richard Boulton of Cheltenham. The chancel roof is a 19th-century copy of the 14th-century roof from the Guesten Hall at Worcester Cathedral, now at Avoncroft Museum. The Whittal chapel contains a 1920s reredos and organ.

St. Mary's church has a fine collection of 19th- and 20th-century stained glass. The east window and other chancel windows showing scenes from the Life of Christ are of 1855 by Michael O'Connor. The west window is also by O'Connor and shows the Evangelists and Apostles. The window over the north door is of 1890 by Wyndham Hughes, showing Faith, Hope and Charity. Two windows in the south aisle showing the Corporal Acts of Mercy are by Evans of Smethwick in memory of a churchwarden, William Awdry. The clerestorey windows, which show the Benedicite, by John Hardman are a memorial to a former vicar, Thomas Claughton, who became the first bishop of St. Albans. A further window by Hardman & Co. of 1902 is in the south aisle. A window under the tower was glazed in 1904 as a memorial to John Brinton, carpet manufacturer, who undertook the restoration of the tower. The remainder of the windows in the north aisle are by James Powell and Sons of Whitefriars in London, who also designed the glass showing the Virgin, Joan of Arc and Florence Nightingale in the Whittal Chapel in 1927.

The monuments include several 15th-century memorials which reflect the prestige of this church during the late Middle Ages. There is a fine brass with three figures, being Sir John Phelip, who died in 1415, and Walter Cokesey who died in 1407, with their wife Matilda Harcourt. She is shown in contemporary costume between her two husbands, who wear armour. Above are the remains of a crocketed ogee-shaped triple canopy and their family arms. Below is a latin inscription. A large tomb chest is built into the wall at the east end of the south aisle as the memorial of Joyce Beauchamp who died in 1473. She was the widow of Walter Beauchamp and daughter of Walter Cokesey. It has been much damaged, but has a large canopy with four projecting niches, each with a canopy and draped statue, now headless, representing the Annunciation, Trinity and St. John the Baptist. Inside is a panelled vault. Below the effigy are angels carrying shields. This part of the south aisle was a chantry founded by Joyce Beauchamp and dedicated to St. Catherine. Her brother, Sir Hugh Cokesey, who died in 1445, has a memorial in the chancel with his wife Alice. The effigies are of alabaster in a projecting recess with cresting above the four centred arch.

Thomas Blount, founder of the school, was a principal servant of the Earl of Leicester, favourite of Queen Elizabeth I. On his death in 1568, he was buried in the chancel, where he was subsequently joined by his wife Margery, who died in 1595. He is shown with his head on his helm, whilst she wears widow's attire, and behind are shown their four children and an infant. Their son, Sir Edward Blount, who died in 1630, has a memorial with his two wives, Mary Neville and Mary Wigmore. He is depicted lying on his side, above his wives, all in contemporary costume. There are numerous other memorial tablets dating from the 18th to the 20th centuries, whilst on the floor amongst the ledger stones is one to Sir Ralph Clare of Caldwell, who was a Royalist opponent to Baxter's preaching during the Civil War period.

The Civil War saw a brief skirmish in the churchyard, and the memorial stone outside to a town crier, who died in 1628, is supposed to have been damaged by bullets. The churchyard opens on to the ring road through great iron gates, which are 20th-century in the Georgian style. The war memorial of a bronze angel with a child is by Alfred Drury, whilst the statue to Richard Baxter by Thomas Brock of 1875 was brought here from the Bull Ring. By the chancel are the remains of the medieval churchyard cross.

KIDDERMINSTER   ST. BARNABAS, FRANCHE

Franche is a residential suburb on the north side of Kidderminster, and the church which stands on the Wolverley Road is a chapelry of St. Mary, Kidderminster in whose parish it stands.

The small red brick nave and chancel has a south porch and tower that once carried a spire. The church was built in 1871 to designs by Chamberlain and Martin in a late Early English style, and was paid for by the curate of St. Mary, H. Fortescue, along with the church of St. James.

KIDDERMINSTER   ST. GEORGE

This large limestone church stands to the east of the town centre, on the Birmingham Road. It was built between 1821 and 1824 as a chapel of ease to the parish church and represents the eastward expansion of the town with industrial developments in the early part of the 19th century.

St. George's church has a tall thin west tower with a large high nave, aisles, and short chancel with vestry. It is a Commissioners type church, built in the Perpendicular style by Francis Goodwin. Goodwin's previous buildings were classical, such as his addition of the steeple to St. Paul's church in Birmingham, but St. George is very similar to All Saints church in West Bromwich; the only two churches by Goodwin to have a tower. Typical Goodwin features include the large pinnacles, rose window and the west front with its cavernous porch. He worked hard to keep the symmetry of his buildings, and seems to have used very similar plans; indeed, St. George is very like the well proportioned Holy Trinity church at Bordesley in Birmingham. The tower has long thin bell openings, and the west doorway is very high. There are also entrances at the west ends of the aisles. At the east end is a rose window with cast iron tracery. The five Perpendicular style side windows have transom bars part way up, which indicate the level of the former galleries inside.

The interior is no longer Goodwin's work, as it was destroyed by fire in 1922. The galleries, which were supported by iron piers, not unlike those at Hartlebury, have gone, and the plaster ceiling has been replaced. Yet the result today is light and airy with a variety of 20th-century fittings.

KIDDERMINSTER   HOLY INNOCENTS, FOLEY PARK

The first church of the Holy Innocents was built in 1888 as a timber mission church for the Foley Park area in the southern part of the new parish of St. John. It was demolished and replaced by the present structure in 1938. The church is in the Byzantine style, which was fashionable with many suburban churches at this time. A second mission chapel dedicated to St. Stephen was established in Mill Street for the people of the north end of the parish, but this was demolished in the early 20th century.

KIDDERMINSTER   ST. JAMES

The former church of St. James was built in the Horse Fair to the north of the town centre, as a chapel of ease to St. Mary's church in 1872. The architect was Davis of Kidderminster, and the church was paid for by the curate, H. Fortescue, who also founded the church at Franche. It is a small brick building which has been used by the Salvation Army since its closure in 1977.

KIDDERMINSTER   ST. JOHN THE BAPTIST

On the Bewdley Road near the hospital stands this curious church, built in the 19th century to serve the new western suburbs of the town. It is a large building with a varied roofline, which forms an attractive view from Summer Place.

The church was first built in 1843 as a Commissioners church using blue brick, of which the tower and spire remain. This was designed by the little known Gordon Alexander in a neo-Norman style with simple heavy round arches for details. The octagonal spire has long lucarnes at the base. Alexander's church of aisled nave, transept and chancel with apse was superseded when a new large nave and chancel were built in dark red sandstone to the north between 1890 and 1894 by Julius Chatwin of Birmingham, with both lancets and late Early English tracery. This type of addition, dwarfing the original church, was also undertaken by Chatwin at St. James' church at Handsworth in Birmingham. However, here the south part was reconstructed in sandstone between 1902 and 1904 to give a new Perpendicular style south aisle with clerestorey, outer south aisle, porch on the site of the former transept and a chapel with a small polygonal apse on the site of the former chancel.

The Chatwin interior is High Victorian Gothic with yellow brick walls and polychrome patterning. The church was extensively reordered in 1972, and the south aisle is now used as offices. One window in the north aisle has glass of 1896 by Powell & Co. showing Elijah and St. John the Baptist.

KIDDERMINSTER   ST. OSWALD, BROADWATERS

Situated close to the Wolverhampton Road in this residential suburb, beside a stream below Podmore Pool, St. Oswald's church is now but a fragment of the former building. The 1960s church room is currently used as the church, but the main building with a huge sloping roof of 1964 was demolished in 1981. It replaced a mission church of corrugated iron erected in 1908.

KINGTON   ST. JAMES

Kington lies to the south of the road between Worcester and Inkberrow. It is a small compact village with several 20th-century houses between the brick and timber-framed cottages and farms. The church is at the northern end opposite the Georgian brick Court Farm. The medieval village once extended to the north, and there are the remains of house platforms in a field. During the early Middle Ages the de Lacy family held much of the land around here.

Within the village itself, St. James' church is almost hidden from view by surrounding trees and buildings. However, viewed from the main road about one mile to the north, the timber-framed upper parts of the tower are conspicuous. The tower is at the west end of the nave with a porch and chancel. There are 15th-century square lancet windows with trefoil heads in the stone lower stage of the tower, which also has small side roofs at the base of the timber-framing. The frame is close-studding, making the tower similar to that at Warndon church and the nearby church at Dormston. The tower has braces beside the square bell openings on the sides and a saddleback roof which is only a little higher than the roof of the nave. The nave west gable is also timber-framed, and the nave was extended to the south in the 16th century. The north wall is 13th-century, and is probably part of the original building, of which the earliest documentary reference is 1285. There is one Early English lancet. The windows on the south side were replaced in 1881, when the church was restored by William Jeffrey Hopkins. The plain chancel was largely rebuilt at this time, though the medieval north windows and low side window were retained. The early Decorated style east window is Hopkins' work.

The interior is simple and whitewashed, and is much the result of Hopkins' restoration. There is no chancel arch, and instead the roof is supported by timber braces with carved tracery installed in 1881. The medieval aumbry and remains of carved brackets survive in the chancel. The 13th-century octagonal font has been retooled, and there is a medieval door at the west end. Parts of the former medieval rood screen and loft hang on the south wall of the nave and are incorporated into the pulpit. The remaining fittings are of the late 19th-century, and include a former painted reredos of 1890 now positioned in the nave.

KNIGHTON-ON-TEME   ST. MICHAEL

Knighton-on-Teme, showing the churchyard setting and yew tree

St. Michael's church is isolated in fields together with a farm along a gated road about one mile to the north of the present main centre of population at Newnham Bridge. The almost circular churchyard and ancient yew tree have been taken to indicate that the site of the church may be of Celtic origin, and certainly the surrounding deserted medieval village site points to this formerly being a place of greater significance. Even so, Knighton was a chapelry of Lindridge until it became a separate parish in 1843.

The removal of the rendering from the walls in the early 20th century has revealed a building of sandstone and tufa, of a type found elsewhere in the Teme Valley, as at Eastham and Clifton. There is a nave and chancel with a large bell turret on the west end. The tall Norman nave was lengthened to the west in the 13th century, and there are two lancet windows of this date. The stone surround to the tower was built later in that century, with a small plain doorway. Of the Norman nave, there are flat buttresses and the tall north and south doorways. The north doorway is blocked, but the spectacular south doorway is set in a projecting feature with blind arcading above. The doorway has shafts to the sides, and block capitals with roll mouldings on the corners, very similar to those at Stockton church. The arch also has a roll moulding and carved saltire crosses. The late 12th-century chancel has Norman lancet windows on the north side, but the lancets on the east end date from 1910 when the chancel was restored. The windows on the south side and the priest's door are Decorated and of the 14th century, and the low side window is of similar date, and has a restored shutter inside. The restored windows in the eastern part of the nave are early 14th-century and were probably installed to cast better light onto the rood loft whilst a further Perpendicular window was inserted to the west of the south door.

Inside, the church is very charming. The plain whitewashed walls of the nave direct attention immediately to the stonework at the east end. The Norman chancel arch is imposing. It is similar to the south doorway with shafts and a roll moulding inside a line of carved saltire crosses with rosettes. To the sides at the levels of the capitals are double splayed blind arcades. They are plain with shafts and capitals. Were they to contain statues or paintings of saints? The chancel beyond is scraped to the stonework, and includes a sedilia in the sill of the south window which was discovered in 1902. The medieval nave roof has moulded tie beams, though the eastern one is 20th-century—a medieval one would have blocked the view of the rood. The rood screen has long gone, but the 15th century painted ceilure above survives, with red and green colouring. At the west end of the nave is a timber-framed wall with an ogee-headed doorway leading into the tower and vestry. The tower itself has massive timbers, like those at Mamble church, concealed behind panelling which is made up of the 18th century box pews to form a vestry. The pew numbers can still be seen on the former doors.

The 18th-century fittings also included a gallery at the west end of the nave which was removed in 1884. The font is late 17th-century with a baluster shaft, there is a 17th-century communion table, and the communion rails are 18th-century. Most of the other furnishings are 20th-century, including a Nicholson organ of 1909. Most of the glass is 20th-century, but a north window contains some 14th-century fragments of grisaille work and border designs. The Barber memorial windows in the nave date from 1885. In the north-east corner of the nave is a memorial tablet with arms to John Cecill, High Sheriff of Bristol who died in 1697.

Outside in the churchyard, next to the huge yew tree, is the cross, with a 14th-century base. It contains a niche to hold the pyx with a worn canopy head decorated with crockets.

KNIGHTWICK   CHAPEL

Isolated on a low hill to the south of Knightsford Bridge stands this small chapel of nave and chancel under one roof, with a timber bell turret at the west end. It was built in 1879 in the early Decorated style, and designed by an unknown architect. There was a medieval church on this site, but it was replaced by the church of 1856 at Knightsford Bridge which serves both Doddenham and Knightwick (see separate entry). This chapel was built to serve the burial ground which continues to be used.

The inside is very plain, but contains the round Norman font with its carved zig-zag decoration from Doddenham church. There is a 17th-century memorial tablet on the west wall to Grace Lane, the niece of Jane Lane, who helped the future King Charles II to escape after the Battle of Worcester in 1651.

KYRE WYARD   ST. MARY

On the Herefordshire border, south of Tenbury, Kyre is a scattered village with the church set away from the main road. It forms a remarkable group with Kyre Park House, the tithe barn of 1618, and a medieval dovecote. Kyre Park was owned by the Pytts family from the 16th to the 19th century, and they shaped the house and grounds into their present form. They acquired the remains of the fortified manor house next to the church, which had been built by the Wyard family, and gradually rebuilt it between about 1600 and 1800. The grounds were landscaped in the 18th century, though no evidence has been found to support the suggestion that it was the work of Capability Brown. Today the view west from the church is towards the house and across these grounds, all of which have been recently restored after years in institutional use. The church is linked to the house by a small wooden cloister passage added by the Baldwyn Childes family, when they owned the house in the 19th century. Close by to the west are almshouses founded in 1675 by Anne Pytts, and Parsonage Farm, which includes the former medieval tithe barn.

The church has an unusual appearance with a nave and chancel, to which have been added a large south chapel with the timber bell turret and small spire on the west gable. At the end of the cloister on the west end of the nave is the medieval timber porch. The nave and chancel are mainly Norman, and the foundations of a former apse within the present east end were discovered during restoration between 1992 and 1994. On the north wall of the nave is a Norman lancet window and a blocked doorway. The south chapel and east end of the chancel are 14th-century with Decorated windows with cusped Y-shaped tracery and reticulation on the east side.

The interior has been restored and limewashed. The large chancel arch of 1833 replaced the smaller Norman opening. The chancel contains the medieval piscina, aumbry and two small recesses which may have contained reliquaries. The Decorated arch to the chapel is now partitioned. The roofs are all 14th-century. The small font is 13th-century but has been retooled. At the west end of the chapel are traces of 14th-century wall painting, and on the west jamb of the south window is painted a female saint, thought to be St. Clare. The background work with quatrefoils is very fine. The communion rails are 18th-century, and the present nave panelling and pews are made out of the 18th-century box pews. There is a bier dated 1682 in the chapel. The 19th-century stained glass includes a figure of St. George and the arms of the Pytts family in the east window, and the windows of the chapel illustrate the phrases 'I am the Way, the Truth and the Life'.

The memorial tablets include one of black and white marble with an oval inscription surrounded by a wreath to Edward Pytts who died in 1672. Another black and white tablet with twisted columns commemorates Catherine Pytts who died in 1702, whilst a straight-sided sarcophagus is the memorial to Jonathan Pytts, who died in 1807. The baroque style Harman memorial dates from the 1960s.

Wall painting in a window jamb at Kyre Wyard

LEIGH   ST. EDBURGA

This large parish south of the River Teme formerly included parts of Malvern Link. Today the main centre of population is at Leigh Sinton. Leigh church stands close to the River Teme and next to Leigh Court, with a group of converted farm buildings, and its huge tithe barn with a sweeping tile roof. The barn, which is thought to be the largest cruck timber-framed barn in England, was built in about 1300 by Pershore Abbey who held extensive lands here. Indeed, the church at Leigh originated in Anglo-Saxon times as a daughter monastery to Pershore Abbey, and the estates at Leigh were confirmed to Pershore in a charter of 972 by King Edgar. The church was dedicated to St. Edburga, whose relics were brought to Pershore Abbey in the 1050s. Leigh Court was a residence of the abbots of Pershore until the Dissolution of the Monasteries, when it passed to the Colles family who sold it to the Devereux family in the 17th century. Treadway Nash, the Worcestershire historian, became vicar here in 1792.

The church is of red and grey sandstone, and has a tower with porch at the west end. Beyond is a nave and chancel and a large south aisle. The earliest part of the building is the Norman nave, with flat stepped buttresses along the north wall, though the length and height are suggestive of Anglo-Saxon building of the eleventh century. Over the north door is a Norman round arched recess with roll moulding and saltire crosses, and scalloped capitals on small shafts. This once contained a statue which is now inside the south aisle; a similar recess and figure can be found at Rous Lench church. This entrance to the church from the abbot's house must have been impressive. The nave has pairs of lancet windows of the late 13th-century. The chancel is late Norman, and has flat buttresses between lancet windows, which

The mid-11th century Christ in Benediction, now set in the east window recess in the south aisle of Leigh church

were altered and made pointed in the 13th century. Perhaps this work was undertaken by masons from Pershore Abbey, the chancel of which was rebuilt at about this time. The south aisle has 13th-century lancets in the east wall, which was the east wall of a south transept. In the 14th century the transept and narrow late Norman south aisle were extended into a large Decorated aisle. The south wall of this aisle was rebuilt in 1855, and a new east window was also put into the chancel in the Decorated style. The battlemented tower dates from about 1400, and has Decorated bell openings and a west doorway with a restored Perpendicular west window. The Perpendicular timber porch contains a piscina, probably from the south aisle, which was reset as a stoup in the 19th century.

The interior is impressive, and much larger than the exterior would suggest. The arcade of late Norman sandstone piers and pointed arches are the most striking feature. The chancel arch has simple capitals with scallops. A similar arch leads from the chancel to the south aisle. The arcade has round piers, scallop capitals and single step arches, whilst the piers at the east and west ends have capitals with crockets. This all points to a date at the very end of the 12th century, similar to the tower arch in Bredon church and the west end of Worcester Cathedral. Pershore Abbey, which undertook the building of the church, was pioneering new church architecture at the time. Indeed it is probable that the masonry of the nave dates back to the 1050s when Pershore Abbey may have rebuilt and rededicated the church to St. Edburga. The blind arches above the present chancel arch are perhaps a survival of late Anglo-Saxon work, in which case these late Norman arches would pierce earlier walls.

In 1970, the sculpture from the north doorway was set in the east window recess in the south aisle. It is very beautiful and shows Christ in Benediction carrying a staff with a cross; the drapery is finely carved. It has been dated to the mid-11th century, making it not only a very early example of sculpture, but also more animated and less stylised than other contemporary pieces. It may have been moved to the north doorway from a dominant position above the chancel arch when the arch was rebuilt in the late 12th century.

The surviving section of the 15th-century rood screen once extended with a loft for the full width of the church. It is decorated with carved roses and quatrefoils, and has Perpendicular style tracery. It was repainted in 1855 by a curate, Edward Bradley, who was also known as the author Cuthbert Bede. The rood loft stairs also

The memorial to William Colles, d.1615, and his wife, Mary Palmer, d.1602, in the chancel

survive in the aisle. The font is a round Norman bowl, carved with scallops and zig-zag, set on a 19th-century stem and base. At the west end of the south aisle is a group of medieval floor tiles, with a few more on the chancel steps. There is also a medieval squint by the chancel arch. There is a 16th-century communion table, and 17th-century communion rails, but most of the remainder of the fittings are 19th-century, which gives the interior a Victorian gloss. These include the stone reredos in the chancel and the Nicholson organ, brought from St. Edmundsbury Cathedral in 1971.

The glass is also mainly Victorian, but a few medieval fragments are apparent in the tracery lights of the south aisle windows. The three lancets in the chancel have glass of 1866 by Francis Barnett of Leith showing the Good Shepherd, the Sower, and Galilee. The east window is a memorial to the Day family, and the west window of 1858 shows the four Evangelists.

The south aisle contains a restored Decorated tomb recess, but the finest monuments are in the chancel. On the south side is Edmund Colles, who died in 1606. His effigy and tomb chest are painted, the chest having several Renaissance motifs such as caryatids and strapwork. Opposite are William Colles, who died in 1615, and his wife Mary Palmer, who died in 1602. Their figures are also painted and are shown kneeling, both facing east. The children are on the tomb chest, and the monument has a large round arch and canopy. Also on the north side is the imposing stone memorial to Walter Devereux, Viscount Hereford, who died in 1659, with his wife Elizabeth Knightley. The effigies lie beneath a canopy which rests on round columns. Their kneeling children are shown on the tomb chest. Above is the memorial to Essex Devereux, who died in 1639. It appears quite precarious, particularly as his daughter is shown perched at the front. He kneels at a prayer desk opposite his wife, Ann Courteen, below a canopy with their family arms. Essex Devereux drowned in the River Teme with a friend, George Freke, who is commemorated by a tablet in the nave close to the font.

In the churchyard is the base of the medieval cross, and on the south side of the tower are the remains of a large painted sundial.

LICKEY   HOLY TRINITY

High on the Lickey Hills between Bromsgrove and Birmingham, the village of Lickey is mainly a suburban development of the 19th and 20th centuries. The church is close to the obelisk erected as a monument to the eighth Earl of Plymouth, and much of the surrounding woodland was leased by the earls to the City of Birmingham as recreational open space. This gives the village something of the feel of a resort.

Holy Trinity church was built in 1856 of grey sandstone, and was designed by Henry Day, who also restored the churches at Cofton Hackett and Feckenham. It is of Early English style with lancet windows and a bellcote on the east gable between the nave and chancel. The nave is aisled with a porch, and the chancel has an organ loft and vestry. The interior is in the same style, and whitewashed. The Rowlands memorial window is the work of Bromsgrove Guild craftsmen.

LINDRIDGE   ST. LAWRENCE

Lindridge church is in a commanding and almost isolated position above the River Teme, close to the Worcester to Tenbury road. The school and vicarage are by the church with a large Georgian house, but the main village is a mile to the east at Eardiston.

This is the third church on the site. The medieval church, which was destroyed by fire, had a timber bell turret like that at nearby Knighton-on-Teme. The second church fell victim to subsidence on this steep site, and the present church was built in 1861. It is a large dark sandstone building with a south-west tower and spire, aisled nave and chancel. The south aisle has gables, and the style is late Early English. The design was that of Thomas Nicholson, the diocesan architect for Hereford, who designed and restored many churches in Herefordshire.

The interior is typical of the later 19th century, with fittings of that date, including the font of alabaster, which has an unusual tracery design on the sides. There are four 17th-century brass plaques with arms to the Penell family, who lived at Woodston in the parish. A large monument to Arthur Onslow, Dean of Worcester, who died in 1817, is elaborately carved—above a sarcophagus is an obelisk, with sun rays and an angel on a cloud.

The tower contains a sanctus bell from the old church, thought to date from about 1475.

LITTLE COMBERTON   ST. PETER

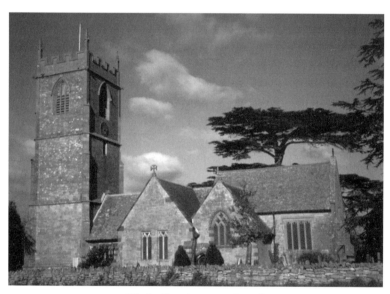
Little Comberton church

Little Comberton is an attractive village with many timber framed cottages and houses lying to the north-west of Bredon Hill. Land here, like neighbouring Bricklehampton, was held by Westminster Abbey during the early Middle Ages and then passed through the hands of the Beauchamps and Savages along with Elmley Castle. Finds of pottery, glass and coins near the church indicate an established Roman settlement here.

St. Peter's church is of limestone and has a proportionally tall west tower, relatively low nave with north porch and high chancel with south transept and chapel, north chapel and vestry. The resulting rooflines are most attractive. The nave is Norman and has three reset lancet windows, one of which is decorated with rope moulding. Another window is 14th-century. The Norman north doorway is most unusual. The tympanum has a carved cross, either side of which are four unexplained whorls, presumably carved features in a painted design. The porch carries the date 1639 and has graffiti of the outlines of hands, claimed to be those of newly married brides. The chancel and south chapel transept were built in 1886 using some medieval material, including the Decorated east window, and a Perpendicular north window with a hood mould, the stops of which are carved with letters P and N, whilst at the centre is the letter S between two oak leaves. Could this be a reference to the Savage family? The 17th-century north chapel was rebuilt in 1886. The nave and chancel are divided by a timber-framed gable of 1886, replacing the medieval structure. The work of 1886 is all by William White in memory of the rector, William Parker, who served here for 56 years. The tower is a beautiful 15th-century piece of work with pinnacles, battlements and gargoyles above the Perpendicular bell openings and west window.

The interior is very much the product of the 19th-century alterations. There is a high oak arch between the nave and chancel, and polychrome pillars to the transept and chapel arches. By contrast, the tower arch is Perpendicular with simple capitals. Amongst the mainly Victorian fittings are some 15th-century tiles with arms, two medieval piscinae, and the recut 14th-century font. The reredos which shows the Ascension was carved in 1900 by Richard Houghton of Worcester, and there are oak panels in the chancel of 1892 by Thomas Collins of Tewkesbury.

*The Norman tympanum on the north doorway,
with its unexplained whorls*

There are some fragments of medieval glass, including some heads in a nave south window. Further fragments, along with some 18th-century arms are in the south transept window. Another medieval head is incorporated into a north window in the nave which was installed in 1888 in memory of Rector Parker. Another window of this date to Parker is on the north side of the chancel by Powell & Co. of London. The east window glass shows scenes from the Life of Christ.

The First World War bronze memorial is inscribed with famous lines by Rupert Brooke, and nearby a brass to William Abell killed at Obourg in 1914, shows a soldier lying on the battlefield. There is also an early 19th-century tablet to the Shekell family in the chancel.

LITTLE MALVERN   ST. GILES

The priory church at Little Malvern must be one of the most beautifully situated churches in England (see also illustration p.8). It stands on the lower slopes of the east side of the Malvern Hills, below British Camp, with woodland ascending steeply behind. The views to the east across the Severn Valley are spectacular. The priory was founded as a daughter house to Worcester Cathedral in about 1125. It remained small, with about 12 Benedictine monks, until its dissolution in 1534 when there were just five. The monastic buildings and land passed to Henry Russell in 1539, whose family and their descendants

Little Malvern Priory from the south-east

the Beringtons, have lived there ever since. Little Malvern Court contains the 14th-century refectory, and in the grounds are the landscaped remains of the medieval fishponds. The Russells and Beringtons were recusant Roman Catholics and in 1862 built the Catholic church of St. Wulstan a little to the north, where, in 1934, Sir Edward Elgar was buried.

The sandstone priory church is approached from the north across a small, pretty churchyard. It was formerly cruciform, but now consists simply of the east end which now forms a nave and chancel together with the crossing tower. Ruined walls are visible to the north and south which are the remains of chapels and transepts, and in the east end of the former nave is a small single storey annexe. The remains of the south wall of the nave south aisle contain a Norman doorway which once led to the cloisters, and it is thought that the nave had arcades, as still survive at Great Malvern Priory. The outline of the nave is marked in the private drive of Little Malvern Court. The tower stands on three blocked Decorated arches which opened into the nave and transepts. There are small quatrefoil openings in the middle part, whilst the belfry has panelling and large bell openings. The tower is like a simpler version of that at Great Malvern Priory, and was once also crowned with battlements and pinnacles which were probably removed at the Dissolution and replaced by the present pyramid roof; perhaps it was the intention to demolish the tower. The body of the church, the former chancel, has 14th-century lower walls with blocked later Perpendicular arches, above which are high clerestorey windows. The east end has long Perpendicular windows to each side of the east window, all with transoms. In the blocked arches are further Perpendicular windows, which seem to have been reset from the side chapels after the Dissolution. The rebuilding of the east end and tower was undertaken by Bishop Alcock of Worcester between 1480 and 1482 and who, when he visited the priory in 1480, was so appalled by the state of affairs that he sent the prior and monks for two years' correction at Gloucester Priory. Alcock then wrote to them in 1482 to say that he had rebuilt the church, and the monks returned.

The entrance to the church is via the west annexe from which a doorway leads into the base of the tower. The height of the interior is impressive and light, whilst the old woodwork gives a most attractive atmosphere. There are numerous architectural fragments from the remains of the priory, including a reset Norman capital by the entrance. Behind the altar are two blocked doorways which once gave access to a Lady Chapel or vestries beyond the east end. In the side walls are blocked squints connecting with the side chapels. The 19th-century wooden ceiling incorporates reset 15th-century bosses and a border of quatrefoils.

There is an octagonal font, which may be a reused medieval pillar base. Dividing the present nave and chancel is a Perpendicular screen, with part of the rood beam lowered to make a cornice. It has carved vine decoration. The ten stalls which were once beneath the tower contain misericords which have been defaced, but the carving on the handrests survives, including two pigs eating from the same trough, and several grotesque human faces. Another survival is a medieval carved wooden figure of a man, though its origins are unknown. At the west end is a large 19th-century gallery containing the organ.

There are many medieval tiles in the chancel, which were probably made in Malvern during the 15th century. Designs include heraldry, parts of Latin inscriptions, the names of Evangelists and the instruments of the Passion. Two of the windows contain 15th-century glass. The tracery in the window on the north side in the blocked arch contains God the Father from a Coronation of the Virgin. The east window glass commemorates the restoration of the priory by Bishop Alcock. The six lights below the transom contained the portraits of the Yorkist royal family, of which the figures survive of Prince Edward (later King Edward V), Queen Elizabeth Woodville, Princess Elizabeth (later Queen to King Henry VII) and her sisters Princesses Cecily, Anne and Katherine. King Edward IV has been lost. Above was probably a line of figures of saints, of which the lower half of St. Ecgwin of Evesham remains. In the tracery are coats of arms, including those of the King, Prince of Wales and Bishop Alcock.

Amongst the architectural fragments there is the side of a 15th-century tomb chest with panels that contain four figures, probably weepers, beneath canopies. There is also a separate head of a knight which may have come from the same monument, itself perhaps once standing in the north chapel. The hatchments are those of the Russell and Berington families.

The church possesses a 15th-century crucifix now made into a processional cross, and in the tower is a 14th-century bell.

LITTLE WITLEY   ST. MICHAEL

The mainly 19th-century church at Little Witley

To the east of Great Witley and the Court, Little Witley is a compact village around a cluster of lanes to the south of the Worcester to Tenbury road. The church is tucked away in the south-west corner. In the Anglo-Saxon period, Little Witley was part of the large parish of St. Helen's in Worcester.

The earliest parts of the present red sandstone building are of 13th-century date, including the lower courses of the north and west walls, and much of the south wall. The blocked Early English north doorway has a simple moulding. The previous church appears from 19th-century illustrations to have had an Early English nave and chancel, but was rebuilt with a nave and apsidal chancel, along with a vestry and porch, and a bell turret on the west end.

The architect for this work was Abraham Perkins of Worcester Cathedral and he provided the church with Early English style details throughout. The windows are both lancets with Y-shaped tracery. The bell turret has a short stone spire, and is unusual in being set at an angle to the building with the west end projecting over the wall, and supported by a bracket. There are Early English style shafts on the turret, bearing a great similarity to those around the east end of the cathedral. The carvings on the corbels, capitals, font and pulpit are the work of Mrs. Sale, the wife of the incumbent at Holt, in whose parish Little Witley was at the time. In the 1930s her adopted daughter, Mrs. Berkeley, recalled that Mrs. Sale carved 114 pieces for Little Witley church in the entrance porch of Holt Rectory. The interior with its 19th-century fittings has great charm and has been restored, with the attractive paintwork to the roof timbers of the apse giving colour to the east end.

LONGDON   ST. MARY

In the Middle Ages, Longdon was one of several places held by Pershore Abbey to be given to Westminster Abbey, and from 1335 the tithes went to help finance the rebuilding of the church there. The parish is a rural one on the southern edge of the county. In the western part is a large low-lying area known as Longdon Marsh which was tidal until navigational improvements were carried out to the River Severn in the 19th century. The village stands on a low ridge and surrounds the church.

Only the lias stone tower survives from the medieval church, to which is attached the rendered brick nave and stone porch, apsidal chancel, organ recess and vestry. The tower is probably early 14th-century, and has unusually tall bell openings of two lights with Y-shaped tracery and transom bars. They are almost identical to those on the old church tower at Upton-upon-Severn, and represent a local architectural trend. The stair turret, pinnacles and spire were added in 1826, and probably replace a similar but smaller spire. The top of the spire was rebuilt in the 1970s. However, the medieval church had fallen into such great disrepair by the 18th century that the nave was replaced in 1786. The classical brick preaching box of the period is finely proportioned and has a large round arched window on either side of a central Venetian window. By the 19th century the nave was considered unfashionable for worship by the High Church movement, and in 1870 the vicar, Anthony Lefroy, designed a new Gothic south porch and blocked the west doorway. He also planned to coat the nave in stone and to convert the classical windows to Gothic ones. The Italianate Hoarwithy church in Herefordshire is the ultimate example of the conversion of a classical church of this type through the benefaction of the incumbent. At Longdon church in 1870, the vicar merely added the Norman style chancel, whose round-arched windows display a sympathy with those of the nave.

The interior is remarkably harmonious, and very appealing—at the west end is the early Decorated tower arch, with no capitals, but chamfers which fade into the sides of the arch. The nave is light and the chancel darker, thus emphasising in one setting the difference between churches of the 18th and 19th centuries. The nave was refitted when the chancel was built along with the organ loft recess, whilst the west gallery removed. Of the Georgian fittings, the 18th-century pulpit survives. It is of inlaid wood, with a back panel and concave sided canopy, which was made from the base, when the pulpit was moved in 1870. The baroque chandeliers date from 1789 and were formerly one piece. The font is probably late 19th-century, and the remainder of the fittings are of this date or later. The stone floor was laid in 1969. The iron gates of 1972 to the tower by Michael Farrar-Bell are very fine.

The west window has colourful glass releaded into a new pattern in 1972, also by Farrar-Bell, whilst the chancel windows contain glass of 1870 by Heaton and Butler showing the Life and Works of Christ. However, the central lancet glass was replaced in 1944, as a memorial to Catherine Weiss, and is of the Virgin and Child.

The earliest memorial is a brass to William Brugge of Eastington Hall, who died in 1523, and his wife Alice. There are several 19th-century memorial tablets and ledger stones, and a larger monument by William Stephens of Worcester with a sarcophagus shown in front of an obelisk to Thomas Parker, who lived at Longdon Hall, and who died in 1794.

LOWER MOOR   ST. THOMAS

On the gravels of the Avon Valley, between Fladbury and Wyre Piddle, lies the straggling village of Lower Moor. The present parish of Hill and Moor is attached to Fladbury, and amongst the timber-framed cottages at the centre of the village a small church was built in 1869. The architect was Frederick Preedy, and the building is a plain mission church, like a parish hall. It has just a nave with lancet windows of the Early English type.

LOWER SAPEY   ST. BARTHOLOMEW OLD CHURCH

The valley of Sapey Brook is a remote and beautiful area to the west of Clifton-upon-Teme. The church at Lower Sapey lies at the end of a narrow track alongside the brook and adjacent to a timber-framed house. Its remoteness has essentially saved the church. It was replaced by a new church in the village at Harpley in 1877, and was due to be demolished to a height of six feet—the frequent fate of abandoned churches in the 19th century, such as Grafton in Herefordshire—but the destruction was never carried out, and instead the church was used for farm storage. It featured in the Churches at Risk campaign in the 1970s and was eventually restored through the efforts of local fundraising, and is now vested in the Churches Conservation Trust. Since 1984 occasional services have been held with the congregation seated on bales of straw.

The Domesday Survey records a priest here in 1086, and indeed the nave and chancel built of sand-stone and local tufa, which make up the church, are basically Norman work. The windows include three Norman lancets, an Early English east window, a Decorated south chancel window, and an early 19th-century window at the west end which formerly lit the gallery. The wide pointed window in the nave is probably 18th-century. The north and priest's doorways are blocked but the timber south porch is 15th-century and shelters a simple Norman doorway, which has scalloped capitals and a 15th-century door.

The inside is simple, empty and whitewashed. The chancel arch was removed in the early 19th century and replaced by a timber tympanum. The plaster ceiling is 18th-century below medieval roof timbers. There are traces of wall paintings, including a lion on the south wall, which was probably from a Royal arms. At the west end is the base of the font now at Harpley church, and there are aumbries in both the north and south walls of the chancel. Only the restored gallery remains of the early 19th-century fittings which included box pews and a three decker pulpit.

The belfry is a simple internal structure in the west gable of the nave, where boarded louvres allow the sound to escape. An earlier medieval belfry of this type survives in the nave of Warndon church. On the south wall are the remains of a scratched Mass dial.

LULSLEY   ST. GILES

Lulsley church is now a private house, having been converted in the 1970s after being made redundant, though the graveyard is still accessible. Several of the fittings are now in the church at Alfrick. The village is a scattering of houses and farms close to the River Teme between Alfrick and Knightwick. It is a quiet place, only accessible by a long narrow loop road. Jabez Allies, the antiquary and folklore historian of Worcestershire, was baptised here in 1787.

The present red sandstone church, which replaced a medieval church on the same site, was built in 1892 by Henry Rowe, architect of St. Oswald's Hospital and Chapel in Worcester. It has a nave and chancel with a timber bellcote and spire at the west end. The windows and doorways are in the early Decorated style.

MADRESFIELD   ST. MARY

The Lygon family have lived at Madresfield Court since at least the 13th century, and held the title Earl Beauchamp from 1815 to 1979. The Court today is a splendid mixture of Tudor and Victorian brick archi-tecture inside a moat, and includes a chapel decorated in the Arts and Crafts style with work by several members of the Bromsgrove Guild. The house appears particularly fine when approached from the east with the Malvern Hills behind. Evelyn Waugh visited Madresfield regularly in the 1930s, and it seems to have been the inspiration for *Brideshead Revisited*.

The medieval church stood immediately to the south-west of the Court. It was a small building with nave, chancel and a small timber bell turret at the west end. A new church was built on the same site in 1852 by Edward Pugin, son of Augustus, but by the 1860s it had already become unsafe, and was demol-ished. A plaque in the grounds of the Court marks the site.

The present church was built in 1866 on a new site to the west in the estate village. Victorian brick cottages and a school make up a short street and the sandstone church with some polychrome decoration forms an impressive focal point. The nave and chancel are attached to a north-west tower and spire, a south porch, and an organ chamber with vestry lie on the north side of the chancel. The style is Decorated

Madresfield—Preedy's tower with its pinnacles and lucarnes to the spire, with, in front the well of 1866

and parts of Pugin's church were reused, particularly the east and west windows. Henry Lygon, fifth Earl Beauchamp paid for the work and commissioned the architect, Frederick Preedy. However, he died before it was finished and his brother, Frederick, the sixth Earl instructed Preedy to add the tower and spire with its impressive pinnacles and lucarnes.

The interior is a period piece of the 1860s—lofty and spacious with many contemporary fittings, but in which the Decorated style predominates. The chancel roof structure is reused from the nave of the 1852 church, whilst the nave roof is supported by a series of corbels carved with the Doctors of the Church. The pulpit and font both date from 1852. In the chancel, the reredos of Caen stone, with statues of Eve and the Virgin, contains an unusual painting of the Last Supper. The large Nicholson organ is of 1867. The chancel arch has a screen by Preedy, and above is a painting of the Last Judgement with the text of the Ten Commandments. The vestry contains a piscina made from the 18th-century font of the first church.

The glass in the west window was moved from the second church and shows Christ in Majesty with the Last Judgement. The other windows of the nave have glass showing saints, including St. Wulstan and St. Edburga, along with Reginald Bray, benefactor of Malvern Priory. The windows are memorials to members of the Lygon family. The east window glass shows Paradise, and was designed in 1918 by Henry Payne of Birmingham.

A collection of simple tablets are memorials to the earls Beauchamp and the Lygon family. The first earl was Member of Parliament for Worcestershire from 1780 to 1806, and the seventh earl was Mayor of Worcester in 1895. Living abroad from 1931, the seventh earl was probably the model for Waugh's Lord Marchmain. Under the west window is a bronze monument by Feodora, Countess Gleichen, to Edward Lygon and Richard Somerset who were killed in the Boer War in 1900. The figures of Obedience, Loyalty and Fortitude are under mosaic canopies in the Art Nouveau style.

Outside in the churchyard are several Lygon gravestones, including that of Hugh Lygon, who died in 1936 after collapsing and hitting his head on a stone in Bavaria. The character of the flamboyant Sebastian Flyte in *Brideshead Revisited* seems to have been derived by Waugh from him. On the east wall of the church is a carved crucifixion in memory of George Munn, rector from 1856 to 1906. The well by the porch with pretty ironwork mechanism and corona was sunk in 1866 as a water source for the builders and was subsequently used for baptismal purposes.

MALVERN   PRIORY CHURCH OF ST. MARY AND ST. MICHAEL

The Perpendicular Malvern Priory church from the north-west

The setting of Malvern Priory is beautiful and striking. It stands at the centre of the town on the eastern slopes of the Malvern Hills, higher up which can be had some of the best views of the priory. To the north of the church is a large graveyard with beautiful mature trees, to the south the site of the Benedictine monastery is now occupied by the Abbey Hotel. The monastic buildings have virtually disappeared, but the church has survived almost intact in its medieval state. When the monastery was dissolved in 1539, the people of Malvern, then a small village outside the priory gates, bought the church for £20 to replace their derelict parish church of St. Thomas, which stood in the north-west corner of the churchyard. The relative poverty of the community meant that many of the pre-Reformation furnishings and stained glass windows were not removed and replaced, although subsequent neglect took its toll on the building.

The details of the foundation of the monastery are confused. In the 15th century, a muddled story grew up that it was established by St. Werstan, who fled to Malvern when Deerhurst Priory in Gloucestershire was sacked by the Danes in the early 11th century. However, it seems more likely that it was founded in about 1085 by Aldwin, a monk from Worcester, who established a hermitage on the present site. The subsequent priory was built on land belonging to Westminster Abbey, to which it remained dependent to the consternation of successive bishops of Worcester; there was a serious dispute over jurisdiction between Worcester and Westminster in 1282. At the Dissolution, the monks fought hard to save the monastery with petitions and even bribes, but were unsuccessful.

The church is constructed from a motley range of coloured sandstones. It is cruciform with an aisled nave and chancel, central tower, north transept, porch and truncated south transept. The south transept and Lady Chapel at the east end are the only parts which did not survive the Dissolution. The main impression is of a Perpendicular church but there are traces of the Norman building visible on the outside—the south wall was less easily rebuilt in the 15th century as it joined the monastic buildings, and it retains a plain Norman doorway with columns, which led from the south aisle to the cloister. Part of a Norman eastern arch in the destroyed south transept also survives, along with late Norman capitals from the former crypt beneath the Lady Chapel. The Lady Chapel itself was rebuilt in the Decorated style, but the rest of the Norman church was rebuilt in the Perpendicular style.

The 15th-century building work is very stately. The chancel was rebuilt between about 1420 and 1460. It has large clerestorey windows with typical Perpendicular tracery and transoms, and a huge east window, which was probably completed by 1440. The battlements are plain. The tower is very similar to that at Gloucester Cathedral, and may well be the work of the same mason, John Gower. The Gloucester tower was complete by 1457, and this tower may have followed immediately, being finished by 1460. It

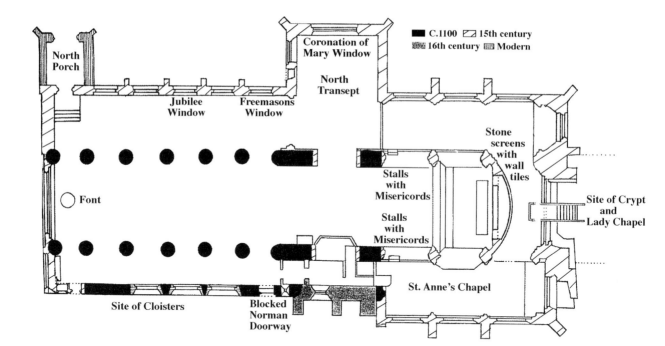

Plan of Malvern Priory

has panelled sides, canopied bell openings and beautiful traceried pinnacles and battlements. Similar battlements can be found on the nave, which also has long clerestorey windows and a large west window to complement that at the east end. The nave was complete by 1490 and the north transept by 1501 when the windows were also glazed. The windows in the south aisle were inserted in 1841, whilst the north porch was rebuilt in 1894.

It is a surprise on entering the church to see the solid Norman arcades of the nave beneath the large clerestorey windows. The piers are short and the arches have steps, whilst the heavy round capitals are similar to those in the nave of Tewkesbury Abbey in Gloucestershire. There are also traces of Norman work at the crossing from a former tower. The effect of the Perpendicular windows is to make the space feel light, whilst the medieval glass softens the brightness to be found in Perpendicular churches with completely clear windows. The upper parts of the tower arches are Perpendicular, along with the Lierne vault. The chancel was also to have been vaulted, and springers can be seen between the windows. It is otherwise richly decorated with carved stone panels. There are vaults to the chancel aisles, but the chancel has a flat wooden ceiling like that of the nave. However, the nave ceiling was rebuilt by Sir George Gilbert Scott in 1860. A blocked doorway in the east wall led to stairs giving access to the crypt and the unusual wide arch to the former Lady Chapel contains an ogee headed doorway, similar to the entrance to the Lady Chapel in Gloucester Cathedral.

The Priory is justly famous for its 15th-century glass, notably in the east window, chancel clerestorey windows, St. Anne's Chapel in the south chancel aisle, the north transept, and the west window. The glass was installed over some 60 years, with the east window glazed in about 1450 and the north transept window in 1501. It is probable that the east window glass is by John Thornton of Coventry, son of the designer of the great east window of York Minster, whilst the north transept window was given by King Henry VII in 1501 and is likely to be the work of the Westminster glazier, Richard Twyge. It seems likely that the glazing was planned by the monks, who then persuaded donors to follow the scheme, as it is so very uniform. The king was Lord of Malvern Chase, and aside from the gift of Henry VII, King Richard III gave the west window when he was Duke of Gloucester. Other donors included local families, such as the Corbets, Walwyns, Blounts and Ferrers. There were also ecclesiastics, like Prior Richard Dene, and John Alcock, Bishop of Worcester, who also contributed much to Little Malvern Priory. Many of their heraldic arms appear in the glass. The glass in St. Anne's Chapel and the south chancel clerestorey was rearranged by the medievalist and author of ghost stories, Montague Rhodes James in 1910, whilst the rest was restored by Gordon McNeil Rushforth between 1915 and 1919, and formed the basis for his book *Medieval Christian Imagery*. After storage during the Second World War, the glass was restored to its present positions by the organist, L. Hamand, who also produced a book on the subject.

The east window shows the Passion of Christ and the Resurrection, with figures of the apostles. The clerestorey window on the north side of the chancel nearest the tower shows the legend of the foundation of the priory, with donor figures and scenes. In the south chancel clerestorey windows can be seen Crucifixion scenes and four of the nine orders or choirs of angels. The north transept window depicts the Coronation of the Virgin (see also Little Malvern), along with scenes from Christ's early life and figures of Prince Arthur, King Henry VII and his chief councillor, Reginald Bray, who was also a benefactor to the priory. The transept west window contains a panel depicting the Last Supper and figures of saints. The west window of the nave also depicts saints including St. Lawrence and St. Christopher. St. Anne's Chapel has medieval glass in its southern windows, with 33 Old Testament scenes which were once in the nave clerestorey—it is helpful to see depictions of the Creation, Noah, Abraham and Moses at eye level. Particularly notable too are the figures of angel musicians to be found around Prince Arthur in the north transept and in the east window. There are many other fragments of medieval glass, especially in the north chancel aisle, and a further window in the north aisle with scenes from the Life of Christ.

The glass in the east window of St. Anne's Chapel commemorates Queen Victoria's Diamond Jubilee of 1897 and is by Charles Eamer Kempe. Other important glass of more recent date includes the window in the north aisle, designed by Thomas Camm in 1887 for Queen Victoria's Golden Jubilee. This shows the Jubilee of the Nations, with the ceremony at Westminster Abbey, including a portrait of her grandson, Kaiser Wilhelm II. Also in the north aisle is a window showing King Solomon with the temple, given by the county freemasons in memory of their Provincial Grand Master, Augustus Godson, who died in 1906.

Of the medieval furnishings to survive, the stalls and miserecords in the chancel are the most signif-

icant. The canopies and upper parts of the stalls have been lost, but the arm rests and misericords have fine carved detail. The misericords show the Labours of the Months, which are similar to those in Ripple church and Worcester Cathedral, and date from between about 1450 and 1480. The other misericords are a century earlier and show a variety of mythological and domestic scenes, including three rats hanging a cat, a legendary beast called a cockatrice, and a sick man being attended by his doctor.

The 15th-century stone screens behind the altar incorporate a semi circular chamber, accessed by two doors. Its purpose is unclear, but it may have been a vestry or a trea-

Malvern Priory—the south of the nave showing the blocked Norman doorway in the south aisle

sury, where the priory's relics could have been visited by pilgrims on feast days. The back of the screen and the north chancel aisle contain a unique collection of medieval wall tiles, which, along with the large number of floor tiles, are the products of kilns that were located near the priory, kilns which supplied tiles to most of Worcestershire's churches. The wall tiles are rectangular, and many have architectural designs. Other tile designs include heraldic arms of families, England, France and a Staffordshire knot, the monogram HS and a crowned M for the Virgin. The inscription on the so called Friends Tiles reminds the reader that it is better to give to the church during a lifetime than to entrust the gift to executors of the will after death. The Victorian tiles on the floor of the church are copies of several of the medieval tile designs.

The font has a plain Norman bowl, and there is a 15th-century piscina in the north chancel aisle. The medieval brackets in St. Anne's Chapel now carry statues of St. Anne and St. Ursula by Celestino Pancheri of the Bromsgrove Guild. The pulpit is of 1864 by Scott, whilst the brass lectern dates from 1877. The reredos, which shows the Nativity, was designed in 1884 by Sir Arthur Blomfield, architect of the church at Upton-upon-Severn. The present organ is by Rushworth and Dreaper of Liverpool and is housed in a case of 1927 by William Caroe.

A chantry chapel near St. Anne's Chapel contains fragments of medieval sculpture, as well as the tomb slabs of Walcher, the second prior, and Prior William Wykewane. To the north of the main altar is the effigy of an unidentified 13th-century knight, shown with a shield and battle axe rather than a sword. Opposite is the large monument to John Knottesford, who died in 1589, and his wife, Jane Knightley, who died in 1582. He had purchased the monastery buildings from John Pinnock, who had acquired them from the king at the Dissolution and they are shown lying on the tomb chest in contemporary costume, with their children on the base. Their eldest daughter, Anne, who gave the monument, is shown as a large kneeling figure at a prayer desk.

Other monuments and tablets include a memorial in the north transept to John Dandridge, who died in 1785, and is shown with members of his family. It was produced by Sir Richard Westmacott in about 1830. There is a resting pilgrim shown at the base. Peter Hollins designed the tablet in St. Anne's Chapel of a woman seated by an urn to commemorate Thomas Woodyatt, who died in 1811. He also designed the memorial in the nave to Sophia Thompson, who died in 1836, which shows the head of a woman reclining on a couch. The tablet to Sir Henry Foley Lambert, who died in 1872 and was grandson of Lady Emily Foley, the town's great benefactor, was designed by Sir George Gilbert Scott. There are several ledger stones of various dates in the floor, whilst the war memorial was designed by William Caroe.

One 14th-century bell survives in the tower, whilst the clappers of several other bells are preserved on a 17th-century panel in the porch. To the west can be seen the priory's gatehouse straddling Abbey Road, and although much restored in the 19th century, incorporates much of the medieval gateway to the monastery buildings and now houses Malvern Museum. Of the other monastic buildings only the timber-framed Guesten Hall survived the Dissolution until it was demolished in 1841.

In the churchyard to the north is the base of a medieval cross, with a niche for the pyx, such as can also be found at Broadwas and Knighton-on-Teme churches.

MALVERN   ST. ANDREW, POOLBROOK

Poolbrook Common lies at the foot of the hills and the extensive Malvern Common. Poolbrook Road runs along the centre with brick cottages and houses to either side. St. Andrew's church lies east of the common, and has a gabled bellcote on a substantial buttress with lancet windows making up the west front. The church has a nave with south aisle, a porch, chancel and vestry, and was constructed in the Early English style in 1885 to designs by Sir Arthur Blomfield, architect of Upton-upon-Severn church. It was built as a memorial to Edward Chance of the glass manufacturing family from Stourbridge.

Amongst the many 19th- and 20th-century fittings inside, is a font designed by Frederick Preedy for St. Mary Magdalene's church in Worcester in 1877, and brought here in 1981. The pulpit came from St. Matthias church in 1881. The organ is by Nicholson and there are Godwin tiles on the chancel floor. The previous font with an inscription dating it to 1724, which had been found by the Reverend Henry Foster in Northumberland, was placed in the churchyard.

MALVERN   ALL SAINTS, THE WYCHE, MALVERN WELLS

At the north end of Malvern Wells on the edge of the common, All Saints church stands close to the entrance to the railway tunnel under the hills. The site was given by Sir Henry Foley in 1900 and the church was consecrated in 1903, just after the church of the Ascension opened at Malvern Link, replacing a mission chapel of 1865 by Wyche Cutting at the top of the hill. The church was designed in local stone by the local architect, Troyte Griffith, and has a nave with an apsidal chancel and small bell turret. The style is Early English and there are several lancet windows.

The interior is brick-faced and contains some early 20th-century glass, showing St. Michael and scenes from the Life of Christ, alongside scenes of the Battle of the Somme as a memorial to the First World War. The first vicar of the new parish was Canon W. Buchanan-Dunlop, a noted local historian. Since the closure of St. Peter's church, All Saints church has served the whole of Malvern Wells.

MALVERN   ASCENSION, MALVERN LINK

Inside the church of the Ascension, Malvern Link

The area between Malvern Link and North Malvern was extensively developed during the late 19th century, and this church comes as a surprise amongst the streets of terraced houses at the junction of Somers Park Avenue and Albert Park Road. The tall nave and chancel have a rather bleak exterior with rendered walls, broken by limestone buttresses and dressings, with lancet windows. There is a thin tower at the west end with a curious four gabled roof, and square sanctus bellcote at the division between nave and chancel.

The church was built in 1903 in memory of the Venerable Arthur Livingstone by Walter Tapper, architect of several Arts and Crafts churches throughout the country. The windows are Early English style lancets, high on the walls, in pairs in the nave but single in the chancel. There are triple lancets at the west and east ends.

The elegant interior has whitewashed walls with the lancets making a clerestorey, linked to each other by a wall passage lined with little Early English style columns. The nave is roofed with a pointed tunnel vault, whilst the chancel has a rib vault of brick. There is an air of great simplicity offset by the division of the nave and chancel by a large metal rood screen under the arch. It was designed by G. Bainbridge Reynolds. There are other fine 20th-century furnishings including banners by Ian Thompson.

MALVERN   CHRIST CHURCH

Christ Church stands above Barnards Green close to Great Malvern Station and Malvern Girls College. It is a large church of 1875-76 with a west tower supporting a tall broach spire, an aisled nave and chancel, with a south porch in front of an unusual south gable. The architects were T.D. Barry and Sons of Liverpool, who used the Decorated style and the church has similarities to their church at Bengeworth. The foundation stone on the south side of the tower was laid by Lady Emily Foley who gave the land on which the church is sited.

The spacious interior contains glass in the east window of 1892 by Charles Eamer Kempe showing scenes from the Crucifixion and the Resurrection, which was a memorial to the first trustees of the building. Other glass of the same period is by Coxwell, Chance and Wilmot, as well as Clayton and Bell. St. Francis and Florence Nightingale are depicted in the memorial window to Grace Tucker, an incumbent's daughter who died in childhood.

MALVERN   HOLY TRINITY, LINK TOP

Above Malvern Link by the junction of Newtown Road the hill suddenly begins to rise more steeply. Holy Trinity Church stands at this point in a churchyard enclosed by yew trees. It was built in 1850 to 1851 by Samuel Dawkes of Cheltenham, who also did much of the 19th-century building work at Witley Court, and enlarged in 1872 by George and Henry Haddon, who designed one of the boarding houses at Malvern College. The church is of buff coloured stone with a nave and chancel. There is an octagonal eastern turret with a short spire. The style is Early English, and the clerestorey windows have cross gables.

The interior has numerous 19th- and 20th-century fittings. There are windows of 1873 glazed by Ward and Hughes, and the east window glass is of about 1902 by Charles Eamer Kempe.

MALVERN   ST. MATTHIAS, MALVERN LINK

The parish of St. Matthias was formed in the 19th century out of the southern part of the parish of Leigh, when Malvern Link developed around the Worcester to Hereford railway. The church rises above the terraced houses near Malvern Link Station and stands in a large churchyard.

The substantial Malvern stone building has an aisled nave and chancel with a north porch and south west tower. The first church was built in 1844 to 1846 by Sir George Gilbert Scott, which today comprises the chancel and four eastern bays of the nave and aisles. Scott's porch was later moved to its present position. The church was extended to the south in 1858 and a new tower added in 1862, before it was much altered and given new east and west windows in 1880 to 1881 by a London architect, F.W. Hunt. The building work was undertaken by Thomas Collins of Tewkesbury who constructed many Victorian Worcestershire churches. The present tower with battlements, pinnacles and a higher stair turret was added in 1899. The church is in the early Decorated style with lancets and tracery, and the clerestorey windows alternate between two and three lights. The statue of St. Matthias and other sculpture was carved by William Forsyth of Worcester.

The interior has many interesting late 19th- and early 20th-century high Anglican fittings, particularly the screen, which has a dado painted with figures of saints by nuns from the Convent of the Holy Name in Malvern Link in about 1918. The fitting of the Lady Chapel by Richard Boulton of Cheltenham in 1934 was paid for by the vicar, Henry Wilmot Hill, from the sale of his moth collection. The screens in the chapel are the work of Robert Thompson, the 'Mouseman' of Kilburn in Yorkshire which, like his furnishings at Ilmington church in Warwickshire, are carved with his distinctive mouse signature. The Nicholson organ dates from 1873. The glass in the east window of the south aisle is of 1877 by Clayton and Bell, and four other windows in the south aisle showing scenes from the Life of Christ are by Mayer & Co. The glass in the main east window is by Charles Eamer Kempe, who also installed two further windows in the chancel in 1884, one of which shows St. Matthias.

MALVERN   ST. PETER, COWLEIGH

Under the shadow of North Hill, St. Peter's church stands on Cowleigh Bank, which rises steeply from Malvern Link. It is a Malvern stone church without a tower, and so is not easily seen from any distance. The aisled nave and chancel have a bellcote in an unusual position at the east end of the north aisle. It was built in a late Early English style in 1863 to 1866 by George Street, architect of Hagley church. The windows have plate tracery, and the unusual clerestorey windows are half quatrefoils under round arches.

Malvern—St. Peter, Cowleigh by George Street

The interior is typical of the mid-19th century, with Early English arcades. The simple round piers and capitals support pointed chamfered arches. The walls are of buff sandstone ashlar blocks which change to rough blue granite above the arcades. Amongst the many 19th- and 20th-century fittings is the pulpit designed by Street with columns of different coloured marbles on the front.

MALVERN   ST. PETER, MALVERN WELLS

St. Peter's church is at the centre of Malvern Wells, surrounded by several large Victorian properties on the side of the main road. Malvern Wells developed as a separate resort with its own water cure in the early 19th century, but never enjoyed the success of Great Malvern. This area was formerly part of Hanley Castle parish, but being over three miles from the parish church, a new church was provided at the expense of the vicar, Peter Boissier. It was begun in 1835 and completed in 1836.

The building is typical of the 1830s, and has a nave, transepts and chancel in the Early English style with large lancet windows. The steep slope of the hill to the east meant it was necessary to build an undercroft beneath the chancel. The architect was Robert Jearrad, who had designed Christ Church, Cheltenham. The church closed and was sold in the 1990s, when the fittings were dispersed—including a Norman style font, a reredos by Forsyth, and a lectern and pulpit carved by a vicar, Francis Hopkinson. The stained glass remains. The east window is of 1865 by Heaton, Butler and Bayne, another window by John Hardman of 1887 shows Mary Magdalene anointing Christ's feet. A south window has glass of 1885 by William Morris to a design of Edmund Burne-Jones showing the Good Shepherd.

The war memorial in the churchyard was designed in 1919 by the Arts and Crafts architect, Charles Voysey. Above the polygonal base and shaft is a pediment with Voysey's lettering. Two local houses, Perrycroft near Colwall in Herefordshire and Bannut Tree Farm at Castlemorton, are also his work.

MAMBLE   ST. JOHN THE BAPTIST

Mamble—the remains of the Blount Chapel

The name Mamble appears to be derived from a Welsh word for hill, and the village is beautifully situated on a hillside west of Clows Top with fine views into Shropshire. The area had small coal mines in operation up to the 19th century, but the parish today is mainly agricultural and centred around the small village just off the Bewdley to Tenbury road.

The church lies along a narrow lane in the village centre, and is set in a churchyard with several large trees. The layout seems unusual when approached from the east. Attached to the chancel is a ruined chapel, and the nave is concealed from view by a vestry and a south aisle with a pitched roof. The porch projects from the aisle, and beyond is a belfry with spire at the west end of the nave. The church is mainly built of grey sandstone, but the ruined chapel is of brick, whilst the belfry and spire are timber-framed, with weatherboarding and shingles. The timber-framed porch has brick in-fill. The earliest masonry, of about 1200, is in the nave, which has Early English lancets at the west end and on the north side, where the north doorway is now blocked. There are similar lancets in the chancel, but the east window and those in the south aisle are early Decorated with Y-shaped tracery. The porch was added in the 17th century and the south aisle extended eastwards to make a vestry in 1880.

The ruined chapel was built by the Blount family who lived at Sodington, now a farm to the south-east of the village. They were recusant Roman Catholics after the Reformation, and this chapel of about 1560 represents a typical addition by such a family to a church at this juncture, similar to the Sheldon chapel at Beoley and the Berkeley chapel at Cotheridge. It is unusual in Worcestershire to find building of this date in brick, and the lower courses with their pattern in blue bricks represent some of the earliest brick construction in the county. The Blounts had left Mamble by the 19th century, and although the upper parts of the walls were repaired about 1800, the chapel has been abandoned and closed off from the church. Upkeep has remained the responsibility of the family, and some restoration work is now planned.

The interior is attractively plain and whitewashed. There is an early Decorated arcade with round piers and arches with steps and chamfers. The chancel arch has capitals carved with foliage, more elabo-

Mamble—the massive timbers of the belfry

rate moulding to the arch, fillets on the piers, and probably dates from the early 14th century. The west end of the nave is partitioned by a timber-framed wall, similar to that at Knighton-on-Teme church, concealing the massive timbers of the scissor-framed belfry supports. The date of this structure is uncertain, but it seems to be early, possibly even 13th-century, and as it is built independently of the stonework of the surrounding nave walls, it is possible that it may pre-date them. Was it a separate belfry structure, as can be seen at Pembridge in Herefordshire? If so, has it been moved? Perhaps it was a temporary feature which became permanent and incorporated into the present turret and spire?

The fittings are almost all 19th-century, but the plain round font is Early English. Supports for the former west gallery can be seen on the timber-framed west wall. The east window contains a panel of beautiful 14th-century stained glass, showing the Crucifixion on a background of blue quarries divided by red bands. Other windows contain early 20th-century glass showing St. George, St. Michael and the Resurrection, whilst the war memorial window depicts St. Oswald and St. Alban.

The 14th-century tomb chest recess in the south aisle has an ogee arch and contains the worn remains of a carved skeleton shown lying on a mat. This has been moved here from the Blount Chapel, and is from the memorial to Thomas Blount who died in 1561. The rest of the monument has disappeared except for a worn inscription and some arms which are still on the ruined walls. Sir John Blount, who died in 1510, and his wife, Katherine Corbet, are represented on a brass in the chancel. He is shown wearing armour whilst she wears widow's clothing, but the children have been lost. There is a 14th-century effigy of a knight, probably Sir William Sodington, who died in about 1325, and who is shown with both hands lying on his body and without a shield, which is unusual on an effigy of this type.

There is a 15th-century bell in the tower. Some late medieval vestments thought to have been used in the church were preserved by local Roman Catholics and are in private hands.

MARTIN HUSSINGTREE   ST. MICHAEL

Martin Hussingtree is a small village lying between Droitwich and Fernhill Heath. The curious name refers to two separate manors, which were joined together in the Middle Ages. Pershore Abbey held estates here in Anglo-Saxon times, but along with many of their lands, such as Little Comberton, they were gifted to Westminster Abbey during the reign of King Edward the Confessor. The church is located next to the 17th-century court, former Georgian rectory and converted barns at the end of a lane to the west of the main road.

At the west end of a sandstone nave and chancel which are under the same roof is a small timber bell turret with short spire. There is a south aisle and north porch. One Norman lancet window survives in the chancel. Another chancel window is Perpendicular, and the Perpendicular east window has a date stone above which is inscribed 1625. This could mean that this is an example of very late Perpendicular style work or it could be that it is a restoration date. The medieval carved head above is a reused corbel. In 1857 Frederick Preedy planned a south aisle to replace a south transept but this was not built until 1883—even then it is unclear whether Preedy's design was actually used. However, the bell turret and rebuilt medieval porch are by Preedy and date from 1857 when he restored the church.

The interior is very much the result of Preedy's restoration, and has an oak arcade between the nave and aisle. Aside from the medieval font, the fittings are 19th- and 20th-century, and include the pulpit and communion rails of 1858 by Preedy.

There are several memorial tablets including one to Thomas Tomkins, the assistant licenser of books to King Charles II. He was involved in a debate over granting a licence for *Paradise Lost* by John Milton. At a time when the Divine Right of the monarch had been so recently re-established following the execution of King Charles I and the rule of Oliver Cromwell, there was grave concern over the publication in Milton's work of the phrase 'perplexes monarchs', but Tomkins eventually granted the licence. He was the step-nephew of another Thomas Tomkins, a composer, who was choir master and organist at Worcester Cathedral until 1649 when cathedral music ceased under Cromwell's orders. Many of his compositions were drawn together to form the work *Musica Deo Sacra*. Tomkins lived here from 1649 until his death in 1656 with his son Nathaniel, who was a prebend at the cathedral.

MARTLEY   ST. PETER

Martley—the effects of restoration and the influence of the Arts and Crafts movement

The church at Martley has a tower built of a most striking orange red sandstone. It is best seen in the evening sunshine, and is unlike any other church in the area. A lane leads south from the village to the church, which stands close to a spring known as St. Peter's Well, suggesting a pre-Christian origin for the site. To the east of the church is the Old Rectory, which contains the remains of a 14th-century timber-framed hall. Martley is a significant local centre between Worcester and the Teme Valley, its importance being reflected as a royal manor until 1196. It was then held by the Despencer and Mortimer families during the Middle Ages, and eventually passed to the Foleys of Witley Court.

The tower is at the west end of the nave and chancel, to which are attached a porch and vestry. The body of the church is also of sandstone, but here it is light red and grey. Indeed on the nave are significant remains of banding of stones in the two colours to make polychrome decoration, particularly so on the north side. These walls have flat buttresses and are Norman work of about 1150. There are also two similar Norman doorways both on projecting sections of the walls, which have a column to each side, and roll mouldings to the arches with bands of saltire crosses and lozenges. The north doorway is more easily visible because the timber porch added on the south side in 1884 obscures some of the south doorway. The chancel was largely rebuilt in the early 13th century and has two Early English lancet windows on the north side. It is probable that the east window is contemporary with a chantry chapel which was established in the south side of the chancel in 1315—it is Decorated with cusped Y-shaped tracery. There is similar tracery in the windows on the south side of the chancel and throughout the nave. The tower is Perpendicular with typical west window and bell openings, it has battlements and pinnacles, and was possibly built by the widow of Hugh Mortimer who died in 1460. The vestry was added in 1875, and the church was restored by Charles Nicholson in 1909.

It is this restoration which has made the interior so appealing in an Arts and Crafts way, blending medieval and modern. The walls are tall and mainly whitewashed, there is a quarry tile floor and the 14th-century roofs have been restored. There is no chancel arch, though the roofs are divided by a 17th-century timber-framed tympanum, which is now open. The medieval rood screen and loft were destroyed in 1829, and the present oak screen and loft erected in 1909, making use of the medieval rood loft stair. The large blind arch nearby, close to the eastern window of the nave, has never been satisfactorily explained. Other medieval features include the stoup outside the south doorway, the damaged 14th-century piscina with carved heads, several heraldic tiles on the chancel steps, including the arms of Henry Prince of Wales, later King Henry V, and those of Gloucester Abbey, and the central part of a medieval altar stone now incorporated in the present altar. In the chancel are two 17th-century houseling benches, predecessors of communion rails. The organ case has Arts and Crafts style painted decoration and there are royal arms and commandment boards. At the west end the statue of Christ was carved in the 1980s from a conifer in the churchyard.

No medieval glass survives, but several of the nave windows have glass by Charles Eamer Kempe. However, the church has a wonderful group of medieval wall paintings. The earliest is the 13th-century masonry pattern with quatrefoils on the north wall of the chancel. Chevrons are used to decorate the window surrounds, whilst further chevrons continue around the east window, either side of which are two elaborate 14th-century canopies. On the lower part of the east wall is some drapery with a series of beasts painted at the tops of the folds, including a fox, a hare, a stag, a wolf and four dragons. The south wall of the chancel seems to have been painted for the chantry of 1315. The donor and an angel are painted in the jamb of the south-east window with the arms of the Mortimer, Despencer, Clare and Camoys families, and there is an Annunciation. On the north wall of the nave are traces of a scene, probably the Adoration of the Magi, along with St. Martin dividing his cloak for a beggar.

The earliest memorial is a plain sarcophagus on the north side of the chancel with traces of a carved staff on the lid, which may mark the burial of an abbot of Cormeilles in France, who held the parish living during the Middle Ages. The elaborate effigy of a knight is probably Sir Hugh Mortimer, who held the manor in the 15th century, for it is finely carved with contemporary armour and has the emblems of the House of York on the collar. The front of the tomb chest, with carved angels holding shields, now

Martley—medieval wall paintings in the chancel

forms an overmantel to the fireplace in the old rectory. There are several ledger stones on the floor of the chancel, and a tablet to George Nash, who died in 1840, has a Greek sarcophagus by Joseph Stephens of Worcester.

In 1829 a 13th-century incense boat and sacring bell were found underneath the pulpit, rare survivals of medieval worship. Priests serving the chantry in the chancel also taught here in the 14th century and, some years after the Dissolution, the Chantry School was refounded in 1579. By the 19th century it was housed in the buildings to the north of the churchyard, and the name has been continued by the present school in the village.

MIDDLE LITTLETON   ST. NICHOLAS

Middle Littleton, showing the Perpendicular south chapel

In the heart of the market gardening area of the Vale of Evesham, North and Middle Littleton form one parish to the north of South Littleton. St. Nicholas's church lies between Middle and North Littleton, and with the Manor House and the Tithe Barn forms a group of grey lias stone buildings. The massive barn was built in the 13th century for Evesham Abbey, which held the manor until the Dissolution. It is now in the hands of the National Trust.

The church has limestone dressings to the lias walls. The tower is at the west end of a long nave and chancel and there are a transept and vestry on the north side with a chapel and porch to the south. The lower part of the tower is Early English with lancet windows. The belfry is Perpendicular with characteristic bell openings, gargoyles, battlements and pinnacles. The nave, chancel and north transept all date from about 1300, of which the north doorway to the nave and one lancet window on the south side survive. The lofty porch formerly contained a parvis. The Perpendicular south chapel, which adjoins the porch, has a low pitch roof and battlements. It was built by Thomas Smith to contain his monument and brass, and is mentioned in his will of 1532. The vestry was added in 1871.

The long, whitewashed interior was restored by Frederick Preedy in 1871, when new arches were inserted between the nave, chancel, transept and aisle. The ornate tower doorway is 14th-century with large spandrels carved with foliage. There are blocked arches to either side. Similar elaborate doorways can be seen in the towers at Offenham and South Littleton churches. There is a round Norman font, with a line of carved lozenges on sloping sides, similar to the font in Suckley church, and Decorated piscinae survive in the chancel and transept. The nave has a set of benches with Perpendicular traceried ends, and similar panels have been incorporated into the pulpit. On the sill of a north chancel window and on the floor of the transept are several medieval tiles, some with the arms of Sir John Talbot. Fragments of medieval glass are reset in the east window. The reredos and roofs are all of 1871 by Preedy.

Outside the remains of a medieval Mass dial can be seen on a south-west buttress, whilst nearby are the shaft and steps of the churchyard cross. The lychgate was designed by Preedy.

NAUNTON BEAUCHAMP   ST. BARTHOLOMEW

At the west end of the village, which has many timber-framed houses, the small lias stone church stands opposite the timber-framed former rectory. Naunton Beauchamp is situated on low ground by Piddle Brook between Upton Snodsbury and Pershore. The surrounding land was held by the Lyttleton family in the 16th century, and the farmhouse at Naunton Court, which stands across the fields to the west, has a stone bay window which is the sole surviving part of an attempt to rebuild the property on a grander scale.

The nave and chancel are under one roof and the church also has a west tower and timber porch. The gaunt tower is 15th-century with a Perpendicular west window and bell openings, a parapet and short pinnacles. The nave and chancel were rebuilt in 1767 but were refurbished and the chancel shortened in 1897 by William Jeffrey Hopkins. On the north side, the windows retain the Georgian Gothic Y-shaped tracery, whilst those to the south and east were renewed in the Perpendicular style.

The interior has been scraped, and has the illusion of being a restored medieval church, but only the tall Perpendicular arch to the tower is original. The font has a 14th-century bowl, and there is a 17th-century communion rail. The pulpit, which dates from about 1550, has linenfold panels, with balusters at the angles, and leaf motifs on the top row of panels. The rest of the fittings date from the 1897 restoration or are more recent. The brass lectern of 1896 is by Jones and Willis.

The memorial tablets include one to Humphrey Lyttleton, who died in 1624, which has a typical surround of the period and a poetic inscription. He is also commemorated on an incised stone at King's Norton church in Birmingham, where his first wife is buried.

NETHERTON   CHAPEL

Netherton lies to the east of Elmley Castle below the northern slopes of Bredon Hill. Until 1864 it was in the parish of Cropthorne which is some two miles to the north, and a chapel was built here in the 12th century. It seems that Netherton never developed as a settlement and by the later Middle Ages the chapel is recorded as being in need of repair. By the 17th century it had been converted into a house and by 1738 was being used as a barn. The chapel is now a ruin in the private garden of the farmhouse at Netherton, though it can be seen from the lane to the hamlet.

The limestone ruins consist of a nave and chancel and are late Norman. Much of the north wall has now gone. The north doorway has shafts with keels, and an arch ornamented with carved zig-zags and rosettes, a design also to be found in Bredon church. There are two lines of crenellation with triangular merlons and hexagonal features, which may have been carved by the same mason as the present west doorway at Eckington church. The south doorway has a tympanum of between about 1175 and 1200, which was reset in the early 20th century. It has an unusual carved dragon with outspread wings, long tail and a raised head with an open mouth, and is derived from the medieval legend of the sawfish or serra, which spread its large wings when chasing ships. This would have been a very awe-inspiring doorway in the 12th century. There are also two Norman windows with roll moulding on the south side, whilst a third window from the north side is now reset in a nearby farm building. The chancel was rebuilt in the early 13th century, and one Early English lancet remains. Part of the crude piscina survives by the south-east window. The east window of one light dates from the late 13th century.

There was a plain chancel arch over which stood a 13th-century gabled double bellcote on the east gable of the nave. This collapsed about 1907, demolishing the entire wall. The fallen stones were cleared away in 1920 when the ruins were made safe.

Newland's rich interior with medieval style frescoes of the 1870s

On the approach to Malvern from Worcester, the road passes over Newland Common. To the south, amongst the chestnut trees is an unusual group of buildings with a stone church set amongst groups of red brick cottages, the spire of the church complementing the gate tower of the houses. The core of these buildings are the almshouses founded through the will of the third Earl Beauchamp of Madresfield in 1853 to accommodate 12 poor men and women who had been agricultural workers. These were built in 1862, to which have been added the Lygon Almshouses of 1889, St. Barnabas Clergy Houses in 1900, and other more recent homes all in the same estate cottage style. At the centre are the hall and library, which are connected by a cloister to the mortuary chapel and St. Leonard's church, consecrated in 1864. The plan is based on a medieval college or monastery, and follows the ideas of the medieval Gothic Revival pioneered by the Roman Catholic Earl of Shrewsbury and Augustus Pugin around Alton Towers and Cheadle in Staffordshire. This, the Beauchamp Community, is a High Anglican version and the architect was Philip Hardwick, who was employed by Earl Beauchamp on the alteration of Madresfield Court. Much of the planning behind the church and the community was the work of the incumbent, James Skinner, a beleagured member of the Oxford Movement who came to Malvern away from Protestant opposition in London.

The church of St. Leonard is no longer the parish church, but serves the Beauchamp Community. It has a nave with porch and chancel, to the south of which are a chapel and tower with spire. To the west the building immediately abuts the chaplain's house which was formerly the infirmary, whilst the cloister leads from the tower to the mortuary chapel. The mortuary chapel is the surviving part of the 14th-century timber-framed chapel of St. Leonard which stood in the present graveyard to the south east of the Community, and which was reconstructed on this site with brick infill panels after its demolition. Other timbers were used in the building of the lychgate. The medieval chapel site is now marked with a large cross—it was a small building with a porch and timber bellcote, and must have been very similar to the church at Besford. St. Leonard's chapel was attached to Malvern Priory, but was restored and endowed by the More family at the Dissolution. The remaining portion which makes up the Mortuary chapel can now only be entered from within the Community, via a wide double door for the biers—it is simply furnished and has many exposed timbers between whitewashed walls. By contrast, the sandstone St. Leonard's church with its Decorated style doors and windows, with much cusped tracery and numerous crockets on the spire, is very much the Victorian ideal of a 14th-century style church.

The sombre exterior means that the highly elaborate interior comes as a surprise, and successfully recreates the effect that a medieval church with all its

The reconstructed 14th-century timber-framed mortuary chapel

paintwork and ornamentation would have had on those entering. The walls and roof are covered with painted decoration, and there are paired Italian marble columns to the chancel and south chapel. In the chancel arch is an ironwork screen on a marble base. The altar piece and pulpit are of stone, whilst the floor is tiled in a medieval style pattern. At the west end a large gabled oriel window, projecting into the nave, looks out from the former infirmary and allowed sick inmates to watch services. Next to this is the font that dates from *c*.1200. It is drum-shaped and carved with a band of dogtooth, and came to the medieval chapel from the former church of St. Thomas which stood next to Malvern Priory. Above, is an ironwork pulley in typical Gothic Revival form used to move the font cover.

The wonderful medieval style frescoes were executed by Clayton and Bell in 1877. On the north wall of the nave are three Miracles—the Feast at Cana, the Loaves and the Fishes, and the Raising of Lazarus—above the eight Corporal Acts of Mercy. On the south wall are four Parables—the Good Samaritan, the Great Supper, the Talents with the Pharisee and the Publican—above the eight Beatitudes. On the west wall can be seen the Pool of Bethesda above Christ with the Wise and Foolish Virgins, and to the left of the window are figures of St. Leonard and St. James. Under the window is a smaller scene showing the sick man being let down through the roof. Over the chancel arch is a Judgement scene with Eve and the Virgin, which replaces the original scene by Frederick Preedy of 1865. The east end has the Resurrection and the Ascension on the north wall, with Melchizedek and Aaron by the credence table. The remainder of the north wall is covered by the Entry into Jerusalem above six Virgin Martyrs. On the south wall are the Nativity and the Adoration of the Magi. In the south chapel are the six Doctors of the Church and a vine with Figures of Our Lord. Women from the Bible, including Dorcas, Rebekah and Rachel can be found on the south and west walls, whilst St. Asaph and St. Christopher are on the organ. Eli, Samuel and other figures from the Old Testament are by the sacristy door. The nave roof is painted with the chains of St. Leonard whilst that in the chancel has the four elements. The stained glass in the chancel windows is of 1864 by Hardman & Co.

NORTH PIDDLE   ST. MICHAEL

The Piddle Brook passes through an area of low-lying ground between Upton Snodsbury and Flyford Flavell, with the scattered village of North Piddle to the south of the Worcester to Inkberrow road. The church is on sloping ground to the east together with a couple of farms that mark the site of the medieval settlement.

The lias stone church has a nave and chancel with north porch and south vestry. The bellcote is at the west end. It replaced the medieval church in 1876, and was designed by the Worcester architect, Henry Rowe, who was also responsible for the church at Lulsley. The style is early Decorated with lancets and Y-shaped tracery. The porch is of timber reused from the old church. The vestry was added in 1893.

The plain white interior contains many contemporary fittings, including a pulpit and lectern by Rowe. In the chancel the piscina is a reused 13th-century corbel carved with the head and shoulders of a man.

The font bowl is probably also late 13th-century. In the vestry are reset some 15th-century floor tiles.

NORTON AND LENCHWICK   ST. EGWIN

Norton, to the north of Evesham, has a village street running north-east from the church with many attractive timber-framed houses dating back to the 16th century. It lies about a mile to the east of Lenchwick, with which the church is shared. Lands in Norton were given to Evesham Abbey in the late 8th century and stayed in their possession until the Dissolution, before passing through the Bigg and Craven families in the 17th century. During the 19th century the exiled Duc d'Orleans lived at nearby Woodnorton.

The church was consecrated or rededicated in 1295 by the Bishop of St. Asaph, as was Bretforton church. Today it is a limestone building with west tower, nave, north transept and vestry, south porch and chancel. The tower is Perpendicular with a square-headed west window and bell openings, gargoyles, battlements and pinnacles around a low saddleback roof. The nave has some 13th-century masonry in the north wall and some Perpendicular work, including the large north window which was moved here from Bengeworth old church when it was demolished in 1870. The chancel is Perpendicular, whilst the north transept is 14th-century and has a Decorated window to the north, but otherwise Perpendicular windows. In 1844 an extensive restoration was undertaken with the rebuilding of the south wall of the nave and the porch in the Perpendicular style. The south doorway was reset, and has an unusual Perpendicular arch, made into a half hexagon shape from three stone blocks. The vestry was added in 1906.

The spacious interior owes much of its character to the 1844 restoration. A chancel arch was constructed, and arcades, which are thought to have divided the present nave to give side aisles, were removed. To the north of the chancel arch are the remains of a medieval squint, and the chancel roof contains 15th-century beams. The sedilia and chancel fittings are 19th-century, but incorporate some 16th-century linenfold panelling. The pulpit is early 17th-century with Gothic decoration. The Perpendicular font is octagonal and carved with quatrefoils. The beautiful stone top of the lectern, carved from Purbeck marble, was found in 1813 near the site of Evesham Abbey and was installed here in 1865 on a base made by William Forsyth of Worcester (see illustration on p.14). The story behind this top is similar to that of the lectern at Crowle church—it is thought that it might have been the lectern made for the abbey's chapter house in the time of Abbot Adam between 1160 and 1191. Between pieces of carved foliage is the figure of a bishop holding a crozier in his left hand. He is facing the congregation and giving a blessing with his right arm. On the other side below the book rest are angels' heads. At the west end of the church are the royal arms of King George II, but the remaining fittings are 19th- and 20th-century.

The north window to the chancel may contain some medieval fragments of glass amongst the design of the Annunciation and installed before 1891 by the vicar, Narcissus George Batt. The east window has 19th-century glass with subjects from the Old Testament, including Moses with the Ten Commandments. The memorial window to Mrs. Thompson is of 1871 by Clayton and Bell, whilst that to Mrs. Ashmore is by George Rogers of Worcester.

The window in the south-west part of the nave is in memory of Mary Boulter, daughter of a former rector, who died aged nine in 1906. It shows St. Luke painting St. Cecilia at the organ with, above, Mary Boulter walking along the River Avon towards the bell tower at Evesham. The Kaye memorial window in the nave is by Burlison and Grylls. Only the figures are left of Frederick Preedy's glass of 1862 showing St. Paul before Agrippa.

In the north transept are three large memorials. The effigy of Thomas Bigg, who died in 1581, lies next to that of his wife, Maudlen Hoby, who died in 1574. He is wearing armour and the effigies have been damaged. On the chest, decorated with strapwork, are the kneeling figures of their six children. Maudlen Hoby was sister to Sir Philip Hoby, who obtained from King Henry VIII much of the land held by Evesham Abbey at the Dissolution. The large kneeling figures, which face one another across a prayer desk, are Sir Thomas Bigg, who died in 1613, also shown dressed in armour, and his wife, Ursula Throckmorton. The monument has black columns supporting a large canopy with heraldic shields. Their nine children are shown below—those shown as smaller died in infancy. Behind the memorial are the blocked remains of a Perpendicular window. The sculptor was probably Ephiphanius Evesham, who may also have made the Hanford memorial in Eckington church. Another Sir Thomas Bigg, who died in 1621, has a memorial of alabaster with four black columns and a flat canopy with heraldic shields. He is shown lying down and wearing armour. The hatchment, armour and pennants in the transept are from the Craven family, who acquired the manor at Norton from the Biggs. Other tablets include those to the Boulter family commemorating deaths in 1908 and 1912, which have lettering by Eric Gill.

In the churchyard are three headstones by Gill, also to members of the Boulter family. The lychgate is made from the Perpendicular north door of the nave which was removed when the window was brought from Bengeworth in 1870.

NORTON-BY-KEMPSEY   ST. JAMES THE GREAT

To the south-east of Worcester, the parish of Norton is becoming increasingly developed with housing. Close to the M5 are the surviving parts of Norton Barracks which were built in 1876 and housed the Worcestershire Regiment until 1970. The church lies a little to the east in the old village centre. The parish also includes Hatfield and Littleworth.

St. James's church stands in a large graveyard and is built of lias stone with sandstone dressings. It has a chancel with vestry to the north, nave and large south aisle with porch and a tower at the west end. The nave has a mainly Norman north wall, which includes a blocked plain north doorway and one lancet window. It was extended to the west in the 13th century, where there is an Early English lancet. The chancel may include some Norman stonework, but the medieval features are all 14th-century. The tower is also 14th-century, but the belfry was reconstructed in the 19th century with Decorated style bell openings, and a parapet with quatrefoil tracery and pinnacles around a low pyramid roof. The Norman south doorway was reset when Ewan Christian added a new south aisle and porch in 1874-75. Christian also restored the remainder of the church and put in a new east window. His other work in Worcestershire include the restoration of Kempsey church and the chancel of St. John in Worcester.

The interior has whitewashed walls and has an essentially Victorian character. The chancel arch, with no capital piers, is probably a copy of the medieval one, whilst the round piers and chamfered arches of the arcade are in a late Early English style. The fittings almost all date from the late 19th-century, and the colours of the Regiment are laid up in the south aisle as a reminder of the presence of the former barracks. In a north window of the nave are some panels of 17th-century glass. The Norman tub font has been recut to make it octagonal.

There are several memorial tablets. A monument to Thomas Brewer, who died in 1810, shows a woman in mourning kneeling by a pedestal, whilst an inscription of 1845 with drapery on a sarcophagus commemorates the Hooke family.

The tower contains a 15th-century bell. In the churchyard are a number of military graves of soldiers from the Regiment.

ODDINGLEY   ST. JAMES

Oddingley church has a wonderful setting which evokes thoughts of the passage of time. It is approached by an avenue of trees which passes a farm and the site of the medieval village. From the churchyard, views past a timber-framed cottage extend over the Worcester to Birmingham canal, the railway and the M5. Oddingley was part of the extensive parish of St. Helen in Worcester in the Anglo-Saxon period, and a church is first recorded here in 1288. In medieval and Tudor times the land was held by the Crown, before passing to the Wintours of Huddington, the Foleys of Witley and the Galtons of Hadzor.

The church is built of lias and has a west tower, nave with porch and transepts and a chancel. The medieval building was partly reconstructed in 1851 by R.C. Hussey, architect of several Warwickshire churches, with an endowment from the Galton family, and it is therefore appropriate that this church now houses several artefacts from the redundant church at Hadzor. The body of the church is basically 15th-century, and the Perpendicular

The interior at Oddingley showing the Perpendicular timber arch opening into the south transept

priest's door, east and side windows of the chancel have been preserved. The simple tower with plain bell openings has a pyramid roof and is 17th-century. The porch was rebuilt in 1860, incorporating some medieval timbers. A 15th-century stoup can be seen next to the south door.

The interior has an unprecedented charm. There is much 19th-century work including the roofs, but there are many earlier features that have been restored. A Perpendicular arch of timber opens into the south transept with characteristic mouldings. On the eastern side is a small opening which now leads to the pulpit, but which formerly would have given access to the rood loft stairs. In the chancel is a 15th-century piscina, and the Perpendicular octagonal font is carved with roses and fetterlocks on alternate panels. From the 17th century survive the plain benches, the communion rails and an iron stand, used to hold an hour glass to time the sermon. There is a similar example in the church at Bishampton. The 18th-century chamber organ came from Hadzor church.

There is a collection of pieces of mainly 15th-century glass in two chancel windows. The north window shows the Coronation of the Virgin. In the north light of the east window are the arms of Richard, Duke of York, who was killed in 1460, and his wife, Cecily Neville. They are above part of a

The hourglass

figure of St. Catherine and a figure of a priest, the inscription for which is now missing, but has been recorded as referring to William Harries. Two small half figures are of donors, John and Joan Yarnold. In the centre is an archbishop, probably Thomas Becket, but the inscription has been lost and replaced by one for a missing figure of St. Martin. The bishop in this light is probably St. Wulstan. In the south light are the arms of the Mortimer family, part of a figure of a female saint, a head of Christ with the crown of thorns, and two further donors, shown as husband and wife. An inscription beneath them refers to John Harries, another priest, who is also shown kneeling in vestments at a prayer desk.

A brass on the south wall of the nave was brought from Hadzor church. It is in the medieval style and commemorates Richard Cameron Galton, who died in 1866. He is shown with his wife and children kneeling beside him, and was the youngest son of John Galton who restored the church in 1851.

The memorials include a ledger stone in the chancel to a rector, George Parker, who was murdered in 1806 after a dispute over tithes, the murderer escaping through the woods. Almost 25 years later a skeleton was discovered when a nearby barn was demolished. This was identified as Richard Hemming, a Droitwich carpenter, who had been hired to shoot the rector by a local farmer, Samuel Evans, who had since died. After an inquest and trial in Worcester, three other men were acquitted of being accessories both to the murder of George Parker and Richard Hemming. The story of the Oddingley murders became well-known in 19th-century Worcestershire.

OFFENHAM   ST. MARY AND ST. MILBURGH

Land at Offenham to the north-east of Evesham, was granted to Evesham Abbey in the 8th century, and the church's dedication to St. Milburgh is a reminder of the village's Anglo-Saxon origins. Court Farm is the site of a favourite residence of the abbots of Evesham, to which Abbot Lichfield retired after the Dissolution. It was a crossing place on the River Avon in the Middle Ages, and although subsequently bypassed by other routes became an important market gardening centre in the 19th century, specialising particularly in strawberries and cabbages. In the centre of the large village near the church are several timber-framed cottages and a tall maypole.

The lias church has a west tower, nave with south porch and north aisle, and chancel with north vestry. The tower is 15th-century with Perpendicular bell openings, gargoyles, battlements and tall pinnacles. The rest of the church was rebuilt in 1861/2 by Frederick Preedy in the Decorated style, though there is a curious circular window at the east end of the north aisle. The roof tiles are laid to form a polychrome pattern in the manner of William Butterfield.

The interior is all Preedy's work and includes his choir stalls, reredos and alabaster pulpit, which has an open parapet with columns in different coloured marbles. The reredos is also alabaster and by Preedy. The Perpendicular font has survived and is decorated with quatrefoils and flowers. At the west end the tower arch is similar to those in Middle and South Littleton churches—it is Perpendicular and made up from two large spandrels with foliage designs and a floral frieze. Is the connection between these arches related to the patronage of these churches by Evesham Abbey?

The east window of the north aisle, and three other north aisle windows all contain glass of 1864 by Preedy.

OMBERSLEY

ST. ANDREW

Ombersley is a large village to the north of Worcester. The main street was bypassed in the 1970s and has an attractive assortment of mainly timber-framed houses, on the western side of which stands the church in a large graveyard. Beyond the church are the grounds of Ombersley Court. The Sandys family took possession of the manor of Ombersley in the 1560s, when it was granted by Queen Elizabeth I to Edwin Sandys after he became Bishop of Worcester. Bishop Sandys was fiercely Protestant and went on to become Archbishop of York, whilst two of his sons were very influential in the establishment of the Puritan communities in North America, through the Pilgrim Fathers and the Virginia Company. The present house was completed in 1726 for the first Lord Sandys.

From the 8th century until the Dissolution, Ombersley was held by Evesham Abbey. The medieval church, dedicated to St. Ambrose, stood to the south of the present building. Today only part of the chancel survives as the mausoleum of the Sandys family. It is of deep red sandstone with 13th-century walls to the north and south that contain Early English lancets with cusped heads and deep mouldings. New east and west walls were built about 1830 in the early 19th-century Gothic style with battlements. The rest of the medieval church was demolished at this time, but had a tall spire on a substantial tower at the south-west corner of an aisled nave with a timber porch and dormer windows.

Inside the old chancel, the lancet windows have shafts and the blocked outline of the square Tudor east window is visible. There are an Early English piscina and triple sedilia and the 17th-century communion table is also preserved. There are many memorial tablets to the Sandys family; particularly notable are those to Edwin, Lord Sandys, who died in 1797, which has a bust by Joseph Nollekens, and to Samuel Sandys, who died in 1685, by William Bird, and which has a carved surround and cherubs. Close to the old chancel is the 15th-century base to the churchyard cross decorated with quatrefoils. The shaft has an ornamental top of the 18th-century.

To the north stands the present large sandstone church, which was begun in 1826. Funds were raised by the parish and by Lady Sandys, who was also Dowager Marchioness of Downshire. The architect was Thomas Rickman, who designed an aisled nave and chancel with transepts. The vestries are beside the chancel and there is a tower with spire at the west end. Rickman used the Decorated style, as he would at nearby Hartlebury in the 1830s, and Ombersley is one of the first churches to explore the architectural correctness which would become more apparent during the Gothic Revival. The Decorated style tracery varies between the different windows, and the church has an interesting medieval style outline with varied rooflines and battlements with pinnacles. Ombersley demonstrates Thomas Rickman's wish to combine well studied medieval architecture with the new technical progress of the early 19th century. The tower at the west end has bell openings with Decorated style canopies, above which is a recessed spire connected to the pinnacles by innovative flying buttresses.

There are three entrances at the west end in the manner of the Commissioners churches. Those on the sides lead into lobbies with staircases to the galleries. The interior is lofty with rich colours to the ceiling with its plaster rib vault, introduced by J. Homery Folkes in his restoration of 1957. The arcades are of a Perpendicular type without capitals, though the shafts and the quatrefoil design below the clerestorey windows are of the Decorated style. The galleries are above the aisles behind the arcade, but the interior has a more medieval Gothic feel than the classical proportions of Hartlebury church.

There is a further gallery at the west end with three music stands, which were used by the choir before the organ was improved, and the choir stalls set up in the chancel in 1896. The area below the gallery has been sealed off with glazing. The box pews survive, along with the Sandys family pew, complete with a fireplace. There is a cast iron Gothic stove on the north side by Robert Howden of London. The coloured glass is contemporary with the church, and there are Commandment and Creed tables painted to each side of the east window. The royal arms of King Charles II, dated 1660, has been placed over the chancel arch. The font was a gift in 1888 from the Sandys family. The organ was installed in 1829 by John Gray of London, and enlarged by Nicholson in 1862. There are many small memorial tablets around the church interior, with charity boards at the entrances to the galleries. The east side of the churchyard has fine iron railings, which are contemporary with the church.

ORLETON   ST. JOHN THE BAPTIST

Orleton is a hamlet in the Teme Valley between Stanford and Eastham. The medieval church was a chapelry of Eastham and was rebuilt in 1816 as a small brick building with a nave, chancel and short west tower. The nave side windows are slightly pointed in a Regency Gothic, whilst the east window has intersecting cast iron tracery. The church was converted into a house in the 1970s, but remains an important landmark in this section of the valley.

OVERBURY   ST. FAITH

St. Faith's church serves Overbury and Conderton, two villages on the southern slopes of Bredon Hill. Overbury is an exceptionally pretty village with limestone houses and cottages close to the church and Overbury Court. During the 18th and early 19th centuries there were several water mills in Overbury which produced flour, paper and silk thread. The Court was rebuilt by the Martin family in 1738, and is home today to their descendants, the Holland-Martins. In medieval times the manor and church were held by Worcester Priory, who had received it as a gift from the Mercian royal family in 875.

Overbury church from the south-west

Conderton, with its Iron Age hillfort, is thought from the origins of the name to have been settled in Anglo-Saxon times by migrants from Kent. Overbury parish was also linked to Alstone, Teddington and Little Washbourne in Gloucestershire until parochial reorganisation in 1986. In the Middle Ages the church was responsible for St. Faith's church at Berrow in the west of Worcestershire.

The limestone church stands in a beautiful graveyard next to the Court, entered through a lychgate designed as a war memorial by Sir Herbert Baker in 1921. It is next to a small stream. The church has an aisled nave with porch, and a central tower beyond which is the chancel. The nave is concealed from view, but is Norman, and the 12th century aisles were widened during the 14th century and given Decorated windows, one of which survives at the east end of the north aisle. The porch was added in 1850 and the aisles rebuilt in 1879-80. The south doorway is late 12th century and has a round arch with several mouldings, supported by capitals with carved scallops and spirals, and keeled shafts. It can be compared with other very late 12th-century work in the west of England, as at Wells Cathedral. The chancel is Early English with lancets on the side walls. The east wall was rebuilt with an elaborate Perpendicular window in the 15th century. The roofspace of the chancel, above the vault, was used as a dovecote in the Middle Ages, providing an important source of food for Worcester Priory. Other examples of dovecotes in churches are at Elkstone and Leonard Stanley in Gloucestershire. The Perpendicular tower has pinnacles and battlements with gargoyles; the one on the north-west corner being replaced in 1989. The bell openings were renewed in the 17th century.

The south doorway was fitted with glazed doors engraved by Bryant Fedden of Winchcombe in 1973. The interior is stripped to the limestone and rather dark, but is beautifully presented. The nave arcades are Norman with round piers and scalloped capitals supporting square abaci and arches with single steps. The south arcade is a little earlier with dogtooth carving to the hood mould. On the inner side of the north arcade three carved heads are reset. Above the spandrels are Norman lancet windows making a clerestorey which now opens into the aisles. The chancel is splendid—the Early English lancets have shafts to the sides and the surrounds are moulded. It has a vaulted ceiling of two bays and has shafts with stiff leaf capitals, and keeled ribs with bosses, carved to show the Crowned Virgin and a serpent with the head of a woman, presumably Eve. Below the east window are sixteen Perpendicular niches with tracery. The rebuilding of the tower in the 15th century meant that the chancel vault had to be altered a little at the west end. The tower vault itself was rebuilt in 1880. There is a stair in the north-west corner which also gave access to the rood loft. The nave has a medieval wagon roof, whilst part of the medieval screen has been incorporated into the pulpit, with traceried panels and the remains of a cornice carved with a vine. The bench ends also have Perpendicular traceried panels with carved figures and beasts. The font is Norman and is shaped like a goblet. Part is carved with two figures standing with outstretched arms, one of whom holds a church, divided by a panel with a symmetrical scroll design, and there is also a dove and cross with a floral pattern. It has been reworked and the stem made octagonal, but it is similar to the lead fonts found in some Gloucestershire churches and to that at Coleshill in Warwickshire. The cover is 17th-century. In the chancel are two medieval red painted consecration crosses. The remaining furnishings are 19th- and 20th-century, including the choir stalls of 1880.

In the south window of the tower are fragments of 16th-century glass. There is a window of 1880 by Heaton, Butler and Bayne, and in 1881 four windows showing Prophets and Evangelists were installed by Burlison and Grylls. The east window is also their work of 1885, as is a window of 1893 showing Faith, Hope and Charity.

In the south aisle is a 13th-century coffin lid with a carved cross, and there are several 18th-century memorial tablets to the Agge, Darke and Martin families. The tower contains a late 15th-century bell dedicated to St. Giles cast by Robert Hendley of Gloucester.

PEBWORTH   ST. PETER

At the centre of the most easterly parish in Worcestershire, Pebworth village stands on a hilltop close to the Warwickshire and Gloucestershire borders. Several timber-framed and brick cottages cluster around the church, which is surrounded by large trees within the graveyard. Pebworth is the only Worcestershire place to feature in the local rhyme about Shakespeare's villages:

> Piping Pebworth, Dancing Marston,
> Haunted Hillborough, Hungry Grafton,

Dodging Exhall, Papist Wixford,
Beggarly Broom and Drunken Bidford.

St. Peter's church is built of limestone and is mainly Perpendicular. It has a west tower, nave with north porch and south aisle, and a chancel. The earliest part is the north wall of the chancel which is 13th-century with one Early English lancet. The tower has battlements, but the tracery of the large west window has been removed and replaced by 19th-century lancets. In the nave roof on the south side are 19th-century dormer windows which were provided to let in more light.

The 15th-century porch contains stone seats, and the medieval north door opens into the white-washed interior. It is charmingly light and airy. Most features are Perpendicular including the tall arches to the tower and chancel, and the arcade with octagonal piers and small hollows in the middle of the diagonal sides. There is an ornate canopied niche in the south wall of the aisle, which was mentioned as new in the will of Edmund Marten in 1528. There is a further smaller niche beside the chancel arch, close to the surviving staircase to the lost rood loft. The roofs are 15th- and 16th-century with moulded tie beams.

The low Perpendicular font is octagonal with carved quatrefoils and floral decoration and there are Perpendicular piscinae in the chancel, nave and aisle. The pulpit is made up from 17th-century woodwork, and the communion rail is of the same date, though some balusters are missing. The pews are early 19th-century Gothic and have doors. On the north and west walls are the remains of medieval and post-Reformation paintings.

In the chancel is a worn effigy of a 14th-century priest, near to which are displayed the plain chalice and paten discovered in his grave. There are several memorial tablets including one to Robert Martin, who died in 1629, carved with columns, strapwork and skulls and painted with roses. Another Robert Martin, who died in 1720, is commemorated on a tablet by Edward Woodward, architect of St. Swithin's church in Worcester. It has pilasters, a pediment and an urn with two cherubs' heads below the inscription. The Shekell family, who are also commemorated in Little Comberton church, have a tablet of about 1825 by Lewis of Cheltenham. In the churchyard is the base of the medieval cross.

PENDOCK   OLD CHURCH

The church is a landmark beside the M50, yet the approach from the Ledbury to Tewkesbury road still gives a strange sense of remoteness despite the adjacent motorway. The medieval village was mainly to the north of the church, but now there are few other buildings except the 17th-century Prior's Court. In the Middle Ages much of Pendock was in the possession of Worcester Priory, and was associated with their lands at Berrow held by Overbury Manor. By the 19th century the centre of population had become centred on Pendock Cross about one mile to the west, and a mission church was built there which is now used as the main place of worship.

The old church is redundant and maintained by the Churches Conservation Trust. The lias stone church has a nave and chancel with north porch, vestry and west tower. Both chancel and nave are late Norman with the surviving south and north doorways. The latter is more ornate with scalloped capitals, a zig-zag decoration to the arch, and a hood mould with pellets, similar to those at Queenhill and Ashton-under-Hill. The present windows are restored 14th-century Decorated, and part of a further medieval window survives on the east wall of the nave which would have given extra light to the rood loft above the chancel arch. The plain west tower is 14th-century with a Decorated window and bell openings and has a pyramid roof. The timber porch is 16th-century, whilst the vestry is Victorian.

The interior is homely and whitewashed. Both the cross-battened doors are medieval. The chancel arch is now pointed, but was once rounded and has probably been widened. The shafts to the sides have scalloped capitals, which are decorated with crosses similar to those at Pirton, whilst the zig-zag carving on the abaci is similar to that at Beckford and Eldersfield. A few sections of the extensive medieval wall paintings are exposed above the chancel arch. The lower part of the medieval rood screen survives with traceried panels, and concealed in the south-east

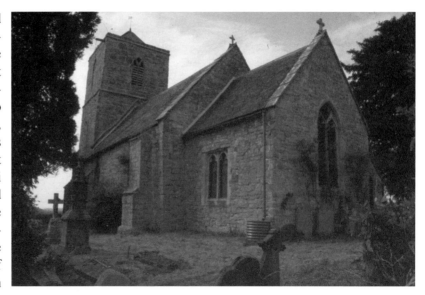

Pendock Old Church

corner of the nave is the blocked rood loft stair. The tower arch is Decorated. The 16th-century pews have linenfold panelling. The piscina is medieval, whilst the choir stalls contain 16th-century woodwork, and the communion rails are 17th-century. Under the tower are 18th-century boards with the Creed and Lord's Prayer, and a Commandment Board dated 1851. The chamber organ with a classical case is Georgian. The windows contain 19th-century glass, including one on the north side of the nave by John Hardman of 1897 showing the Light of the World. The east window with the Resurrection and the Ascension is probably of 1847 by Warrington. The west window, perhaps by Heaton, Butler and Bayne, is of 1887 and a memorial to William Symonds—a 19th-century rector and noted local geologist, as well as being author of two historical novels *Malvern Chase* and *Hanley Castle*. His daughter, Hyacinth, who is represented by the flowers in the glass, married the botanist, Joseph Dalton Hooker, who was commemorated on a bronze memorial in the nave after his death in 1911.

PENDOCK CROSS   THE REDEEMER

By the late 19th century, the centre of population in Pendock parish had almost entirely shifted from around the old church to the area around Pendock Cross, about one mile to the west. This mission church was built in 1889 as a temporary structure, but is still very much in use. It is an excellent example of a mission church, and can be compared with that at Crossway Green near Hartlebury. However, it is unusual in that it is built completely of timber, with an absence of corrugated iron so often found in these churches. The black and white nave and chancel are under a single roof, and supported by substantial wooden buttresses. There is a south porch and a bellcote with a short spire at the west end. The style is late Perpendicular, which is echoed in the homely timber-lined interior where the wooden structure can be seen to have warped with age. It is filled with mainly contemporary fittings, and has great atmosphere.

PENSAX   ST. JAMES THE GREAT

High on the hills to the north of the Teme Valley, Pensax is a small village which developed as a result of small scale open cast mining from the 17th to the early 20th centuries. The church is approached by a foot-path from the lane opposite the early Gothic revival Pensax Court. Pensax was part of the parish of Lindridge until 1843. The unusual name is derived from the Welsh 'pen' meaning head of a valley, whilst the second part refers to the Saxons.

The medieval church was demolished in the 19th century, but its outline can still be seen to the south of the present church. This has a nave, west tower, chancel and vestry. The nave and tower are of 1832-33 by Thomas Jones, a little known architect, who has used the Perpendicular style in an accurate medieval manner, unusual in a Commissioners type church of this date. The entrance is in the south side of the tower, and there are finely detailed Perpendicular style windows. The chancel was rebuilt in 1891 in a Perpendicular Arts and Crafts style.

The plain interior is very wide and was much restored during the 1980s. The fittings date mainly from the 1891 addition and are in the Arts and Crafts style. The chancel has a low iron screen and a reredos painted with angels, St. George and St. James, while the communion rails are the work of Bromsgrove Guild craftsmen. The east window has glass depicting the Parables by Christopher Whall, designer of the west window in the church at Upton-upon-Severn. Under the tower are a collection of memorial tablets to the Clutton family of Pensax Court, and in the churchyard is buried the author, Arthur Clutton-Brock.

PEOPLETON   ST. NICHOLAS

Peopleton is on low-lying land between Pershore and Worcester close to Bow Brook. The village has expanded with housing during the 20th century, but there are several timber-framed cottages and houses. The church is at the south end and overlooks open countryside next to Bowbrook House, built in the early 19th century by the Norton family and now a school.

At the west end a low brick tower rises from the roof of the nave. There is also a chancel, south vestry and a porch. The body of the church is of lias stone. There are two 13th-century lancet windows in the chancel with a priest's door, and two Decorated windows at the west end of the nave. In the eastern part of the nave are two Perpendicular windows in red sandstone. The chancel also contains two 17th-century windows. The tower was built into the nave about 1845 to replace a timber belfry. It has lancet windows and a pyramid roof.

The interior has a moulded Perpendicular chancel arch, and 15th-century wagon roofs to the nave and chancel. The chancel also contains a Decorated piscina. The octagonal font is Perpendicular on a more recent base. The communion rail and table are 17th-century, and at the west end of the nave is reset the 15th-century rood beam from the vanished screen. It is carved with vine leaves and grapes. The remainder of the furnishings are 19th- and 20th-century, and there is a window in the chancel with glass of 1939 by Archibald Davies of the Bromsgrove Guild showing contemporary children with the Virgin and Child.

There are several memorial tablets including one to Mark Dingley who died in 1682. It is carved with 'memento mori'—perhaps significant as he died in the same year as he bought the manor at Peopleton and moved from the family seat at Charlton.

PERSHORE ABBEY CHURCH OF THE HOLY CROSS AND ST. EDBURGA

Pershore Abbey: the crossing tower and south transept

The town of Pershore lies between Worcester and Evesham. It has a street of Georgian buildings along the main route, but two of the town's most prominent features are not easily seen on passing through—the River Avon flows around Pershore with extensive flood meadows to the east and south of the town, whilst the golden limestone abbey stands in a park behind the buildings on the west side of the centre.

Before 716, a monastery at Pershore seems to have been endowed by King Ethelred of Mercia. The monks followed the Benedictine Rule from about 970, but in 976 were expelled during a period of resentment against the growth of monasticism and some two-thirds of the monastic estates were confiscated by Earl Alfhere of Mercia. These lands eventually passed to King Edward the Confessor in the 11th century as endowment for his foundation at Westminster Abbey, and St. Andrew's church was founded for the use of the tenants of the Westminster estates. Sometime after a fire in 1002 and before 1020, the monastery church was rebuilt, the foundations of this building being discovered beneath the present structure in 1996, of which a section has been left exposed. By 1020 the abbey was dedicated to St. Mary and St. Edburga—Edburga (or Eadburga), an abbess in Winchester, was the grand-daughter of King Alfred and after her death in 960, some of her relics were brought to Pershore where a cult developed and several churches on the monastic estates, including Leigh and Abberton, were dedicated to her. Pershore Abbey prospered in the Middle Ages, but was dissolved in 1539. The townspeople, who had held services at an altar dedicated to the Holy Cross in the nave, decided to abandon the nave and purchase the east end of the abbey as a parish church for £400, and this is almost all that survives today. The majority of the buildings were demolished and the stone bought by Sir John Russell of Strensham.

Today, a somewhat truncated Pershore Abbey consists of the crossing with the tower above, part of the north transept with a vestry, the south transept, the aisled chancel with an apse, side chapel and small

170

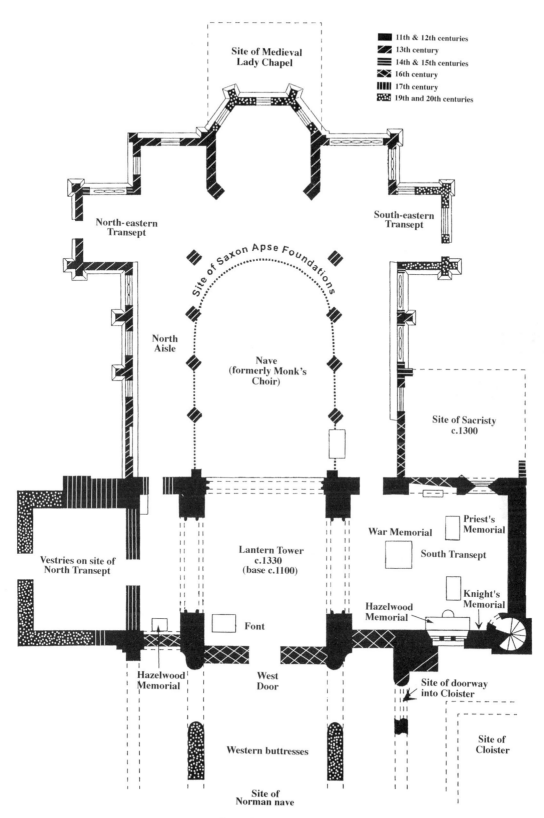

11th & 12th centuries
13th century
14th & 15th centuries
16th century
17th century
19th and 20th centuries

Site of Medieval
Lady Chapel

North-eastern
Transept

South-eastern
Transept

Site of Saxon Apse Foundations

North
Aisle

Nave
(formerly Monk's
Choir)

Site of Sacristy
c.1300

Priest's
Memorial

War Memorial

South Transept

Vestries on site of
North Transept

Lantern Tower
c.1330
(base c.1100)

Knight's
Memorial

Hazelwood
Memorial

Font

Hazelwood
Memorial

West
Door

Site of doorway
into Cloister

Site of
Cloister

Western buttresses

Site of
Norman nave

Plan of Pershore Abbey

eastern transept. Nothing remains above ground of the monastery except for traces from the arcading in the slype and the roof line of the dormitory on the south wall of the south transept, along with the blocked doorway from the church which stood at the top of the former night stairs. A further roof line can be seen on the west wall of the transept, which marks the position of the cloisters, which were entered from the church by the Decorated doorway in the ruinous fragment of the south aisle wall. The massive south transept dates from the 12th century, and has Norman flat buttresses to the corners. Below the roof is a line of corbels, many of which are carved with heads, and there is some fine Norman intersecting blind arcading with projecting zig-zags to the gable, which is probably a decorative feature relating to the end of the Norman barrel vault inside. It is similar to the east end of Halesowen church in the West Midlands. On the east side is a blocked Norman arch, which led to an apsidal chapel that had been demolished by about 1300. The Norman north transept must have looked very similar, but it collapsed in 1686, and was replaced by a small lean to structure with a square headed window in a very late Perpendicular style. On the west side of the south transept is a 15th-century Perpendicular window.

At the base of the tower, the Norman arches on the west side of the crossing give an indication of the impressive appearance of the demolished Norman nave. The arches are tall, and those to the side aisles are narrow, so the high piers of the nave arcades with a small triforium and clerestorey would have made the nave at 180 feet in length, very similar to those at Gloucester Cathedral and Tewkesbury Abbey. Indeed, they were probably built by the same masons. The present west doorway and window date from the 19th century. Above the Norman crossing rises the impressive 14th-century tower. The upper stages are ornamented with much carved ballflower, typical of this date. The lantern part has unusual Decorated tracery in the windows, similar to the tracery in the chancel of Madley church in Herefordshire, and above a line of carved crenellation the Decorated style windows and blind arches have canopies. There are many similarities between this tower and that at Salisbury Cathedral in Wiltshire. The large pinnacles which rise from the plain parapet date from 1871. The tower has a low pyramid roof, covered with copper, which stands out in views from afar. Concerns for the structure resulted in the construction in 1913 of the huge flying buttresses at the west end. The vestry on the north side was added in 1936.

The architectural history of the chancel is complex. The Early English eastern chapels and low eastern transepts are part of a rebuilding of the early 13th century. This included the Lady Chapel, which was demolished at the Dissolution; its site now occupied by the Early English style three sided apse, which was built in 1847. The chancel was rebuilt after a fire in 1223, and with the chapels has several characteristic Early English lancet windows, as well as three stepped lancets in the north aisle. However, there are two Decorated windows in the south aisle, and there are 14th-century flying buttresses with crocketed pinnacles, which date from the rebuilding of the chancel vault after another fire in 1288. These buttresses are in contrast to the simple Early English clerestorey windows, and the corbel table which appears to be very similar to that on the Norman south transept. On the south side a blocked arch once led from the aisle to St. Edburga's Chapel, which replaced an apsidal Norman chapel in about 1300. Parts of the Decorated vaulting, together with a sedilia and an aumbry can be clearly seen on the transept east wall.

The initial impression on entering is of the great height of the interior being disproportionate to its present length. The large plain Norman arches of the crossing are similar to those at Tewkesbury Abbey, though there are carved capitals, rising above which is the 14th-century lantern with traceried panelling. This was revealed when Sir George Gilbert Scott removed the lower vault during his restoration of 1862-64. Scott replaced the ringing chamber with the platform at a giddy height in the centre of the lantern.

There is much Norman work in the south transept. The arches leading to the chancel aisle and the former chapel are lower than those to the nave aisle, and above them are blocked openings to a triforium and an upper chapel. Again, the Norman arrangement was similar to those at Gloucester Cathedral and Tewkesbury Abbey. There are passages in the east and south walls of the transept with Norman arcaded

The chancel with its vault looking east

openings into the church, some of which have scalloped capitals beneath plain abaci and arches. Arches carved with a zig-zag from a blind arcade survive towards the base of the walls, similar to the transept of Hereford Cathedral. Some of the piers are enriched with incised zig-zag decoration.

The Norman barrel vault has gone, though outline evidence of it can be seen at the top of the staircase turret in the corner of the transept. The Norman Pershore Abbey was one of only three churches in England, along with Durham Cathedral and Lindisfarne Priory in Northumberland, to have been fully vaulted in stone. The vault was renewed sometime after the fire of 1288, and has moulded ribs and carved bosses with foliage and heraldic arms. There are further Norman arches and traces of a barrel vault in the remains of the north transept.

The chancel is the great glory of the interior of Pershore Abbey. The arcades date from the rebuilding of about 1230 after the fire of 1223. They are similar to the arcades at Wells Cathedral in Somerset. The composite piers are lozenge-shaped with several shafts, and carry capitals carved with stylised stiff leaf designs which are richer than those on the shafts of the aisle walls. It could be that the aisles were rebuilt a little earlier, in about 1210. Above, the triforium and clerestorey are incorporated together in triple lancets, and those at the east end are blind above the entrance to the earlier Lady Chapel. Indeed, the surviving Early English west bay of the Lady Chapel has several shafts of Purbeck Marble, similar to those at the east end of Worcester Cathedral, and it is interesting to note that the chancel was rebuilt from west to east resulting in an awkward join at the Lady Chapel arch. The fire of 1288 caused the collapse of the Norman tower and the subsequent reconstruction of the chancel vault. It is a fine and very early Decorated lierne vault, with moulded ribs, and 41 bosses carved with more naturalistic foliage than the capitals below. There are several representations of the Green Man as well as other grotesque and animal heads.

Many of the furnishings date from just after the 1862 restoration. However, the font is Norman, and shows Christ and the Apostles beneath intersecting arches which have beaded decoration. The font is weathered after being in the garden of the Nash at Kempsey from about 1840 until it was returned to the church in 1920 on a base designed by Harold Brakspeare. A Perpendicular stone reredos can be seen in the blocked eastern arch of the south transept. It has been reused as part of a later canopied monument which no longer exists. Part of a wooden screen in the north transept is inscribed with the name of Abbot Newton and dates from 1435, and three of the stalls on the south side of the church are medieval. Part of a medieval wall painting showing a large figure can be seen on the south east pier of the crossing. However, the painting by Clayton and Bell above the altar, which illustrates the dedication of the Abbey along with that in the blocked nave arch showing Christ in Majesty with SS. Peter and Paul dates from 1865. They are a memorial to the vicar, Richard Williamson. There are some 15th-century floor tiles in the south-east chapel, which show the arms of the Diocese of Worcester, the Beauchamp and Boteler families, and three chalices. An 18th-century charity board is interesting for the details it records of the terms of the Smith Charity. Several of the sanctuary furnishings date from 1962 and represent the only work in Worcestershire by the popular architect, George Pace, well known for his restoration of Llandaff Cathedral in Wales after the Second World War. In 1997 much of the floor was re-laid in attractive black and white stone.

No medieval stained glass survives, but several windows contain Victorian glass by various artists. Clayton and Bell were responsible for 11 windows designed in 1864, including those in the apse and the west windows, which show the childhood of Christ. The Scobell memorial windows in the aisles and the clerestorey windows show Dorcas and the four Evangelists are also their work of between 1869-73. Two windows in the south aisle of 1870 are a memorial to Edwin Ball and show the history of the abbey, which were designed by a former curate, Canon Wickendon and made by Hardman & Co. of Birmingham. Hardman also installed the Bartlett memorial window in the south-east transept which shows Christ blessing children. A window in the north aisle of 1870 in memory of Francis Davis and the east window of the north-east chapel showing Mary and Martha of 1879 in memory of Clendon Dawkes are by Lavers and Barraud. The window showing the Life of St. Peter in the north aisle of 1898 and the Woodward memorial window on the east side of the south-east transept of 1879 showing Christ are by Mayer and Co., whilst the east window in the south-east chapel depicting The Annunciation is a memorial to John Hilditch Evans by Charles Eamer Kempe.

There are numerous memorial tablets around the interior, but four notable monuments can be found in the transepts. An effigy of a knight, dating from about 1280 is unusual in that it shows the buckles connecting the breast and back plates of the armour, and in that the figure holds a horn. The man commemorated is not known, but may be a member of the Harley family. The effigy is weathered from being in the churchyard. A second effigy shows a priest, possibly Edmund Hert, Abbot of Pershore from 1456 to 1479, with his head resting on a mitre, indicating that he had resigned before he died. A large memorial with a round arch, classical columns and a large armorial crest on the flat canopy commemorates Fulke Hazelwood, who was living at Wick in about 1570, and his wife Dorothy Hungerford. Their own kneeling figures have disappeared, but three sons and six daughters are shown. A tenth child is shown facing out, either representing an infant death, or an older child who predeceased the parents, and is shown welcoming the others to Heaven. A longer memorial is to their son, Thomas Hazelwood, who died in 1598. He is shown lying beneath a flat canopy with heraldic arms, with his widow, Elizabeth Dineley, kneeling at his head, and their son, Francis, kneeling at his feet. An inscription is on the back wall. The monuments were moved to the transept in 1864. There are also hatchments to the Cradock, Probyn and Bedford families. In the centre of the south transept is the large war memorial.

The Bedford family lived at Abbey House, a large early 19th-century Gothic building, which stood to the south of the abbey until it was demolished in the 1930s. From 1914 to 1926 the house was occupied by a community of Anglican Benedictine monks, who moved to establish Nashdom Abbey in Buckinghamshire. The house was probably the successor of the 'New Lodging' granted to the last abbot, John Stonywell at the Dissolution, and its estate, much of the present Abbey Park, probably represents the extent of the monastic enclosure. The great gateway was probably at the south end of the Newlands, where the timber-framed Almonry, successor of the medieval almonry, is located. The medieval cross base was brought here from Wyre Piddle in 1844.

It should also be noted that a 12th-century bronze censer was discovered in 1840 in the abbey grounds, whilst an early 11th-century censer cover in the shape of a tower with a Rhenish Helm was discovered when a nearby cellar was excavated in about 1770. Now in the British Museum, it is inscribed with the maker's name, Godric, this is a remarkable reminder of the importance of Pershore Abbey during Anglo-Saxon times.

PERSHORE   ST. ANDREW

Across Church Walk from the east end of the abbey is the attractive limestone church of St. Andrew. It has a projecting south-west tower with a large south aisle and porch, to the north of which are the nave, north aisle and chancel. The church had not been used for regular worship since 1943, and the graveyard to the south is now a public garden. It was adapted for use as a parish centre in 1971. Its proximity to the abbey is explained by its foundation in the 11th century to serve the tenants of land in Pershore, which had been taken from the abbey by King Edward the Confessor to endow the foundation of Westminster Abbey. Possession of several estates in the surrounding villages such as Bricklehampton had also been transferred.

The tower is Perpendicular with a pyramid roof and battlements, some of which are rather attractively missing. It has a fine west window and bell openings, as well as gargoyles and grotesque animals carved on the steps of the buttresses. On the south side is an image niche. The west window of the nave is decorated with reticulated tracery. The north aisle was rebuilt and widened in the 14th century and has a simple north doorway which is now glazed. There is a gable on the roof to accommodate a larger three light window, which may mark the site of a chantry chapel as at Allensmore in Herefordshire. In the 14th century the chancel was rebuilt, and was subsequently restored in the 17th century. It is probable that there was a south transept which was replaced by the south aisle about 1430. The brick porch is of 18th-century date.

The interior is now a jumble of rooms divided by the breezeblock walls of 1971—a meeting room and a kitchen have been formed out of the south aisle and chancel. The north arcade is the earliest surviving part of the building, dating from between 1170 and 1190, with round piers which have trumpet scallop capitals and plain pointed arches. The original south arcade or arch to the transept must have been in line with the south wall of the chancel, but this was replaced about 1430 when the new south aisle was built, making the nave narrower than the chancel. Tha arcade has unusual crenellation on the capitals. The arcades were also altered in the 18th century when galleries were installed, but then were restored in 1887 by Sir George Aston Webb. There are piscinae in the chancel and south aisle, and a Perpendicular canopied niche by the large window in the north aisle which is supported by a corbel carved with an angel. There are medieval wagon roofs in the nave and chancel, but almost all the furnishings have been removed, though some pieces of panelling from a screen survive. The glass of the Walters memorial window in the north aisle is of 1899 by W. Pearce of Birmingham. On the east wall of the north aisle is part of a stone carving of a male figure, possibly holding a stole, which could be a portrait of a saint. It may be 9th-century in date, and is perhaps from a carved frieze reused from the earlier abbey buildings.

PINVIN   ST. NICHOLAS

Pinvin is a typically large Vale of Evesham village just north of Pershore which developed during the 19th and 20th centuries. Pershore station lies in the parish. A lane from the main street leads via fields to the small church, which was once a chapel to Pershore Abbey.

The church has a nave and chancel with a bellcote and south porch as well as a large vestry on the north side. The Norman nave is of lias, with one round-headed lancet window. The Norman north doorway is only visible from the inside, whilst the south doorway is ornamented with two stepped rounded mouldings, similar to arches in Worcester Cathedral. The other nave windows are 15th-century, but restored. The chancel was altered in the 18th century when the two square side windows were installed, and has a mainly 20th-century east window. The 17th-century limestone porch incorporates an

Early English stiff-leaf capital over the doorway. Is this reused stone from Pershore Abbey? The curious triangular bellcote and vestry date from 1884-85.

The interior is plain with whitewash, which in the nave covers extensive medieval wallpaintings. Some were exposed on the south wall in two sections in 1855. Traces of several layers in the eastern section include parts of 14th- and 15th-century scenes showing the Adoration of the Magi, the Crucifixion, the Resurrection and the Ascension at the lower level with the Annunciation and Salutation above, and a border of red dragons at the top. These are overlayed at the west end by the remains of a late 15th-century figure of St. Roch, to whom prayers were said in times of plague. St. Roch lived in 14th-century France, and was reputed to have been healed of the plague whilst on pilgrimage—he is shown with a plague spot on his leg. The

Medieval wallpainting in the nave of Pirton church

western section has unidentified medieval painting and the remains of 17th-century text. The octagonal font is Norman, and has a series of blind round-arched panels, which probably contained painted images of saints. The visible part of the nave roof includes a medieval tie beam and wall plates, whilst the remainder of the timbers are still under plaster. In the 19th century, a large chancel arch was built to replace a small Norman arch with squints such as still survives at Wyre Piddle. The furnishings are mainly 19th-century, but the pulpit incorporates the legs of a 17th-century communion table. The chancel windows contain panels of 20th-century glass.

PIRTON   ST. PETER

South of Worcester, Pirton is reached by small lanes and remains secluded. The name is based on the Anglo-Saxon word for pear tree, and whilst there are now fewer orchards in this part of the county, it remains a distinctly agricultural area. Both Pirton church and Court lie away from the small village centre. The Court was held by the Folliott family in the Middle Ages, and then passed to the Earls of Coventry at Croome, who owned it until the mid-20th century. It is a beautifully ornamented Tudor timber-framed house.

The church is situated on top of a ridge with fine views from the Indian Bean Tree in the pretty churchyard towards the west across the Severn Vale to Malvern. The nave and chancel are of lias, whilst the tower is timber-framed. The Norman nave also incorporates the base of the former central tower at the east end. Its position is marked by a massive plinth in the side walls, and the base of the stair turret which was retained as access to the rood loft. It seems that the tower either collapsed or was dangerous, as large cracks can be seen on the north side and it was replaced by the present tower, which was built outside the north doorway of the nave probably in the 16th century. It has close-studded timbers with a tall pyramidal roof, and is supported to the sides by aisles with crucks. This tower is more like the timber towers of churches in Essex or Hertfordshire, than the other Worcestershire towers such as Warndon and Cotheridge, although parallels can be drawn with the earlier belfries at Mamble and Knighton-on-Teme.

The Norman south doorway projects from the nave wall, and though it has been heavily restored, it has scalloped capitals and abaci carved with a Z-shaped design. There are Norman flat buttresses, and a Norman window on the north side. The Decorated west window was restored in the 19th century. The 14th-century chancel also has a restored Decorated east window; the side windows had their tracery replaced with a brick plate tracery in the 18th century and there is a medieval low side window. Although the interior has been scraped to the stone, it blends with the many interesting features. A further Norman window can be seen in the north wall, next to a doorway, concealed from view externally by the tower. The chancel arch is also Norman with a stepped arch and shafts to the piers. Above is a carved Norman figure set with the feet pointing upwards. This is St. Peter placed upside down in the manner of his crucifixion. Similar Norman carvings can be seen on the chancel arch at Rowlstone in Herefordshire. The former tower and rood loft stairs have been much rebuilt inside, but close

The timber-framed tower at Pirton

by are the foundations of the west wall and arch from the Norman tower. A carved Norman corbel is reset above the south doorway and an early Norman Mass dial is reset over the north doorway.

The plain font is also Norman, and around it are placed a group of medieval floor tiles. The north and south doorways both have early medieval ironwork. The roofs of both nave and chancel have medieval timbers. The pulpit and communion table are both 17th-century. Under the tower is the 18th-century clock mechanism.

The memorial tablets include one in the chancel to Elizabeth Lole, the rector's wife, who died n 1664. Outside in the churchyard is the base of the medieval cross.

Information is displayed in the church about the Pirton Stone, which is now at the Ashmolean Museum in Oxford. This stone, which measures some five inches by four inches was found in the church and is thought to have been a die for casting pilgrim tokens in the Middle Ages. The mould has a design showing the Crucifixion with the Virgin and St. John, and tokens bearing this design would have been purchased by pilgrims visiting a shrine. Its presence in this church has not been explained.

POWICK   ST. PETER

The village of Powick is situated on a hill beyond the meadows by the River Teme just outside Worcester's south western suburbs. The meadows, or Powick Hams, extend eastwards to the River Severn and were the sites of the battles of Worcester in 1642 and 1651 which marked the beginning and end of

The transepts at Powick church contain Norman masonry

the Civil War. The medieval Powick Bridge, which was severely damaged in the battles, was superseded by the present bridge in 1837. The mill nearby was built as England's first hydro-electric station in 1894.

Powick church is on the hilltop in a large churchyard overlooking the meadows. It is approached from the village by a driveway to the west end. The church is built of sandstone with an aisled nave, transepts, chancel and west tower. The earliest parts of the building are the transepts with late Norman lancets on both the east walls. It would seem that this was once a large cruciform Norman church, similar to nearby Kempsey. The chancel was rebuilt in the 13th century and has three Early English lancets at the east end, and two further lancets in the south wall. There are three lancets on the east wall of the north transept with a trefoil light above making plate tracery of the late 13th century. The aisle windows are Decorated and there is a blocked south doorway. At the angle of the chancel and the north transept is the late medieval rood loft stair turret. The end windows of the transepts are Perpendicular, as is the tower, though the west door was created in the 19th century. The church was restored in the 18th and 19th centuries. It is unclear what damage it may have sustained during the battles, but the south wall of the tower is definitely pitted from use as target practice for musket fire on the eve of the battle of 1651.

The spacious interior has been scraped back to the stonework. The arcades are Perpendicular with ornamental chamfering to the piers, and double chamfered arches. There is a panelled Perpendicular tower arch. The arch leading from the south aisle to the transept has the remains of a

The interior of Powick looking north-east

178

13th-century arch with a keeled shaft. In the east wall of the south transept is a small blocked Norman arch, only visible from inside, which was perhaps the entrance to a chapel or an apse or may have been a recess for an altar as at Ripple. The Early English lancets in the chancel have shafts inside. There are medieval timbers in some of the roofs.

The medieval rood loft stair survives by the north transept, but the present rood screen dates from 1845, though it incorporates some medieval woodwork. The side screens, pulpit and stalls are also of this date. Some of the bench ends are 15th-century, and the octagonal font is Perpendicular, carved with quatrefoils and floral motifs. The south transept now contains the organ and vestry.

In the north transept is the fine monument by Thomas Scheemakers to Mary Russell, formerly Cookes, who died in 1786. She is shown semi-reclining in a classical manner with one breast exposed. On the sarcophagus is a beautifully carved roundel with the young mother teaching her child to play the spinet, whilst to the left and right are carved musical instruments. This monument was unfortunately damaged by the collapse of the memorial above, which was to Sir Daniel Tyas, who died in 1673, and his wife Elizabeth. The tablet had two allegorical figures standing to the sides, with two more on the pediment. Tyas was an apothecary in Worcester, and mayor in 1639 and 1643, being knighted in 1644 for his services in defence of the city during the first battle. Another tablet commemorates, with a long Latin inscription, William Cookes, the brother of Sir Thomas Cookes who founded Worcester College in Oxford. Other stones commemorate members of the Russell family. The armorial banner in the north transept once hung above the stall of Admiral Compton Domville in the Henry VII Chapel at Westminster Abbey—the admiral is buried in Powick churchyard.

QUEENHILL   ST. NICHOLAS

It is unclear whether Queenhill takes its name from the Welsh 'cwm' describing the valley by the church, or from the fact that it was a royal manor in the eleventh century. Despite the close proximity of the M50 to the church, this is still a remote place, which can only be reached by narrow lanes from the Upton to Gloucester road. Queenhill church now also serves Holdfast, a hamlet to the north, where there was once a chapel, though this was in ruins by the 16th century. St. Nicholas' church was itself once a chapel to Ripple church across the River Severn.

The churchyard is set amidst fields and is shielded from the motorway by trees and shrubs. The church has a nave and chancel with a vestry and west tower all of local lias. The 19th-century timber south porch protects a Norman doorway with shafts, scallop capitals and a zig-zag arch similar to the doorway at Pendock. Much of the nave masonry is Norman, but the chancel was rebuilt in the 13th century with chamfered sandstone lancets to the sides. The east window consists of three lancets grouped under one arch, in the manner of the windows in the chancel at Kempsey. The tower is 14th-century, but the saddle-back roof was added, along with the vestry, when Sir George Gilbert Scott restored the church in 1855. This was funded by the Dowdeswell family of Pull Court in Bushley, who at the same time also altered many nearby houses.

The interior has been severely stripped to the stone and appears deceptively 19th-century. In the nave north wall is a reset Norman lancet window head, placed upside down, whilst the nave roof has 14th-century tie beams. Medieval fittings comprise the late Norman font base carved with cable moulding, a Perpendicular screen, and what may be part of the medieval rood beam with a carved vine is incorporated into the 17th-century pulpit. The communion table and rail are also 17th-century. In the north windows of the nave there is some 14th-century glass including fragments of a panel showing St. Anne and the Virgin, and the three lions which made up the Arms of England before 1340. The east window has glass of 1892 by E. Franklin, showing Christ holding a lamb, with Moses and St. Peter.

By the south door there is an incised slab which was once in the chancel with the figures of Henry Field and his two wives Anne and Sybil. He died in 1584 having moved to Holdfast Manor from King's Norton near Birmingham. In the chancel is a small brass of 1624 to Nicholas Barnes inscribed 'If any one asks who lies within this tomb, Tell them that Nick Barnes hath taken up ye roome'. Outside in the church-yard is the base of the medieval cross. It is thought that the view from the porch inspired Edward Elgar's composition of *The Apostles*.

REDDITCH   ST. GEORGE

St. George's is an area of Victorian housing which developed around Beoley Road on the east side of Redditch town centre with the growth of needle manufacturing in the late 19th century. Land for a new church was given by the Windsor family, and the building was erected in 1876-77 to designs of Frederick Preedy. It stands today in a cul-de-sac surrounded by trees, a short distance from the Roman Catholic church of Our Lady of Mount Carmel, which includes part of a church designed in 1834 by Thomas Rickman, the architect of Hartlebury and Ombersley churches.

The church of St. George is a large sandstone building, with an aisled nave and chancel with clere-storey, and a small bellcote over the east gable of the nave. There is a large south porch. The north aisle was completed in a late phase in 1898 by a different architect. The style is mainly Early English, with plate tracery in the west window, which has a circular opening above the lancets. Other lancets are both grouped and single. In the aisles there is some early Decorated style tracery.

The interior is very lofty with plain exposed stonework. The capitals to the piers were never carved with the intended stiff leaf decoration. There are many late 19th- and early 20th-century fittings and several stained glass windows. The organ in the gallery dominates the west end and was brought here from Queen's College, Oxford.

REDDITCH   ST. LUKE, HEADLESS CROSS

The name Headless Cross is a corruption of Headley's Cross. This large southern suburb of Redditch lies on the ridge between the town centre and Astwood Bank, and consists of terraces of cottages for needle-workers and fishing tackle makers which grew up in the 19th century. The area has been further developed since Redditch became a new town in the 1960s.

St. Luke's church is less obvious as a landmark than either of the Victorian or 20th century water towers nearby. It is, however, complemented by the Methodist Church, which was rebuilt in 1897 with an openwork spire to the tower. St. Luke has no tower, but a bellcote at the west end of the aisled nave. It also has a chancel and apse. Standing back from the street, the west front is impressive with a Norman style portal and unusual rose window, similar to the east window at Spernall church in Warwickshire. The church was originally constructed in 1843, but was enlarged and much rebuilt by Frederick Preedy in 1867-68. He retained the south and west parts of the previous church, and added a north aisle with organ chamber. Some of the window tracery dates back to 1843. On the east end he added the apsidal chancel, which has a stone vault inside.

The interior has paintings by Preedy in the chancel with signs of the zodiac above the large figures of a censing angel, St. Augustine, St. Peter, St. Mary, St. John, St. Paul and St. John Chrysostom (Archbishop of Constantinople). The painted reredos is also by Preedy and shows the Entombment of Christ. There is also much painting to the roofs. The furnishings are 19th- and 20th-century. Preedy installed stained glass in most of the windows between 1870 and 1875, though he had designed the west window in about 1860. A brass memorial of 1914 to a former rector, Sydney Baber, is the work of Bromsgrove Guild craftsmen.

REDDITCH   # ST. PETER, IPSLEY

St. Peter, Ipsley, showing the south arcade now filled with windows

In 1931 Ipsley was transferred from Warwickshire, and by the early 1970s it had been completely absorbed into Redditch new town. A few older houses remain in the district, and on a hilltop to the east of the River Arrow, but to the west of the line of the Roman Icknield Street is a deserted medieval village site. Here too, St. Peter's church and the remaining parts of Ipsley Court now form an historic nucleus to an essentially 20th-century settlement. The court was held by the Huband family from Norman times to 1740, when it became the home of Samuel Landor, whose family included the poet Walter Savage Landor. He frequently mentioned Ipsley in his poems.

The church today consists of a west tower, nave and chancel, for ironically the building was reduced in size in 1785, when the aisles were demolished and the arcades blocked up. Windows were put into the arches, and some of the masonry from the aisles seems to have been incorporated into the former rectory. The new town has meant expansion is once again necessary, and a new room was added in the 1980s to the north side of the church. The Perpendicular west tower has battlements and a fine west window and is of a type found throughout Warwickshire.

The south aisle appears to have originally been built in the 13th century, with an arcade of two round piers either side of an octagonal pier still exposed internally. One capital has a carved human head with tendrils. The north arcade is later, probably 14th-century, with octagonal piers and chamfered arches. A tall Perpendicular arch leads to the tower. The chancel arch and much of the east window date from a restoration of 1867, when the church was given a new roof. Most of the fittings are 19th-century, but there is an unusual 14th-century font. It is heptagonal, similar to that at Warndon church, and is decorated with ballflower and crenellation. The elaborately carved 17th-century pulpit came from Eastnor in Herefordshire, and there is a carved panel of similar date showing the sacrifice of Isaac possibly from the former woodwork in the church. The stained glass in the east window was given in 1887 in memory of Charles Dolben, the rector's son, after his death from cholera whilst working as a priest in India. A second window given by the family shows the Resurrection, whilst a window of 1899 has a Nativity scene.

The interior of the church was once dominated by a large Renaissance style memorial of the 1580s to Sir John Huband and his wife, which was destroyed during the restoration of 1867. However, incised alabaster slabs survive to Nicholas Huband, who died in 1533 and is shown in armour, beside his wife Dorothy, who died in 1558 and is seen wearing contemporary costume. Another slab thought to commemorate Sir John Huband, who died in 1563, and his wife, Mary, who died in 1551, has no inscription.

REDDITCH   MATCHBOROUGH CHURCH

In Redditch New Town during the 1970s, the only existing church building was St. Peter's church at Ipsley. It was decided to build an interdenominational church in Matchborough, which was funded jointly by the Methodists and the Church of England. The brick building is a typical 1970s design with huge sweeping roofs and long wooden mullioned windows.

REDDITCH   ST. PHILIP, WEBHEATH

Webheath is on the south-western fringe of Redditch in the former Forest of Feckenham. It was formed out of the parish of Tardebigge, as the village grew in the 19th century with cottages occupied by needle-makers, and was further developed with extensive 1930s suburban housing.

St. Philip's church was built between 1869 and 1870, at the expense of Lady Windsor of Hewell. The architect was Frederick Preedy, who used the Decorated style, with traceried windows to the nave, chancel and porch. There is a bellcote on the east gable of the nave.

The interior has many contemporary fittings. Of particular note is the reredos by Preedy made with Italian marble given by Lady Windsor, which has mosaic work and a cross with angels. The east window glass is also by Preedy, whilst a south window has glass of 1871 by the Belgian Jean-Baptiste Capronnier.

REDDITCH   ST. STEPHEN

The parish church of Redditch stands in Church Green at the heart of the town. Redditch developed as a needle manufacturing centre, particularly during the 19th century, and there are several industrial buildings and Victorian houses as evidence of this. However, Redditch changed dramatically after it was designated a New Town in 1964—there has been considerable expansion across the Arrow Valley to the east, but also a complete rearrangement of many parts of the old town.

St. Stephen's church can trace its origins back to the gate chapel of Bordesley Abbey, an important Cistercian monastery situated next to the River Arrow to the north of the present town. It was founded in 1138, and the monks were instrumental in bringing metalworking to the area through the abbey's mill, which has been studied as part of the archaeological excavation of the site. The gate chapel stood at the entrance to the west side of the abbey precinct and was a small 14th-century building with Decorated windows and a bellcote. Excavations have revealed its plan and the layout of the burial ground, with its 17th-century gravestones. The gate chapel was renovated by the Earl of Plymouth and Nathaniel Mugg in 1687, and served as the church for the small community of Redditch. By 1805 the chapel was once again in decay, but as the centre of Redditch had moved to the hilltop, the Chapel on the Green was built in 1808 on land given by the Earl of Plymouth. It was a plain brick building with a cupola, which had to be extended in 1816 and again in 1827 as the town grew.

It was eventually decided that the church should be rebuilt, and the present sandstone building was erected by Henry Woodyer in 1854-55. Funds were limited and the church is less elaborate than his other works, such as St. Michael at Tenbury Wells. It is in the Decorated style and has an aisled nave with a north-west tower with a slender spire, which dominates views of the town on account of its position at the top of the hill. In 1893-94 a new chancel with chapels and vestry was designed by Temple Moore at the expense of the rector, Canon Horace Newton. This part is in the Perpendicular style with a clerestorey, low pitch roof and a sanctus bellcote.

The interior has been much changed with reordering during the 1970s and 1990s to increase community use, and much of the nave is now partitioned into smaller spaces. The nave arcades are Decorated in style but with plain octagonal piers. The chancel arch and arcades have the Perpendicular characteristic of being without capitals. The ribbed plaster vault in the chancel is Temple Moore's design. The 19th-century furnishings include the partly gilded iron chancel screen of 1890 by Hardman & Co., and a pulpit installed by Canon Newton, whilst the font cover is the work of the Bromsgrove Guild.

In the south aisle are two windows by Kempe and Tower, and a window showing the Nativity is by the Belgian Jean-Baptiste Capronnier. In 1870 the west window by Frederick Preedy was installed. It shows the Corporal Acts of Mercy—a memorial to Lady Windsor of Hewell. A further window of the same year by Preedy depicts the scene 'Suffer Little Children'. The windows showing St. Stephen and St. George are of 1890 by Burlison and Grylls, who also made the Sarson's memorial window in 1889.

In the vestry are some medieval floor tiles from Bordesley Abbey, and there is a brass tablet from the previous church commemorating the benefaction of Nathaniel Mugg in restoring the chapel; he was buried in the chapel graveyard in 1712. In the churchyard are some stones which may have come from the abbey. Today, St. Stephen's is closely linked with the ecumenical centre, Trinity Church, in the adjacent Kingfisher Shopping Centre.

RIBBESFORD   ST. LEONARD

Ribbesford today is a small hamlet beside the River Severn opposite Redstone Rock and close to Bewdley bypass. The church is picturesquely sited next to Ribbesford House, a largely Tudor building with turrets much altered by Lord Herbert of Chirbury in 1820. The House was used as the Headquarters of the Free French during the Second World War and has since been converted into flats. The large 17th-century brick barn is most attractive. St. Leonard's church was the parish

The extraordinary timber south arcade at Ribbesford

church of Bewdley until 1853, and thus is large in relation to the present settlement.

The red sandstone church has a nave and chancel with large north and south aisles. At the west end of the nave is a timber bell turret. There is also a timber north porch and a vestry. The west end of the north aisle represents the remains of the Norman nave, and in the remaining section of 12th-century wall is the north doorway. This has capitals with carved interlace decorated by dots, and to the west is a stone panel carved with a bird, which is of the Herefordshire School of Sculpture type, and similar to the panels at Eastham and Stockton-on-Teme. The abaci have chequer and zig-zag patterns, and there is roll moulding to the arch. The tympanum is carved with an archer and two beasts, one of which is large and monstrous, the other small like a fawn or a hound. Does this represent the struggle of goodness to overcome the evil beasts? The south doorway has been reset in the south aisle and has eroded columns, capitals and panels. The nave and south aisle are 15th-century and have Perpendicular windows and a west doorway. The south aisle was added later. Much of the east end of the chancel and north aisle was rebuilt in the Decorated style in 1877 after the church was struck by lightning. This was much criticised at the time by the art critic and architectural writer, John Ruskin, who favoured the church being allowed to remain ruinous. The porch is prettily painted in blue, white and grey and has turned balusters. It is dated 1633 and carries the initials TM and HW. The bell turret is a 19th-century reconstruction.

The interior is spacious and light, despite the scraped stone walls. The principal feature is the 15th-century timber south arcade, which has octagonal piers fashioned to look like Perpendicular stonework and arches made up from curved braces. Ruskin was keen to see this retained had the church remained a ruin in 1877. The two west bays of the north arcade are Perpendicular, whilst the eastern part was rebuilt in 1877 to replace two Norman arches, which must have joined the 12th-century nave to a south chapel. There is no structural division between the nave and chancel.

There are further medieval survivals, including two Perpendicular canopied niches in the north aisle below two corbels, which were formerly supports for the roof. In the south aisle is a Perpendicular piscina. In the blocked south doorway are a number of pieces of reset Norman sculpture, including fragments of round shafts carved with plaiting. This is very similar to the Herefordshire School work in the west window at Kilpeck in Herefordshire, but can also be compared to carving on the font at Siddington in Gloucestershire. There is also some zig-zag carving. This sculpture came from either the Norman south doorway, the chancel arch or the arcade. A projection in the south wall marks the position of the rood screen and loft, and there is a staircase with two doorways. The present dado screen incorporates tracery panels from the medieval screen, with carved foliage, angels and heads. Further carving from the screen has been set into the pulpit, with scenes from folk tales and fables, such as a pig pulling down acorns, a dancing pig and the fox preaching to the geese from *Aesop's Fables*. The lectern is made up of 17th-century woodwork. The remaining fittings are 19th- and 20th-century.

At the west end of the south aisle is a window containing 15th-century glass, including a figure of St. George and angels with musical instruments. Fragments of heraldic glass include the arms of the Acton and Peverell families, and the royal arms of King Edward IV. The west window was designed by Edward Burne-Jones and made by Morris and Co. in 1875. It is pre-Raphaelite and shows two minstrel angels with a woman offering her cloak to a poor girl. It was given by Alfred Baldwin, the Stourport ironmaster and father of Prime Minister Stanley Baldwin, in memory of his mother-in-law Hannah Macdonald. Burne-Jones was another of her sons-in-law, whilst a further daughter was mother of Rudyard Kipling. Other examples of this type of glass can be seen in Wilden church. The east window of 1926 is a memorial to the family of Archdeacon Winnington-Ingram of Hereford, and shows the Triumph of Christ.

At the west end of the north aisle are three medieval coffin lids with carved crosses, one of which has the arms of the Mortimer family across the shaft. There is a memorial tablet to John Soley, who died in 1604, and his wife who died in 1639, with classical features. The large medieval style brass in the south aisle, with an effigy underneath a canopy, is to Captain Francis Winnington-Ingram who died in 1843. There are several other tablets to the Winnington-Ingram family of Ribbesford House. A further tablet commemorates Peter Prattinton, who died in 1840, after a lifetime of antiquarian research; his collections are housed at the Society of Antiquaries in London. In the turret is a 13th-century bell—the earliest to survive in Worcestershire, though there is one of similar date at Oldberrow, formerly in this county but now in Warwickshire.

Ripple church from the north-west

This large parish on the east side of the River Severn is on Worcestershire's southern boundary with Gloucestershire. In the early Middle Ages, the Croomes, Upton-upon-Severn and Queenhill were all chapelries to Ripple church, which suggests its origins were as an Anglo-Saxon minster. It is probable that Ripple, with its Scandinavian name meaning strip of land, is a settlement of Danish or Jutish origin and may be connected in some way to Ripple in Kent. The village prospered during the medieval period under the patronage of the Priory of Worcester, but had declined by the 17th century as Upton rose in importance. The church stands at the east end of the village, close to the small square with its medieval cross, and next to the large former Georgian rectory. The M50 is only a couple of fields away, yet the village remains quite secluded.

St. Mary's church is built to a cruciform plan mainly from the local lias. It has an aisled nave of six bays, a clerestorey and north porch, a central tower with transepts and a chancel. The tower, transepts, nave and aisles date from the late 12th century, and represents the transition from Norman to Early English architecture. The arches are pointed, and the arcades elegant, yet there are some round-headed

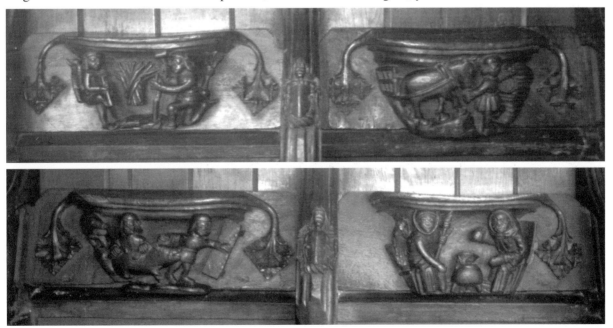

Misericords at Ripple carved in the 15th century

windows, whilst the carvings on the capitals of the crossing arches are a mixture of Norman beasts and Early English foliage. The chancel was rebuilt in the 13th century, and has fine lancet windows of red sandstone to the sides in groups of three under single arches. At the east and west ends of the church are Perpendicular windows, and a further 15th-century window at the east end of the northern clerestorey was inserted to throw light onto the former rood screen. In the 18th century an extra level was added to the tower, above the bell openings, with a classical Georgian balustrade. At this time the porch was given an upper room in a plain, almost medieval style.

Although the interior is largely scraped back to the stone walls, it is spacious and elegant with the crossing arches and arcades of about 1200. The transepts have round-headed recesses on the east walls, perhaps for the altars of the chantry chapels. Medieval fittings include the 13th-century font and some fragments of a screen, but most significant are the 15th-century stalls in the chancel with their 16 misericords. They were installed by Worcester Priory for the use of the Augustinian canons who took services here and said Mass in the chantries. The misericords are carved with representations of village activities for each of the 12 months, and include hedging and ditching, sowing, reaping and killing a pig. The most unusual is that for July, which shows a dispute over the weight and quality of bread loaves at Lammas, the Loaf Mass. Four further misericords have symbols of the four elements—light, dark, heat and water— which gave a successful harvest. The moon with a face is particularly appealing. The communion rails are 17th-century, but the remainder of the fittings are mainly 19th-century. The organ was brought here from Tewkesbury Methodist church in 1985.

In a chancel window are fragments of 15th-century glass from the east window, which was destroyed by fire during the Reformation. Some of the glass was discovered during the 18th century near the altar along with a damaged censer. Some medieval wall painting has been discovered in the north transept during recent restoration work. The present glass in the east window shows the crucifixion and was installed about 1888 in memory of the Empson family by Bryans of London. Charles Eamer Kempe designed the west window glass depicting the Nativity in 1885.

Amongst the memorial tablets are brass plates in the chancel to John Woodward, who died in 1596, and to his grandson William Woodward, who died in 1668—the Woodwards owned land in Ripple from the 16th century. John Woodward is recorded as a Yeoman of the Guard to both King Philip, Spanish husband of Mary Tudor, and to Queen Elizabeth I. A further tablet to a former rector, John Holt, who died in 1734 is by Thomas White of Worcester, sculptor of the trophy and some of the figures on Worcester Guildhall.

Severe structural problems in the tower and transepts and at the west end have meant that a thorough restoration of the church has been carried out during the late 1990s. Outside in the churchyard is the base of the medieval cross.

ROCHFORD   ST. MICHAEL

The church at Rochford is in the lower part of the village next to the River Teme, downstream from the site of the ford by the rocky cliff which gives the place its name. Today the main centre of population is at Upper Rochford on the road from Tenbury Wells to Martley. The church is visible across the river from the main Tenbury to Worcester road near Newnham Bridge, but it is necessary to pass through Tenbury to reach Rochford, where the church is approached through a farmyard.

The red sandstone church consists of just a nave and chancel with a vestry, a timber-framed porch, and a bell turret with a small spire. It was a possession of the Abbey of Lyra in Normandy from 1066 until the suppression of alien monastic houses in England in 1416, when it became affiliated to Tenbury church,

The restored Norman church at Rochford

and passed into the hands of the Carthusian Priory at Sheen in Surrey until the Dissolution. The nave is mainly Norman masonry, and the north doorway has two shafts with capitals carved with scrolls beneath abaci carved with plaiting and interlace. The tympanum shows the Tree of Life and is reminiscent of the tympana at both Dymock and Kempley churches in Gloucestershire and Kilpeck church in Herefordshire. Below is cable moulding, whilst the arch is carved with rosettes and projecting zig-zag. The doorway dates to about 1150, and is set in a projecting piece of wall, similar to those at Martley or Knighton-on-Teme, in which exposed position it has unfortunately become weathered. There are two Norman lancet windows in the nave and a further one in the chancel, whilst the south doorway and chancel windows are Decorated. The church was extended to the west when the vestry and bell turret were added in the 19th century.

The interior is very much the result of the 19th-century alterations and restoration. However, the Norman chancel arch has carved projecting zig-zag, and there is a restored 14th-century piscina in a south window of the chancel. The many 19th-century fittings include the font and the organ with its mahogany case and brass inlays of about 1810—it has a double headed eagle and foliage on the top. On the north wall are the royal arms of George I and II, similar to those at Eastham. In the nave are boards with the Commandments, Creed and Lord's Prayer. The east window contains glass by William Morris and Co., dating from after 1863, which commemorates the death of a child. It shows the Adoration of the Christ Child with two angels set in clear quarries in the lancets with further angels in the tracery. It is very different to later Morris glass designed by Edward Burne-Jones.

ROCK   ST. PETER AND ST. PAUL

Rock church has a splendid hilltop setting in the south west corner of this very large parish in Wyre Forest, which includes Far Forest and Heightington. The main centres of population are at Callow Hill and Bliss Gate, whilst around the church at Rock Cross are a few timber-framed cottages and several 20th-century houses. On the south side of the churchyard are the earthworks of the manor house of the Tosny family. The church was founded on land given to the monastery of St. Evroul in Normandy before 1102 by Ralph Tosny to atone for the destruction of the town. Ralph also founded a priory on the family estates at Astley. Like other English property of St. Evroul, Rock passed to the Carthusian monks at Sheen in 1416 when alien monastic houses were suppressed.

The large green sandstone church has a nave and chancel with a vestry, south aisle and chapel, and a west tower. The nave and chancel survive from a large Norman church dating from about 1170 and founded by Roger Tosny. The north wall has some very interesting Norman features. The restored north portal projects from the wall and to each side of the doorway are three shafts. There is zig-zag carving on the outer bands similar to the doorways at Astley and Beckford, whilst the capitals are carved with scallops, and one face which is similar to those at Holt. The abaci have carved detail, and the arch has projecting zig-zags, crenellation lobes, and rolls with radiating rays. Both nave and chancel have flat buttresses, and below the roof the corbels are decorated with heads, similar to those at Astley. Above the string course the Norman lancet windows have shafts to each side with capitals which are a mixture of plain blocks, scallops and carved foliage designs. The windows are each accompanied on the nave to the east by a blind arch also with shafts. The reason for this is unclear, but they could have served as niches for statues. The vestry was added to the north side of the chancel when it was extended eastwards in the late 13th century. The reticulated east window is Decorated

The Norman chancel arch at Rock

and there is also a Decorated low side window in the north wall of the nave. The tower and south aisle were added in 1510 by Sir Humphrey Coningsby and the tower retains its Perpendicular battlements, bell openings and west window, but the south aisle was rebuilt in the 19th century with Decorated style windows. It still has a low pitch roof, battlements and a Perpendicular west window.

The lofty interior is stripped back to the stone and is dominated by the impressive Norman chancel arch with shafts to the jambs. Each side has one larger central shaft with a smaller shaft facing east and two smaller ones facing west. The capitals are carved with entwined trails, a centaur and a boat with a cross representing St. Peter. Above the carved abaci are projecting and diagonal zig-zags on the arch. This is fine Herefordshire School sculpture and the arch has many similarities to the chancel arch at Rowlstone in Herefordshire. Built into the north wall of the nave are several fragments of Norman sculpture, which by their similarity to the carving on the north doorway may have been placed there from the south doorway which was removed with the addition of the aisle. However, it is also possible that there were unused stones from the original time of construction, which were built into the wall and remained plastered over until the stone was scraped during restoration. The chancel roof has 14th-century timbers including wind braces, whilst the nave has a wagon roof with 15th-century tie beams. The Perpendicular tower arch has concave sides to the responds, similar to the tall octagonal piers of the south arcade and the shorter piers in the south chapel. These are very similar to the piers in St. Mary's church, Kidderminster, and date from 1510.

The Norman cauldron-shaped font is carved with nine rosettes linked by clasps, and is similar in style to the font at nearby Bayton. In the south chapel is a medieval altar stone. To either side of the main altar are two decorated niches, which may once have contained statues. The reredos, chancel seats, parclose screens and stone pulpit inlaid in red marble, are by Frederick Preedy, and were installed when he restored the church in 1861. The other furnishings are all 19th- and 20th-century, but the earlier village stocks and whipping post are preserved at the back of the church.

The north chancel and south chapel windows contain glass of 1861 by Preedy. In the south chapel is an incised slab depicting, in his Mass vestments, Richard Smith, a priest who died in 1554. The tomb chest in the chapel was installed by Sir Humphrey Coningsby, the builder of the aisle and tower, for his father Thomas Coningsby, who died about 1498. It is ornamented with shields in quatrefoils and has traces of the original paint.

ROMSLEY   ST. KENELM

Romsley church, showing the miniature Perpendicular tower

Almost a mile west from the village of Romsley on the Clent Hills is the small church of St. Kenelm. A legend, which has since been discredited, claimed that Kenelm, the boy king of Mercia, was murdered in the Clent Hills by his sister in the 9th century. A holy spring rose on the spot. He was declared a saint and the majority of his relics were kept at Winchcombe Abbey in Gloucester-shire, though a shrine and some relics, including his head in silver gilt, remained here. The site attracted many pilgrims in the Middle Ages whose offerings were an important source of revenue for nearby Halesowen Abbey. A hamlet called Kenelm Stowe grew up around the well and the church, but this has now disappeared and the church is left isolated. The church was richly furnished before the Reformation.

The church consists of a small west tower and a nave and chancel with south porch. Beneath the chancel is an undercroft, which has no features except a blocked arch in the south wall but once held St. Kenelm's shrine. The nave and chancel are Norman. In the medieval timber-framed porch is the south doorway which dates from about 1150. The tympanum shows Christ crowned and seated with a ring around his raised right hand; angels are holding the mandorla. The theme is similar to that of the door-ways at Pedmore near Stourbridge and Rowlstone in Herefordshire, as well as the remaining fragment of the tympanum at Chaddesley Corbett, whilst the carved drapery is similar to Herefordshire School sculp-ture at Fownhope in Herefordshire. Around the figures is a wide border with the loosely entwined tails of serpents, perhaps based on Anglo-Saxon decoration. The arch is of red sandstone and is the only complete arch with carved beakheads in Worcestershire, and contrasts with the brown tympanum. High on the south wall is placed a further piece of worn 12th-century sculpture, showing a saint. The chancel was altered in the 14th-century and has a Decorated east window and north lancet. The slim tower was built in the 15th century, perhaps to replace an earlier bell turret, and rests on two large buttresses which project from the west wall and are joined by an arch. Large animal gargoyles protrude from the corners. The belfry has bell openings of one light with canopies to the sides over blank openings. Above are panelled battlements, pinnacles and more gargoyles.

The attractive homely interior is now simply furnished and there are stone seats to the side of the nave. On the left side of the chancel north window are the remains of a painted figure of the 14th century, and there are traces of other wall painting. The glass in the window showing Faith and Peace is by Edward Burne-Jones, whilst the east window showing Kenelm with Christ and the Disciples was the gift of Prime Minister, William Gladstone. He was a frequent visitor to nearby Hagley Hall, as his wife was the sister of Lady Lyttleton. The window showing scenes from the Life of St. Kenelm is of 1915 by one of the Camm family.

ROUS LENCH   ST. PETER

South of Inkberrow is the estate of Rous Lench. The village has many timber-framed cottages around a green beneath a hill which rises up to a brick tower above Rous Lench Court. The tower was built in an Italianate style by the owner of the Court in the late 19th century, the Reverend William Chafy, while the Court is a mixture of 16th-century timber-framing and neo-Tudor work of about 1840. It was home to the Rous family, and then the Rouse Boughtons from the late 14th century. At the bottom of the garden, next to the green, the church stands in a graveyard with several mature trees.

The restored Norman church at Rous Lench

St. Peter's church is built of grey sandstone and has a nave and chancel with a bellcote on the east gable of the nave. To the north is an aisle with an apsidal east end, and a north chapel with vestry. The nave and chancel are Norman, whilst the bellcote was added in the Norman style by Frederick Preedy in 1884 to 1885. The northern parts were all built in the Norman style by Preedy at this time at the expense of Chafy. There are several genuine Norman features to be seen from the outside—the reset north doorway with its scalloped capitals; the three window heads of the north chapel with their different carved designs; and the south doorway with a carved shaft to each side and projecting zig-zag to the arch. This doorway has no carved tympanum, just a large plain stone, but above the doorway is a niche with shafts carved with foliage, and an arch with zig-zag. In the niche is a seated figure of Christ in Blessing, surrounded by a cusped almond-shaped mandorla. It probably dates from between 1140 and 1150 and has been compared to carving at Castor church in Cambridgeshire and on the Prior's Door at Ely Cathedral. A similar niche can also be seen at Leigh church. The chancel was rebuilt in the early 13th century, and the former Early English east window is now the west window of the north aisle. The nave has a Decorated west window.

The interior is quite dark and very much the result of Chafy's benefactions. However, the north arcade is late Norman. It has three arches, parts of which are stepped, on round piers with scalloped capitals. The chancel arch is also Norman although it was partly rebuilt during Preedy's alteration of 1884-85. At the south-east corner of the nave is a turret which contains the rood loft stair. The octagonal font is Perpendicular and there are medieval credence shelves in the nave and chancel. The interior is dominated by Chafy's Italianate Romanesque altar canopy at the east end of the north aisle, behind which the apse

The memorial of 1719 to Frances Rous

has skylights for dramatic effect. The Gothic screen was installed in 1885 along with the Tudor style chancel seats and kneeling desks. There are two late 16th-century pulpits. The painting showing the Feast in the House of Simon is Venetian and of about 1600 in the style of Tintoretto. There is a collection of sculptural fragments found during the alterations, including an Anglo-Danish stone from about the 9th century, of unknown origin but perhaps from a cross. It has carved birds and interlace on one side, a man carrying a sickle on another, and entwined serpents on the remainder. Other pieces include further Norman window heads, one of which has entwined tendrils. Along with the tympanum at Billesley in Warwickshire, this is an example of the Herefordshire School of Sculpture which is a considerable distance to the east from the main centre of the school's works.

In the north chapel are several monuments which were moved from the chancel in 1886. A large tomb chest with two effigies commemorates Edward Rous, who died in 1611 and his wife Mary Haseling, who died in 1580. Edward's feet rest against a large Moor's head, whilst Mary's rest on a dog. Around the chest is a cartouche with strapwork, in front of which are shown their son and three daughters kneeling. The son, Sir John Rous, was captured at the Court by the Royalists during the Civil War and died in prison at Warwick in 1645. His monument is a chest with black columns, a plain canopy and a coat of arms. There are no effigies, but the memorial also commemorates his wife, Hester Temple. A large memorial of 1719 to Frances Rous shows her seated holding a heart, next to an urn with two doves on top. Each side has Corinthian columns supporting an open pediment below which is a medallion showing her husband being carried by cherubs. Frances was the daughter of Thomas Archer, the architect of Birmingham Cathedral, from Umberslade Park in Warwickshire. There are also memorial tablets to Sir Thomas Rous, who died in 1676, and Sir Edward Rous, who died in 1677.

RUBERY   ST. CHAD

Rubery lies on the A38 between the Lickey and Waseley Hills at the point where Worcestershire meets Birmingham. It is easy to dismiss it as a suburb, but it grew in the 17th century as a nail making centre in a remote part of the parish of King's Norton. No houses of this period remain, and the buildings are all 19th-century or later. The church is by the shopping centre in the middle of Rubery.

St. Chad was first built as a chapel of ease to St. John's church, Bromsgrove. It was a mission church constructed in the Tudor style in 1895, taking its dedication from St. Chad's Well in Holy Well Lane, which is supposed to have been visited by the saint. The church was rebuilt in 1958 by Lavender, Twentyman and Percy, and is typical of the period, contrasting with their pre-war church at St. Martin, Ettingshall in Wolverhampton. It has a low pitch roof and side walls with grid like windows. There is no east window but a patterned brick wall inside, whilst there is an octagonal chapel to the south of the altar and a vestry to the north. These orientations are for church ritual, for in fact the church is aligned north to south. There is a separate modern campanile. A lead figure on the exterior was brought here from the former war memorial made by the Bromsgrove Guild.

RUSHOCK   ST. MICHAEL

Rushock is a scattered village to the south-east of Kidderminster. Close to the church is Rushock Court on the site of the house where the recusant Roman Catholic priest, Father John Wall of Harvington Hall was arrested in 1679. He was executed at Worcester on the same day as John Kemble was martyred in Hereford, being the last Roman Catholic priests to be put to death in England.

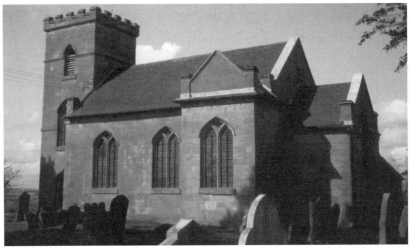

The late Georgian church at Rushock

The medieval church was rebuilt on the same site in 1758 by Roger Eykyn. It consists of a nave with short transepts and a small chancel. At the west end is a low battlemented tower. The church is very much in the mode of 18th-century ecclesiastical building, but the Y-shaped tracery and Gothic detailing including the ogee arched doorway suggest that it may have been altered in about 1800. The church was restored in 1872 when the east window was replaced, and the glass of 1876 was the gift of the rector. The interior is quite plain and has the feel of an early 19th-century Commissioners church. The date of the octagonal font is uncertain.

SALWARPE   ST. MICHAEL

Just less than a mile from the southern edge of Droitwich, Salwarpe lies at the end of a lane close to the River Salwarpe and a restored stretch of the Droitwich Canal. The approach to the village from the east passes the timber-framed Salwarpe Court which was probably built by Sir John Talbot in the early 16th century. During the Middle Ages Salwarpe was held by the powerful Beauchamp family.

St. Michael's stands close to the Court in a churchyard with a number of trees. It is built of sandstone and has a west tower, aisled nave, chancel, south porch and vestry. The battlemented tower is Perpendicular, and there are Decorated windows in the north aisle, but from the outside everything else appears to be 19th-century work in the Decorated style. The chancel was rebuilt in 1848.

The interior has the overall feel of 19th-century restoration and rebuilding, but the nave arcades show that part of the late Norman masonry remains. The three eastern arches date from about 1200, with round piers and abaci, supporting simple stepped pointed arches. The western arches are separated from the arcades by rectangular piers that may mark the position of the Norman west wall of the nave. The west end of the present nave may have been the site of the earlier medieval tower, for there are springers from arches across the aisles at this point. The Norman chancel arch was replaced by the present arch in 1848. The tower arch is panelled and Perpendicular.

The chancel incorporates a sedilia with two round arches dating from about 1530. The north aisle wall contains a medieval cross shaped niche which may once have held a crucifix, and there is a Decorated tomb recess. The south aisle has a piscina and a Perpendicular screen with single lights; the north aisle screen has been restored. There were chantry chapels at the ends of the north and south aisles, one of which was probably founded by William Richeport, rector from 1367 to 1401, whose effigy is believed to be that in the chancel. At the west end of the north aisle are some medieval floor tiles, several of which have heraldic designs, including the arms of the Talbot family. Many of the remainder of the fittings are 19th century, including the reredos by Powell & Co. of London, which shows the Last Supper. The stained glass in the east window, and of another window, is of 1863 by Hardman & Co.

The effigy, probably of William Richeport shows him holding a chalice and wearing vestments with fine carved drapery. There is a lion at his feet, and angels by his pillow. A memorial on the opposite wall is to Thomas Talbot of Salwarpe Court, who died in 1613, and his wife, Magdalene Wyvell. They are shown kneeling, facing each other across a prayer desk, with their son and two daughters kneeling below. A tablet in the south aisle with twisted columns commemorates Olave Talbot who died aged 18 in 1681. Below is a memorial to her mother, Elizabeth Talbot, formerly Gower, who died in 1689. It is of black and white marble and has two figures of Charity with a Biblical inscription from Acts.

SEDGEBERROW   ST. MARY

This large Vale of Evesham village, just east of the A46 not far from Bredon Hill, has developed around the brook-like River Isbourne. The village contains several timber-framed houses, including an altered but rare example of a small medieval cottage. The present manor cottages stand on the site of the medieval manor house of Worcester Priory, which held land at Sedgeberrow through the Middle Ages.

The church stands in a secluded graveyard in the centre of the village. It is built of limestone and consists of a lofty nave and chancel under one roof, with a north porch, large south vestry and slender west tower with spire. The tower and spire are unusual as they are octagonal from the base, and would seem to date from the time of consecration in 1331, but it has been suggested that the medieval west wall of the nave is of Anglo-Saxon origin, which would help to explain the height and width of the church. The body of the church is uniformly Decorated in style, and was restored to a pure 14th-century state by William Butterfield between 1866 and 1868, contrasting with his other Worcestershire church at Alvechurch, which is a period Victorian rebuilding. The east window has reticulated early Perpendicular tracery of about 1400, whilst each side of the church has four of Butterfield's tall Decorated style two light windows. The north doorway is 14th-century and has the remains of a stoup. The vestry was added in 1900.

The interior is large and symmetrical. Butterfield has created a medieval style place of worship with some tiling to the walls and furnishings including the sedilia, the screen with a stone base and restored wooden upper section, and the reredos of three parts with Decorated style canopies and mosaics with stone and tile. To the sides of the altar are two 14th-century image brackets and there are two piscinae of the same date, including one for a nave altar. The font is of about 1200 and has a round bowl on a stem. In the north window of the chancel is a panel of 14th-century stained glass showing a man holding a church, thought to be the founder Thomas de Evesham. There are several 18th-century memorial tablets.

Outside, the limestone lychgate incorporates pieces of medieval stonework removed during Butterfield's restoration. A medieval scratched Mass dial can be found on the exterior.

SEVERN STOKE   ST. DENYS

This pleasant village lies on a winding section of the Worcester to Tewkesbury road on the eastern side of the flood plain of the River Severn. The church stands at the end of a lane close to the timber-framed Rose and Crown Inn, with a fine view of the Malvern Hills to the west.

The lias stone church has red sandstone dressings and consists of a nave with south aisle and porch, a south transept, and chancel. The tower is in the position of a north transept. The nave is Norman and has one small lancet on the north wall and flat buttresses to the west end. The lower part of the tower was built around 1300, and has a Decorated window on the north side. The upper parts were added about a century later and have battlements and a higher stair turret. The windows in the south transept are also Decorated with reticulation on the east side, and the south window has an example of an early Decorated style quatrefoil. The south aisle is also 14th-century, as is the chancel, which has an early Perpendicular east window.

Inside the medieval porch are springers for the corners of a vault, which seems never to have been built although there is a blocked doorway to give access to a chamber from the aisle. The main body of the church is large and rambling, and although it was scraped back to the stone after a flood in 1886, it is quite light. The 14th-century arcade has four Decorated arches, with angular piers which have rounded projections. The south transept arch is also Decorated.

Most of the fittings are 19th- and 20th-century, including the carved pulpit and reredos, but the font dates from about 1400. In the south transept windows are fragments of medieval glass including the arms of the Beauchamp family, a head of a female saint with a blue nimbus, and another saint with a red robe. A small piece of wall painting survives at the east end of the south wall of the nave. The doorway in the north wall of the nave has been blocked and now contains medieval floor tiles, and there are fragments of Norman stonework to the east, which perhaps come from another doorway. There is a 17th-century communion table by the charity boards in the south aisle.

In the Gresson memorial window by the organ is glass of about 1924 by Archibald Davies of the Bromsgrove Guild. The memorial tablets include a monument with a low urn by Lewis of Cheltenham to James Barker who died in 1851. There is also an inscription to Richard Somers of Clifton, in the north of the parish, who died in 1598. The Somers family held much land in Severn Stoke during the Middle Ages, and a tablet commemorates John Somers with a Latin inscription by his son Lord John Somers, who was Member of Parliament for Worcester in 1689 and became Lord Chancellor. John Somers the elder is reputed to have fired shots at the minister in the pulpit of this church during the Commonwealth period.

Outside in the churchyard is the base of the medieval cross, with a niche for the pyx. Some stones beneath a south chancel window are carved with quatrefoils, the purpose of which is unkonwn.

SHELSLEY BEAUCHAMP   ALL SAINTS

Shelsley Beauchamp is on the opposite side of the River Teme to Shelsley Walsh in a secluded part of the valley between Clifton-on-Teme and Stanford Bridge. To the north are the heights of Woodbury Hill, on the summit of which are the earthworks of an Iron Age hillfort. The setting of this church is very beautiful, with the surrounding woodlands in the valley, and next to the attractive former rectory and barns.

All Saints is built of red sandstone and has a west tower, nave with south aisle and porch, and a chancel. The plain tower is late 14th-century with Decorated bell openings, stair turret and plain parapet with pinnacles. The body of the church was rebuilt between 1846 and 1848 by a local architect James Cranston, who also restored the church at Clifton-on-Teme. A little like Frederick Kempson's church at

Harpley, it shows changing styles between the early Decorated nave and aisle, with the windows having cusps and quatrefoils, to the plain Early English style of the chancel with lancets including a triple lancet for the east window.

Inside is all Cranston's work with early Decorated style arches although the tower arch is 14th-century. The corbels of the chancel arch are carved with hands holding bunches of grapes. The fittings are mostly 19th-century, including the stone altar. However, the font dates from about 1200, and what seem to be parts of a medieval pulpit are incorporated into a chancel seat. There is also part of the base of the medieval rood screen. The stained glass in the central lancet of the east window is of 1896 by William Wailes, whilst the side lancets contain glass by John Hardman. There are two 13th-century dugout chests with iron fittings.

Outside in the churchyard are the base and shafts of the medieval cross. The eastern belfry opening of the tower contained a sanctus bell until 1846. Surviving examples of bells in this position can be seen at Fladbury and Bishampton.

SHELSLEY WALSH   ST. ANDREW

Shelsley Walsh: the 15th-century rood screen
and attached parclose screen

St. Andrew's church is in an isolated position on the wooded west side of the Teme Valley and is approached by the drive to the Court House, once home to the Walsh family. Shelsley Walsh has found fame since the early 20th century, as from 1905 the Midland Automobile Club hill tested cars on the modified steep bridle path up the bank from the Court House. Famous drivers have included Raymond Mays and Sir Malcolm Campbell.

The church is surrounded by a garden-like graveyard and is largely built of tufa. This is formed by limewater passing through moss in the sandstone, and comes from Southstone Rock a little to the north in Stanford parish. The nave and chancel are under one roof with a timber bell turret and short spire at the west end. There is also a timber north porch. The nave is Norman, with one tiny lancet window remaining on the south side, and a north doorway, which has a shaft to each side with scallop capitals, with a plain tympanum surrounded by an arch with projecting zig-zag. The north wall of the 13th-century chancel was rebuilt in the 16th century. In 1859 the church was restored by the London architect, George Truefitt, who rebuilt the bell turret and removed the dormer windows. He also installed the Early English style lancet and plate tracery windows. The church was again restored in 1908, when many of Truefitt's alterations were removed, and most recently renovated in 1980.

The north doorway is the only entrance, and the door and lock are both medieval. A long recess in the jamb is to take a wooden beam bolt. The footscrapers and umbrella stand are by Truefitt. The interior is scraped to expose the tufa. The roofs are medieval, the wagon roof of the nave giving way to the chancel roof with its tie and collar beams, and large openings with cusped sides in the apex. The ceiling boards are painted blue with gold stars. Nave and chancel are divided by the late 15th-century rood screen, with linen-fold panelling and single lights with intricate tracery, and of which the top rail is elaborately carved. Attached to the south-west is an identical parclose screen, enclosing a former chantry chapel. The west face of the rood screen is undecorated at the base, indicating the position of the altar in the chapel. The screens give a good impression of the internal divisions of a medieval church. Above the rood screen is the 15th-century rood beam with a carved vine trail, and surmounted by a cross of 1859. The metal candlebeams are by Truefitt, removed in 1908, but reinstated in 1981. However, Truefitt's stone pulpit, font and fireplace were removed and broken up in 1908, though the altar, sedilia, lectern and pews with distinctive decoration survive. The 12th-century font was brought back into the church in 1908. The present pulpit is of 1908 by Sir Ninian Comper. There are 15th-century tiles on the chancel floor, many of which make up a design of a large cross. The east window contains glass by William Wailes of about 1850, whilst the small Norman window glazed with a figure of St. Andrew is of an uncertain 19th- or early 20th-century date.

On the south side of the chancel is a 14th-century coffin lid carved with a cross. Opposite there is a memorial tablet with heraldic arms to Elizabeth Plampin who died in 1730. Nearby is the wooden tomb chest to Francis Walsh, who died in 1596, and his wife Alice Cornwall. The sides have pilasters and panels with blank arches around shields with the arms of the Walsh, Cornwall and other families. The memorial to Thomas Walsh in the nearby church at Stockton-on-Teme is very similar.

SHRAWLEY   ST. MARY

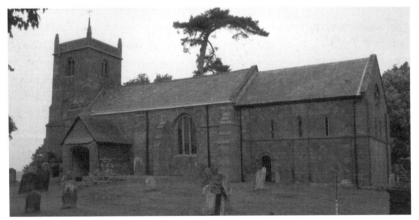

The much altered Norman church at Shrawley

Shrawley is a pretty, straggling village to the west of the River Severn between Holt and Astley. In the Norman period the manor was held by the Tosny family as were Astley and Rock, before it passed to the Beauchamps for most of the Middle Ages. During the 18th and 19th centuries much of the land belonged to the Vernon family from Hanbury, but in the 1650s an ironworks was established on Dick Brook at the north end of the parish by Andrew Yarranton, who smelted much Roman iron slag from Pitchcroft in Worcester.

St. Mary's stands on a sandstone outcrop to the south of the village, and there is a dramatic drop on the east side of the graveyard. The nave, chancel, and west tower are built of red sandstone, whilst the porch and vestry are mainly of brick. It is basically a Norman building but has been much altered during the 18th and 19th centuries. The side walls of the chancel are 12th century and have three lancet windows, of which the middle one is in a projecting flat buttress. Similar windows in buttresses can be seen on the tower of Fladbury church. These windows have a slight stepped chamfer around them which may indicate that they had shutters. The string course on the south side is carved with zig-zag, whilst on the north it is cable moulding, the zig-zag string course also continues along part of the south side of the Norman

Norman font and 17th-century cover at Shrawley

nave. The north doorway has trumpet scallop capitals and there is a Norman lancet in the wall nearby. The capitals of the south doorway are carved with waterleaf, and billets on the hood mould indicate a date of about 1180. However, this doorway was modified in the 15th century when a higher arch was installed with floral carving in the spandrels, and the eastern shaft partially removed and replaced by a Perpendicular panelled stoup, which has subsequently been damaged. The Norman arch to this doorway appears to have been altered again in the 18th century, which may have been the time when the arch to the priest's doorway in the chancel was lowered.

The frames of the 14th-century nave windows survive, but the tracery was replaced by mullions and clear glass in the 18th century. The south-west window was enlarged at this time to allow more light onto the gallery. A dormer window on the north side was removed in 1921, whilst the 19th-century Decorated style window was inserted in the wall to replace a Georgian Gothic window with ogee curves. The church had battlements added in the 15th century, of which only a fragment remains at the west end, at the same time as the pitch of the nave roof was lowered. The present porch is a 16th-century replacement of the medieval one, and the very pretty vestry with Gothic windows was added to the north side in the early 19th century. The tower was built in the 17th century, but altered and given a new west doorway in about 1845. The east wall of the chancel was also rebuilt in the Norman style in 1845 and has two lancets beneath a circular window, and continues the string course from the side walls.

The interior shows a contrast between 18th-century improvements in the nave and 19th-century work in the chancel. Shrawley is very similar in this to the other church on the Vernon estates at Hanbury. The whitewashed nave has a brick floor with ledger stones. The box pews and west gallery are early 19th-century, but the pulpit is 17th-century. The Norman font has trumpet scallop carving and a conical 17th-century cover. The royal arms are Georgian dating from before 1816. The nave contrasts to the scraped stone chancel, which is entered through a Norman style arch of 1845 that replaces a pointed arch of about 1200. The chancel contains a large 14th-century aumbry. The 19th-century painting behind the altar is by Walter Starman, and there is a glass of the same period in the east windows showing the Annunciation, with angels in the upper circular window. There are several memorial tablets to members of the Vernon family, which make an interesting link with the monuments in Hanbury church.

Outside there is a scratched Mass dial on the south side of the church, and a large 14th-century base to a cross, with spurs cut to the angles.

SOUTH LITTLETON   ST. MICHAEL

This Vale of Evesham village is larger than its two neighbours, North and Middle Littleton. There are terraces of late Victorian brick houses, similar to Badsey, but many older cottages and houses survive on the main street. Opposite the church is the fine 17th-century brick house, Hathaways, with its cupola and arched chimneys. The local historian and avid collector of natural history specimens, Robert Fisher Tomes lived in the village.

St. Michael's stands amongst trees in a large churchyard, well back from the busy road. It has a west tower, nave, porch, chancel, north transept and vestry, and in plan is very similar to the church at Middle Littleton. The Perpendicular tower has very weathered gargoyles and battlements and was used as a dove-cote in the 16th century, like the tower at Birlingham church. The nave and chancel were much rebuilt by Frederick Preedy in 1883, but incorporate an Early English two light window in the chancel and a lancet in the nave. The Early English priest's doorway has a hood mould. The timber porch is 19th-century but incorporates 16th-century woodwork and shelters the plain Norman south doorway. The blocked Norman north doorway is almost concealed externally by a lean-to structure.

The interior is painted white and largely the work of Preedy. However, the tower arch appears to be a reused cusped window head, and has a similar effect to the tower arches at Offenham and Middle Littleton. Preedy replaced the Norman chancel arch and squints with the present arch, and designed the roof structures. The Norman font bowl is carved with bands of arrowheads and cables, and has rosettes and a cross on the sloping sides. The damaged pillar piscina in the chancel may be Norman, and there is a later medieval piscina in the transept. The pulpit incorporates Perpendicular woodwork, and many of the bench ends have traceried Perpendicular panels as well. There are 15th-century heraldic tiles in the north transept floor and the north chancel window contains fragments of medieval glass, including some heads, one of which is thought to represent St. Anne. Two other chancel windows have glass by John Hardman; one in the 14th-century style, showing St. Michael of 1886, and one of 1888.

The tower contains two 15th-century bells and the medieval churchyard cross base holds a 20th-century shaft.

SPETCHLEY   ALL SAINTS

Spetchley Park, immediately to the east of Worcester, has belonged to the Berkeley family of Berkeley Castle in Gloucestershire since 1605 and is crossed by the Worcester to Inkberrow road. The church and stables are beside the road close to a little cast iron footbridge, whilst the present house, Spetchley Park, completed in 1818, is to the south of the church and contains its own Roman Catholic chapel. On the opposite side of the road, the Berkeleys commissioned Augustus Pugin to build a brick school in the Gothic Revival style in 1841, a very significant piece of Victorian architecture in Worcestershire.

The church is of lias stone with grey sandstone dressings and has a west tower with timber porch, nave, and chancel with south chapel. The earliest parts of the building are the nave and chancel with 14th-century cusped Y-shaped tracery to several of the windows. The tower, with square bell openings and battlements, was built into the west end of the nave in the 17th century, probably to replace a timber structure. A round-headed doorway was inserted in the west end and the south doorway blocked. On the north side of the chancel is a striking domestic mullioned bay window added in the 16th century, whilst the south chapel was built in 1614 as a burial place for the Roman Catholic Berkeleys. The Decorated windows were reused but the chapel has a 17th-century doorway, battlements, pinnacles and carries the Berkeley arms on the west end. The east window is 19th-century in the Decorated style.

The entrance is through the timber porch, which was moved from the south doorway, under the tower and into the simple whitewashed nave. Ahead is the late Decorated chamfered chancel arch, which has no capitals. Beyond, the chancel opens up into the south chapel through a large arch with stone piers and a moulded wooden beam. The chapel is filled with Berkeley monuments.

Many of the fittings are 19th-century, including the pews, pulpit, lectern, communion rails and charity boards, but the font is Norman and there is a 13th-century dug out chest. The communion table and reredos panelling are 17th-century. Recently pre-Reformation wall painting showing part of a figure has been uncovered behind the panelling. There are some medieval floor tiles in the chancel, some of which have heraldic designs. In the nave window tracery are fragments of medieval glass, while a north chancel window has glass of 1860 by John Hardman showing the Annunciation. The windows in the Berkeley Chapel also contain Hardman glass—a Resurrection of 1874 in the east window, continued in the south window of 1876, as well as figures of a bishop, St. Robert and St. Catherine.

The memorials include the unused 16th-century tomb of John Slade in the bay window; Slade was actually buried at Hindlip in 1597. The window and tomb are a later version of the type of medieval bay window in St. John's church, Bromsgrove. The window and the Berkeley Chapel have 19th-century wrought iron railings. Most imposing is the central monument to Sir Rowland Berkeley, who died in 1611, and

Spetchley: the memorial to Rowland Berkeley, d.1611, and his wife Katherine Heywood in the Berkeley Chapel

his wife Katherine Heywood. They were the first of the Berkeley family to live at Spetchley as from 1606. The effigies are on a large alabaster tomb chest under a dramatic coffered arch with obelisks. Behind is the memorial to their son, Sir Robert Berkeley, who died in 1656. He was a judge and a royalist, whose house at Spetchley was destroyed by Cromwell in 1651, and he is shown as a reclining figure in his judge's robes. Further monuments are to Thomas Berkeley, who died in 1693, and his wife Ann, who died in 1692, and to another Robert Berkeley, who died in 1708 and his wife Elizabeth. This large monument has cherubs, urns and drapes, and is placed across the south-east corner of the chapel. All these memorials carry interesting heraldry relating to the Berkeley family, and there are large hatchments on the wall. Amongst the other memorial tablets are brass plates to Ann Smyth, who died in 1638, and William Smyth, who died in 1658.

The tower contains four 15th-century bells, one of which is dedicated to St. Peter. Beside the former south doorway is a scratched Mass dial. Spetchley church has been restored and maintained by the Churches Conservation Trust since 1987.

STANFORD-ON-TEME   ST. MARY

The road from Witley to Bromyard crosses the Teme at Stanford Bridge, where the 20th-century bridge and another narrow bridge of 19th-century ironwork stand side by side. The church is in a prominent position on the valley side with superb views from the churchyard across the parkland of Stanford Court. The Court was home to the Salways until the 17th century, when it passed to the Ingram and Winnington families. The 18th-century house was rebuilt after a fire in 1886. About one mile to the south, by the road to Shelsey Walsh is Southstone Rock. This cliff was the source for tufa, a stone formed by lime water passing through moss in the sandstone, which was used in several churches in the valley, such as Eastham and Shelsley Walsh. The cliff was also the site of a medieval chapel and hermitage to St. John, which was in the possession of Evesham Abbey.

St. Mary replaced a medieval structure which was located by the Court, and was built in 1768-69 to designs by James Rose, who also added the tower and spire to the church at Chaddesley Corbett. It is of sandstone and has a west tower, nave and short chancel with small transepts. The exterior looks rather bleak, especially as the tower has a plain parapet. The detailing is Georgian Gothic and Stanford is one of a group of local country churches in this style, yet keeping the plan and proportions favoured in classical churches. The ultimate example of this is at Croome D'Abitot, but this plain building with its Y-shaped window tracery is similar to the church at Rushock. Here at Stanford there is intersecting Y-shaped tracery in the east window. There are also quatrefoil openings to the sides of the tower.

The interior is entered through a west porch and doorway under the tower, similar to that at Croome. Although the ceiling has 18th-century coving, the paintwork and heavy stained glass in the windows make the interior quite dark and give it more of a Victorian feeling. Some 18th-century fittings do remain amongst the 19th-century pieces. The east window glass of 1893 shows scenes of the Garden Tomb. Other dark 19th-century windows have glass showing Christ and the Virgin.

Stanford church is rich in memorials. To the left of the altar, and preserved from the medieval church, are the effigies of Sir Humphrey Salway, who died in 1493, and his wife Joyce Strelley. He is shown wearing armour with his head on a helmet and his feet on a lion's tail. Underneath, on the sides of the tomb chest, are shown seven sons and three daughters kneeling under canopies with ornate crocketed ogees. There are several memorials to the Winnington family, although a bust by Louis Roubilliac of Thomas Winnington who died in 1746, is no longer kept in the church. He was shown above a sarcophagus on lions' feet, and was known as a supporter of Walpole whilst a Member of Parliament and Lord of the Treasury. There are identical tablets to Edward Winnington, who died in 1791, and his wife who died in 1784 and at the west end medieval style brasses with kneeling figures to Edith Winnington, who died in 1864 aged 18, and Thomas Winnington, who died in 1869 aged 21.

There are two 15th-century bells in the tower.

STOCKTON-ON-TEME   ST. ANDREW

One mile upstream from Stanford, Stockton church is surrounded by farms with converted hopkilns close to the Worcester to Tenbury road. The hilltop location and remains of a circular churchyard point to Celtic Christian origins of the site, and amongst the headstones in the churchyard are stumps of massive yew trees.

This is a very pretty church with nave, chancel, west bell turret and porch. The sandstone nave is Norman and has a south doorway with single columns to the sides, with large spurs and ribs on the corners of the square capitals. The arch has a roll moulding and carved saltire crosses. Above the doorway is a worn carved stone panel with a large four legged beast of the Herefordshire School type also found at nearby Eastham. The nave north wall was largely rebuilt in 1845, whilst the medieval chancel was replaced by a brick structure in 1718, which is now painted cream. The bell turret is of timber and weatherboarded, whilst the timber porch is 14th-century.

The west end of the scraped stone nave has been partially partitioned off for community use, but the main feature to which the eye is drawn is the Norman chancel arch. This is very similar in style to the south doorway, with a roll moulding, but with scallop capitals. To the south is a squint, which may suggest

The Walsh tomb in the chancel

there was once a chantry with altar at the south-east corner of the nave. Above are further Herefordshire School type panels with a lion and a roundel showing the lamb and cross. The white painted chancel contains some 15th-century tiles with parts of Latin inscriptions, benches with linenfold panelled ends from the nave, and 18th-century communion rails. The nave roof is 15th-century, whilst the octagonal font is early medieval. The 20th-century stained glass includes an east window based on an Italian painting, with figures of St. Andrew, St. Oswald and St. Wulstan.

On the wall of the nave is a small brass to William Parker who died in 1508. He is shown in Italian clothes with a robe of fur, but the accompanying figures of his two wives have disappeared. The family were landholders in Stockton at the time. The chancel contains a large coffin lid, carved with a cross with truncated branches, which is inscribed in memory of Ralph de Dunelm, who was instituted as rector at Stockton in 1284. The stone was found in 1933 being reused as the top of the chest tomb of Thomas Walsh, who died in 1593. This wooden tomb chest with a back wall and canopy is painted grey with classical turned columns, which are also used unusually in horizontal positions to form panels. The monument is similar to that of his cousin, Francis, at Shelsley Walsh. Thomas was the son of another Thomas Walsh, who was Chancellor of the Exchequer to King Henry VIII.

STOKE BLISS   ST. PETER

Stoke Bliss was in Herefordshire until 1897. The parish has scattered houses and farms in attractive countryside south of Tenbury Wells. The church was founded by the Mortimer family in the 12th century, and was attached to the nunnery at Limebrook, close to the Welsh border by Presteigne, until the Dissolution. It has a sandstone nave and chancel, with south aisle and porch tower with spire and a north vestry, and is situated on a steep bank above a narrow lane.

There is 12th-century masonry in the north wall of the nave to which the chancel and south aisle were added in the 13th century with Early English lancets. The south-east window of the aisle has a gable, and was probably added in about 1300 to give extra light onto the rood screen. In the chancel, a window on the north side has wooden tracery, and there is a low side window with a rebate for a shutter, similar to that in the church at Knighton-on-Teme. The vestry was added in 1815, then in 1845 the church was restored, the windows with late Early English style plate tracery inserted, and the tower and spire built to replace a bell turret.

The attractive light interior has features or furnishings from most periods. The south arcade is plain Early English with round piers, moulded capitals and chamfered arches. The west bay was added when the tower was built in the 19th century. The chancel has an Early English piscina. The Norman font is drum-shaped with plain arch panels which were possibly once painted with figures. The Perpendicular rood screen has single lights with tracery in a rose pattern. The pulpit is dated 1631 and has typical carved lozenges, flowers and round arches. The lectern, dated 1635, also has round arches, together with small carved figures and dragons, and is inscribed with the name of the then churchwarden, Roger Osland. The remainder of the fittings are mostly 19th-century, but the east window is filled with very striking 20th-century glass.

STOKE PRIOR   ST. MICHAEL

Details of the outside of the Early English tower at Stoke Prior

The large parish of Stoke Prior, once held by Worcester Priory, also included Finstall and the eastern part of Bromsgrove until the 19th century. The church is situated between the centres of population at Stoke Heath, Stoke Pound and Stoke Works, of which the latter grew to fame from 1852 as the development of the entrepreneur, John Corbett, when he moved the improved salt extraction process here from Droitwich and created a model village. The salt works and most of the housing have gone, but the Corbett Institute survives. The church stands to the north-east of Stoke Works, on its own in a large graveyard set in a pretty valley.

The large green sandstone building has an aisled nave with south porch and north vestry, a chancel with north chapel and sacristy and a massive south tower, which carries a red tiled broach spire. Much of the nave is late Norman, including a window on the south wall, close to the south doorway, which has a round arch with roll moulding above capitals, covered with an unusual design of plain leaves, and a column to each side. The hood mould has an unusual pattern with carved lobes. To the left, beside the capital, is a stone carved with interlace, which appears to be a reused piece of Anglo-Saxon work, possibly from a cross.

About 1200 the chancel was rebuilt with a chapel to the north and tower to the south, which itself has a chapel in the base with a lean-to projection on the east side to house the altar. The chancel of this date has been replaced, but a lancet window is apparent on the north wall of the north chapel. The tower is one of the best pieces of Early English architecture in Worcestershire after the east end of the cathedral, with which it is closely connected in style, and is perhaps the work of the same masons. There are stone shafts to the small doorway and to the blind arches and windows on the south and east sides, all of which have typical Early English pointed arches. The stone shafts are reminiscent of the work in Purbeck marble in the cathedral, and can also be found on the windows in the tower base at St. Andrew in Droitwich. The

202

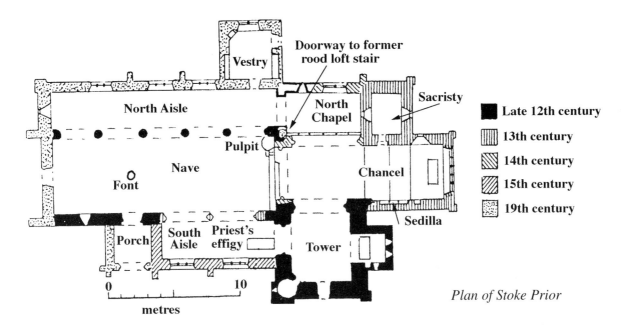

Plan of Stoke Prior

■	Late 12th century
⦀	13th century
⧅	14th century
▨	15th century
⬚	19th century

bell openings are similar lancets with shafts, beneath a plain 19th century parapet with carved trefoils to the base. The bulk of the tower is derived from Norman architecture, along with the flat buttresses, which are enlarged in the south-west corner to incorporate the stair turret.

The south aisle was added in about 1250, but improved in the 15th century with Perpendicular windows and battlements. The Early English chancel has flat buttresses to the corners, but the Decorated windows were installed in the 14th century. Also in the 13th century, the sacristy was added to the north side, which then inspired the eastwards extension of the north chapel to join up to it in the 14th century with a further Decorated window.

The north aisle was rebuilt in 1848 by Harvey Eginton, when the Early English style vestry was added. It was rebuilt again in 1894, after John Loughborough Pearson had been commissioned by John Corbett to report on the condition of the church. The lower part of a blocked Norman doorway was incorporated in the rebuilding, which also included the west wall, porch and the tracery of the east window.

The interior, scraped back to the sandstone, is equally complex. The 12th-century north arcade has five arches with round piers carrying plain capitals and abaci. The arch leading from the north aisle to the north chapel is a little later of about 1200, and the chancel arch has carved trumpet scallop capitals and a double chamfered arch. The flat bands of the shafts, or fillets, continue into the capital, a 13th-century feature also to be seen in the porch at Halesowen church. There are similar mouldings on the arches of the tower, which also have capitals with trumpets and crockets. The eastern projection to the chapel under the tower has a rounded tunnel vault. The south arcade is typical Early English work of about 1250, and has two arches with round piers which have four attached shafts supporting round abaci and heavily moulded arches. The sacristy of similar date has a four part vault supporting the vestry above. There is a blocked Early English lancet on the west side. Whilst the roof of the south aisle is 15th-century, the nave roof was replaced in 1894, and some of the timbers from the aisle roof were used to make the statue of St. Michael in the north aisle.

The octagonal font is Perpendicular, with a symmetrical design of carved leaves to the base, and the bowl has four angels carrying shields along with a baptism scene. The chancel contains a 14th-century piscina and the triple sedilia with carved grotesque heads as corbels. The 17th-century communion table is now in the south aisle. The organ was installed in the north chapel in 1895, when the medieval roof loft stairs were removed, leaving a blocked doorway by the chancel arch. The chancel has 19th-century fittings, except for the communion rail and reredos which were designed by Eric Gill, and the woodwork in the chapel under the tower is by Celestino Pancheri of the Bromsgrove Guild.

Also in lancet windows beneath the tower are some fragments of medieval glass brought from Malvern Priory in 1895. A window depicting St. Michael and the Dragon was installed by Chance for John Corbett, who also commissioned glass by William Chance for 18 further windows in the church. The east window glass showing Christ and the four Evangelists is by Sebastian Evans, and was given in 1860 as a tribute to John Corbett, who had just ceased to employ women and children in the saltworks. A further window in the chancel contains glass of 1904 by Bryans of London.

In the south aisle is a 13th-century stone effigy of a priest, along with brass plates to Henry Smith, a London draper, who died in 1606, as well as to Robert Smith, who died in 1609. He is shown kneeling with his two wives, Thomasin Dedicote and Susan Pyke, accompanied by their 11 sons, six daughters and the family arms.

The lychgate at the entrance to the churchyard is made from the timbers of the former medieval porch.

STONE   ST. MARY

Stone is situated to the east of Kidderminster, on the side of a bank with extensive views to the west. Older houses and cottages surround the church, including Stone House with its renowned cottage garden to the north (see p.21). Until the 16th century, the parish was a chapelry of neighbouring Chaddesley Corbett.

The present grey sandstone church has a nave and chancel with west tower and spire. It was built in the Early English style of the Commissioners in 1831 to replace a medieval church, and has long windows, especially the lancets to the tower. The tower has a parapet with pinnacles, behind which rises the short octagonal spire. The chancel was lengthened in 1899, when it was rebuilt in memory of a lieutenant in the Royal Navy, J.E. Russell, by his mother, Mary Creese. It is in the Perpendicular style, and the windows have traceried transoms.

The white interior is quite plain, with many 19th- and 20h-century fittings. The font of 1900 is by William Forsyth, whilst the pulpit of the same date is by Richard Houghton. There are fragments of medieval glass, including the heads of angels and a saint, as well as a roundel of 17th-century glass. The east window has glass by Charles Eamer Kempe of 1900 which shows Christ appearing to the Disciples by Lake Tiberias. There are brass plates with heraldic shields to a vicar, William Spicer, who died in 1656, and his wife, Ursula Ruggeley, who died in 1663. Amongst the memorial tablets is one to John Peel, Dean of Worcester, and a monument to Benjamin Gibbons, who died in 1863, by Peter Hollins. It is old fashioned for its date and similar to an 18th-century memorial with a pedestal, urn and cherubs.

The churchyard contains a memorial to Hannah Hill, who died in 1788, with its fine pedestal and urn. Nearby is the base of the medieval churchyard cross, whilst at the gate is the early 16th-century church house, with close studded timber-framing. This is almost certainly the house built on land in the churchyard by the patrons of the church, the collegiate church of St. Mary, Warwick, to endow a chapel to the Virgin Mary. A grant was made to Thomas Forest, Keeper of Dunclent Park in Stone, to build the house. Forest's brass can be seen in Chaddesley Corbett church.

This village on the Worcester to Pershore road has expanded with several new houses in the late 20th century. The church lies along a lane to the east surrounded by several 17th- and 18th-century timber-framed and brick houses. Until the 16th century, Stoulton was a chapelry to Kempsey, and it is unusual in this area that the church should be dedicated to St. Edmund, an East Anglian king and martyr, whose relics were at Bury St. Edmunds in Suffolk.

The lias and limestone church consists of a nave and chancel with a west tower and north porch. The nave and chancel are Norman of between 1130 and 1140, and have several flat buttresses and small lancet windows. Some of the windows have been slightly altered at a later date. The north and south doorways are both in projecting sections of wall. The south doorway has a column to each side with block capitals and roll moulding to the arch. Above are two blind rounded arches with scallop capitals to the shafts. The concept is similar to the doorways at Bockleton, Eastham and Knighton churches in the Teme Valley area, but unlike those doorways, the feature at Stoulton is to the full height of the wall. Remains of a Mass dial can be found to the side. The north doorway is similar, but obscured by the porch which was rebuilt in 1848. There are blind arches above, but the arch to the doorway has a single step. On the eastern jamb are the remains of a consecration cross.

In the 14th century a south window of the chancel, and a north and south window of the nave were replaced in the decorated style. The other nave windows date from 1848, and the east window was installed at that time in the Decorated style, into the east wall of the chancel which had been rebuilt with brick in 1799. The limestone tower was built in 1936 to 1937 in the Perpendicular style as a memorial to Hamilton Kingsford, vicar from 1867 to 1912. The original timber tower was destroyed by fire and replaced by a brick structure in 1799, but this had much decayed by the 1930s.

The interior gives a good sense of the scale and proportions of a Norman village church, though it is now light, airy and whitewashed. The simple Norman chancel arch has survived, and has a single step. On the sides are grooves marking the position of the rood screen. The nave roof has 14th-century timbers, with arched braces. At the apex are carved braces forming a quatrefoil and two trefoils, in a similar fashion to the roof at Shelsley Walsh. The Norman font is round and tapers, is carved with a wavy band and pellets just below the rim, and stands on a 20th-century base. Most of the furnishings date from the 1848 restoration, but there are 17th-century communion rails and table. The reredos depicting St. Edmund and St. Wulstan is a memorial to John Mylius, who was killed at the Somme in 1916. In the vestry is a large fragment from a 15th-century cope embroidered with fleur de lys, and the figure of a saint thought to be St. Oswald. There are some fragments of medieval glass in a south chancel window, whilst the east window glass was moved from St. Helen's in Worcester in 1953. It shows the Virtuous Wife and Christ blessing children, and was a memorial to Madeleine Chaytor in 1906.

The memorial in the chancel is to William Acton, landowner of nearby Lower Wolverton Hall, who died in 1814. It is by Michael Crake of London, and shows a woman standing by an urn on a pedestal with the initials on a roundel. Above used to hang a medieval sword and helmet belonging to the Acton family. There are also several ledgers and tablets to the Acton and Vincent families, and an 18th-century hatchment with the Acton arms hangs in the chancel. The war memorial in the nave is by the Bromsgrove Guild.

Outside is a tablet on the wall to the east of the south doorway commemorating George Allen, vicar from 1608 to 1657.

STOURPORT-ON-SEVERN   ST. MICHAEL AND ALL ANGELS

The Staffordshire and Worcestershire Canal was begun in 1766 near where the River Stour flows into the River Severn. The engineer was James Brindley, who had designed the first canal in England in 1761. A bridge was first built over the Severn in 1775, and the town developed between the village of Mitton and the Severn as a rival to the port of Bewdley, which became increasingly marginalised. Several late Georgian streets retain their brick houses, but Stourport subsequently developed as both an industrial and a tourist town during the 19th and 20th centuries.

St. Michael's church is the fourth church in the hilltop churchyard site above Mitton Street, which with one timber-framed house, marks the location of Mitton. Initially there was a medieval chapel in the parish of St. Mary, Kidderminster, which was replaced in 1782 by a small brick church in the classical Georgian style with a tower, designed by James Rose, architect of the church at Stanford-on-Teme. The foundations of this church have formed a feature in the graveyard since its demolition in 1912.

At that date it was succeeded by an ambitious Gothic revival church a little to the north. Only the outer walls of the aisles and porch now remain as the building became unsafe and was demolished in 1980. One of the reasons for its state was that it was never completed—the nave and aisles were paid for by the vicar Benjamin Gibbons, and designed by Sir George Gilbert Scott, but they were not started until after Scott's death. This work was then overseen by John Oldrid Scott, and the nave was finally conse-crated in 1910, but the west tower with spire and the chancel were never built as the result of a dispute between Benjamin Gibbons and John Brinton, of the Kidderminster carpet manufacturing family, who lived at Moor Hall in the town. The aisle walls are in an ornate 14th-century Decorated style, and the south porch has a vaulted ceiling, canopied niches and a cusped arch to the doorway. The rood loft turret has been left as a feature at the east end of the south wall. The present single storey church was built in 1980 at the east end with the site of the nave making a driveway. It is a contemporary brick building with wooden windows and a tiled roof.

In the churchyard are several Georgian memorials reflecting the growth of Stourport, including a series of wrought iron memorials to the Baldwin family which were made at their factory nearby.

STOURPORT-ON-SEVERN   ST. BARTHOLOMEW, ARELEY KINGS

Today the village of Areley Kings, on the west bank of the River Severn, is a suburb of Stourport, but at the northern end the church is still in a rural setting. It stands on a hilltop next to the rectory and church house in a large graveyard, with splendid views across the fields and woods to the north and west.

First mention of this church seems to come in the late 12fth century poem, the *Brut*, which describes the history of Britain from the time of its legendary founder, Brutus. The work is powerful, telling the stories of the Arthurian Court and King Lear in English for the first time. The author, Layamon, describes himself as priest of Areley, and indeed his existence is recorded in a contemporary inscription on the base of the font, which was discovered in 1886.

This find was made when the medieval nave was replaced by a large Decorated style nave and north aisle designed by Frederick Preedy. The medieval chancel and 14th-century tower porch were retained; the south doorway is much restored but may contain some 12th-century work, whilst the 14th-century porch houses the remains of a stoup. The tower above has Decorated bell-openings. The chancel is partly Norman, with one restored 12th-century window on the south side. There is a 13th-century priest's doorway, but the upper parts of the east wall with the east window were rebuilt in brick in 1796. The vestry, to the north of the chancel, contains reused medieval masonry, including the former west window.

Areley Kings—a 14th-century tower porch

The doorway is a copy of the previous north door.

Inside, the spacious 19th-century nave and aisle contrast with the small medieval east end. The fittings date mainly from the 19th and 20th centuries. Exceptions are the Norman font base, with the Layamon inscription (though the bowl is Victorian), a medieval aumbry in the chancel, a small 17th-century figure of Time from a sundial, and some 18th-century memorial tablets. There is some good colourful 20th-century glass, and the Norman window contains a figure of Layamon dated 1899.

The picturesque timber-framed church house is 16th-century, and has a jettied first floor. It may have been built as an ale house, or it could have been accommodation for the priest, which was superseded by the fine 17th-century rectory.

STRENSHAM   ST. JOHN THE BAPTIST

Strensham today is well known for its service station on the M5, but deserves to be better known for its church, which stands on a hilltop to the east. Today the church is isolated, with only the old rectory and a few houses nearby. However, Strensham Castle used to stand to the west, being held by the Russell family from the 13th century, but was destroyed by the Parliamentarians after Sir William Russell served the Royalists as Governor of Worcester. A moat near the stone Moat Farm now marks the site of the castle. The Russells built a new home at Strensham Court in Upper Strensham, which has since been demolished, leaving just the stables and the brick almshouses founded in 1697 by Sir Francis Russell. Treadway Nash, the Worcestershire historian, had acquired Strensham by 1795. The centres of population are now Upper and Lower Strensham, which were separate manors in the Middle Ages.

St. John's church has a nave and chancel, with south porch and north vestry, and a west tower. The tower is of lias whilst the walls of the church have been plastered and painted white during the restoration of the church by the Churches Conservation Trust, in whose care it has been since 1991. Prior to then, the church was in a poor state of repair with roofs of corrugated iron. The building is architecturally quite simple. The late 14th-century west tower has battlements and a square stair turret on the south-west corner, Decorated bell openings and a Perpendicular west window. The nave has Perpendicular windows, though the south wall was rebuilt in the 18th century, and the chancel has a Decorated east window. The medieval porch has a scratched Mass dial over the doorway. The vestry was added in the early 19th century.

The whitewashed interior is impressive for the width of the nave. The plain chancel arch is 14th-century. The wagon roof of the nave is plastered and has tie beams, one of which has a large boss of a flying angels carrying the arms of the Russell and Lytton families. The pews are 16th-century with linen-fold panelling, and the nave walls are panelled and have fitted hat pegs. Beside the chancel arch is the 17th-century family pew of the Russells. The Communion Table is 17th-century, the pulpit is 18th-century, but the plain font is Norman. The gallery at the west end is a reconstructed rood loft, dating from the end of the 15th century. It has two posts and spandrels carved with leaves, above which are 23 canopied panels with painted figures, and although these were much restored in 1875 they give an indication of the richness in colour of medieval church furnishings (see rear cover). The panels show Christ in the centre with three archbishops and 19 saints, including St. Blaise with a woolcomb, St. Edmund with an arrow, St. Erasmus with a windlass and St. Antony with a pig. The panel showing St. John the Evangelist includes a representation of the Devil emerging from a chalice. The nave is floored with 15th-century tiles with designs including the arms of the Berkeley and Beauchamp families, Gloucester Abbey, Bishop Carpenter of Worcester and Abbot Elyot of Bristol. During the restoration layers of wall paintings from medieval scenes to 18th-century text were discovered behind the monuments.

The organ in the gallery was made by Thomas Casson in the 19th century, and to each side are boards with the Creed, Commandments and Lord's Prayer. Over the chancel arch are the royal arms of King George II and two hatchments. There are some panels of 18th-century glass in the west window, and the east window has glass showing the Good Shepherd by Cox, son and Buckley of 1890. The glass in a nave south window of 1903 shows the Ascension by Ward and Hughes, and the south chancel window has glass of 1918 depicting the Good Samaritan by Florence Camm in the Arts and Crafts style.

The church has an outstanding collection of monuments. The earliest is a brass in the chancel floor to Robert Russell, who died in 1390, which shows a knight in armour, with his feet resting on a lion. A similar brass commemorates John Russell, who died in 1405. A small brass on the chancel wall is to Robert Russell, who died in 1502 and his wife Elizabeth Baynham; the associated brass of their five daughters has been lost. Sir John Russell, who died in 1556, and his wife, Edith Unton, are shown kneeling, on a brass with their heraldic arms, on the east wall under a stone canopy. The large elaborate stone memorial on the south wall of the chancel is to Sir Thomas Russell, who died in 1632 and his wife, Elizabeth Spencer, who died in 1618. The alabaster effigies lie on an open fronted chest with a baroque coffin below. The column bases have carved strapwork and skulls, whilst the tops of the round columns support a flat canopy, above which are globes and a broken foliated pediment surrounding their arms and crested helm. Behind the effigies is an arch with strapwork and an inscription highlighting the favourable marriages of their children. Their son, Sir William Russell, who died in 1669, with his wife Frances, are, by contrast, commemorated in a simple chest and memorial tablet, perhaps reflecting their loss of fortune during the Civil War.

Sir Francis Russell, who died in 1705, and his wife Anne Lytton have a large memorial in white and black marble. He is shown in contemporary costume, part reclining with his wife kneeling at his head and gesticulating upwards to where his coronet is being carried on a cloud by two cherubs. They did not have any sons, and the long inscription concentrates on Sir Francis and the line of the Russells at Strensham. Their daughter, Anne, Lady Guise was given a huge memorial when she died in 1734, which required part of the chancel ceiling to be heightened. The classical design includes her semi-reclining figure. Sir Charles Trubshaw Withers, of Worcester, who died in 1804 is also commemorated here by a coloured marble tablet with seated allegorical figures. He was married to Frances Russell, the last of the family.

The nave contains a tablet with an urn to Anne Dauncey, who died in 1733, and was another Russell descendant. Other tablets include those to the Taylor family, local landowners. There is also a tablet of 1830 by Robert Ashton junior to Samuel Butler, author of the satirical poem *Hudibras* which explores the extremes of Puritanism, and who was born in Strensham in 1612 and died in 1680.

SUCKLEY   ST. JOHN THE BAPTIST

The large Victorian church at Suckley

Suckley is a large parish on the western edge of Worcestershire which once also included Alfrick and Lusley. It has a scattered village with several large houses and farms dating from the 17th and 18th centuries. The church stands on a low hill near the centre with views of the surrounding hills and countryside from the church-yard.

The large grey sandstone church has an aisled nave, porch, chancel and north transept with a west tower. It was built in 1878 to 1879 by the Worcestershire architect, William Jeffrey Hopkins, in the style of the late 13th century with plate tracery to the east window. However, the tower with its Decorated style west window and bell openings is altogether later in appearance. It is crowned with battlements, eight pinnacles and a pyramid roof. The site is early, and this very urban looking church replaces a lengthy medieval church which had a timber-framed west tower, not unlike that still to be seen on the church at Knighton-on-Teme.

The interior is lofty and 14th century in style. The chancel arch is supported by corbels carved with foliage and birds. There is a 14th-century recess with carved ballflower decoration in the chancel, which may have been an Easter Sepulchre. The piscina is also Decorated, and has a trefoil head with ballflower. The Norman font survives, and is carved with lozenges between roll mouldings. It is similar to the design on the font in Middle Littleton church. The cover is 17th-century, and the pulpit contains 17th-century woodwork with arched panels.

Under the tower are gathered several memorials from the old church, especially to the Gower, Oliver and Ballard families, as well as to the Romney family of Tundridge and the Freeman family of Gaines in the parish. A brass plate at the back of the recess in the chancel commemorates a former rector, Thomas Littleton, who died in 1665.

In the churchyard is the base of the medieval cross, with a niche for the pyx, similar to the cross at Broadwas.

TARDEBIGGE   ST. BARTHOLOMEW

The large parish of Tardebigge lies between Bromsgrove and Redditch and indeed, until 1855 actually included Redditch. The curious place name is not fully understood, but a suggested meaning is big or high tower, and certainly this is reflected in the present dramatic situation of the church on a hilltop over-looking the Worcester to Birmingham Canal and the long flight of locks. Tardebigge village is by the grounds of Hewell Grange, a large 19th-century house built by the first Earl of Plymouth, and St. Bartholomew's church is an estate church, on the lands which the Windsor family took along with

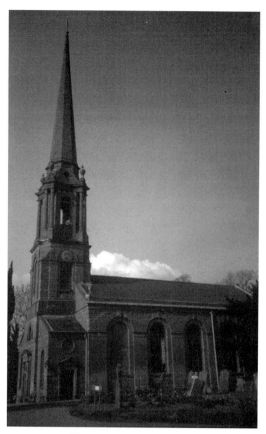

*Francis Hiorn's tower
and nave of 1777 at Tardebigge*

Bordesley Abbey after the Dissolution, as an exchange for Stanwell in Middlesex with King Henry VIII. Medieval Tardebigge was held by Bordesley Abbey.

The medieval church dated mainly from the 12th and 13th centuries, and had a partly octagonal tower. It stood a little to the south of the present church, astride the county boundary at that date with the chancel in Warwickshire, but the rest of the building in Worcestershire. The church was surveyed by the historian, Thomas Habington who, in the early 17th century, was exiled to Worcestershire following his involvement in the Gunpowder Plot, and so examined the chancel from across the boundary! Habington's descriptions are useful because in September 1775 the tower collapsed and much of the church was destroyed.

The present church was built of sandstone in 1777 by Francis Hiorn from Warwick. Hiorn's nave and tower survive to which have been added an apsidal, but still classical, chancel designed by Henry Rowe of Worcester, and built by Thomas Collins of Tewkesbury. The nave is of classical proportions with round-headed windows, and a contrast to the Gothic churches Hiorn designed at Tetbury in Gloucestershire, Stony Stratford in Buckinghamshire and the East Gate Chapel in Warwick. The west tower and spire are very tall and make a conspicuous feature in the parkland landscape. The square classical tower gives way to a baroque belfry with concave walls and pairs of columns in the corners which support urns as pinnacles below the octagonal spire. The tower and spire are very similar to those at Over Whitacre church in Warwickshire of 1766, which may also have been designed by Hiorn.

The interior, although quite plain and light in the manner of Georgian churches, was refitted in the 19th century. The three decker pulpit, box pews and side galleries have gone, but the west gallery remains, now with the royal arms of Queen Victoria, along with the family pews of the Cookes and Windsor families. The chancel of 1850 is sympathetic in style to the nave, although there are some medieval style carved capitals. The font is of 1850 in a Norman style, with Biblical scenes carved on the bowl. The communion rails are by Hardman & Co. Much of the chancel woodwork was made in the early 20th century by craftspeople from the Plymouth estate, who met regularly at Tardebigge village hall, now a public house. The choir stalls, reading desk and reredos were worked there, the central panel of the latter being to the design of the first Earl of Plymouth. The bronze lectern was designed by 1907 by Amy Walford of the Bromsgrove Guild. The pulpit, lectern and bishop's stall date from the 1960s and are by Celestino Pancheri of the Guild, who also designed the west doors. The 1930s prayer desk is by Frederick Etchells. The organ of 1819 was moved to the chancel from the west gallery in 1878.

The east window contains glass of 1922 showing the Ascension, the upper part being the design of the Earl of Plymouth, the lower that of Alfred Pike. Amy Walford designed the memorial window to the wives of Thomas Dixon showing Faith, Hope and Love. The north window glass in a Flemish Renaissance style as appropriate for a Georgian church was designed in 1894 by Heaton, Butler and Bayne. There are 19th-century floor tiles by Minton.

A fragment of the great memorial to Henry, Lord Windsor who died in 1605, which Habington described as 'glorious', is preserved at the west end of the nave. However, the early Windsor memorials were otherwise destroyed with the old church, but on the east wall of the nave is a monument to Sir Thomas Cookes and his wife, Mary Windsor, who died in 1693. It is a classical piece with twisted columns to the sides of the three-quarter figures in an oval. She is shown bare breasted in the classical manner of the day, which may be the source of the unlikely story that she suckled her husband when he was in prison to save him from starvation. Sir Thomas Cookes refounded Bromsgrove School in 1693. The memorial to Other Archer, sixth Earl of Plymouth, who died in 1833, is of white marble by Francis Chantrey of 1835, whose monument to Mrs. Digby can be seen in the Lady Chapel at Worcester Cathedral. It shows a woman in mourning, beside a pedestal and urn, with a book and chalice.

Outside, the base of the medieval churchyard cross now supports a memorial in Portland stone to Baroness Windsor. On the north side is a memorial to Captain William Emmott of the Worcestershire Yeomanry Cavalry, who died in 1865, having fought in the Battle of Waterloo and the Peninsular War. As a mark of esteem, the Earl of Plymouth presented an engraving of his portrait to every member of the regiment. Nearby are the monuments of Sir Augustus and Lady Walburga Paget, Sir Augustus being ambassador to several European countries in the 19th century, and that of the first Earl of Plymouth, who designed the glass and reredos panel in the church. Outside the churchyard is the school building erected by Harriet, Baroness Windsor in 1818, to replace the Magpie Inn, which in turn was probably on the site of the medieval church ale house.

TENBURY WELLS   ST. MARY

Tenbury Wells is a small market town beside the River Teme, where the boundaries of Worcestershire, Shropshire and Herefordshire all meet. It was granted a charter in 1249 and developed as an important local market. In 1839 a mineral spring was discovered by the main street, and the town had a short-lived period as a spa. Amongst the half-timbered buildings are several former hotels and the remains of the curious Gothic spa building designed by James Cranston, architect of Shelsley Beauchamp church. Away from the main street, and accessible through alleyways or from Church Street, St. Mary's church stands in a precinct-like churchyard beside the River Teme, by which it has frequently been flooded.

The red sandstone church has a west tower, nave, large aisles and porch, and a chancel. The west tower is Norman with twin bell openings, similar to Harvington church, but that to the north has a water-leaf capital, and like the west doorway was probably reset when the church was rebuilt in 1770. On top is an 18th-century parapet with pinnacles which surround a pyramid roof. The nave of 1770 was rebuilt after severe flood damage in 1865 with aisles in the Decorated style by Henry Woodyer, who had designed St. Michael's church nearby nine years before. Much of the 14th-century masonry of the chancel has survived but has been refaced and incorporated into Woodyer's work.

The whitewashed interior appears to be of pure Victorian Decorated style, with Woodyer's quatrefoil piers to the arcades, and his elaborate western opening for the organ chamber with a doorway and arch divided by a pillar below, together with a large reticulated arch above. During restoration work to the chancel in 1864 part of an Anglo-Saxon cross shaft was discovered in the masonry, where it must have been incorporated into the Norman church. The cross shaft can now be seen in the north aisle and dates from the 10th century; it is carved with interlace and serpents. It is possible that the cavity on the shaft once held a small relic. In the north wall of the chancel is a Decorated Easter Sepulchre, which has cusped tracery and trefoils in the canopy, and below the shelf are trefoil-headed panels. It is likely that these were once painted to show the sleeping soldiers outside Christ's tomb, similar to those carved on the sepulchre at Hawton church in Nottinghamshire. The back of the recess may also have been painted with a representation of the Garden Tomb, but today there is an effigy here. Apart from the 19th-century fittings, the reredos of 1961 is in the Perpendicular style, carved by Robert Pancheri of Bromsgrove. There is also a single chained book preserved from the former chained library, and several architectural fragments including trumpet and water-leaf capitals from the medieval church. The glass in the east window is by Hardman & Co.

The effigy now in the Easter Sepulchre is a miniature cross-legged knight holding a heart. It was found amongst stonework in the church in 1824, and could be a member of the Sturmy family, who held a manor here at Sutton Park until about 1430. The mittens in mail are an unusual feature of this monument.

The large effigy of a knight is probably that of Sir John Sturmy who died in about 1300, for the Sturmy arms are carved on his shield. The chest tomb was erected in 1581 as a memorial to Thomas Acton and his wife Mary Lacon, who lived at Sutton Park to the south of the town. The alabaster effigies have finely detailed costume

St. Mary, Tenbury—Easter Sepulchre which now houses the effigy of a knight holding a heart

and his feet rest on a boar. The chest is carved with tapering pilasters, between which are oval niches with figures of their two sons and a daughter, Joyce, who married Sir Thomas Lucy of Charlecote in Warwickshire, famous for his prosecution of William Shakespeare for poaching deer on his estate. A large monument to William Godson, who died in 1822, is by John Bacon junior and Samuel Manning. It has a large obelisk with sunrays, clouds and an angel above a woman grieving on a broken column.

TENBURY WELLS   ST. MICHAEL AND ALL ANGELS

St. Michael's church is an extraordinarily un-English sight as it is approached across the common to the south-west of Tenbury Wells. It has the height, apse, rose window and steep pitched roofs of a small French cathedral. The church owes its existence to Sir Frederick Gore Ouseley, who became Precentor of Hereford Cathedral in 1855, and who founded a college here as a choir school in 1856 to promote musical development, as part of the growing revival of Catholic worship and tradition in the church after 1840. Much of the funding came from the Rushout family of Burford in Shropshire, where a friend of Ouseley's was rector. The college church also served a new parish, properly known as Old Wood, and so it has remained a parish church since the college closed in 1985. Today the college buildings are occupied by a Spanish school.

The architect of this group of sandstone buildings was Henry Woodyer, who was a pupil of William Butterfield and who developed the Decorated style in a flamboyant French way. The college buildings are like a French monastery with their cloister, and steep roofs with narrow pointed dormer windows.

The church has an aisled nave with clerestorey, porch, transepts and a chancel with polygonal apse and is linked to the college buildings by a cloister. Woodyer's elaborate Decorated style tracery can be seen in the limestone work of the windows, and the church should be compared with Woodyer's work at Highnam in Gloucestershire or the Convent of St. John the Baptist at Clewer in Berkshire. There is much fine carved detail to the exterior such as on the corbels, gargoyles and buttresses with angels, saints and foliage in the Decorated style. There is no tower but the bells hang in an arched recess on the west front.

Woodyer's large Decorated style church of St. Michael, Tenbury Wells

The interior is lofty and elegant, as the exterior would suggest, and is indeed modelled on a 14th-century cathedral. The walls support a wooden vault. It is painted in the chancel with Biblical emblems and is supported by corbels carved with musical instruments. The arches in the arcades and recesses are in the Decorated style, many with carved foliage. The sedilia has a crocketed canopy with cusps, and a back wall with carved floral diaper work. The credence table has ballflower decoration.

Many of the fittings were installed in the church in 1856. In the fashion of a medieval collegiate church the choir is under the crossing. The screen, pulpit and lectern are also notable along with the reredos, which was designed to reflect a medieval shrine. The font in the north transept has a huge oak cover whilst nearby is a recess for the baptism register, and a well, now covered, from which water was drawn for baptism. The organ was originally designed by Ouseley but rebuilt by Henry Willis in 1873. The floor has medieval style tiles by Minton. There is a portrait of Sir Frederick Gore Ouseley in the north transept. The stained glass of saints in the porch of 1897 is by Lavers and Westlake, and there are fragments of medieval glass which were placed in the cloister in 1935, but the rest of the glass is by Hardman & Co. of Birmingham. The west window shows Christ in Majesty, whilst the windows in the aisles illustrate stories of Christ's healing. In the clerestorey are the emblems of St. Mark and St. John, Christ with the cross, and St. Veronica. In the north transept are the Baptism of Christ and Christ with children, along with Miriam and St. Cecilia. The Lady Chapel has miracles and the martyrdom of St. Thomas. In the south choir aisle is an Annunciation. The chancel windows show angels with musical instruments. The apse windows depict the angelic choirs, as well as Christ with St. Michael at his feet, and the figures of St. Raphael and St. Gabriel.

There are several memorial plaques, including brasses to Sir Frederick Gore Ouseley and the chief benefactor, Georgina Rushout. Musicians commemorated include John Stainer, composer of *The Crucifixion* and George Robinson Sinclair, organist, whose initials appear in Elgar's *Enigma Variations*.

In the churchyard is the tomb of the founder, Ouseley, who died in 1889, by Sir George Aston Webb, with the gravestones of wardens and others associated with the college. St. Michael's is a remote but remarkable legacy from the 19th century.

THROCKMORTON   CHAPELRY

*Throckmorton: a simple church with a central tower,
reached by a path across a field*

Throckmorton church stands almost alone in the fields. Much of the village disappeared in 1940 when Pershore airfield was laid out, and today there are a few cottages around the road junction, the 16th-century timber-framed Court Farm to the east, and the church. Next to the church is a moat which may have surrounded an earlier manor house, which with Court Farm belonged to members of the Throckmorton family from the 14th to the 20th centuries. Thomas Throckmorton was Constable of the Beauchamp's castle at Elmley Castle, and his son, John, was standard bearer to King Henry V. Sir John Throckmorton's brass is in Fladbury church, which is the parish church of Throckmorton. Through his wife, Eleanor Spiney, the family acquired Coughton Court in Warwickshire, which became their main home.

The grey lias church is a simple building with an atmosphere which reflects its rural situation, approached by a path across a field. It consists of a nave with south aisle, central tower and chancel. The chancel is late 13th-century with later Early English windows and a priest's doorway. On the north side of the nave is a window of similar date, which has three stepped lancets with cusps. The tower is 13th-century, but has a 15th-century belfry with Perpendicular bell openings, gargoyles, battlements and pinnacles. The south aisle was much rebuilt in 1894 yet retains Perpendicular windows.

The entrance is on the south side, with the north and west doorways being blocked. The interior is quite plain, with a whitewashed nave and the east end scraped back to the stone. The arcade between the nave and aisle is oddly irregular, with a lower small arch in the middle in line with the doorway. There are round piers with pointed chamfered arches and carved heads in the spandrels. The fittings are all 19th- and 20th-century, except the Norman font which seems to have been altered in the 13th or 14th century.

TIBBERTON   ST. PETER AD VINCULA

The long, straggling village of Tibberton extends from the Worcester to Birmingham Canal to the church, which stands on a hill next to the large timber-framed Rectory Farm. There is much 20th-century housing in the village, a result of its location some four miles east of Worcester. Evelench Farm in the parish was used by recusant Jesuit priests from Worcester during the late 17th and early 18th centuries, reflecting the faith and influence of the Wintour family at Huddington and the Berkeleys of Spetchley.

St. Peter was re-built in 1868 by William Jeffery Hopkins. It has a nave and chancel of lias, with a timber porch and west bell turret, which carries a short spire. There are lancet windows in the early Decorated style. The interior is brick-faced, with some decoration in black and yellow, not unlike Hopkins' church at Abberton. The fittings are mainly contemporary but the reworked font may be 13th-century. There are several memorial tablets including three Georgian examples with urns.

TRIMPLEY   HOLY TRINITY

Trimpley church was founded as a chapel to St. Mary's church in Kidderminster. It is in the centre of the village, to the north of Bewdley, high above the River Severn, in pretty countryside with fine views across the valley to the Wyre Forest. Trimpley Reservoir nearby is part of the water supply system for Birmingham.

The sandstone church was built in 1844, with an endowment from Joseph Chillingworth, by Harvey Eginton, architect of Catshill church and St. Michael's church, Broadway. Here the Norman style has been used, and the church has a nave and chancel in one, with an apse to the east, and a west bellcote. The west front is quite elaborate with a rose window above the doorway, a window similar to that at Headless Cross church in Redditch. The Norman style is exaggerated in the carvings on the doorway and lancet windows, with plenty of large zig-zags.

The interior contains many 19th- and 20th-century fittings. There had been a medieval chapel at Trimpley founded in about 1370 by the Attwood family and dedicated to the Assumption of the Blessed Virgin Mary, which has disappeared.

UPPER ARLEY   ST. PETER

Upper Arley stands on a hillside by the east bank of the River Severn. Until 1964 it was well known for its chain ferry across the river, but this has been replaced by a footbridge giving access from the village to Arley station and the Severn Valley Railway. The approach to the village by road is along a cul-de-sac past the parkland of the former Arley Castle, a medieval style house built by the second Earl of Mountnorris in 1844 with turrets and battlements, but demolished in the 1970s. The estate had belonged to the Lyttleton family of Hagley, and the previous house had been their dower house. Upper Arley was in Staffordshire until 1895, and today is on the border with Shropshire.

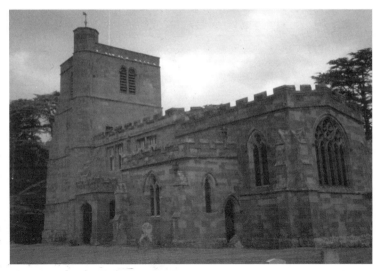

Upper Arley: the south porch and vestry with massive tower beyond

The red sandstone church stands above the village by the entrance to the park. It has a massive west tower, nave and chancel, with north aisle and chapel, and a south porch and vestry. The south wall of the short nave has Norman masonry. The north aisle was added in the 14th century with Decorated windows. A clerestorey was added to the nave in about 1500 by Sir William Lyttleton and has Perpendicular windows, battlements and a low pitched roof. It is like a smaller version of the great clerestorey on St. Mary's church in Kidderminster. Lyttleton also added the north chapel to the chancel. The medieval chancel was much rebuilt between 1885 and 1887, when the vestry and porch were added. The tower was built in the 16th century, with a south-western stair turret and plain parapet. It was altered in the 18th century, when the bell openings were inserted.

The interior is attractively compact. Fragments of Norman stonework have been reset in the 12th-century south wall. The north arcade and the chancel arch are Decorated, but the north chapel arcade was replaced in 1885. The nave has a fine 16th-century roof, and there is a later 16th-century arch to the tower.

The fittings are mainly 19th- and 20th-centuries, including floor, pews and organ chamber, as well as the early 19th-century font, a gift of Lady Valentia. In the north chapel is an 18th-century communion table, and a Georgian Gothic carved communion rail of between 1750 and 1775. The late 18th-century stone Commandment panels are now in the tower. There are also some medieval floor tiles in the north chapel, but sadly little trace now remains of the medieval Doom painting recorded as being over the chancel arch in the 19th century. The east window glass of 1887 is by Charles Eamer Kempe.

The 14th-century effigy in the north chapel is of a knight thought to be Walter de Balun, whose heraldic arms appear on the shield. He was the first husband of Isolda Mortimer, and was killed in a tournament in 1270 on his wedding day. A tablet to Sir Henry Lyttleton, who died in 1693, has a carved skull, trumpet and torch at the bottom. He was a Royalist, and taken prisoner at the Battle of Worcester in 1651. A tablet by Stephens of Worcester commemorates Viscount Valentia later Earl of Mountnorris, who died in 1841. His successor, the builder of the castle, was a keen traveller and naturalist with a passion for fireworks.

UPTON SNODSBURY   ST. KENELM

The main road from Worcester to Alcester passes over the hill at Upton Snodsbury close to the church. A long history of settlement is reflected in the eroded remains of a small Iron Age hillfort on a higher hill to the north, whilst in the south of the parish is the site of an Anglo-Saxon cemetery. The church stands at the centre of the village with several timber-framed cottages to the south and west. The churchyard is raised above the surrounding roads, and a path leads to the church under arches of yew.

The tall tower stands at the west end of the nave with south aisle and porch, and a chancel. It is built of lias and was very extensively restored by William Jeffrey Hopkins in 1873-74. The earliest masonry is the nave north wall with a blocked doorway and Early English lancet windows. The chancel is mainly the work of Hopkins, yet retains an unusual Decorated window on the south side with stepped lancets and ogee curves. Hopkins copied the design in the north window. The tower is Perpendicular with a parapet and short pinnacles. The bell openings on the south and west sides are off-centre to

Upton Snodsbury: the Perpendicular south doorway

allow for the stair. The south aisle and clerestorey are late Perpendicular, and quite simple if compared to contemporary work at Rock or Claines. The aisle has a low pitched roof and the windows have shallow arches with square heads in the clerestorey. The south doorway has a square surround with spandrels carved with heraldic arms. The heavy door is contemporary with cross battens. It is sheltered by a 19th-century timber porch.

The interior was scraped to the stone in 1949, though traces of wallpainting survive in the south aisle. The south arcade is quite low and has octagonal piers and shallow Perpendicular arches. One of the capitals is carved with a small barrel, the rebus of the Lyttleton family, who held land here in the 16th century. The aisle has 16th-century roof timbers and bosses. There is no chancel arch, but the 19th-century rood screen contains some late medieval tracery. The other fittings, especially the pews and organ case are typical of the later 19th century, but the octagonal font is Perpendicular with carved quatrefoil panels enclosing the symbols of the Evangelists, a head and a rose. There are some fragments of medieval glass in the north chancel window, but the reminder of the glass is 20th-century. The 17th-century chest shows the names of the churchwardens—the spelling of Armell Greene being corrected from Ormell, with little attempt to conceal the mistake.

In the churchyard can be seen the decayed base of the medieval cross.

UPTON-UPON-SEVERN   OLD CHURCH

The riverside town of Upton was a thriving port serving Herefordshire from the Middle Ages. By the 18th century the town had more or less its present compact appearance, its development being restricted by the extent of the surrounding flood meadows. The fine main streets are lined with timber-framed and Georgian buildings. At the north end the tower of the former parish church stands near the present bridge. On the opposite side of Church Street, a range of Georgian houses incorporates the manor house, successor to the site of a possible former fortified manor identified to the west.

The medieval bridge and church were seriously damaged during the Civil War, when in 1651 Cromwell's forces captured Upton from the Royalists in a successful move to get troops on to the west bank of the Severn prior to the Battle of Worcester. The medieval red sandstone church tower survives, and dates from the early 14th century. It has a Decorated west window and long transomed bell openings like those at nearby Longdon. There is a Decorated arch on the east side which once opened into the nave. The medieval church was probably founded by the Boteler family of Ripple, and had a chancel with side chapel, between which was placed a memorial to William Boteler and his brother, part of which is preserved in the present church.

The damaged medieval church was replaced between 1756 and 1757 by a large tall nave, the roofline of which can still be traced on the eastern bell openings. The nave had round-headed windows with semi-circular openings to light the galleries. At the east end was a small, low chancel with a vestry on the north side and a vestibule to the south. The east window was of the Venetian type. Inside there were galleries on the north, south and west sides to which second tiers were later added. The church was built of limestone from the demolished church of Holy Trinity, Westgate Street in Gloucester, its architect being the local John Willoughby. Today only the south door to the nave survives with a pediment and provides access to the Heritage Centre in the tower. The church was demolished after years of disuse in 1937.

However, the most famous feature of the church is the upper parts of the tower which were added in 1769 to 1770 to replace the medieval spire (see front cover). A white octagon with blank round panels carries a copper cupola with a lantern on top. It was designed by Anthony Keck, architect of Bevere House, the Infirmary and Old St. Martin's church in Worcester. In place of pinnacles, urns can be seen on the corners of the tower. This is Upton's most distinctive feature giving the skyline of the town a continental appearance. It is known locally as the Pepperpot.

The old churchyard was restored in the 1960s, when the remains of the nave and chancel were consolidated beneath a grassy mound. In 1921, the former market cross, which had stood in the grounds of Ham Court, was brought here as a war memorial. Close by is a bronze bust to Admiral Sir William Tennant, who was in command of the Mulberry Harbours used in the invasion of Normandy in 1944.

UPTON-UPON-SEVERN   ST. PETER AND ST. PAUL

The present parish church of Upton stands at the opposite end of the town from the old church. The view from the west across the meadows and cricket field towards the honey-coloured church is very attractive. It was built of Hornton stone in 1878-79 in the front garden of a fine late Georgian house, which has been the rectory since 1895. The land and much of the funding for the new church was provided by George Edward Martin of Ham Court, whilst much of the drive to move from the outdated 18th-century church came from the rector, Robert Lawson. The architect was Sir Arthur Blomfield, who used the Decorated style, as he did on his other church in the county at Wribbenhall in Bewdley. It was built by Thomas Collins of Tewkesbury. The church has an aisled nave, chancel with side chapel, vestry and organ chamber, whilst the north-west tower supports a commanding octagonal broach spire. It is a very regular building, though the two sides of the chancel are different. The east and west windows are large Decorated style features.

The interior is rather grey with Decorated style arcades and chancel arch. The north chapel is now partitioned off. A central feature is the spectacular corona of spirit figures of 1987 by Anthony Robinson. The west end of the church is divided by the former Perpendicular style rood screen from St. Mary Magdalene church in Worcester, carved by William Forsyth in 1876, and brought here after that church closed in 1976. The carved oak sedilia is also by Forsyth of 1870, whilst the lectern and bishop's chair were made by Rattee and Kett in 1872. The reredos was designed by Blomfield in 1895. A table in the nave has the 18th-century wrought iron base from the altar of the old church, but the remainder of the fittings are 19th- and 20th-century, and include a Nicholson organ.

Two windows on the south side of the chancel have glass of 1881 by Heaton, Butler and Bayne, who also designed the east window glass in 1884 showing the Te Deum. The Holloway memorial window in the south aisle is also Heaton, Butler and Bayne glass of 1899, and shows the anointing of Christ's feet by Mary Magdalene. Their glass can also be seen in the Lawson memorial window nearby which is of 1900 and depicts the raising of Lazarus. The west window glass was installed as a memorial to George Edward Martin after 1906. It shows the Creation and the Benedicite with figures including St. George, St. Edward the Confessor and St. Martin (the choice of saints reflects his name), and is by Christopher Whall, who designed notable glass in Ashbourne church in Derbyshire and the Lady chapel of Gloucester Cathedral. There is other 19th-century glass in the aisle windows.

Several memorial tablets were moved here from the old church, particularly to the Bromley family, who held the manor. The worn effigy of William Boteler is but a fragment of a large destroyed memorial from the medieval church, which was discovered on the old church site in the 19th century. There are tablets by Eric Gill to George Edward Martin, who died in 1906, and his wife, Henrietta, who died in 1914.

UPTON WARREN   ST. MICHAEL

Close to the M5, and by the River Salwarpe, Upton Warren nevertheless remains an isolated place. The large waterlogged gravel pits to the east are now a nature reserve, but the church is to be found with a few houses along a lane west of the A38. Badge Court, a timber-framed house nearby, was home to the Cokeseys who held the manor before the Wintours of Huddington.

The sandstone church today has a nave, chancel and south tower with spire. The earliest part is the 13th-century tower with plate tracery to the Early English bell openings, which are surrounded by roll moulding. Above the battlements is a short octagonal Decorated spire. The lower windows are also Decorated, and represent improvements of the 14th century. The chancel has some 17th-century masonry and a date stone of 1664, but was rebuilt in 1724, when the east window was installed. The nave has a low pitched roof and Y-shaped tracery to the windows and dates from 1798. It is in a similar Georgian Gothic style to the alterations at nearby Rushock church. The blank west wall is rather bleak.

The interior is late Georgian, but there is a Decorated arch leading into the tower. The west gallery with music stand dates from 1798, but the fittings are mainly 19th- and 20th-century. The east window has glass of 1880 by Taylor and O'Connor illustrating the Book of Revelation, Pevsner describing the glass as 'uncommonly horrible'. An 18th-century flute displayed in the church was part of the church orchestra. A stone of 1669 records the charity of John Sanders. The tower contains medieval bells.

WELLAND   ST. JAMES

South of Welland, Castlemorton Common stretches towards the hills as a reminder that this is part of Malvern Chase and that much of Welland was unenclosed until the 19th century. The present church is at the crossroads at the centre of the village, but this reflects the movement west of the settlement, for the medieval church was situated by Welland Court and the Old Vicarage. The outline of the simple structure is traceable at the end of a lane south of the Upton road in a deserted graveyard.

The present church of 1875 is a large urban looking building with walls of Malvern stone, which have a harsh appearance as at Guarlford church. The aisled nave has a chancel and south-west tower with a spire. The architect was J. Hugall, who also designed the nearby school, master's house and vicarage. The style is of the transition from Early English to Decorated.

The interior is typical of the period, with arcades which have piers of striped buff and blue stone, supporting Early English style capitals. The fittings are 19th- and 20th-century. The east window glass is perhaps by Hardman & Co., whereas a window in the south aisle has glass of 1895 by Charles Eamer Kempe showing an angel leading St. Peter from prison. A further window was brought from the mission church of the Good Shepherd at Upper Welland in the 1970s. A miniature 17th-century travelling font survives from the old church. Also from the old church is the memorial tablet to Thomas Evans who died in 1671, which has scrolls and a curved, open pediment.

WEST MALVERN   ST. JAMES

The setting of West Malvern is spectacular, high on the north-western slopes of the hills with views across Herefordshire towards Shropshire and Wales. The small village developed as Malvern became a fashionable resort in the 19th century, with several large houses taking advantage of the views. The church is next to St. James and the Abbey School, the former mansion of the Howard de Walden family.

The first church was built between 1841 and 1843, as a chapel of ease to Mathon church below the hill and now in Herefordshire. It was designed by Harvey Eginton, architect of Trimpley and Catshill churches. By the 1870s it was too small, was demolished, and the materials used in the construction of the school across the road. The new church was built between 1870 and 1871 to the designs of George Street. It is of Malvern stone, with a nave, chancel and south tower with a saddleback roof, transverse to the roofs of the church. The style is early Decorated, but the chancel has five stepped Early English style lancet windows. A baptistry was added at the west end between 1924 and 1926 by Gillespie.

The typical interior contains many 19th- and 20th-century fittings, including brass communion rails of 1870 by Sir George Gilbert Scott, given to the church by the patron, Westminster Abbey, where they were formerly in the Henry VII chapel. The glass includes one south aisle window by William Wailes and several by Hardman & Co., dating from between 1873 and 1886, showing the Corporal Acts of Mercy, St. James and St. John, and the Crucifixion, with scenes from the Life of Christ in the east window.

WHITE LADIES ASTON   ST. JOHN THE BAPTIST

The unusual name of the village is a result of the tithes from the parish being paid to the nunnery of Whistones in the Tything in Worcester. Whistones was a community of Cistercian nuns who wore undyed or white habits. The site is now occupied by the Royal Grammar School, but the remains of the nunnery church can still be seen next to the house called Whiteladies.

St. John's church stands at the north end of the scattered village, which has a mixture of timber-framed cottages and 20th-century housing. It is set back from the road and is approached down a pretty avenue of yews. The lias building has a nave, chancel and north aisle, whilst there is a Home Counties style weatherboarded timber bell turret at the west end with a spire, and a timber porch. The nave and chancel are mainly Norman, with small lancet windows surviving in the south walls. The simple Norman south doorway has been extensively restored. The other windows are Decorated and Perpendicular. A north aisle was added in 1861, and the porch in 1865.

The whitewashed interior has a large 19th-century Norman style chancel arch, which replaced a much smaller opening. The aisle extension also gives the church a greater sense of width than is perceived from the exterior. There are many 19th-century fittings, but the duodecagonal font with thin rolls to the angles is probably 14th-century. In about 1920 a depiction of angels by a stream with flowers was painted over the chancel arch by Millicent Anderson, but this has now been completely lost. There are several 18th-century memorial tablets, including one to Thomas Elrington, who fought at Culloden in 1745, before serving in North America and the West Indies. A brass to a former vicar, Henry Martin Sherwood, commemorates his incumbency of 71 years at White Ladies Aston from 1839-1911.

WHITTINGTON   ST. PHILIP AND ST. JAMES

Crookbarrow Hill is more usually known in Worcester as Whittington Tump. It is a landmark close to the M5 and has unexplained origins, though is most probably a natural feature which may have been modified as a motte. Evidence of Roman settlement has been found close by, and today there is a brick and timber farmhouse at its foot on the site of the manor.

The church stands in the village on the opposite side of the Worcester to Pershore road. Despite the immediate proximity of the city, it retains a rural atmosphere. The present church is the successor of a timber-framed chapel, which was probably of 14th-century date, and similar to the surviving church at

Besford, though with close-studded timbers to the walls. It had a nave, chancel, south porch and bell turret at the west end. The chapelry was part of the Anglo-Saxon parish of St. Helen's church in Worcester, which extended from Little Witley to Huddington and also included Warndon.

The present church is of lias and was built in 1842 to the design of Abraham Perkins, the cathedral architect who also built Doddenham church and worked on that at Wichenford. It is like a contemporary Commissioners church, and has lancet windows in the Early English style, with a nave, chancel, south porch and thin bell turret at the west end.

The interior has recently been restored. It has white walls, a west gallery and there are Gothic box pews to the nave. The royal arms of King George II have been retained. Several windows have glass of the 19th century as memorials to the Holden family. The east window glass is thought to have been designed by Frederick Preedy.

Perkins, the architect, was buried in the graveyard in 1873, whilst the artist Benjamin Williams Leader lived next door at Whittington Lodge and gave land for the extension of the graveyard in 1884. He based a sketch called *April Day* on a view of the churchyard before the extension.

WICHENFORD   ST. LAWRENCE

Wichenford is a scattered village to the east of Martley. The church stands in fields close to Laugherne Brook, not far from Wichenford Court, a fine late 17th-century brick house which incorporates parts of an earlier manor house, and has a timber-framed dovecote next to a large barn. The present house was built by the Washbourne family whose memorials are in the church.

The impression is of a 19th-century church of red sandstone, containing a nave and chancel with a porch vestry and west tower with a spire. Indeed, much work was done in 1863 by Abraham Perkins, architect of Whittington church, when the south porch, vestry and belfry with stone broach spire were added. The work is in the early Decorated style, but the nave and lower part of the tower are medieval Decorated, whilst the 13th-century chancel is Early English.

The interior is much the result of Perkins' restoration with black and white roofs and contemporary fittings. There is a medieval piscina in the south wall of the nave, and there are some fragments of Norman sculpture. The east window has glass of 1863 by William Chance of Smethwick. The glass in three other windows are also by Chance, and were the gift in 1866 of Admiral Richard Britten, benefactor of the church at Broadheath. One shows the Presentation in the Temple. The north chancel window, the Day memorial, has glass of 1893 by Hardman & Co., and incorporates the piscina and credence table in the stonework. The Jones memorial windows of 1902 on the south side are also by Hardman.

There is a memorial in the nave to John Washbourne, who died in 1615, and his wife Alice Robinson, who survived him, remarried, and lived until 1655. The painted effigies are shown lying in contemporary costume on a chest which has their two daughters and a son shown kneeling on the side. John's father, who died in 1633, also John Washbourne, erected a memorial in the chancel in 1631 to commemorate his family and his father Anthony Washbourne, who died in 1570. It is a large standing painted monument in wood with the two effigies of himself and his father, dressed in armour, lying beneath the kneeling figures of John's two wives, Mary Savage and Eleanor Lygon, who are shown with flat arches above under a straight canopy. It is interesting to compare this with the wooden memorials at Shelsley Walsh and Stockton-on-Teme.

There is a late 15th-century bell in the tower.

WICK

ST. MARY

Across the River Avon from Pershore lies the small village of Wick. There are several timber-framed cottages around a loop road at the foot of the hill from Pershore Horticultural College. The very attractive timber-framed house, Wick Manor, opposite the church, was remodelled in 1923 from a Georgian house.

The limestone church has a nave and chancel, with north aisle, porch, vestry and organ chamber, as well as a timber west bellcote. The core of the building is medieval, and there are plain Norman windows and a south doorway which have been reset. However, the aisle was rebuilt by Samuel Whitfield Dawkes in 1861, and the chancel was extended to the east in 1893. The 19th-century windows are in the Decorated style.

The stone interior retains several medieval features. At the west end is a blocked arch, which may be a Norman survival. The arcade is Norman, and is thought to be a late Norman rebuilding of plain early Norman round arches. The arches are now pointed, and the round piers carry simple capitals with square abaci. The nave has a Perpendicular wagon roof.

Amongst the 19th-century fittings are the Norman font, which carries a Victorian inscription. The Communion Rail is 17th-century. There are several windows by Charles Eamer Kempe and his successor, including one in the chancel of about 1890. The Woodward memorial window of 1905 is by Mayer & Co.

The medieval base to the churchyard cross has a top added in 1911, which along with the lychgate are thought to have been designed by George Bodley.

WICKHAMFORD

ST. JOHN THE BAPTIST

In the Vale to the east of Evesham, Wickhamford retains several timber-framed houses in the centre of the village. The church stands towards the northern end along a side lane by the manor. The manor house is a timber-framed building dating from the 16th century and stands on the site of a grange of Evesham Abbey, which held lands here from the 8th century until the Dissolution. The manor passed to the Throckmorton family, who sold it to Sir Samuel Sandys in 1594.

The pretty limestone church is small with a nave, chancel, south porch and west tower. The chancel is 13th-century, and Early English lancet windows survive in the side walls. The east wall and window were rebuilt along with the nave in the 14th century, where there are Decorated windows on the north wall. The south wall of the nave was reconstructed in the 17th century, and has a square-headed mullioned window. The tower was completed in 1686 in a late Perpendicular style with a west window, battlements and pinnacles. The bell openings are in the Decorated style. The plain porch is 18th-century.

The whitewashed interior is an excellent example of a survival of a medieval church adapted for post Reformation worship. It remained unaltered during the 19th century, and was gently restored by George Lees Milne in 1949. Some medieval features remain. The chancel arch is Decorated, and the nave roof has a carved Perpendicular beam at the east end surviving from the canopy of honour to the former rood screen. There is a plain medieval font, now restored to the nave, and a piscina in the chancel. Traces of a wall painting, believed to be a 13th-century Virgin and Child have been found on the east wall of the chancel. The core of the woodwork in the pulpit is medieval, and some Perpendicular traceried panels from the sides are now under the tower.

However, it is the 17th-century furnishings which fill the interior. The medieval pulpit has 17th-century panels with carved saints and cherubs. Below are the clerk's and reader's desks making the three decker arrangement. The next pew has six 17th-century carved Flemish panels, whilst the remaining pews, some of which on the south side are boxed, have reused 16th-century linenfold panelling. There are

17th-century gates to the chancel in place of the screen. Above are painted the royal arms of King Charles II. The chancel is mercifully free of 19th-century choir stalls. There is a 17th-century wooden panelled font with the Griffin from the Sandys arms on the cover. The 18th-century communion rails are in front of a communion table, which is made up from 17th-century woodwork. The west gallery, for singers, has 17th-century carvings on the front. These were believed to have been brought by the Sandys family from a London church. Under the tower is a cupboard with painted panels from Ribbesford House.

The chancel is dominated by the huge memorial to Sir Samuel and Sir Edwin Sandys who both died in 1623. It is a double monument with the effigies lying beneath a long straight canopy, which has quatrefoils carved underneath in an unusual late survival of the Gothic style, also to be found on the Savage memorial at Inkberrow church. The heraldic arms are above.

Sir Samuel Sandys, son of Bishop Sandys, who bought the manor, died three weeks before his son, Sir Edwin. Sir Samuel is shown with his wife, Mercy Culpeper, who died in 1626. He is wearing armour with his feet resting on a griffin. She wears widow's costume, and below are shown their four sons and seven daughters. Sir Edwin was the eldest son, and he is shown in a similar way to his father with his wife, Penelope Bulkeley from Beaumaris in Anglesey, who lived until 1680. Beneath are their five sons and three daughters. A ledger stone on the floor commemorates Penelope Washington, who married Sir Edwin's son, Samuel. She was the daughter of Henry Washington, who fought for the Royalists in the Battle of Worcester. The heraldic arms have elements of the famous Washington stars and stripes. A tablet to George and Helen Lees-Milne of 1966 has lettering by Reynold Stone.

WILDEN   ALL SAINTS

Wilden—glass to the design of Sir Edward Burne-Jones

Wilden is situated in the Stour Valley between Stourport and Kidderminster and formed part of Kidderminster parish until the 19th century. The Baldwin family ironworks were here and some of the buildings can still be seen opposite their former home, Wilden House, a little to the north of the church. Stanley Baldwin, the Prime Minister, was the only son of Alfred Baldwin who built the church at his own expense.

The brick church stands next to the school in a large churchyard. At the gate is a clock tower, erected as a memorial to Alfred Baldwin. The church was designed by William Jeffrey Hopkins and built by Cook of Hartlebury in 1879-80. It has a nave and chancel, with a north vestry and double bellcote on the west gable, and is in the Decorated style. The south porch is of timber.

The interior is faced with brick, and has good contemporary fittings, including an organ by Henry Willis of London. The timber roofs are in the medieval style. However, the church deserves to be better known for its windows, which were all designed by Alfred Baldwin's brother-in-law, Sir Edward Burne-Jones. The story of this pre-Raphaelite glass is similar to that of the window in memory of Hannah MacDonald, Baldwin's mother-in-law, in Ribbesford church. The glass was made by Morris and Co. after the death of both Burne Jones and William Morris, and was installed between 1900 and 1914. The east window commemorates the happy marriage of Alfred

Baldwin to Louisa MacDonald, and shows a child, representing Stanley, setting out on life's journey with a guardian angel, beneath the figures of Christ, St. Martin and St. George. The lancets on the south side of the chancel given by Roger Beck in 1902 show a minstrel angel, St. Cecilia playing the organ, and Miriam holding cymbals, .

The eastern window on the south side of the nave showing Joshua was given by the Directors of Baldwins in 1909, whilst the adjacent characteristic Morris foliage commemorates Louisa Baldwin.

Fortitude, along with Triumph, here represented by King Ethelbert, are shown in glass of 1903 also on the south side of the nave, whilst a further window has glass of 1914 depicting the Good Shepherd. The west window has Paradise with angels, whilst glass on the northern side includes a figure of Enoch, installed in 1907 in memory of Enoch Baldwin. Samuel and Timothy are also represented in glass of 1909, whilst a figure of St. Agnes was installed in 1907 in memory of Louisa Baldwin's sister, Agnes MacDonald, who had married the artist, Sir Edward Poynter.

WOLVERLEY

ST. JOHN THE BAPTIST

The large parish of Wolverley is to the north of Kidderminster, by the border with Staffordshire. It formerly included Cookley and Broadwaters. There is much suburban housing on the south side of the village, near the sandstone pound, but the centre close to the River Stour and the canal remains remarkably unspoiled.

It is dominated by the church on a rocky sandstone outcrop. The road and paths to the church are hollowed into the rock, whilst many of the houses have cellars cut into the rocks, all of which is reflective of nearby Kinver where houses are built into the rocks of Kinver Edge. The village centre surrounds the Georgian Gothic style buildings of the former Sebright school, now houses, whilst the timber-framed Bury Hall, next to the church, was once also part of the school and is now a distinctive group of houses. Sebright School was founded by William Sebright, a local man who became a London merchant and who left property in London to endow the school on his death in 1620. The school

The imposing Georgian church at Wolverley

had closed by the 1980s. Wolverley was also the birthplace in 1706 of the printer John Baskerville, who became famous for his distinctive typeface often used in bibles and prayer books.

The imposing church is of red brick, and consists of a tower, nave and chancel, with a vestry, organ chamber and porch. It was built in 1772 with funds from Edward Knight, one of the wealthy family of ironmasters who lived at Lea Castle, and replaces and medieval church which stood on the same site. The nave and tower have battlements and large round-headed windows in larger blank arches. However, the east window has three stepped lights in the style of later Victorian work. Indeed, the chancel was altered in 1882 when Ewan Christian raised the roof. The organ chamber and vestry were added to the south side in 1887, and the south porch was built in 1889.

The interior is painted distinctively and is the product of 19th-century refurbishments. The three galleries remain from the 1772 design, although these were altered in the 19th century and refronted in 1937. The six-sided font with Gothic tracery has been retained from the old church. The present pulpit and lectern date from 1881, but the sounding board from the previous pulpit, dated 1638, hangs on the gallery. There is a chained copy of Bishop Jewel's *Apology of the Church of England*, written in 1562. The royal arms of George I and II are on the gallery, and there are several charity boards recording gifts, including those of the Sebright family. In 1887 the Nicholson organ was removed to its present position, whilst the pews were installed in 1889.

On the north side of the chancel are two windows with glass by Morris and Co., which were designed by John Henry Dearle in 1899 as a memorial for the Elkington family. The east window glass of 1882 with scenes from the Life of Christ is a memorial to the Hancocks family, whilst a window on the south side showing St. James was installed as a memorial to the Knight family in 1900 and designed by Clayton and Bell.

The battered late 14th century effigy of a knight is probably that of Sir John Attwood of Wolverley Court. Legend states that he was found chained in the grounds after being imprisoned on crusade, having been miraculously returned from the Holy Land by a swan. His wife had presumed him dead, but cancelled her wedding to another man when the unrecognisably ragged man in chains produced half a wedding ring, broken when the couple parted, which matched the half retained by herself. The chains in which he was supposed to have been bound were displayed for a long time in the parish. The impressive collection of 18th- and 19th-century memorials include tablets to Humphrey Bate who died in 1741, and Sarah Hurtle who died in 1771. The latter is in a rococo style with cherubs by an urn. The memorial to John Hurtle, who died in 1792, is by John Nelson of Shrewsbury and shows an urn in front of an obelisk. Helen Knight, the wife of Edward Knight who financed the building of the church, died in 1801 and is commemorated on a tablet by John Flaxman. It shows her praying, yet semi-reclined, on a classical type relief with gothic quatrefoils in the surround. The memorial to Mary Smith, who died in 1804, has an urn in front of an obelisk in coloured marbles, whilst that to John Smith, who died in 1824, has an urn and drapery by Peter Hollins of Birmingham. There is also an urn with drapery on the tablet to John Hancocks, who died in 1849. There are hatchments with the heraldic arms of the Brown and Brown-Westhead families of Lea Castle.

WORCESTER   THE CATHEDRAL & CITY CHURCHES

There is possible evidence for a Christian community at Worcester as early as the 4th century. Certainly the establishment of the cathedral here by the later Anglo-Saxon period represents Worcester's growing importance as a regional centre. The medieval cathedral priory was the focal point of religious life in the shire and diocese. Pilgrims came to the shrines of St. Oswald and St. Wulstan, and then later the cathedral was the burial place of King John and the Tudor Prince Arthur. It also led the way in local architectural developments. Connections can be made between the work of masons at the cathedral and at several local churches, particularly those on monastic or episcopal estates. The 13th-century additions to Stoke Prior, Kempsey and Bredon churches bear strong similarities to the east end of the cathedral, which was rebuilt after 1224. The cathedral's early Perpendicular central tower was begun in 1374, and understandably influenced the stylistic development of towers in the diocese in the 15th century, as at Malvern

Priory, culminating in the fine early 16th-century bell tower of Evesham Abbey, but also quite notably in the beautiful towers to be found in present-day Gloucestershire.

The cathedral had a turbulent history through the Reformation and political upheavals in the 16th and 17th centuries in common with other Worcestershire churches. Civil War damage and subsequent neglect led to repairs and alterations in the 18th century, which were then swept away in the vigorous Victorian restoration. This 19th-century work, and particularly the alterations of Sir George Gilbert Scott, is also echoed in the substantial restoration of many county churches.

The city churches, which surround the cathedral, have also had a chequered history. Ten of the churches described here began as pre-Reformation foundations within the medieval city wall. Of these, at least three—St. Alban, St. Helen and St. Peter the Great—appear to be of early Anglo-Saxon origin. Only St. Helen and St. Alban retain their medieval appearance, whilst another four—All Saints, St. Nicholas, Old St. Martin and St. Swithin—were rebuilt in the 18th century, giving Worcester one of the finest groups of Georgian churches outside London. St. Michael-in-Bedwardine and St. Peter-the-Great were rebuilt in the 19th century, but have since been completely demolished, while of St. Andrew only the spectacular tower and spire remain. St. Clement was replaced by a 19th-century church to the west of the river, close to the fine medieval church of St. John-in-Bedwardine. The suburban areas outside the city wall have developed from the 16th century, and now contain a number of 19th-century churches, of which St. Paul and St. George are particularly noteworthy. The unusual 1960s circular church of Holy Trinity and St. Matthew forms part of Worcester's considerable expansion since the Second World War. The developing city has also caught up with the medieval settlement of Warndon, with its remarkable church of St. Nicholas, while by contrast the church at Claines retains a fragile independence from the urban sprawl, which has encroached over much of the southern part of its parish.

WORCESTER   ST. ALBAN, DEANSWAY

It is easy to miss St. Alban's church, as it stands next to the large 20th-century College of Technology building, beside busy Deansway. Now used as the Maggs Day Centre for the Homeless, this small church is the only one in Worcester to retain its early medieval form. Constricted by property and streets until the 1950s, and with only a tiny parish of relative poverty which extended over the site of the present college building, there was neither the need nor the resources for expansion.

St. Alban's may have very early origins. The dedication to a late Roman Christian martyr has been used to suggest this, but the evidence is not conclusive. It is possible that the inhabitants of the fourth century defended enclosure around the area of the present cathedral established a church here by the 6th century, but the church was almost certainly in existence by about 720, along with a church of St. Margaret, which stood further west towards the river. These churches, along with the early cathedral established by Bishop Bosel in 680 and minster church of St. Helen, formed the important early Saxon Christian community at Worcester. By the 11th century St. Alban's was held by Evesham Abbey, and considerable rivalry with the church of St. Helen, to which it was once perhaps formerly a chapel, was resolved at a synod in 1092 held by Bishop Wulstan when the supremacy of St. Helen's was upheld.

The red and green sandstone church consists of a nave and chancel in one, with a north aisle. The walls have slightly irregular alignments, perhaps dictated by the former streets and adjacent buildings. There is a small bellcote on the west gable of the nave. The south wall is at least early Norman in date, and contains a small circular window at the east end, which was restored in 1920. A narrow blocked doorway below has a flat lintel, and to the west is a small blocked window of similar type. The age of these is unknown and the style ambiguous, and it has been suggested that they could be Anglo-Saxon work. The wall today is dominated by the large Norman style windows and doorway which were inserted in 1821. The doorway perhaps copies the original, part of which survives inside. A fragment of this doorway with carved zig-zag is now in Worcester City Museum. The windows of the north aisle have been reconstructed in the Norman style, whilst the east window is three stepped Early English lancets, which were also much restored in the 19th century.

The interior is partly subdivided for its present use, but is dominated by the north arcade of four bays, which has two round Norman piers and later pointed chamfered arches. The capitals have scalloped trumpets, whilst at the west end is a carved head of Christ with the Crown of Thorns, which may be a copy of medieval work. A Perpendicular piscina was uncovered during the 1920 restoration. There are no longer any furnishings in the church; the Norman font has gone, along with the 17th-century pulpit, as well as some communion rails formerly in Lower Sapey church, whilst the 17th-century font cover is now in All Saints church. The church was much refitted whilst James Henry Wilding was rector between 1840 and 1862. He was a follower of the High Church movement and founded St. Alban's home and orphanage, which later moved from the parish to Diglis. The buildings and chapel there are now part of King's Junior School. The east window glass showing the Crucifixion and the glass in the circular window at the west end showing the Baptism of Christ are a memorial to him of 1863 by Frederick Preedy. A First World War memorial window in the north aisle has a figure of St. Alban.

To the west of the church stood Worcester's most substantial late medieval town house, Warmstry House, which became in turn the first porcelain works from 1751 and Dent's glove factory in the 19th century before being demolished in the 1950s. It was built by the Warmstry family, of whom the memorial to Francis Warmstry who died in 1589 can be seen in the church. It is a small tablet with heraldic arms. Other memorial tablets include that to Edmund Wyatt, who died in 1684, which has an elaborate surround, and to Marcia Wyatt, who died in 1595, which has heraldic arms. The Wyatts were an important clothier family who founded almshouses in Friar Street, and these memorials are a reminder that for much of its history St. Alban's has been at the centre of Worcester's trade and industry.

WORCESTER   ALL SAINTS, DEANSWAY

All Saints church is in a very striking position at the head of the 18th-century route to the city from the west. Whilst current traffic is diverted to other streets, the 18th-century traveller approached the city via New Road, the Severn Bridge and Bridge Street which were laid out by John Gwynne between 1769 and 1792. The medieval church had been rebuilt in the Georgian style earlier in the century, but its origins seem to be linked to its position and the river crossing. Although first mentioned in documents of 1125, the church was probably founded in Anglo-Saxon times. It stands at the north end of a parcel of land or 'haga', which was granted by Bishop Waerfirth to ealdormen Aethelred and Aethelflaed in 904, within the recently constructed northern defences of Worcester. Perhaps the church was founded as a gate chapel on the route leading from the city across the river. A market area developed by the church at the foot of Broad Street, where cattle and agricultural produce were traded through the Middle Ages. The sense of a market place can still be felt to the north of the church in that area of the junction between Broad Street and Deansway, which was known as All Hallows until the 20th century. Until the 19th century the church was closely abutted by timber-framed and brick houses, and there was a conduit in the street.

The church today has a west tower, with an aisled nave and short chancel under one roof. The earliest surviving masonry appears to be the remains of a Norman arch visible in the north buttress to the tower. The red sandstone tower base is part of the rebuilding work of after 1450, and is the only significant part of the medieval church to survive. The Perpendicular west window is similar to that at St. John's church.

The east window and restored tower at All Saints, Worcester

The medieval church had been badly damaged in the Civil War, and extensively repaired. Some further medieval stonework can be seen reused in the south wall, where it contrasts with the limestone of the Georgian building. The upper parts of the Perpendicular tower appear on early 18th-century engravings of Worcester, but were rebuilt along with the rest of the church between 1739 and 1742 by Richard Squire and William Davis, whose names are recorded on a stone inscription in the tower.

The Georgian work is baroque in character. The first level of the tower has pairs of rusticated strips and round-arched windows, whilst the upper level has twin bell-openings and pairs of pilasters. The balustrade and urns were replaced in 1992. The church is six bays long with round-arched windows to the aisles, and an impressive entrance on the north side, with Doric pilasters supporting a frieze and pediment. As at St. Swithin's, the east end is the main façade, with the large round-headed east window beneath a gabled pediment, which is supported by pairs of Doric pilasters to the sides. In the pediment is a carved bust of Bishop Hough who contributed £1,000 towards the rebuilding from his personal money. The aisles have eastern doorways with circular windows above, and rusticated strips to the sides. The half gables are stepped and curved.

The beautiful and spacious interior is not altogether expected. At the west end the Perpendicular tower arch contrasts with the Tuscan columns which divide the nave and aisles. The nave ceiling has a low semi-circular vault whilst the aisle ceilings are flat.

The arrangement of fittings is largely the result of the restoration of 1888 by Sir George Aston Webb, architect of St. George's church, when the galleries, organ and three decker pulpit were removed, the box pews were adapted to make the present seating, whilst the remainder became panelling around the walls and pier bases. However, the present pulpit incorporates 17th-century panels, the communion rail is 18th-century, and there is a beautiful 18th-century wrought iron sword rest, which would once have been attached to a mayor's pew, similar to that in St. Swithin's church. The church also has an unusual 17th-century chained bible.

Aston Webb designed the gilded iron screens to the sides of the chancel, and many other fittings date from about the time of his restoration. The altar piece by Charles Ford Whitcombe is of 1903, and has painted panels showing Joseph and St. John the Divine by Frank Smallpiece of Birmingham, as a memorial to Josephine Jane Arthure. The painting above of 1867 is by Josiah Rushton of Royal Worcester Porcelain. The main font is of 1901, whilst the Norman font is from St. Andrew's church, and a 17th-century cover from St. Alban's church. The 19th-century lectern by William Forsyth is from St. Helen's church, and several furnishings in the north aisle are from other closed city churches, in particular St. Andrew and St. Nicholas. The east window glass which shows the Last Judgement is of 1891 by Powell & Co., whilst the end aisle windows contain collected fragments of 15th-century glass, including the heraldic arms of the Berkeley and Andrews families.

The extensive collection of memorial tablets includes one with twisted columns and a painted half figure to Samuel Mathew, who died in 1676. The kneeling figures with a prayer desk in the south aisle west window are of Edward and Joan Hurdman; he died in 1621, was Worcester's first mayor, and is shown wearing his robes. The figures were originally on a larger monument in the previous church. A tablet over the south doorway was erected during the incumbency of William Cleiveland between 1758 and 1794 to record the grant of money from Queen Anne's bounty, which was established to assist poorly endowed churches. This fine city church is also noted for its peal of twelve bells, and remains in use.

WORCESTER   ST. ANDREW, DEANSWAY

St. Andrew's spire is one of the chief features of views of Worcester, particularly from the river. Sadly the tower and spire are all that remain, as the rest of the church was demolished in the 1940s, after many years of disuse. Whilst the earliest known reference to the church is in the mid-11th century, it seems likely that it was an Anglo-Saxon foundation as, with the adjacent All Saints, it stands within the area of an important plot of land granted by Bishop Waerfirth to two ealdormen in 904. The parish was always small, about ten acres, and after a period of prosperity with the cloth trade in the Middle Ages, went into a long period of relative poverty and decline, leading to its virtual clearance in the early 20th century. During the 19th century the area was noted for the number of inhabitants involved in the gloving industry, and the slender spire earned the nickname the Glover's Needle, by which most local people refer to it today. The churchyard has been extended to form public gardens which slope down to near the river, whilst to either side are the substantial 20th-century buildings of the College of Technology.

The 15th-century red sandstone tower was refaced with limestone in the 18th century, in a similar fashion to the tower of St. Swithin's. There are a large Perpendicular west window, bell openings and battlements. The medieval spire was destroyed by lightning in 1733, and rebuilt in 1757 by Nathaniel Wilkinson in the medieval style, but with a classical Corinthian capital at the top. The present top is a copy, and the original can be seen in the gardens. The spire is 155 feet high, and had to be repaired after wind damage in 1778 and again in 1799. There are many colourful local stories about the repairs, such as a local barber shaving customers on top of the scaffolding in 1801, and further restoration was done in 1870 with the aid of a kite. Wilkinson is also recorded as having rebuilt the spires at the churches of Ledbury and Ross-on-Wye in Herefordshire, and Mitcheldean in Gloucestershire.

The red sandstone is very evident in the base of the tower, which is all that survives of the interior. The late 15th-century Perpendicular arches show that the aisles embraced the tower, and there are canopied image niches on the eastern side of the piers. Above, the springers are all that remain of the nave arcades. The tower has a lierne vault, with a little-known series of 32 fine bosses, which are carved with scenes of the Annunciation, Epiphany, Trinity and the Coronation of the Virgin, along with 14 saints including St. Andrew and an unusual image of St. Philip with three loaves, representing his role in the miracle of Feeding of the Five Thousand. Several other bosses have grotesque faces, whilst one shows a man and his wife, who were probably the donors. Their names are not known, but they are likely to have been wealthy clothiers in the medieval parish.

The wooden bosses from the roofs of the church are now divided between Avoncroft and Worcester City museums. The aisled nave and chancel were quite short in proportion to the tower and spire. The nave and aisles were mainly 15th-century, whilst the chancel masonry was probably mainly 12th-century, though it was much restored in 1886. The font and some other furnishings are now in All Saints church, but a variety of monuments to members of several prominent Worcestershire families who played a role in the city's trade and industry, such as Cokesey, Oldnall, Street and Nash, have been lost.

WORCESTER   ST. BARNABAS, RAINBOW HILL

The parish of St. Barnabas was, like St. George and the other north Worcester parishes, formed out of Claines parish in the 19th century. From the arrival of the railway in Worcester in the 1850s, there was much housing development on Rainbow Hill, and by 1874 services were being held in the chapel of the newly laid out Astwood Cemetery. In 1881 a mission church was opened in Albany Road, and by 1885 St. Barnabas' had been built.

The church is a brick building with an aisled nave, transepts, apsidal chancel and a bellcote on the west gable. There is no tower, and so the church does not dominate the area of terraced housing in the manner of St. Mary Magdalene. It was designed in the later Early English style by Ernest Day, a local architect chosen on the strength of his economical design for Hounds Lane School, which formerly stood by St. Andrew's church in the city. In 1908, a vestry was added by the Arts and Crafts architect, Charles Ford Whitcombe.

The large interior is also brick-faced with sandstone dressings. The fittings are mainly late 19th- and early 20th-century. The font has carved panels designed by William Forsyth, the pulpit is of 1890 by Jonathan Brazier of Bromsgrove, the builder of the church, whilst the screen dates from 1921. The earliest stained glass window was installed by Frome Selwood in 1890 in memory of Ellen Barker, whilst the Bird memorial windows of the apse show the Resurrection in the centre dating from 1894, with St. Paul and St. Barnabas to the sides added in 1929.

The church forms a group with the brick vicarage of 1888 by Alfred Rowe, architect of the Hop Market Hotel, whilst the former schools to the north dating from between 1892 and 1912 have been replaced by the present school and housing.

WORCESTER   ST. CLEMENT, HENWICK ROAD

St. Clement is an unusual Norman style church of the 1820s

The parish of St. Clement forms the northern part of Worcester on the west side of the River Severn. The church in Henwick Road stands next to the railway and level crossing, and was built between 1822 and 1823 by Thomas Lee of London, replacing a medieval church which stood on the east bank of the river, just within the city walls. This church is first mentioned in the early 12th century, and after it was demolished in 1823, two Norman arches survived on the site until later in the 19th century. It was a small church, with a nave, chancel and large north aisle. A wooden belfry appears to have been added to the west end to replace the medieval tower, which was destroyed during the Civil War when this part of the city wall, with which the tower was integrated, was demolished.

After numerous repairs in the 18th century, it was decided to replace the church with a building on Henwick Hill where it would not be prone to flooding, as the site by the river flooded regularly. The earlier church can be seen on several 17th- and 18th-century illustrations of the city, and is particularly conspicuous next to the medieval bridge.

The present church is of brick and stucco, has a west tower with side annexes, wide nave and chancel. It was built in the Commissioners' manner, but is unusual for its Norman style. The large windows and three doorways at the west end all have Norman style ornament with zig-zags and roll mouldings, and the west façade has intersecting blind arcading. The tower was once crowned with pyramid-like pinnacles but only the stumps remain. In 1879 the chancel was lengthened and an organ chamber and south chapel added all in a complementary style by Frederick Preedy. Because of the slope of the land there is a crypt below the east end.

The interior is refreshingly light with three white painted galleries. The Norman style chancel arch has corbels carved with angels. The furnishings are mainly later 19th-century, and include a Norman style screen, a pulpit of 1879 by Preedy, a font with alabaster columns of 1885 by William Forsyth, who also carved the reredos of 1890. In 1884 the chancel walls were decorated by Forsyth with designs by Preedy, but these are now covered over and the church interior was altered and redecorated in the 1920s by Charles Nicholson.

The east window has stained glass of 1890 by Hardman & Co. A window of the Good Shepherd in memory of Benjamin Harber is of 1898 by Camm & Co. of Smethwick, and another window showing St. Clement preaching commemorates five men who were drowned in an accident in a vat at a distillery.

There are several memorial tablets at the west end, some of which were transferred from the previous church. One by George Truefitt is in memory of John Davies, rector from 1816 until his death in 1858. Aside from overseeing the new church, he is known for the foundation of the Watermen's church including a floating chapel off North Quay, along with the Mariners' church in Gloucester Docks. After Davies's death a new Watermen's church was built by the site of the old St. Clement's church. It was constructed with iron sheets and had a small tower and spire, and the barge was reused as a schoolroom next door. The site was cleared in 1947.

WORCESTER   CHAPEL OF ST. CUTHBERT, LOWER WICK

The lower walls of a large barn at Manor Farm, Lower Wick are the remains of the chapel of St. Cuthbert. Land to the west of the River Severn, which became the manors of Wick, bounded by the River Teme and Laugherne Brook, was granted to the bishops of Worcester by King Offa of Mercia in 790. By the time of the Norman Conquest the inhabitants worshipped at two chapels, St. Cuthbert's and St. John's, which were served by St. Helen's church. By the 13th century, St. Cuthbert's was the parish church, but during the 14th century, with the development of St. John's suburb at the west end of the causeway leading to Worcester Bridge, St. John's had become the more important church. St. Cuthbert's was closed in 1371, and used as a barn on a farm leased from the cathedral priory.

The Norman church was of three bays with a nave and chancel under one roof. Considerable portions of masonry survive with remains of flat buttresses and part of a doorway. However, in about 1500 a large timber upper barn store was added, and new windows and doorways inserted into the lower walls. After the Dissolution the farm became Crown property and was held by the Bromley family until the 18th century when it passed to the Vernons. During the 17th and 18th centuries the barn was also used as a poorhouse, and an iron grille which survives at one of the windows is thought to be associated with its use as a temporary home for prisoners from Worcester gaols suffering from gaol fever—typhus—at this time. The western brick extension and the hop kilns with their louvres were added by the Hopkins family in the 19th century. Their eldest son, who died of tuberculosis, is commemorated by an unusual memorial in St. John's church. A Norman font found buried in the yard is now in Crown East church.

WORCESTER

ST. GEORGE, BARBOURNE

The fine west front of St. George, Worcester

The church of St. George is set strikingly at the east end of St. George's Square. The whole composition of the brick church and late Georgian houses with mature gardens around the Square is delightful. The construction of the Square is part of the story of the expansion of Worcester during the early 19th century, with several planned developments in the rural areas around the city. This was the parish of Claines, and a chapel of St. George was built in the Square in 1830. It was a Commissioners type building, which became a separate parish church in 1862. The church became too small for the rapid population growth in the Barbourne area in the late 19th century, and by 1889 plans for a larger building were drawn up. In 1893 the old church was closed and demolished. By 1895 the present church had been consecrated, with the foundation stone of the old church placed above that of the new one.

The architect of the present St. George's church was Sir George Aston Webb, who extended the churches at Claines and Alfrick, and who went on to design the library at Malvern College. It is generally regarded as one of his finest churches. The west front makes an excellent focal point for the Square. It is of a mellow brick with stone dressings, and is in the Perpendicular style favoured by Arts and Crafts architects. The low pitched gable has a battlemented turret on either side with a short shingled spire. The turret features do not continue to the ground, unlike most medieval turrets. Below, the large Perpendicular west window is set in a recess, similar to the west window of Tewkesbury Abbey, though here there is a west porch beneath. The overall effect is based on the great Perpendicular chapels of St. George at Windsor Castle or of King's College in Cambridge. Beyond the façade the brick nave and chancel are aisled and have transepts all with Perpendicular style windows, of which those in the transepts are very tall. There is a large five light Perpendicular window at the east end. The vestry is on the north side of the chancel.

The interior is high and spacious, with arcades and a clerestorey to the nave and chancel. The three arches to the nave arcades are almost round, in an Arts and Crafts fashion. Between the arches, triangular shafts extend to the roof, between the clerestorey windows which have two lancets to each bay. The chancel is differentiated by a more extensive use of stone facing, and two lower panelled Perpendicular arches lead to the chapels on each side.

There are many attractive late 19th-century furnishings—in the south chapel is a reredos from the old church of 1868 by James Forsyth. There is a rood screen of 1895 by William Forsyth, whilst the communion rail, chancel screens and gates are by Starkie Gardner of London. The organ case was built by Thomas Collins of Tewkesbury in 1902 to Aston Webb's design. The decoration and angels are by H. Spence of London. The stained glass of the east window is by Charles Eamer Kempe, who also designed the Virgin and Child in a window in the south chapel in 1897, along with the Crucifixion in a window in the north chancel chapel. Of the same date are two windows at the west end, given by Aston Webb, and designed by Kempe. Kempe's work can also be seen in the figures of St. Anne and St. Elizabeth in the south chancel chapel of 1898.

The statue of St. George outside was carved in 1903 by William Forsyth to the design of W. Firth of London. The parish was united with that of St. Mary Magdalene when that church closed in 1977, and the single storey Magdalene Room in the southern part of the churchyard was then built for community use.

WORCESTER   ST. HELEN, FISH STREET

Since 1957 St. Helen's church has housed part of the County and Diocesan Record Office. Its central position in the city on the High Street makes it very important visually in the townscape. The origins of the church are uncertain, but its location just within the line of the late and post Roman defences and its dedication to Helen, the mother of the Roman Emperor Constantine, have given rise to the suggestion that it could represent evidence for the existence of a Christian community at Worcester in late Roman times. It may have been the place of worship for a British Christian community during the pagan Anglo-Saxon period, as Worcester and the River Severn were on the boundary separating the two cultures between the 4th and 6th centuries. Indeed no pagan Anglo-Saxon burials have been discovered west of the city. The earliest documentary evidence for the church comes in the synod to resolve the dispute between St. Helen's church and the nearby church of St. Alban in 1092, by which time it was in the patronage of the cathedral, but it is probable that St. Helen's was the principal church in the area before Bishop Bosel established the minster of St. Peter on the site of the cathedral in 680. An indication of the importance of St. Helen's church comes in its large rural parish, which in Anglo-Saxon times included Knightwick and Doddenham, Martley, Little Witley, Holt, Wichenford and Kenswick in the west, Claines, Warndon, Hindlip, Oddingley, Huddington, Whittington, Churchill and White Ladies Aston to the east, and St. John and St. Peter the Great to the west and south of Worcester. The church was an important parish church until it closed before the Second World War, when it was used as a soldiers' club and by the YMCA.

The church has a west tower, aisled nave and chancel and south porch. Though extensively restored, it is largely a red sandstone building which retains its medieval appearance and is a good indicator of how most of the other medieval city churches appeared before the rebuilding work of the 18th century. The earliest surviving masonry is probably in the north chancel aisle, which was built to house a chantry for Stephen Spagard founded in 1288. The remainder of the church was rebuilt in the Perpendicular style in about 1450. During the 19th century fragments of a Norman doorway were recorded in the south wall. The east wall was refaced in 1718 in a gothic style, and was again altered by Frederick Preedy between 1857 and 1863. The south wall was rebuilt, timber porch added, and dormer windows removed from the nave in 1879 when further restoration was carried out by Sir George Aston Webb, who also restored Claines church. The tower was rebuilt with existing masonry between 1813 and 1821.

The 15th-century doors in the south doorway open into the scraped stone interior. Although divided for Record Office use, there are many visible features. The arcades and tower arch are Perpendicular with canted projections to the piers. The nave roof has 15th-century woodwork, and at the east end are two

Perpendicular aumbries and a piscina. The octagonal font is in the Perpendicular style with carved quatre-foils and roses. Most of the 19th-century fittings have been dispersed, such as the lectern now in All Saints church, but the alabaster reredos of 1867 by Frederick Preedy remains. Stained glass in the east window tracery is also by Preedy, whilst two windows in the south aisle are by Lavers, Barraud and Westlake of 1880. The window commemorating Dr. Nash of 1884 in the south aisle is by Ward and Hughes.

There are several monuments, of which the largest is at the east end to John Nash who died in 1662. He is shown in his alderman's robes, in a reclining position, with his head resting on his arm. The large standing monument has twisted columns and garlands on the pediment above the arch, which has cherubs in the spandrels. John Nash was the great uncle of the historian Treadway Nash. Memorial tablets to the Walsgrove or Fleet family, include one to Anne Fleet who died in 1600—it is the earliest monument in the church. The large stone commemorating Dud Dudley was renewed in 1911. He died in 1684, and was the illegitimate son of Lord Dudley, who became a royalist general of artillery and was an important county ironmaster. There are many other tablets and ledger stones, and at the west end are three memorials from the demolished church of St. Michael. Nicholas Archbold, who died in 1660, is shown as a half figure in contemporary costume, whilst the memorial to his wife Margery, who died in 1615, has a figure of time and an hourglass. There is a small brass to Stephen Maylord, who was Clerk to the Chapter from 1610 to 1612.

The peal of bells was sold for scrap in 1951. To the west of the church, the small graveyard is now a car park, and contains the parish hall, which was built in 1890 on the site of the rectory. A 13th-century psalter from the church is now in Exeter Cathedral Library.

WORCESTER   ST. JOHN IN BEDWARDINE

St. John's church is the successor parish church to the chapel of St. Cuthbert within the area of the manors of Wick on the west side of the River Severn. The church was close to the manor of Hardwick, the name of which is kept by the street name Hardwick Close. The name Bedwardine, which was also used to describe the vanished church of St. Michael by the cathedral, probably derives from Anglo-Saxon words meaning table and field, and may refer to the land from which the monastery food was supplied. The suburb of St. John's developed around the church from the 14th century, and still retains a few late medieval timber-framed buildings. The former green at the junction of Bransford Road was the setting for an important medieval fair. After sustaining much damage during the Civil War the suburb was redeveloped in the 18th century, and several buildings have Georgian façades. There is also much 19th- and 20th-century housing.

The red sandstone church is a substantial medieval building, with a west tower, aisled nave and chancel porch and vestries, in an open churchyard and close to the busy road junction in St. John's. The large tower was built in 1481 and has several Perpendicular features including a recessed west window similar to that at All Saints church across the river. The top is crowned with battlements and pinnacles around a pyramid roof with fleche, which replaces a spire destroyed during the Civil War. The south aisle wall is unusual with two large Perpendicular windows under gables, whilst a third gable has two windows below, the lower of which is surrounded by the outline of the former south doorway. The present south-west porch was added in 1841 by an architect named Parsons to house a gallery staircase, and a large north aisle was built with a rose window at the west end, and two tall Decorated style windows in the north wall. The south chapel is mainly Perpendicular. In 1884 the chancel was extended eastwards, and the north chapel rebuilt with vestries and a circular window by Ewan Christian, who had recently extended the church at Norton by Kempsey.

The interior is charming with white painted walls and architecture of many different periods. The earliest part is the nave north arcade with Norman piers, although the round arches were rebuilt and heightened by Parsons in 1841. The arches between the chancel and south chapel are Decorated, whilst the south arcade and chancel arch are Perpendicular, with canted projections and chamfered arches. Christian widened the chancel arch in 1884.

The many 19th-century fittings include a gallery by Parsons of 1841, and a font of 1884, but the squint to the north of the chancel arch is medieval, and a slab with incised crosses in the floor by the chancel arch is possibly a medieval altar stone. The 17th-century communion rails remain in the church.

Fragments of medieval glass are incorporated into the chancel windows, including a crowned head in the east window and the arms of the Muchgros family in a south window.

The east window of 1884 is by Clayton and Bell and shows Christ in Majesty surrounded by saints, which along with figures of St. Oswald and St. Wulstan in the north window and St. Cuthbert and St. John in the south, are a memorial to John Whitmore Isaac of Boughton Park. A window in the north aisle commemorating Albert Buck of 1901 is also by Clayton and Bell. The east window of the south chapel of 1889 showing King Solomon's Temple is by Burlison and Grylls and commemorates Jonathan and Martha Hopkins, whilst the south window of the chapel is of the same date by Lavers, Barraud and Westlake showing the Virgin and St. John the Evangelist in memory of John Swinton Isaac. A window of 1922 showing the Good Shepherd is by Archibald Davies of the Bromsgrove Guild.

The numerous memorials, along with gravestones brought in from the churchyard, include a tablet to Abel Gower of Boughton, who died in 1669, which has twisted columns with allegorical figures below a pediment with cherubs. A tablet in the chancel to the vicar, Walter Carr who died in 1907, shows priests leading their flock to the Heavenly City.

In the porch is the unusual memorial to John Garmston Hopkins of Lower Wick, who died aged 12 in 1871. A photograph of the dead boy lying on a couch is set into the stone. At the east end is a large war memorial, whilst to the north the mainly 19th-century vicarage incorporates part of the earlier timber-framed building visible on the west side, now used as a parish office.

WORCESTER   ST. MARK, CHERRY ORCHARD

With the growing urbanisation of St. Peter the Great parish in the late 19th century, a mission church was established in 1899 to serve the Cherry Orchard area along Bath Road. The church was dedicated in 1903, but did not become a separate parish until 1936.

St. Mark is sited in a grassed churchyard on the west side of Bath Road. It is a brick building with a nave and apsidal chancel which stands on an undercroft. There is a bellcote at the west end.

Amongst the many contemporary early 20th-century fittings is an altar with carvings from the workshops of the Bromsgrove Guild. The bell was brought from the Watermen's church on the site of old St. Clement's church, whilst the 17th-century communion table is from the church of St. Peter the Great.

WORCESTER   OLD ST. MARTIN, CORNMARKET

The former parish of St. Martin lay to the east of the city, largely outside the city walls. Increasing urbanisation in the 19th century led to the creation of a new parish with a church on London Road in 1899. Old St. Martin then became a chapel of ease to St. Swithin. However, since the creation of the city parish, Old St. Martin's church has become just one of two in the city centre still used regularly by the Church of England.

*The Georgian interior of Old St. Martin
which was refurbished in the 19th century*

The medieval church was probably founded in the 11th century. By the time of its rebuilding in 1768, it had a Perpendicular west tower with Georgian urns and a balustrade, and an aisled nave and chancel with gabled Perpendicular windows to the south and east sides, similar to those which survive at St. John's church. The timber-framed porch was two storeyed with an upper chamber. The church's position, close to the city wall, meant that it suffered damage during the Civil War. It was rebuilt in the Classical style between 1768 and 1772 by Anthony Keck, architect of the Royal Infirmary and the cupola at Upton-upon-Severn church. Keck used Staffordshire blue bricks with limestone dressings. The church has a large aisled nave and chancel under one roof, to which the east end forms a plain façade with three round-headed windows below a pediment in the gable. There is a porch to the centre of the south side. The west tower was completed in 1780, and has a balustrade with pinnacles. The church was restored between 1855 and 1862 by William Jeffrey Hopkins, who added the gothic tracery to the east window.

The interior is most elegant and attractive. The aisles are divided by plain Ionic columns, each with a small piece of entablature for a capital. The aisles have groin vaulted ceilings which give way to a flat ceiling in the nave, in a manner similar to James Gibbs's church at St. Martin-in-the-Fields in London. The chancel arch carries a painted inscription, and there is a small opening to each side.

The 18th-century furnishings do not survive, but the panelling around the interior walls is made up from the former pews. The west gallery was installed in 1811, and the 1870s Nicholson organ moved there in the 1920s. The pews were replaced in 1856, but most of the fittings were introduced in the early 20th century under a succession of High Church incumbents. The altar furnishings are French, and the statue of St. Martin probably by the Marquis de Tourney. The Stations of the Cross are a memorial to a former rector, William Beattie Monahan, who died in 1948.

The stained glass includes that showing the Transfiguration in the Colville memorial window in the south aisle, designed by Frederick Preedy in 1857, whilst the window in the north aisle showing St. John the Baptist was given by the Countess of Dudley. The panelling in the church carries numerous brass memorial plaques dating from between 1776 and 1838, which record those buried in the vault below the nave. Several other memorial tablets include one decorated with Freemasons' insignia to Samuel Swan, who died in 1828.

In the tower is a 14th-century bell inscribed with a prayer to St. Martin. The medieval tithe barn stood to the north of the church, on the site of the present Salvation Army building, until it was demolished in about 1915, when the Trinity was widened. Next to it was St. Martin's school from 1883 until its demolition in 1961. To the west of the church is a tiny enclosed churchyard.

WORCESTER   ST. MARTIN, LONDON ROAD

The present parish of St. Martin was created in 1899 by merging part of the former rural section of the parish of Old St. Martin in the city with some of St. Peter the Great. Since the demolition of St. Peter's church in 1976, St. Martin has become the principal church in south-east Worcester.

George Fellowes Prynne, an architect who had been at the office of George Street, was commissioned in 1903 to design the church, along with the parish hall on the opposite side of Victoria Avenue. The parish hall was completed first and was used for services between 1903 and 1911. It is a red brick building with limestone dressings in the same Perpendicular style as the church. The church itself was begun in 1905, consecrated in 1911, and is of red sandstone with limestone dressings. It was built by Braziers of Bromsgrove and has a wide nave and chancel under one roof divided by a sanctus bellcote.

Beneath the chancel is an undercroft housing vestries and offices. There are large east and west windows, which along with the tall side windows in the narrow aisles and double transepts have flamboyant Decorated style tracery in a Perpendicular context. Lack of funds prevented the construction of the south tower beyond the ground floor which serves as a porch. An apsidal south chapel was completed in 1915 as a memorial to the first churchwarden, Francis Barnitt. In 1960 an apsidal west baptistry and porches were designed by F. Potter and Associates of Birmingham and built on foundations laid in 1911. The flat roof and long windows are characteristic of the period.

The large interior is not unlike that of St. George's church, with brick walls and stripes of stone, and a wooden barrel vaulted roof. The floor slopes slightly to the east. The double transepts do not have larger arches than the arcades, which are Perpendicular in style with the arches merging into the piers. The chancel is divided internally from the nave by a low stone screen and a high rood beam, and has a sedilia and piscina, with an aumbry on the north side beneath a large mosaic panel showing the Nativity, erected as a memorial to Mary Barnitt in 1913. The easternmost transepts are filled with a musicians' gallery to the south, and an organ to the north, built by Nicholson in 1928, and refurbished in 1976. The 19th-century stone pulpit came from St. Andrew's church, whilst the wooden font was retained from the temporary baptistry of 1911 at the west end. Most of the windows have clear glass which lightens the interior, but the glass in the side chapel windows is by Archibald Davies of the Bromsgrove Guild. The war memorial outside was erected in 1921.

WORCESTER   ST. MARY MAGDALENE, SANSOME WALK

St. Mary's church is perhaps the most prominent building at the north end of the city centre. It is a large church, and with its tower and spire, rises above the small terraced houses in the Arboretum area. The church closed in 1977, and after many years of uncertainty and near dereliction, was converted into flats in the early 1990s. It had been founded in 1876 to serve the population of the south end of Claines parish, which had become separated from Claines church with the creation of St. George's parish in 1862. Since the Middle Ages people living in the area had the use of the chapel and burial ground at St. Oswald's Hospital in the Tything, and from the 1860s it was hoped to rebuild St. Oswald's chapel as a larger building which would also serve as a new parish church. Negotiations were, however, unsuccessful, and an anonymous donor purchased several building plots for the new church on the new Arboretum development at the junction of Sansome Walk with Northfield Street.

The sandstone church was designed by Frederick Preedy in the late Early English style, with numerous lancet windows. There is, however, some simple tracery and a rose in the windows at the west end of the aisled nave, which was completed in 1877, along with the chancel, organ chamber and vestry.

The tower and spire were added in 1889 to the south side by his former assistant James Samuel Alder, who probably used Preedy's original design. There are lancet windows, and large bell openings in an octagonal belfry, which has four large pinnacles at the corners which lead up to the tall spire with late 13th-century style lucarnes.

The sanctus bellcote between the nave and chancel is a reminder that much of the planning of the church was done by the first vicar, C.H. Pilkington, who followed much Anglo-Catholic practice. There is a large relief over the south doorway showing Mary Magdalene washing Christ's feet, by Herbert Martyn of Cheltenham, and the interior of the church had much sculptural ornament on the nave capitals, credence table, aumbry and reredos in the chancel. Some of the pieces of carving were retained inside the flats when the building was converted, but the fittings have been dispersed or destroyed. The reredos was by William Forsyth, the pulpit of 1881 had panels with St. Mary Magdalene, Moses and Christ holding the blind man, which along with several memorials and ephemeral items are now in Worcester City Museum. The organ was by Nicholson, and the oak rood screen of 1906 is now in the church at Upton-upon-Severn. Almost all the stained glass has gone, including that in the east window which showed the Life of Christ by Hardman & Co. However, despite these losses, St. Mary Magdalene still plays an important role in the Worcester townscape as St. Mary's Court.

WORCESTER   ST. MICHAEL IN BEDWARDINE

There is no longer a church in Worcester Cathedral Close, but the site of the medieval church of St. Michael is marked by a group of ledger stones set in the grass by the war memorial to the north-east of the cathedral. The medieval church was demolished in 1843 and replaced by an aisled Commissioners' type church on the opposite side of College Street. It had no tower but contained stained glass by Hardman & Co. This was in turn closed, became the Diocesan registry from 1910 and was demolished in 1965. The site is beneath the present roundabout.

The medieval church was both parish church for the close and cemetery chapel to the cathedral. It is first recorded in 1268, but was probably of much earlier origin, as either the successor to a series of cemetery chapels on the site dating back to the Anglo-Saxon period, or as incorporating a part of the Anglo-Saxon cathedral church of St. Peter, which was demolished in the 11th century after a new cathedral church of St. Mary was built alongside.

Early 19th-century illustrations show the medieval church to have been of sandstone with the nave and chancel under one roof. Whilst the masonry could have been earlier, the visible windows are Decorated and Perpendicular. A timber-framed tower with a saddleback roof was built at the north-west corner in the 17th century, following the demolition of the medieval cathedral belltower in 1648. This massive octagonal tower had stood at the west end of the church. Next door was the sacrist's house, from which the watching window in the north choir aisle of the cathedral remains. The house was demolished in 1731.

The alterations made to the church interior after the Reformation are featured in accounts, which record payments for the removal of the altar and roof loft, and for the whitening of the walls. The painted alabaster reredos must have been broken up at this time and used in repairs to the walls, as parts of it were found when the church was demolished in the 19th century and are now in Worcester City Museum. Some memorials are now in St. Helen's church and a 15th-century bell is in the cathedral cloisters.

The tower of St. Nicholas' church plays a significant part in Worcester's landscape. It stands at The Cross, which has been the heart of the city's commercial centre since the Middle Ages. The first reference to the church comes in 1256, when an anchoress, Juliana, who had a cell attached to the church, was given permission to extend her courtyard across the street. Several medieval churches provided homes for such devout persons who lived alone and offered spiritual counsel, whilst also serving a practical function such as giving route directions, which would be particularly valuable in this central position. The medieval church has largely disappeared as, with the expansion of Worcester northwards in the 18th century, Foregate Street became a fashionable residential area and this church was one of four to be rebuilt by the prosperous citizens of Worcester. Movements of population and structural problems during the 20th century led to the church's closure in 1992 and subsequent conversion to a restaurant.

The church crypt has from 1988 been used as offices by the Citizens Advice Bureau. It has red and green sandstone walls with rectangular windows of uncertain date, but a doorway on the north side is probably 16th-century. This is the only part of the medieval church to survive, and has probably always been an undercroft, rather than the floor of the previous church as has sometimes been suggested.

The limestone upper parts were built with elegant Georgian proportions between 1730 and 1735. The church has a west tower enclosed within the west end of the nave structure. At the east end is a short apsidal chancel and a vestry. The architect is thought to have been Humphrey Hollins, who is described in church documents as master builder, but who worked from a model. The model was from London architect James Gibbs's *Book of Architecture*, in which were published template designs for use in the building of churches in parts of England where the services of fashionable architects might not be available.

The splendid tower of St. Nicholas is certainly very similar to one of Gibbs's designs which had been an alternative for the church of St. Mary-le-Strand in London. It rises from the west front with a square storey with stepped corners and curved pediments over the windows and clock. The second storey has recessed corners and gabled pediment, above which is an octagonal level with the domed cupola and lantern on the top. The west front below is very fine, with large pilasters, which are also to be found on the first bay of the north and south walls. Above is a large semi-circular pediment containing carved heraldic arms that may be the work of the Worcester sculptor, Thomas White, to whom the design of the church has been attributed in the past. There are certainly similarities between the pediment and White's work at both the nearby Guildhall and Britannia House, and a church at Castle Bromwich in Birmingham with which he was also involved. The west doorway has Tuscan columns with a pediment, and once had a series of semi-circular steps extending out into the street. When the road was widened in the 19th century, these were replaced by a double staircase with balustrade, which in turn gave way to the present recessed stairs. By comparison the rest of the church is plain with round-arched windows.

Although the interior, with its flat ceiling, has been stripped of many furnishings for the restaurant, a number survive. There is an 18th-century baroque baluster font, with four carved cherubs heads on the bowl, and fine Georgian staircases in the west vestibule lead to the tower and galleries. The galleries replaced smaller ones in 1813, and were given fronts with much ironwork by William Jeffrey Hopkins in 1867 when he completely refitted the interior with new pews, pulpit and communion rails. The pedimented Georgian reredos survives in the apse. There are panes of white glass in the side windows which may be as early as the 17th century, but the east window glass dates from 1857.

There are many small 18th- and 19th-century memorial tablets, whilst the crypt contains a memorial to rector William Henry Havergal whose daughter, the hymn writer Frances Ridley Havergal, is buried at Astley church. The first Sunday School in Worcester was opened at St. Nicholas' church in 1785.

The white painted east end of St. Nicholas church makes a conspicuous landmark by the M5 at junction six. It stands next to the converted farm buildings and restored 17th-century brick house of Warndon Court, which until the 1980s stood isolated on a low hill amongst fields. Worcester has now expanded almost to the motorway, and Warndon is today a busy area of the city with housing and industrial estates. The remoteness of the parish until recently has meant that the church remained relatively unaltered during the 19th century. Indeed, it only received a mains electricity supply in 1993. A massive restoration in the early 1990s has secured the building's once uncertain future as a very active church.

The current parish was formed out of the large Anglo-Saxon parish of St. Helen in Worcester, along with many others in the central northern part of the county. During the Norman period a manor house was constructed on the site, held by Hugh Poer. The Norman church was probably built as a manorial chapel, but now lies within the remains of the surrounding moat. The manor was held by the Bracy family during the Middle Ages, but more recently was part of the Berkeley family's Spetchley estate.

The church has a nave and chancel under one roof with a west tower and north porch. The Norman nave and chancel are built of sandstone now plastered and painted white, but stand on a lias base which could be a survival from an earlier church. During restoration a small blocked round-headed arch was discovered at the east end, which gave access to an apsidal structure, of which the foundations were located. This is not fully explained, but could be the remains of a chapel. The outline of the arch is marked in the plaster. The plain north and south doorways with roll mouldings are both Norman. The Norman windows have been replaced; the east window has stepped lancets and is late 13th-century, whilst the side windows are Perpendicular. The west tower was probably added in the early 16th century. It is timber-framed, and has close-studding to the sides and in the base on the west end. The upper parts of the west wall are panelled with curved braces. The saddleback roof is just a little higher than that of the nave. The timber porch is of uncertain date, but could be of a similar age to the tower. It has been restored with later brickwork.

The interior has now been restored and whitewashed, but still retains the atmosphere of a typically cramped church interior before later 19th-century restoration. There is a plastered medieval wagon roof, which has a tympanum dividing the nave from the chancel, and a loft at the west end, which represents the former medieval belfry. It can only be reached from the first floor of the tower via the former bell opening in the west gable. The west wall of the nave has a crudely cut arch leading into the tower, which contains the remains of the former Perpendicular west window. The nave has a quarry tiled floor, and is lined with box pews dating from the 17th and 18th centuries, but restored and altered during the 1990s restoration. At the west end the pews incorporate some simple 15th-century benches, whilst beneath the tympanum on the south side can be seen part of the base of the medieval rood screen.

The chancel has a 17th-century communion table, surrounded by a three sided communion rail, with a communicants pew on the south wall. The floor has some 14th-century tiles, some showing arms of the Beauchamp family, and there are some 18th-century ledger stones. A 19th-century Gothic cast iron stove is preserved and there are commandment and charity boards of similar date. The 15th-century font is heptagonal, like that at Ipsley church, and has a 17th-century cover.

During the 1990s restoration three levels of wall painting were uncovered on the north wall of the nave and some fragments remain exposed, including some pre-Reformation lettering. There are fragments of medieval glass in the tracery of a south window, including the head of a priest, and the panels of early 14th-century glass in the east window are very fine and were restored in 1984. These show the Annunciation and St. Andrew at the top, SS. Peter and Paul at the bottom, whilst in the middle the Virgin and Child are almost identical to the panel at Fladbury church. The Warndon panels are better preserved, and retain the side pinnacles and the finial to the canopy. These two pieces must have come from the same workshop.

Outside, on the south side, a scratch dial can be found on the buttress near the doorway, whilst to the north is the base of the medieval churchyard cross, now surmounted by a simple iron cross. The tower contains a 15th-century bell, together with a bell of 1737 brought from Lulsley church, which is thought to be the last bell cast in Worcester. The brick barn to the north west of the church has been converted to a parish centre.

WORCESTER   ST. PAUL, SPRING GARDENS

By the early 19th century the area known as the Blockhouse between the City Walls and the canal was developing into a dense network of housing and industry. The first church of St. Paul was built between 1835 and 1837, and was of the Commissioners type with a small west tower. However, by 1880 it was too small, and the decision was taken to build a new church to the north. The earlier church was used as a hall, and linked to the new building by a meeting room. It was demolished in about 1960. The present church was designed by Arthur Edmund Street, who took over the practice of his father George Edmund Street in 1881, and built in 1885-86. The church was famous for the ministry of Geoffrey Studdert-Kennedy from 1914 to 1922, nicknamed Woodbine Willie for his role

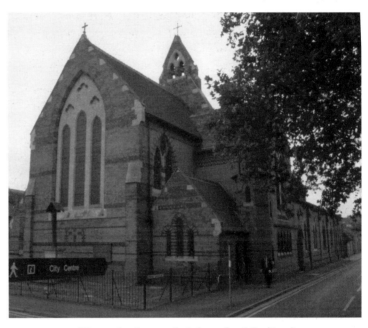

The polychrome brickwork of St. Paul

as army chaplain in France during World War One, when he did much to alleviate the poor conditions of the Blockhouse. With the decline of the area's population from the 1950s, the church became less used and was closed in 1988, when it was leased to the Assemblies of God Congregation who have since done much work to the building.

The church has an aisled nave with clerestorey, a chancel with south chapel, and an organ loft and vestry to the north. The bellcote is on the nave east gable. It is built of red and black brick with limestone dressings, and has polychrome work in the style of William Butterfield. The doorways and window tracery are in an early Decorated style.

Although the large interior has been much altered and subdivided for current worship and use, it is still possible to see much of the original work. The polychrome brickwork and early Decorated features continue inside, and Street designed the sedilia, piscina and aumbry in the chancel, as well as the reredos in the Lady Chapel. The 19th-century font is now close to the pulpit, which has panels painted to show the Life of St. Paul. The nave and chancel are divided by a large wrought iron and brass screen surmounted by a cross.

Several stained glass windows are by Charles Eamer Kempe. The east window of 1886 shows the Crucifixion with St. Paul, St. Matthew, St. John the Evangelist, Isaiah and Jeremiah. The four chancel windows of 1899 show the Doctors of the Church, whilst the Douglas memorial window is of 1905. A south aisle window showing St. Simeon and the Virgin was brought here in 1907, and north aisle windows with St. Barnabas, St. Oswald and St. Edmund were installed in 1901. The Studdert-Kennedy memorial window at the west end of the south aisle was made from cartoons in Kempe's office in 1931. It shows David along with Melchizedek blessing Abraham.

The unusual war memorial outside at the east end was carved in 1921 by G.E. Sprague on the instructions of Studdert-Kennedy, and shows the Crucifixion with Christ looking upwards in victory, rather than with his head turned to the side in pain and sorrow.

WORCESTER   ST. PETER THE GREAT

Today only a plaque by King Street in the car park of the Royal Worcester Porcelain factory can be seen as a reminder of the existence of this church, along with its former school buildings which now serve as a shop and the Museum of Worcester Porcelain. The parish of St. Peter the Great was extensive, reaching from the south-east corner of the medieval city to the boundaries of Kempsey, some two miles to the south. The southern end of the parish with large housing estates is still known as St. Peter the Great.

The church seems to have acquired the suffix 'Great' to distinguish it from the chapel in Worcester Castle which existed between the 13th and 15th centuries, and was known as St. Peter the Less. However, it is probable that St. Peter the Great began as a church recorded in 969 as dedicated to St. Perpetua and St. Felicitas, who were two 3rd century Christian martyrs in North Africa. The location of the church site at the edge of the large Roman cemetery at Diglis, which lay beyond the town boundary, would also support an early origin to this church similar to those of St. Helen's and St. Alban's churches.

The earliest reference to St. Peter's church comes in the 13th century, when between 1204 and 1234 it was transferred to the patronage of Pershore Abbey. The medieval church was recorded in 18th- and early 19th-century illustrations. It had a Perpendicular north-west tower with panelled stonework and pinnacles. The nave and aisles had separate gabled roofs, and appeared to have Decorated windows. The north aisle, however, was timber-framed and the west end of the south aisle had been rebuilt in brick and had a 17th-century mullion window. The church was rebuilt in the Commissioners style between 1836 and 1837 by John Mills. It had a thin, but aisled north-west tower, and a large nave with typical short chancel. The style was Perpendicular. However, the building became structurally unsafe and was closed in 1972, before being demolished in 1976.

Most of the early 19th-century fittings were not preserved. However, several items of interest passed to St. Martin's church, whilst the communion table is in St. Mark. Two of the bells, charity boards, and several memorials are now in Worcester City Museum, including tablets commemorating the Wylde family of the Commandery. Memorials and glass commemorating the Chamberlain family, who established the porcelain works on the present site, along with tiles made in their works, are now in the Museum of Worcester Porcelain. As its demolition was so recent, St. Peter's church is well remembered by many Worcester people, yet its site and connection with the suburb of St. Peter the Great is all too little known.

WORCESTER   ST. STEPHEN, DROITWICH ROAD

This church was built to serve the northern end of Barbourne in the parish of Claines, which developed rapidly during the later 19th century. Land for the church was given in 1861 by Jane Lavender and her sister, Mary Gutch, who came from a wealthy banking family. Set in a spacious graveyard, the red sandstone building was designed by Frederick Preedy and consecrated in 1862, with an aisled nave with porch and chancel with organ chamber and vestry. The massive south-west tower was designed to carry a spire, but Jane Lavender died in 1862 and it was never built. It is now crowned with a parapet and large pinnacles. The south chapel was added after 1918 as a memorial to the First World War. It has a three-sided apse at the east end. The style of the church is later Early English, with plate tracery to several of the windows and those in the clerestorey have two lights divided by a short column.

The interior is lofty and white, with many features typical of Preedy's work. The capitals to the round piers are carved with foliage and dragons. The alabaster reredos, font and stone pulpit are to Preedy's design. The remaining furnishings are mainly later 19th-century including choir stalls with linenfold panelling and carved figures of St. Stephen and St. Andrew on the bench ends.

Preedy's wall paintings at the east end of 1866 have long been covered up, but the stained glass of the east window by him showing the Crucifixion remains and is a memorial of 1862 to Jane Lavender. Preedy also designed the glass in the west window, which shows the Life of St. Stephen, as well as a window at the west end of the north aisle. The Good Samaritan window in the south aisle is a memorial to Josiah Stallard of the Blanquettes. The stained glass in the east lancet windows of the Lady Chapel is by members of the Bromsgrove Guild.

WORCESTER   ST. SWITHIN, CHURCH STREET

The dedication of this church to the 9th century Bishop of Winchester whose relics became the centre of a popular Anglo-Saxon cult, suggests its pre-conquest foundation, which is strongly supported by its situation just within the line of the northern defences of Anglo-Saxon Worcester. The church is first recorded in 1126, and throughout its history has been closely surrounded by buildings and busy narrow streets to the east of the High Street. The parish contained the homes and businesses of wealthy merchants, who funded the rebuilding of the church between 1734 and 1735 by Thomas and Edward Woodward. St. Swithin's remains one of the finest Georgian churches in Britain, and has been maintained by the Churches Conservation Trust since 1977.

The rectangular limestone church has a hipped roof and an eastern façade facing Mealcheapen Street. At the west

St. Swithin, with its classical east façade and Gothic tower

end is the tower. The body of the church is Classical but the west tower is Gothic. Indeed, the Woodwards put a limestone facing onto the lower two levels of the 15th-century Perpendicular sandstone tower. The upper level which was probably octagonal, had to be rebuilt. The exterior features seem to be based on the Woodwards' own church at Chipping Campden in Gloucestershire. Between the Gothic pinnacles on the top, however, there is a Classical balustrade.

The Classical nave and chancel of the church are designed in the fashionable Palladian manner, which reflects the importance of the Woodwards in bringing innovative architecture to this area. The Italianate east end with the Venetian window, fluted pilasters, side entrances and pediments contrasts with the great baroque west façade of St. Nicholas's church, which had only been completed four years before. The eastern façade can be compared

The Georgian interior retains its original fittings

to those at St. John's church, Gloucester, and Bewdley church also designed by the Woodwards, and where the earlier towers were also retained. At St. Swithin, the north wall is also medieval sandstone masonry, but this is barely visible from the street, and is pierced by large Classical round-headed windows to match the south wall, where they are surrounded by more fluted pilasters with an entablature above.

The spacious tower base serves as a vestibule to the interior, where there is a beautifully proportioned space. Well lit and lightly painted, it forms a perfect setting for the wonderful collection of Georgian furnishings, the most complete in Worcestershire. The east end is divided by Doric columns to form a short chancel, to either side of which are panelled vestibules to the eastern entrances. The plaster vault to the ceiling is by contrast Gothic with ribs, bosses and medieval style corbels. The Woodwards also used the Gothic style in the church at Preston-on-Stour, Warwickshire, as well as in the house at nearby Alscot Park, both for the Smith family.

The furnishings focus on the splendid three decker pulpit. It was a very fashionable piece of work, and its similarity to several pulpits in City of London churches perhaps reflects a wish of the Worcester merchants to keep up with the capital. The huge sounding board is suspended from the ceiling by eight carved swags which support a carved and gilded pelican, plucking her breast to feed her young, a popular symbol of piety. Below hang an anchor and serpent to represent the triumph of the Church over evil, whilst the dove represents the Holy Ghost. On the underside of the sounding board an inlaid star can be seen in the woodwork. This degree of iconography is most unusual in a church of this date; was a recusant Catholic amongst those who financed the rebuilding?

The pulpit, clerk's desk and reader's desk all survive, linked by a precarious wooden staircase. Below them is the first of the box pews with the curved mayor's chair, which has more carved swags. Above it is a fine wrought iron rest for the civic sword, similar to that at All Saints' church. The box pews fill the nave, and between them the floor is made up of ledger stones. In a pew at the west end is the baluster font with a mahogany cover. At the east end, the reredos has Doric pilasters, but the pediment was removed when the east window was altered by Harvey Eginton in the mid-19th century and glass by G. Rogers was installed. The communion table has an Italian marble top on a wrought iron base, similar to one in Birtsmorton church. At the west end the gallery contains the organ given to the church in 1692 by William Swift, a grocer and sugar baker in the High Street.

Swift's monument of 1688 was also transferred from the previous church. He is shown with his five sons and five daughters, with cherubs on the pediment. There are numerous memorial tablets of the 18th and 19th centuries, but of particular note is that to Joseph Withers who died whilst he was mayor in 1741, and is shown in a portrait with his wife in a medallion held by a cherub in front of an urn and obelisk. It was designed in about 1770 by John Bacon, who also produced the monument to Richard Jolly in Worcester Cathedral. The tablet to Henry Hope is by Richard Squire, who built All Saints church.

The tower contains three 15th-century bells, and the 18th-century mechanism for the clock, which has a face on the tower and another on the more conspicuous eastern façade, where it stands beneath its own pediment above the window. The drive shaft runs through the roof for the full length of the church. By the tower, on the north side of the small courtyard is the former schoolroom of the Grammar School, which was granted a royal charter by Queen Elizabeth I in 1561, rebuilt in 1735, and moved to its present site in Upper Tything in 1868. The schoolroom is now used as a restaurant.

WORCESTER   HOLY TRINITY AND ST. MATTHEW, RONKSWOOD

This church is situated on the Ronkswood estate, close to the hospital at the top of the hill on the east side of Worcester. This was part of the parish of St. Martin until the 20th century, and the development of land here in the 1950s reflects the movement of population to estates on the edge of the city from the areas of clearance in the city centre. The church is circular and was built of concrete to designs of Maurice Jones in 1964-65. The roof is almost flat and carries a spire in the centre. The rendered walls were formerly chequered and have plain glass windows at the base. There is a church hall built on to the side.

Holy Trinity and St. Matthew—a 20th-century church in the round

Inside, the walls are conical with a gallery, and a chequer board pattern to the brickwork above the windows. The war memorial and gates in the churchyard come from Holy Trinity church in Shrub Hill whose function in east Worcester was taken over by this church. The parish of Holy Trinity was formed out of St. Martin's parish, and the original church built between 1863 and 1865 by William Jeffrey Hopkins on land given by Alexander Sheriff, railway manager and twice Mayor of Worcester, to give the growing eastern portion of the city a church after the coming of the railway in 1850. Indeed, the church was surrounded by industrial and railway buildings. It was demolished in 1969, but its site is marked by the former churchyard railings and trees in Shrub Hill Road.

Holy Trinity church was large and built of sandstone. It had an aisled nave with transepts and a chancel with a polygonal apse. A tower and spire were to be linked to the south side by a cloister, but these were never built. The interior was famous for the nave roof, which was formed from the 14th-century roof of the cathedral's Guesten Hall. This has been reconstructed at Avoncroft Museum. At the church, the roof was supported by corbels carved by Richard Boulton of Cheltenham, whose firm had also done much carving in Worcester Cathedral. Boulton's reredos showing the Last Supper and pulpit showing St. Peter preaching were lost at the demolition, along with the font by William Forsyth. A bowl, perhaps from this font, is currently used as an ornament in the churchyard at Ronkswood.

WYCHBOLD   ST. MARY

The parish of Wychbold was formed from part of the extensive parish of St. Augustine's, Dodderhill during the 19th century. The suburban village is situated along the A38 to the north of Droitwich, its location given away by two radio masts which, at 700 feet, tower above the surrounding landscape. The Droitwich Radio Station was well known in the mid-20th century for its long and medium wave broadcasts.

The church stands in an isolated setting to the east of the village. It is a large sandstone building with a nave and chancel with transepts, porch and a south tower. John Corbett, the Droitwich salt magnate provided the money and land for the vicarage as well as the church, which was completed in 1888. Indeed, subsidence as a result of salt extraction causes the whole building to lean. The architect was Lewis Sheppard of Worcester, who used a late Early English style with some lancet windows along with shafts and moulded capitals to the arches. Jonathan Brazier of Bromsgrove was the builder. It is suggested that they used an original 13th-century doorway to the tower, but the origins of this are unclear.

The large interior is brick-faced and has many 19th- and 20th-century fittings, including screens, altar rails and an altar table by the Bromsgrove Guild. The west window has glass by Evans of Smethwick, which was the gift of John Corbett in 1894. Another window showing the Virgin and Child with St. Richard de Wyche is by Archibald Davies of the Bromsgrove Guild.

WYRE PIDDLE   ST. ANNE

Above the north bank of the River Avon, the village of Wyre Piddle has extensive views of Pershore and Bredon Hill. The village street has several timber-framed and brick cottages near to the restored medieval village cross. Land here was held by the Beauchamp family of Elmley Castle during the Middle Ages, and the church was a chapelry to Fladbury. The church stands along a lane at the west end of the village. In 1989 it was dedicated to St. Anne, as any previous dedication was unknown.

The site of the church was used in the Anglo-Saxon period as a burial ground, and two pagan burials were discovered during the restoration of 1888. The site is one of ancient spiritual significance. The lias stone church consists of a chancel and nave with a north porch. An Early English double bellcote is placed on the east gable of the nave with pointed arches for the bells. The chancel is Norman but has Decorated and Perpendicular windows. The nave was rebuilt in 1888, when it was lengthened at the west end and the porch added.

The compact interior is scraped to the stone. The small, plain early Norman chancel arch is the focal point at the east end of the nave, with a post-medieval squint to either side, giving a better view of the chancel, similar to those in Cotheridge church. Apart from the mainly 20th-century fittings, there are a 12th-century pillar piscina with a scalloped capital and a credence shelf resting on an Early English stiff leaf capital. The stone altar slab is medieval, discovered in the floor during the 19th-century restoration. The drum-shaped font is Norman, and carved with zig-zag decoration and scallops. It is very similar to the font in Abberton church. Carved stones showing part of a beast's head and a foliage design were discovered during the rebuilding of the nave and may be of later Anglo-Saxon date and from the previous church on the site. There are fragments of medieval glass reset in the west window, including canopies and heads, and a chalice with a devil from a figure of St. John the Evangelist. In the chancel are some 15th-century floor tiles with parts of inscriptions and foliage designs, along with a dog, the emblem of the Talbot family. The previous smaller nave had a gallery at the west end, which was erected in 1830.

*Preedy's church of 1862,
with Bidlake's tower of 1903*

Wythall and Hollywood are large villages in the north-east of the county, just to the south of the suburbs of Birmingham. Indeed, until 1853 Wythall was a chapelry in the parish of King's Norton. The church is on the site of the 17th-century chapel and stands to the south-west of the village. It is no longer used and awaits conversion, but the tower is an unforgettable landmark on the approach to Birmingham from Redditch.

The brick church has a nave and chancel, with a south aisle and transept, above which rises the central tower. The church was designed in 1862 by Frederick Preedy, his only substantial church in brick. It is in the Decorated style, with polychrome work in stone and darker bricks of the William Butterfield type, and is similar to Arthur Street's church of St. Paul in Worcester. Preedy's tower was never built, and in 1903 the Birmingham Arts and Crafts architect William Henry Bidlake was commissioned to design the very tall structure seen today. It is in a darker brick to the rest of the church but has stone dressings, with two large shafted early Decorated style openings to each side, making a huge open lantern. Above is a transverse saddle-back roof, with quatrefoils in the gables, and a copper fleche in the centre. In the north-east corner is an octagonal stair turret with a short spire, like a large pinnacle. It was inspired by the church towers of Belgium and Northern France, and is Bidlake's only work in Worcestershire. He is best known for the church of St. Agatha in Sparkbrook, Birmingham.

The interior has exposed brickwork, rather like Butterfield's church at Alvechurch. The arcades and window openings are ornamented with notched bricks. The capitals have carved early Decorated style foliage, and the piers and tower base have ornamental bands of stone. The reredos of stone and marble, showing a Crucifixion with a pelican and the Agnus Dei, is by J. Bland, whilst the brass and iron communion rails are by Skidmore of Coventry. Over the tower arch in the nave, Preedy set in the brickwork a carved white marble cross with the symbols of alpha and omega. Stained glass in the windows includes the west gable window showing the Ascension, and two west lancets with the Nativity and Baptism of Christ by Preedy of 1865, whilst a window in the south aisle of 1862, formerly in King's Norton church, shows the Virgin and Child.

Select Glossary

ABACUS - a flat slab on top of a capital, often decorated with carving.

AISLE - side extensions to the nave of the church (also sometimes used to refer to the walkways between the pews).

ALE HOUSE - a building adjacent to the church constructed in the late Middle Ages for the use of parishioners for church 'ales' or feasts, at which funds were raised for the upkeep of the church.

ALIEN PRIORY - an English priory under the direct control of a continental monastery.

APSE - a semi circular or polygonal projection from the main church building.

ASHLAR - dressed blocks of stone.

AUMBRY - a rectangular medieval recess by the altar, which would once have been a secure storage space for sacred objects. It is rare to find them with their original doors.

BALLFLOWER - a carved decorative projection in the form of a bud usually found on Decorated architecture.

BARREL VAULT - see VAULT

BAY - a vertical section of a building.

BELLCOTE - a small arched structure in which a bell is hung.

BELL OPENING - an opening in the tower, through which the sound of the bells could escape.

BILLET - a rectangular or cylindrical motif.

BOX PEW - an enclosed pew installed in a church between the 17th and 19th centuries. They were numbered and were rented by those who could afford them.

CANOPY OF HONOUR - a large canopy above an altar or rood.

CAPITAL - at the top of a pier, the capital forms a flat bed from which the arches spring. The carved decoration of a capital is likely to be a good indication of the date of the arch.

CARTOUCHE - part of the decoration to a Classical monument, taking the form of an unrolled scroll, on which the inscription is found.

CELURE - an ornamental ceiling above an altar or rood.

CHANCEL - the east end of the church.

CHANTRY CHAPEL - a medieval chapel where mass was celebrated and prayers offered for the soul of the deceased benefactor.

CHOIR - the part of a large church where the choir gathers to sing.

CHURCH HOUSE - a building adjacent to a medieval church used for church burseries, often incorporating an ALE HOUSE.

CLERESTOREY - an upper storey to the nave or chancel usually of a large church, which had windows to give extra light.

COMMANDMENT BOARD - a large board with the text of the Ten Commandments, usually 18th or 19th century.

COMMUNION RAIL - a rail to protect the communion table or altar, first used in the 17th century.

COMMUNION TABLE - a table which replaced the altar in church from the 17th century.

CORBEL - a projecting stone support.

CORBEL TABLE - a line of corbels.

CORNICE - a surround to a ceiling.

CROCKET - a carved decorative projection, sometimes leaf-shaped, to be found on pinnacles and canopies in Gothic architecture.

CUSP - a small point between two curves in later medieval architectural features.

DECORATED - the Gothic architectural style of the period from the late 13th to the late 14th centuries.

EARLY ENGLISH - the Gothic architectural style of the period from the end of the 12th to the late 13th centuries.

EASTER SEPULCHRE - a large medieval recess to the north of the altar, where the Sacrament was kept between Good Friday and Easter Sunday.

FAN VAULT - see VAULT.

GARGOYLE - a projecting stone feature to a parapet, usually containing a water spout, and often carved with grotesque beasts.

GRISAILLE - 13h or 14th century clear glass, which was painted with grey leaf patterns.

HATCHMENT - a panel, usually diamond shaped, on which were painted the coat of arms of a deceased person, and which was left in the church after being carried in the funeral procession.

HOUSELING BENCH - long low wooden bench used as a communion rail.

LADY CHAPEL - a chapel in a large church, with an altar dedicated to the Virgin.

LEDGER - a large flat grave memorial slab, with an inscription.

LIERNE - a short intersecting rib in a later medieval vault (see also Vault).

LOZENGE - a diamond shaped motif.

LUCARNE - an opening in a spire.

LYCHGATE - a gateway, often with a roof, at the entrance to the churchyard. The name is derived from the Anglo-Saxon word *lich* which means corpse—the lich gate marks the entrance place for a funeral procession to the churchyard.

MANDORLA - an oval shaped panel in a painting or sculpture.

MASS DIAL - a sundial set out to give the times at which mass should be celebrated.

MEMENTO MORI - reminder of the inevitability of death.

MERLON - the projecting part of a battlement.

MISERICORD - a wooden seat for a cleric, which is hinged and usually kept vertical as it has a platform on which the occupant could rest when standing. The underside of this platform is sometimes elaborately carved.

NAVE - the main, western part of the church used by the congregation.

NORMAN - the Romanesque architectural style of the Norman period from the mid-11th to the late 12th centuries.

OGEE - an S-shaped curve in Gothic architecture.

PALIMPSEST BRASS - a monumental brass which has been turned over and reused.

PARCLOSE SCREEN - a screen to separate a chapel from the rest of the church.

PARVIS - the room above a medieval porch, which was sometimes used as a priest's accommodation or as a schoolroom.

PERPENDICULAR - the Gothic architectural style of the period from the late 14th to the mid-16th centuries.

PISCINA - a small stone basin in the chancel, with a drain, where the priest could rinse the communion vessels after a service.

PLATE TRACERY - Early English style tracery with openings cut through stone.

PRIEST'S DOORWAY - the small doorway for the priest in the side of the chancel.

QUARRY - a diamond shaped piece of glass.

QUATREFOIL - a carved decorative feature in the shape of four leaves.

REBUS - a pictorial way of depicting a pun on a name, such as a small barrel for Lyttleton.

RELIQUARY - a casket or recess to hold a relic, which was a fragment of the remains of a Saint's body, or an associated artefact.

REREDOS - a solid panelled stone screen behind the altar.

RETICULATION - window tracery with ogee curves linked to give a latticed effect.

RHENISH HELM - a steeple with four gables, usually found in the Rhineland area of Germany.

RIB - a raised band of stone or wood, which strengthens a vault or ceiling.

ROMANESQUE - the architectural style of the Anglo-Saxon and Norman period in England, from the 7th to the 12th centuries.

ROOD - Crucifix, from an Anglo-Saxon word meaning cross.

ROOD BEAM - the beam to which the Rood was affixed.

ROOD LOFT - a gallery above the rood screen, often used by musicians and accessed by the staircase.

ROOD SCREEN - a screen dividing the nave from the chancel in a medieval church, which carried a Crucifix or Rood before the Reformation.

SACRISTY - a room next to the chancel in which valuables and the church plate were stored.

SADDLEBACK ROOF - a gabled roof to a tower.

SANCTUS BELL - a small bell rung at the start of the 'Sanctus' during Mass.

SEDILIA - stone seats in the chancel for the sacred ministers.

SHAFT - the upright part of a pier, above the base and below the capital.

SPANDREL - the area of stonework between the arches of an arcade.

STOUP - a medieval stone vessel, which was placed near the doorway to the church, to hold holy water for the use of worshippers to make the sign of the cross.

STRAPWORK - decoration of the 16th and 17th centuries which had the appearance of intertwining straps.

STRING COURSE - a line of projecting horizontal stonework on a Norman wall.

TESTER - a flat canopy above a pulpit, usually 17th- or 18th-century, to help to project the preacher's voice.

THREE DECKER PULPIT - a pulpit, usually 17th- or 18th-century, with accompanying desks for the clerk and minister, arranged in a stepped formation.

TIERCERON - an intermediate rib in a later medieval vault.

TOWER PORCH - a tower which incorporates a porch in the base.

TRACERY - the open stonework or woodwork in the upper part of a window or opening.

TRANSEPTS - side chapels, often placed to the sides of a central tower, with roofs at right angles to the roofs of the main body of the church.

TRANSOM - a horizontal stone bar in a window.

TREFOIL - a carved decorative feature in the shape of three leaves.

TRIFORIUM - an arched passage in the wall of a large church, above the arcade but below the clerestorey.

TRIPTYCH - three folded panels, painted with religious or family and heraldic illustrations.

TRUMPET SCALLOP - a carved form of decoration, usually found on Norman capitals.

TYMPANUM - either the stone above the lintel and below the arch of a doorway, particularly of the Norman period, or the area of wall, often timber-framed, above the rood screen dividing the nave and the chancel.

VAULT / VAULTING - medieval stone ceilings were constructed as vaults, which become more elaborate as the centuries progressed. Simple Norman tunnel shaped vaults are called Barrel Vaults, whereas more elaborate Decorated vaults had several stone ribs with tiercerons, liernes and carved bosses. These were known as Lierne Vaults. The most elaborate Perpendicular Vaults were Fan Vaults with many more ribs and a cone-shaped effect to the side sections.

VESTRY - the room in which vestments are kept, and where the clergy prepare for a service.

VOUSSOIR - a small wedge-shaped piece of stone in the curved upper part of an arch.

WAGON ROOF - a timber roof constructed in a similar curved manner to the interior of a covered wagon.

WATERLEAF - a carved stylised leaf design of the 13th century.

Bibliography

TWAS = Transactions of the Worcestershire Archaeological Society

Addleshaw, G. & Etchells, F. *The Archaeological Setting of Anglican Worship*, 1948

Alexander, J. & Binski, P. *Age of Chivalry, Art in Plantagenet England 1200 - 1400*, 1987

Allely, L. S*t. Clement, Worcester, the History of the Church and Parish*, 1969

Amphlett, J. (ed) *Thomas Habington, A Survey of Worcestershire,* 1893-4

Archer, M. *An Introduction to English Stained Glass*, 1985

Atterbury, P. & Wainwright, C. ed. *Pugin, a Gothic Passion*, 1994

Baker, N.J. 'The Urban Churches of Worcester - A Survey'. *TWAS*, Third Series, VII, 1980, pp.115-26

Baker, N.J., Dalwood, C.H., Holt, R., Mundy, C.F. & Taylor, G. 'From Roman to Medieval Worcester : Development and Planning in the Medieval City', *Antiquity*, LXVI, 1992, pp.65-74

Barker, P. & Pagett, T. 'Romanesque Carving from St. John the Baptist Church, Hagley and Dudley Priory', *TWAS,* Third Series, XI, 1988, pp.27-34

Barker, P. *A Short Architectural History of Worcester Cathedral*, 1994

Barnard, E.A.B. *The Ruined Norman Chapel of Netherton near Elmley Castle Worcestershire*, 1921

Barnes, G. *Frederick Preedy*, 1984

Barrett, H. & Phillips, J. *Suburban Style*, 1987

Barrett, P. & Wilson, M. *The Book of Pershore*, 1980

Bassett, S. 'Churches in Worcester before and after the Conversion of the Anglo-Saxons', *Antiquaries Journal*, LXIX, pt 2, 1989, pp.225-256

Bennett, J.S.B. *The History of St. Cuthbert's, the Mother Church of St. John's at Bennett's Farm, Lower Wick,* 1980

Betjeman, J. *Collins Guide to English Parish Churches (The North)*, 1968

Bettey, J.H. *Church and Parish, A Guide for Local Historians*, 1987

Beulah, K. *Church Tiles of the Nineteenth Century*, 1987

Binney, M. & Burman, P. *Change and Decay, The Future of our Churches*, 1977

Blewitt, L. & Field, B. *Droitwich, A Pictorial History*, 1994

Blythe, R. *Divine Landscapes*, 1986

Bond, W.L. *From Hamlet to Parish the Story of Dodford, Worcestershire*, 1972

Bottomley, F. *The Church Explorer's Guide*, 1978

Bridges, T. & Mundy, C.F. *Worcester, A Pictorial History*, 1996

British Archaeological Association Conference Transactions, *Medieval Art and Architecture at Worcester Cathedral*, 1975

Brown D.L. 'Archaeological Recording at St. Mary's Church, Kyre Wyard', *TWAS*, Third Series XIV, 1994, pp.193-202

Buchanan-Dunlop, W.R. 'St. Andrew's Church, Worcester', *TWAS*, New Series XIII, 1937, pp.15-27
     'St. Alban's Church, Worcester', *TWAS*, New Series XXVII, 1950, pp.1-14

Burton, J.R. *A History of Kidderminster*, 1890

Chamberlin, R. *The English Parish Church*, 1993

Clarke, B.F.L. *The Building of the Eighteenth Century Church*, 1963

Clifton-Taylor, A. *English Parish Churches as Works of Art*, 1974

Cobb, G. *English Cathedrals; The Forgotten Centuries*, 1980

Coldstream, N. *The Decorated Style, Architecture and Ornament 1240 - 1360*, 1994

Cox, D.C. *Evesham Abbey and the Parish Churches*, 1980
  'The Building, Destruction and Excavation of Evesham Abbey : A Documentary History', *TWAS*, Third Series XII 1990, pp.123-146

Cox, J.C. & Ford, C.B. *Parish Churches*, 1934

Craze, M. *Whittington, Worcester. The History of the Village*, 1977

Crewe, S. (ed) *Visionary Spires*, 1986

Crossley, F.H. *English Church Monuments, AD 1150 - 1550*, 1921

Cunnington, P. *How old is that Church?*, 1990

Dean, D. *The Christian Symbolism of the Zodiac*, 1989

Dickens, G.C.B. & McClatchey, D. (ed) *Diocese of Worcester, 1300 Years : The People of Worcestershire and their Church*, 1980

Dirsztay, P. *Church Furnishings*, 1978

Dixon, R. & Muthesius, S. *Victorian Architecture*, 1978

Duffy E. *The Stripping of the Altars, Traditional Religion in England 1400 - 1580*, 1992

Eames, E. *English Medieval Tiles*, 1985

Edwards, J. 'Some Wall Paintings at St. Peter's Church, Martley', *TWAS*, Third Series X, 1986, pp.59-70

Ekwall, E. *The Concise Dictionary of English Place Names*, 1960

Farmer, D.H. *The Oxford Dictionary of Saints*, 1978

Fletcher, A. *Eckington*, 1932

Frampton, K. *Modern Architecture, A Critical History*, 1992

Freeman, B. *Worcestershire*, 1996

Friar S. *A Companion to the English Parish Church*, 1996

Fryer, A.H. & Jeremiah, J. *Evesham, A Pictorial History*, 1994

Green, B.H. *Bishops of Worcester and Deans of the Cathedral*, 1979

Green, V. *The History and Antiquities of the City and Suburbs of Worcester*, 1796

Grice, F. 'Two Victorian Sculptors—James and William Forsyth', *TWAS*, Third Series XI, 1984, pp.101-106

Grierson, J. *St. Godwald's, A Parish and its People*, 1984

Gwilliam, H.W. *Worcestershire's Hidden Past*, 1991
  Old Worcester People and Places, 1993

Hamand, L.A. *The Ancient Windows of Malvern Priory Church*, 1948

Hammond, C.M. *Wyre Piddle, the Passing Years*, 1981

Harries, J. *Discovering Churches*, 1979

Harris, J. & Lever, J. *Illustrated Glossary of Architecture 950-1830*, 1966

Hart C. *The History and Architecture of St. Paul's Church, Worcester*, 1995

Harvey J. *The Perpendicular Style*, 1978

Harvey, J. *English Medieval Architects*, 1987

HMSO *New Life for Old Churches*, 1977

Hoggard, B. *Bredon Hill, A Guide to its Archaeology, History, Folklore and Villages*, 1999

Hooke, D. *The Anglo-Saxon Landscape - The Kingdom of the Hwicce*, 1985

Houghton, F.T.S. *Worcestershire : The Little Guide* (revised by Matley Moore), 1952

Hurle, P. *Hanley Castle*, 1978
  Upton : Portrait of a Severnside Town, 1979

Jenkins, S. *England's Thousand Best Churches*, 1999

Jeremiah, J. *The Vale of Evesham*, 1997

Johnson, M. *Our English Church Heritage from the Beginning to 1662*, 1987

Kerr, M. & N. *Anglo-Saxon Architecture*, 1983

King, J.F. 'Anglo-Saxon Sculpture at St. Andrew's Church, Pershore', *TWAS*, Third Series, XIII, 1992, pp.129-134

Knowles D. *The Religious Orders in England* (vols. 1-3), 1979

Lang, J. *Anglo-Saxon Sculpture*, 1988

Leatherbarrow, J.S. *Worcestershire*, 1974
    'The Victorians Look at Their Churches', *TWAS*, Third Series, IX, 1984, pp.87-94
    A Brief History of St. Bartholomew's Church, Arley Kings, 1985

Lee, L., Seddon, G. & Stephens, F. *Stained Glass*, 1989

Lees-Milne, J. *Worcestershire, A Shell Guide*, 1964

Livingstone, E. *Concise Oxford Dictionary of the Christian Church*, 1977

Lloyd, R.H. *Bredon Hill and its Villages*, 1967

Mabey, M. *The Windsors of Hewell*, 1984

MacCulloch, D. 'Worcester, A Cathedral City in the Reformation' in Collinson, P. & Craig, J. *The Reformation in England Towns 1998*, pp.94-112

Marchant, S. (ed) *Churches to Visit in Worcestershire etc.*, 1997

Maude, T. *Guided by a Stone-Mason*, 1997

Mayr-Harting, H. *The Coming of Christianity to Anglo-Saxon England*, 1972

Mee, A. *Worcestershire*, 1938

Midmer, R. *English Medieval Monasteries 1066 - 1540*, 1979

Morris, R. *Cathedrals and Abbeys of England and Wales*, 1979
    Churches in the Landscape, 1989

Nash, T.T. *Collections for the History of Worcestershire*, 1799

Osbourne, J. *Stained Glass in England*, 1981

Pace, P.G. *The Architecture of George Pace*, 1990

Palmer, R.A. *St. Cassian's Church, Chaddesley Corbett before and after the Restoration*, 1994

Pevsner, N. *The Buildings of England, Herefordshire*, 1963
    The Buildings of England, Shropshire, 1958
    The Buildings of England, Worcestershire, 1968
    The Buildings of England, Staffordshire, 1974

Pevsner, N. & Wedgwood, A. *The Buildings of England, Warwickshire*, 1966

Platt, C. *The Parish Churches of Medieval England*, 1981

Porter, S. *Destruction of the English Civil Wars*, 1997

Powell, H.J. 'Herefordshire Churches of the Gothic Revival', *Transactions of the Woolhope Naturalists Field Club* XL, 3, 1972, pp.304-311.

Price, E. & Watson, B. 1986 'A Possible Anglo-Saxon Church at Sedgeberrow', *TWAS*, Third Series X, pp.119-122

Redundant Churches Fund, *Churches in Retirement*, 1990

Richards, A. *Braziers, Builders of Bromsgrove 1850 - 1990*, 1996

Richardson, R. *The Book of Redditch*, 1996

Ridyard, S.J. *The Royal Saints of Anglo-Saxon England*, 1988

Rodwell, W. *The Archaeology of the English Church*, 1981

Roelofsz, E. *Through Changing Scenes of Life, A Millennium of History in Ombersley and Doverdale*, 1999

Roper, J. *A History of St. Mary Magdalene's Church, Himbleton Worcestershire*, 1978
    A History of St. Cassian's Church, Chaddesley Corbett, 1978

Rouse, E.C. *Discovering Wall Paintings*, 1980

Salter, M. *The Old Parish Churches of Worcestershire*, 1989

Service, A. *Edwardian Architecture*, 1977

Shawcross, J.P. *Bengeworth*, 1927

Smith, B. *A History of Malvern*, 1978

Thomas, C. *Christianity in Roman Britain to A.D. 500*, 1985

Thompson, J. *The Mouseman of Kilburn : The Story of Robert Thompson and the 'Church Mouse'*, 1979

Thompson, R.D. *Rock,* 1981

Thurlby, M. 'A Note on the former Barrel Vault in the Choir of St. John the Baptist, Halesowen', *TWAS*, Third Series, IX, 1984, pp.37-44.
    'The Abbey Church, Pershore; An Architectural History', *TWAS*, Third Series XV, 1996, pp.147-210.
    The Herefordshire School of Romanesque Sculpture, 1999

Timpson, J. *Timpson's Country Churches*, 1998

Tomkinson, K. & Hall, G. *Kidderminster since 1800*, 1985

Tudor-Craig, P. 'Controversial Sculptures : The Southwell Tympanum, the Glastonbury Respond, the Leigh Christ', Chibnall M. (ed) *Anglo-Norman Studies* XII, 1989, pp.211-231

Turner, J.H. *Worcestershire Register of Countryside Treasures*, 1984

Verey, D. *The Buildings of England, Gloucestershire, The Cotswolds*, 1970

Verey, D. *The Buildings of England, Gloucestershire, The Vale and the Forest of Dean*, 1970

Waite, V. *Malvern Country*, 1979

Walker, R.O. (ed) *The Parish of Shrawley*, 1982
    Witley, Worcestershire, 1985
    Hartlebury, Worcestershire, 1987

Waters, R. & Harrison, N. *The Story of St. Martin's Church and Parish 1911-1986*, 1986

Watt, Q. (ed) *The Bromsgrove Guild*, 1999

Whiffen, M. *Stuart and Georgian Churches*, 1947

Whitehead, D. *The Book of Worcester*, 1976
    'The Georgian Churches of Worcester', *TWAS*, Third Series, XIII, 1992, pp.211-222.

Willis, Bund J. (ed) The History of the County of Worcestershire, I-IV *Victoria County History*, 1906-26

Wilson, D.M. *The Archaeology of Anglo-Saxon England*, 1976

Worcestershire Federation of Women's Institutes (ed.), *The Worcestershire Village Book*, 1988

Index

255